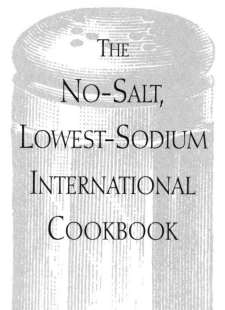

The
No-Salt,
Lowest-Sodium
International
Cookbook

The
No-Salt,
Lowest-Sodium
International
Cookbook

❖ ❖ ❖ ❖ ❖ ❖

Donald A. Gazzaniga
and
Maureen A. Gazzaniga

Foreword by
Dr. Michael B. Fowler, M.B., F.R.C.P.

Thomas Dunne Books
St. Martin's Press ❦ New York

THOMAS DUNNE BOOKS.
An imprint of St. Martin's Press.

THE NO-SALT, LOWEST-SODIUM INTERNATIONAL COOKBOOK.
Copyright © 2007 by Donald A. Gazzaniga and Maureen A. Gazzaniga.
Foreword © 2007 by Dr. Michael B. Fowler, M.B., F.R.C.P.
Preface © 2007 by Jeannie Gazzaniga Moloo, Ph.D., R.D.

www.stmartins.com

Library of Congress Cataloging-in-Publication Data

Gazzaniga, Donald A.
  The no-salt, lowest-sodium international cookbook /
Donald A. Gazzaniga and Maureen A. Gazzaniga ; foreword by
Dr. Michael B. Fowler. — 1st ed.
        p. cm.
  Includes index.
  ISBN-13: 978-0-312-35571-5
  ISBN-10: 0-312-35571-8
  1. Salt-free diet—Recipes.   2. Cookery, International.
I. Gazzaniga, Maureen A.   II. Title.
  RM237.8.G392 2007
  641.5'63–dc22   2007016760

First Edition: November 2007

10 9 8 7 6 5 4 3 2 1

Dedicated to

. . . Everyone who helped with this book, including my wife, Maureen, who deserves top billing for all her hard and very creative work.

Also to everyone at Thomas Dunne Books and St. Martin's Press who has believed in the these books, but especially to Ruth Cavin, our editor, who is the best in the world.

CONTENTS

ACKNOWLEDGMENTS

Without the help of my wife, Maureen, this book may not have happened. Maureen's uncanny research, gathered while traveling to many lands and around the United States, and her ability to pull together recipes with an instinct few have, served us well with ethnic dishes.

Maureen sought special recipes, not hard or difficult to make, but tasty meals without the use of salt or chemicals or additives.

She turned organic on us during this episode. She now buys only organic eggs, meats, and vegetables. She learned about food in other lands and made discoveries that tell us much about why other cultures and peoples eat what they eat. A bowl of rice or a handful of grain often proved to have more calories and nutrients than what we may be accustomed to dining on, and these grains and other ingredients served various cultures very well.

But the upside of her discoveries, and her insistence that she could make some of the most "distant" meals delicious, nutritious, and fun to prepare (without salt), paid off with scores of great recipes in this book.

My specialty in this book turned out to be breads from other lands as well as a few treats, appetizers, and desserts. I was also "assigned" specialty items like English Bangers and Irish Breakfast Sausage.

When Maureen wanted bread from Ethiopia, I researched what was to become one of the best-tasting breads in the book— Ethiopian Spice Bread. And, in order to match a true Ethiopian version of it, we also had to create a special olive oil flavor, brewed, as it were, on our stove top. The oil and the bread came out excitingly delicious.

You'll find recipes for Russian Black Bread that will really tease your palate, and British scones, and breads from many countries, including a steamed bun from China, an idea and direction given to me by my good friend, Ken Chung. Ken owns a large print shop in

Nansa, China, and when I asked him what kind of bread the Chinese had, he laughed. "We don't have bread here, but we do have a steamed bun." So, I got his steamed bun recipe, adapted it for us and, Wow! It's one you have to try. We also turned it into perfect dumplings for another dish in this book.

Our friend in Bangkok, Picha Srisansansee, who used to work on movies and TV projects with me, contributed his best Thai recipe—Peanut Dipping Sauce—and it worked out wonderfully.

We had direct help from friends around the world, and we believe every recipe in this book is worth your effort to prepare.

The great recipes in this book are Maureen's entrées. She was into it and we can thank her for some very enjoyable "nights out" in our own kitchens.

This then, I consider to be her book. Her project. Her success. And I know you're going to enjoy it.

—DON

INTRODUCTION

When Don first thought about putting another book together, he asked me if I'd like to help. My response was an enthusiastic, "You bet." We'd both traveled, and eating ethnic foods was a big and enjoyable part of each trip. So, naturally, we agreed that around the world the no-salt way would be our focus. We accepted the fact that we couldn't include recipes from every country and that we'd have to include some from regional areas of the United States. We also wanted to include a variety of recipes ranging from breakfast to dessert that were both tasty and satisfying. So, our challenge would be to develop recipes that would be representative of some countries, which could be adapted without the use of high-sodium additives.

With our mission in hand, we contacted close friends who also have traveled or who now live in many different parts of the world. Naturally, we tapped them as good sources of ideas for some of the best recipes from their respective areas. Visits to ethnic restaurants in the United States helped us distinguish flavors and ingredients. Also, research about different countries was an invaluable resource.

We learned a lot while doing this project. It is apparent that the recipe trade has been going on for centuries, not unlike any other international trading of goods and ideas. The spice trade, emigrations, and religious observances all have a great bearing on the development of changing ideas about food. Eating, preparation, and sharing food are important parts of all cultures.

Many of our recipes come from Europe, where the diet is usually heavy in meat, fish, dairy, and eggs. They use a lot of root vegetables, particularly in the northern latitudes, where the growing season is short. They also pickle many vegetables and smoke meat for preservation. As one moves south and into warmer climates, the diet changes to what we refer to as Mediterranean. In ancient times, the Romans used the Via Salaria, literally the "salt road," which ran from Rome to Porto d'Ascoli on the Adriatic coast. It was the route by which the Sabines came to fetch salt from the marshes at the mouth of the Tiber

River. We found that by using the same fruits and vegetables, olive oil, herbs, and spices that are part of that wonderful Mediterranean cuisine, we can enjoy their delectable fare without the salt.

Venturing into Asia, we have many recipes from India, where we had fun working with their wonderful spice mixtures. They use cumin, coriander, chilies, ginger, and turmeric abundantly. Delicious *raitas,* or sauces, add so much to their tasty food that we found using salt unnecessary. We saw the same spices used in Africa and followed them to our own American dishes from the South. Many of our African American dishes truly had their roots in Africa, with their stews and soups using root vegetables like sweet potatoes and yams, fresh fish, shellfish, and peanuts. The use of citrus, figs, and dates made for some wonderful taste treats in the Middle East.

Don's tours of duty and the friendships he's made throughout his career brought back fond memories of the Far East. We've included recipes from Thailand, Vietnam, Japan, and China. Don's creative impulses took on the challenge of finding something that would replace soy, hoison, and *nam plah* sauces for these dishes. He was successful, and we know you'll really enjoy these foods again.

We enjoyed the varied cuisines of our own country. It is truly a melting pot. You can find just about anything here, but the various regions do dictate what is found most often, such as delicious fish from the Northwest and spicy Cajun food from the South. Mexican-influenced dishes from the Southwest led us right into Mexico, where it's easy to enjoy meals without salt.

Don is also the baker, and he so enjoyed including some of the world's best-known bread like challah, ciabatta, limpa, Russian black bread, and one of our favorites, steamed buns from China.

We've also included spice mixes that you can make ahead and have on hand. Maureen's Quick and Easy Chicken broth is another make-ahead item to be used in many recipes. We also suggest keeping lemons or limes both for their juice and zest. They really add a boost when cooking without salt, as do flavored vinegars. We borrowed three or four recipes from our previous three books to help you complete your adventure in cooking without salt. If you don't have them, you can pick them up at your local bookstore or at megaheart.com/amazon-link.html.

Please enjoy. We believe the recipes in this book will really enhance your target goals for better health and healthier eating.

—MAUREEN

FOREWORD

BY DR. MICHAEL FOWLER, M.B., F.R.C.P., RESEARCHER,
DIRECTOR STANFORD HEART TRANSPLANT PROGRAM

Salt, usually in the form of sodium chloride or table salt, has been used for the preservation and flavoring of foods since the emergence of modern man. For dietary purposes, salt contains a huge amount of sodium at 2,350 mg per teaspoon.

Sodium ions are crucial for the regulation of fluid balance and for the normal function of most systems including muscles and nerves. Current food production and distribution systems have resulted in a diet that contains excessive amounts of sodium, far in excess of the small intake required to maintain health and at a level that is now considered detrimental to a population at high risk of developing hypertension and heart disease. The lifetime risk of developing hypertension in a developed country is 90 percent and the lifetime risk of developing heart failure 20 percent. The high average consumption of dietary sodium—the bulk of it in the form of sodium chloride, or salt—is accepted as playing an important role in the development of hypertension and the subsequent risk for disease of the heart and blood vessels including heart failure, stroke, and kidney failure. Population studies have confirmed the links between sodium intake (on average two-and-a-half times higher than the reference nutrient intake recommendation in adults and probably even higher in children) and hypertension. The increased recognition and acceptance of the relationship between sodium intake and disease has led to recommendations by The American Medical Association that the maximum total daily sodium intake for healthy adults in the United States not exceed 1300 mg to 1800 mg/day, depending on level of activity* (table salt is sodium chloride and is 40 percent sodium by weight).

For individuals who have developed hypertension, or more significantly heart failure, regulation of sodium intake to much lower

*To see a copy of this report, please visit: www.megaheart.com/salt_homore.html.

levels than those advocated for healthy populations has become an accepted and important part of the therapy for these conditions.

Heart failure is a condition with characteristic symptoms, many of which result from an excessive retention of sodium with subsequent water retention. The accumulation (or buildup) of sodium and water in the lungs is largely responsible for the breathlessness, which is the prominent symptom of heart failure for many patients. The term "congestive heart failure" (CHF) emphasizes the prominent role sodium retention (and the consequent fluid accumulation) plays in the manifestations of heart failure. In its more extreme and severe form, patients will awake with the sensation of drowning, or be unable to lie flat due to the terrifying sensations caused by the "wet" lungs that result as sodium and water fill the lungs. Similar mechanisms are responsible for the ankle swelling experiences by many patients with heart failure, and for the abdominal swelling and discomfort also frequently experienced during periods of decompensation. In the United States there are now more than 1 million episodes of hospitalization for acute decompensated heart failure—the cause for a great deal of suffering in an often elderly population, and principally responsible for the very high costs related to the treatment of heart failure by the Medicare system.

Fortunately, patients with heart failure now have very effective therapies to improve overall survival and to reduce the risk of episodes of decompensation. The effective drugs all tend to reduce sodium accumulation or to actively promote its removal. Diuretics are the class of drugs which act specifically to increase the elimination of sodium by the kidneys. Patients are usually only aware of the impact of these agents on urine production and often refer to diuretics as "water pills." In fact the increased water elimination occurs only as a consequence of eliminating sodium.

The effectiveness of diuretics in relieving the symptoms of heart failure is dependent on sodium intake. Some individuals may be considered to be diuretic resistant and seem to have untreatable heart failure if diuretic therapy is not combined with consistent reduction in salt/sodium intake. Other patients may appear stable until a meal with high-sodium content precipitates an episode of severe decompensated heart failure. Other patients may seem to need a high dose of diuretics and even combination therapy with two types of diuretics in order to reduce the symptoms and physical signs that accompany excess fluid retention in heart failure. These patients are at high risk from electrolyte imbalance or worsening renal function precipitated by high dose diuretics. Many of these potential complications can be avoided if a low-sodium diet is followed on a routine basis with the dose of diuretics appropriately balanced against a consistent low-sodium dietary intake.

Increasing evidence also suggests that a low-sodium diet will not only reduce the risk of developing cardiovascular disease and dramatically reduce the symptoms and risk of hospitalization for heart failure, but that excess sodium in the diet may also influence the progression of heart failure. Experimental studies have shown that the characteristic abnormal and damaging changes that occur in heart muscle in an environment similar to that which exists in patients with heart failure only occurs when experimental animals are fed a diet high in sodium.

For many patients with heart failure and other conditions for which diuretics are required the adoption of a low-sodium diet has led to significant improvements in the number of "good days" and a reduction in the number of "bad days" they experience. For some patients the adoption of a low-sodium diet has meant the difference between recurrence or persistent symptoms of heart failure or an acceptable and stable, mildly symptomatic status. Although the changes in dietary habits required to follow a low-sodium diet are profound, most patients can recognize and appreciate the rewards achieved by improvement in their clinical status.

For most patients, avoiding foods with added sodium added at the time of food processing, not adding salt at the table or while cooking or preparing meals, and making appropriate menu choices from foods prepared in restaurants is all that is required to achieve the low-sodium diet needed to maintain health in heart failure and other diuretic requiring conditions. Initially many patients find that unfamiliarity of such a diet results in diminished recipe choices and leads to concerns that the diet will be bland. Don and Maureen Gazzaniga's cookbooks show that the health advantage of a low-sodium diet can be combined with good-tasting, interesting, and enjoyable food, and have proven to be a valuable and often utilized resource for patients who have come to appreciate the vital importance of reducing the sodium content of their diets.

PREFACE
HEALTH BENEFITS
RICH IN ETHNIC
CUISINES

◈ ◈ ◈ ◈ ◈ ◈ ◈ ◈

By Jeannie Gazzaniga Moloo, Ph.D., R.D.

In this cookbook, you will find recipes with blends of spices and herbs that are unique to cooking around the world. For example, there are dishes using garlic, turmeric, coriander, cloves, cinnamon, sage, or oregano, to name just a few. Gone is the salt, but present in each dish is a blend of flavors that will enhance your palate and bring back the joy to cooking and low-sodium eating.

The health benefits of ethnic cuisines are as numerous as the types and textures of dishes from around the world. Spices and herbs such as garlic and turmeric have powerful antioxidant and anti-inflammatory properties. Inflammation happens in the body when a cascade of inflammatory compounds is released by the body in response to a diet high in sugar or trans fats, being overweight, sedentary, or smoking. Research has shown that a pro-inflammatory state may be related to many autoimmune diseases such as Crohn's disease, lupus, psoriasis, as well as asthma, arthritis, gingivitis, sinusitis, and heart disease. Foods that fight inflammation should be the cornerstone of a healthy diet. Such foods include many of the spices, herbs, fruits, and vegetables used for years in ethnic cuisines around the world.

Some of the more commonly used spices and herbs in this cookbook are cayenne, cumin, garlic, ginger, oregano, rosemary, and turmeric. Cayenne, including chili pepper, paprika, and red pepper, is often used in Mexican or Tex-Mex cuisine. Cayenne contains capsaicinoids that are thought to promote cardiovascular health by lowering blood cholesterol, triglyceride, and platelet aggregation. The capsaicinoids are also being studied as an effective treatment for pain associated with arthritis, psoriasis, and diabetic neuropathy.

Cumin has a nutty peppery flavor that adds zip to Mexican dishes as well as plays an important role in Indian and Middle Eastern cuisines. Cumin is noted for aiding digestion and may have potent anticancer properties.

Fennel Seed is most often associated with Italian cooking. It has its own unique combination of phytonutrients, including flavonoids that provide strong antioxidant properties.

Garlic, often used in Mediterranean and Asian dishes, is known for its cardiovascular protective effects. The allyl sulfides in garlic may reduce cholesterol, make the blood less sticky, help lower blood pressure, and even provide some natural antibiotic effects. To release garlic's potent compounds, you need to smash, mash, or mince it. However, cooking it for a long time or at a high heat may destroy its beneficial substances. To retain some of the biologically active compounds lost when heated, let the raw garlic sit for 10 minutes after crushing.

Ginger is known for relieving nausea, aiding digestion, and countering inflammation. It is commonly used in Asian and East Indian meat dishes, breads, chutneys, and desserts. Ginger adds a wonderful flavor making up for any missed sodium in the dish. Even though dried ginger is a more powerful anti-inflammatory agent than fresh, either version of the rhizome is going to carry health benefits.

Oregano is used in Mediterranean and Mexican dishes, such as lasagne and marinara and enchilada sauces. Oregano is loaded with phytonutrients including thymol and rosmarinic acid that function as potent antioxidants. In this cookbook, you will find oregano in recipes for Basque Chorizo (Spain), Maureen's Easy Enchilada Sauce (Mexico), and Italian Lasagne, to name just a few.

Turmeric, best known as one of the ingredients in East Indian curries, is fast becoming one of the most intensely studied spices, attracting attention for its anti-inflammatory and anticancer effects.

Because it is a concentrated spice only small amounts are typically used in cooking. However, even a pinch of turmeric carries potent health benefits and adds nice color to many meat and vegetable dishes as well as breads.

Cuisines from many countries are made from staples such as beans, lentils, rice, and pasta. Beans are an excellent source of low-fat plant protein. Soluble fiber from foods such as beans, as part of a diet low in saturated fat and cholesterol, may reduce the risk of heart disease. Red, yellow, or green lentils supply complex carbohydrates and healthy amounts of thiamin, vitamin B_6, folic acid, iron, zinc, and potassium. Simmered until creamy, pureed and flavored with garam masala, sautéed onions, tomatoes, cumin, and mustard seeds, lentils taste fabulous and pack a powerful dish as an Indian dal (page 232).

We hope the recipes in this cookbook help you begin your gastronomic tour around the world the low-sodium way.

WHAT IS MEGAHEART.COM?

MegaHeart.com is operated by Donald A. Gazzaniga and a small staff of volunteer helpers. The Web site is committed to enhancing the quality of life for members who have been ordered by their medical practitioner to "cut the salt out." These include heart patients, hypertension patients, those with liver and kidney diseases and Ménière's syndrome, and others wishing to reduce their risk of suffering heart failure—by delivering no-salt/lowered-sodium recipes. MegaHeart also provides links to reliable resources for information relating to heart failure and other maladies demanding a low-sodium lifestyle.

The Web site has a monthly newsletter with fresh new recipes that are not found in our cookbooks. Information also abounds at the site concerning sodium, locations to purchase no-salt-added ingredients, and other helpful information.

You can visit the author at www.megaheart.com and if you have any questions he's always there to help you.

WHERE WE GET OUR NUTRITION DATA

Nutrient data in this book is based on the USDA's SR18. That means it's the eighteenth major change made in their "Standard Reference" for food ratings as of 2006.

The Nutrition Company, www.nutrico.com, supplies our USDA database software to us. The Nutrition Company monitors the USDA's giant resources for all food information, collects their data, collates it, and puts it into a format you and I can better understand.

The Nutrition Company provides excellent software (Foodworks©) at low prices for dietitians, publishers, and cookbook writers, and for you if you're interested in monitoring your intake pertaining to your age, weight, and other factors.

Comparing it with our other books, you will notice some changes in this book in a few ingredients pertaining to their nutrient data. These changes won't significantly affect any of the data in our books, since the changes made by the USDA in most nutrient values either were small or tended to balance each other out.

Following is a list of the nutrients we chose to emphasize in recipes and the reasons why. The nutrients highlighted in recipes include calories, protein carbohydrates, dietary fiber (insoluble and soluble), total sugars, total fats, cholesterol, trans-fatty acids, omega-3 fatty acids, omega-6 fatty acids, potassium, sodium, vitamin K, and folic acid.

CALORIES

Calories listed for each recipe is the amount of energy in the serving size for that particular recipe. Protein, carbohydrates, and fat are the only nutrients that provide calories. Balancing the amount of calories we eat with the amount we expend is critical for healthy weight management.

Protein

Protein is an essential nutrient for maintenance and repair of all cells in the body. Amino acids are the building blocks of protein. Foods rich in protein are meats, beans, eggs, and dairy products.

Carbohydrates

Carbohydrates are the body's primary source of energy. Carbohydrates are found in fruits, vegetables, whole grains, and dairy products. Other components of carbohydrates are dietary fibers, including soluble and insoluble dietary fiber, and sugars. Soluble fiber absorbs water and is often found in fruits and vegetables and whole grains. Research has shown that a diet rich in soluble fiber can help lower blood cholesterol. Insoluble fiber has bulking properties that help keep the gastrointestinal tract functioning healthy.

How Do We Deal With Carbohydrates?

Carbohydrates are found in bread, fruit, starchy vegetables, sugars, and dairy products. Carbohydrates are the body's primary source of energy. All carbohydrates are eventually broken down into glucose, the type of sugar our bodies use as fuel.

If you have diabetes then you know that eating well means controlling your blood sugar and maintaining a healthy weight. Toward that end we have offered suggestions in this book for each recipe. Many can be fit into your daily carbohydrate choices and exchanges. With each recipe we list whether it is acceptable for choices and exchanges or whether you need to adjust the recipe to make it work for you.

You will find one of three offerings with each recipe. They are:

Diabetic Acceptable This allows for proper carbohydrate choices and exchanges. Most of these recipes are well within the 1 to 2 choices ratings.

Generally, one carbohydrate choice equals 15 grams of carbohydrates. Your best bet for figuring choices and exchanges is by getting a copy of *The Official Pocket Guide to Diabetic Exchanges*. This book is from the American Diabetic Association. You can find a copy of this at www.megaheart.com/kit_cookbooks.html or in most bookstores.

Diabetic Adaptable This generally means a recipe contains ingredients such as sugar, rice, and other rich carbohydrate food, which might need substitutes. Usually sugars contain a bulk of a recipe's carbohydrates. Carbohydrate choices are usually within acceptable ranges.

Some recipes in this book may state they are diabetic adaptable but the adaptation may require altering the flavor. Our suggestions to lower the carbohydrates usually alter the flavor favorably. Since sugars have a high level of carbohydrates, many of our adaptations require altering a sauce or other ingredient containing one of the sugar items used, such as molasses, brown sugar, white sugar, or other high-carbohydrate ingredients.

Not Diabetic Adaptable This is not set in concrete, but it does indicate that it might be more expensive to "fix" for a choice than the energy is worth (the expense would be the quantity of Splenda or other sugar substitute needed to help lower the carbohydrates in the recipe). It may also mean that to adjust it would alter the flavors radically and unfavorably, thereby rendering the recipe not as enjoyable as it would otherwise be.

Dietary Fiber (Roughage or bulk)

Dietary fiber includes all parts of plant foods that your body can't digest or absorb. (We use flaxseed meal and wheat or oat bran added to our meals for this.) Fiber is often classified into two categories: those that don't dissolve in water: insoluble fiber, and those that do: soluble fiber.

Insoluble fiber includes whole wheat flour (white, red, or pastry); wheat bran, nuts, and many vegetables are good sources of insoluble fiber. These forms of fiber increase the movement of material through your digestive system and increases stool bulk, so it can be of benefit to those who struggle with constipation or irregular stools.

Soluble fiber includes oats, peas, beans, apples, citrus fruits, carrots, barley, and psyllium. These dissolve in water to form a gel-like material. It can help lower blood cholesterol and glucose levels.

The amount of each type of fiber varies in different plant foods. That's one reason we encourage you to add fiber to any recipe where you believe you can increase it for your own health.

For instance, you can add more fiber to any of our bread recipes, salads, entrées, and desserts. It's easy, simply replace butter or oil using a ratio of 3 tablespoons of flaxseed meal to 1 tablespoon of olive oil or butter. Add oats to your bread recipe or scones or even your breakfast fare. Keep a bowl of flaxseed meal or wheat bran on your table with a spoon. That may remind you to add flaxseed to your morning cereal or your lunch salad. Two tablespoons of flaxseed meal will add 4 grams of fiber to what you eat. By the way, a high-fiber diet may also help you lose weight.

Total Sugars

Sugar (sucrose) is a carbohydrate that occurs naturally in all fruits and vegetables. It is a major product of the process used for plants to transform the sun's energy into food: photosynthesis.

Dietary sugar is found in great quantities in sugarcane and sugar beets. It is from these that dietary sugar is extracted for commercial use. Sugars or nutritive sweeteners also include honey, maple syrup, corn syrup, high fructose corn syrup, fructose, and fruit juice concentrates.

There are a few new sugar substitutes not considered as "potentially harmful" as were some in the past. These are Splenda (sucralose) and stevia, a blend of natural herbs. You can learn more about stevia at www.stevia.net/. And you can learn more about Splenda at: www.splenda.com/.

Splenda, by the way, now has a brown sugar blend that lowers sugar levels appreciably. It is, however, not sugarfree.

Total Fats

Dietary fats are a rich source of energy in our diet. As a food ingredient, fat provides flavor, consistency, and stability, and helps you feel full. Total fats consist of saturated and unsaturated fatty acids. Saturated fats are found in animal fats from meats, eggs, and dairy products. The consumption of too many saturated fats has been linked to heart disease. Unsaturated fats are liquid at room temperature and found primarily in vegetable oils, whole grains, nuts, and seeds. Monounsaturated fats have been shown to help lower cholesterol and other blood fats providing protection against the development of heart disease.

CHOLESTEROL

Cholesterol is a soft, waxy substance found among the fats (lipids) in your bloodstream and for that matter, in all your body's cells. The American Heart Association recommends persons with heart disease should limit dietary cholesterol to 200 mg a day. All animal foods except fat-free versions contain cholesterol. These include meats, eggs, and dairy products.

TRANS-FATTY ACIDS

Trans-fatty acids occur when vegetable oils are hydrogenated. Some trans fats do occur naturally in foods, however, most of the trans fats in people's diets come from processed foods that use hydrogenated vegetable oils as the primary fat source. Most recipes in this cookbook are free of trans fats, with a few exceptions, where trans fats occur naturally in a food.

TOTAL OMEGA-3 AND OMEGA-6 FATTY ACIDS

Omega-3 and omega-6 fatty acids are both essential fatty acids, meaning the body cannot make them so we need to get them from our diet. Omega-3 fatty acids are found in salmon, walnuts, flax, and other foods. Grass-fed beef has a higher omega-3 fatty acid content than does grain-fed beef. Omega-3 fatty acids are known for their anti-inflammatory effects on the body. Omega-6 fatty acids are rich in vegetable oils and animal foods. The typical American diet is often high in omega-6 fats and low in omega-3 fats. The Mediterranean diet, which includes generous amounts of whole grains, fruits, vegetables, and olive oil, and little meat, is a diet much richer in omega-3 fatty acids than is the typical Western diet.

Potassium

Potassium is important for nerve-impulse transmission and fluid balance. It's an important nutrient for normal heart, digestive, skeletal and muscular function. If you are concerned about the potassium content of your diet, discuss this with your physician and registered dietitian.

Sodium

One of my favorite sayings is, "It's not the salt, it's the sodium that matters." Sodium, quite literally, is in nearly everything we eat from apples to zucchini.

Sodium is a mineral needed by the body to keep fluids in balance. The largest source of dietary sodium comes from sodium chloride, or table salt, which can be found in processed foods—and in the salt shaker. Too much sodium can cause our bodies to retain water or fluids, and those fluids in turn put pressure on our systems (heart, blood vessels, kidneys, etc.).

For more information see: www.megaheart.com/sodium_all_about .html.

Vitamin K

Vitamin K acts as a blood thickener. It can decrease the effects of coumadin and warfarin. We list vitamin K for each recipe because of this.

Folate (folic acid)

Folate (folic acid is the synthetic form of folate) is a water-soluble vitamin that helps the body form red blood cells and aids in the formation of genetic material within every body cell. Folate plays a role in reducing blood homocysteine levels, and helps with the formation of red blood cells and cell growth and division. Folate is prominent in the following foods: grains, green leafy vegetables, and fruits including oranges, strawberries, and cantaloupes.

What do the terms used in the recipes mean?

Trace

In our data tag to each ingredient, when you see the word *trace* it means that either the levels are too low to include or are listed as zero by the USDA.

No-Salt-Added (NSA)

This generally means a manufacturer has not added salt to the ingredients in the packaging. It does not mean there isn't any sodium in the packaged food. Check the FDA label for USDA figures.

Filtered Water, Low-Sodium Water

Throughout the world, water varies in levels of nutrients. Many of those nutrients are absolutely necessary for our good health. "Filtered water" means water that has had certain elements, some added by water companies, removed. Chlorine is one such chemical. Other things removed can be toxins, bacteria (like giardia), etc. We do not recommend reverse-osmosis water, since it extracts all the good nutrients with everything else. Bottled, filtered drinking water is probably your best bet if you don't have a filter in your house. Distilled or purified water will have all nutrients out of it. A steady diet of that could negatively affect your health.

Grams (g), Milligrams (mg)

Measurements of weight. A conversion table is available in *The No-Salt, Lowest-Sodium Light Meals Book* and at www.megaheart.com.

Organic Meat, Vegetables and Fruits

Organic refers to the way agricultural products—food and fiber—are grown and processed. Organic food production is based on a system of farming that maintains and replenishes soil fertility without the use of toxic and persistent pesticides and fertilizers. Organic foods are minimally processed without artificial ingredients, preservatives, or irradiation to maintain the integrity of the food.

—Organic Trade Association.*

We recommend that all the beef and dairy products you eat be organic. Beef will be listed as "grass-fed," or "organic." Eggs will usually be listed as "organic."

We know that grass-fed and natural grain-fed wild game make the healthiest eating possible for humans seeking protein through meat. It appears that grass-fed beef ranks right up there with wild game. And one other thing is certain: Organic cattle will not be prone to mad cow disease.

*For more about organics visit the Web at: www.ota.com.

Using This Cookbook with Diabetes Management

Replacements or exchanges for some of our basic ingredients are probably already in your vocabulary.

We figured nutrient data on what you see listed in each recipe.

For some products like nonfat milk, we recommend lactose-free or lactose-reduced nonfat milk. There are no sugars in lactose-free or lactose-reduced milk, and carbohydrates per cup are 11.9 g.

For white granulated sugar, we recommend using Splenda as a replacement, although another product, stevia is also available. See www.sweetleaf.com.

Although we list our recipes as diabetic acceptable or diabetic adaptable, they may or may not meet your specific needs.

Exchange charts are available if you don't already have a few and, of course, plenty of information is available from your registered dietitian and from the American Diabetic Association. See www .diabetes.org.

We have included a long list of foods and ingredients at the back of this book with each ingredient displaying most of the important nutrients in our lives and certainly all those in this book. You can find carbohydrates and other nutrients in that section.

If you need further help adapting our recipes, we suggest you visit with your dietitian or doctor.

If you have specific questions about any of our recipes, visit www.megaheart.com and e-mail us from any of the many contact points provided there.

BREAD IN EVERY CUISINE

Bread is enjoyed around the world. We think you'll be pleasantly surprised with some great flavors in the bread recipes in this book—recipes from Ethiopia, Holland, France and, yes, from a country where bread is not a big thing, China. The Chinese do not have a "bread," but they do have steamed buns, and if you'll make these, you'll fall in love with them.

We also created no-salt versions of Jewish challah, and no-salt bread recipes from Poland, Portugal, Russia, Italy, and Sweden. Please give each a try. We believe you'll fall in love with each of them, too.

WHAT'S NEW ABOUT NO-SALT BREAD MAKING?

When we first started making no-salt bread on a daily basis, the only information available was, "It can't be done."

From commercial flour processors to commercial and retail bakeries, they told us it was not possible. Fortunately, we had been doing it for a long time and knew it was possible.

What we have always wanted to develop however, was a no-salt bread that would stay fresh for as nearly as long as a commercial loaf does.

We also had the challenge of writing bread recipes for those who had heart failure and very little strength to knead bread. Thus, we created breads using bread machines to knead and then bake in our ovens, or knead and bake in the machine. We learned later, however, that low-sodium lifestyles were being prescribed for people with Ménière's syndrome, hypertension, kidney and liver ailments, and other diseases as well. Some could not consume high levels of potassium or vitamin K, others wanted fats as low as possible. And then we learned that a high percentage of heart patients eventually end up with diabetes.

At megaheart.com, we receive hundreds of questions each week about where to find foods without salt, potassium, fat, vitamin K, etc. The challenges kept coming at us, and with each new step our bread recipes were altered to meet as many of the requirements as called for.

We believe that the ethnic-based bread recipes in this book are the best yet and meet most of the above standards.

A good no-salt bread recipe will contain either some or all of these additional ingredients if you want get close to commercial shelf life and texture: ascorbic acid, gluten, vinegar, potato flour (but not always), sugar or Splenda, white or whole wheat flour, granular lecithin (but not always), yeast, sometimes barley malt flour, and any additions the recipe might call for such as fruit or nuts or spices. We also suggest adding a dash or a measurement of granulated onion powder to simulate the "salt kick." Once you get the hang of making no-salt bread, you'll find yourself experimenting and you'll come up with some terrific bread, rolls, buns, and other forms for yourself and your family and friends.

WHAT'S NEW WITH BREAD MACHINES?

Since our first book, *The No-Salt, Lowest-Sodium Cookbook*, bread machines have changed, sometimes for the better, sometimes not. Our highly touted machine back then was the Breadman TR-810. This was a double-paddle bread machine and it worked wonderfully for both small and large orders. It could whip out a six-cup batch of dough with no trouble and bake any loaf with evenly golden-brown crust. It cleaned well, made very little noise, and was such a durable machine that our ten-year-old TR-810 still operates. The marvel of that is that we make a lot of bread, much more than what Breadman probably had in mind. The Salton company took over Breadman and discontinued that model as well as our next choice, the TR2200C. We recommend you visit www.megaheart .com/kit_cabinet.html to learn which of the many current bread machines on the market we recommend for our recipes.

Whichever machine you decide to purchase, we recommend that that it be capable of a 1½-, 2-, or 2½-pound loaf.

Many of the bread recipes in this book are for the bread machine to knead and bake. Others are bread machine–knead with oven cooking. The recipes where you want the machine to knead the dough for oven cooking, are generally from 4 to 6 cups of flour and sometimes with fruit or nuts. It is for those recipes that you want the larger more powerful machine. We also recommend that you remove the dough when using these larger recipes, place it into a lightly greased, room-temperature bowl, cover it with a light cloth, and let it rise in a warm spot. Then follow the recipe from that first rise through the baking.

At www.megaheart.com/kit_cabinet.html, we will always have the latest and best machines on the market listed. (We have no affiliation with any manufacturers.) It's wise to check there before purchasing a new machine.* And if you have any specific questions, please don't hesitate to e-mail us from the site.

*All are available online as well. For links visit www.megaheart.com/wheretobuy.html.

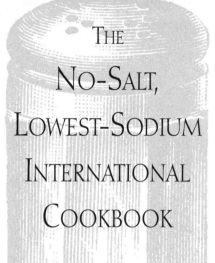

The
No-Salt,
Lowest-Sodium
International
Cookbook

DESSERTS & SWEETS

❖ ❖ ❖ ❖ ❖ ❖ ❖ ❖

Worldwide, desserts and sweets have been a passion for chefs and gourmands for centuries. Especially in Europe the creation of auto-graphed candies, pies, cakes, and other sweets has built reputations for pastry chefs and chocolate companies.

It would take an encyclopedia to list all the known desserts and sweets throughout the world, and an art book of professionally snapped photos to whet our palettes. At least that way we wouldn't devour so many calories.

Unfortunately, if our hearts are in trouble, we can't even think about eating most of them. Too many are loaded with high levels of fat, sodium, and partially hydrogenated oils.

But don't let that spoil your day. In this section, we've pulled to-gether some unique desserts, from spicy Almond Bars (really good) to Italian Cannoli to the best-tasting fruitcake you'll ever eat. Don't run away now just because we said "fruitcake." This isn't one of those dry, commercial types that show up sometimes just when you've ditched your jogging shoes. This one's easy to make, easy to bake, and wonderfully tasty after anointing with brandy and allow-ing it to sit for a day or two. If it wasn't a great treat, we wouldn't have included it.

You'll love our Chocolate Mousse as well, and the German Stollen, and Marzipan-Stuffed Apples.

Everything in our sweets section can be made with Splenda sugar substitute, using equal portions of Splenda for sugar.

❖ One-Crust No-Trans-Fats Pie Shell ❖

ORIGIN: U.S.A.
DIABETIC ACCEPTABLE

When we learned that Crisco had decided to jump on the no-trans-fats bandwagon, we picked up a can and came up with this basic one-crust pie shell. It works well with our pies and has one-half the saturated fats compared to a regular pie shell and no trans fats.

MAKES ONE 9- TO 10-INCH PIE SHELL
SODIUM PER RECIPE: 2.5 MG
SODIUM PER SLICE (8): .312 MG

1   cup all-purpose flour (2.5 mg)
½   cup Crisco's Zero Trans Fat shortening (trace)
4   to 8 tablespoons low-sodium water (trace)

Prepare a pie pan by lightly oiling it.

In a medium mixing bowl, combine the flour and Crisco until the shortening is the size of small peas. Add the cold water a tablespoon at a time, using a fork to mix. When the dough is wet enough, use your hands until the pastry is well mixed and pliable. Roll out the dough into a disk on a floured board to size slightly larger than the pie pan. Roll up the disk on the rolling pan, then unroll over the pie pan. Crimp the edges and discard the leftover dough.

Bake in a preheated oven at 425°F for 10 to 12 minutes

Nutrient Data per Slice (8):
Calories: 166.9. Protein: 1.614 g. Carbohydrate: 11.9 g. Dietary Fiber: .422 g. Total Sugars: .042 g. Total Fat: 12.2 g. Saturated Fat: 3.024 g. Monounsaturated Fat: 5.014 g. Polyunsaturated Fat: 4.065 g. Cholesterol: 0 mg. Trans Fat: 0 g. Total Omega-3 FA: .003 g. Total Omega-6 FA: 0 g. Potassium: 16.7 mg. Sodium: .312 mg. Vitamin K: .047 mcg. Folic Acid: 24.1 mcg.

❖ One-Crust, Butter-Rich Pie Shell ❖

ORIGIN: U.S.A.
MADE WITH UNSALTED BUTTER*
DIABETIC ACCEPTABLE

For one-crust fruit pies.

*See One-Crust Pie shell made with Crisco's Zero Trans Fats shortening. It also has one-half the saturated fats.

1   cup unbleached, all-purpose flour (2.5 mg)
6   tablespoons unsalted butter, softened (9.372 mg)
¼   cup cold low-sodium water (trace)
1   teaspoon vanilla extract (.378 mg)

Prepare a 9-inch pie pan by lightly oiling it.

In a medium mixing bowl, mix together the flour and butter until the butter is the size of small peas. Use either a pastry blender or your finger-tips to do this.

Add the vanilla and 2 tablespoons of the water, mixing with a fork. Add the rest of the water if needed. (If you need even more water, add it only 1 tablespoon at a time.)

Roll the dough out into a disk on a lightly floured board until ⅛ inch thick and slightly larger than the pie pan. Using your flour-dusted rolling pin, and starting at one edge of the crust, roll the crust up on the pin.

Lay the pin on one edge of the pie pan and unroll the dough over the pie pan. Fit the crust into the pan using your hands and crimp the dough along the edges to finish off the shell.

Bake in a preheated oven at 425°F for 10 to 12 minutes.

Nutrient Data per Serving (8 slices)
Calories: 134.7. Protein: 1.705 g. Carbohydrate: 12 g. Dietary Fiber: .422 g. Total Sugars: .115 g. Total Fat: 8.792 g. Saturated Fat: 5.495 g. Monounsaturated Fat: 2.252 g. Polyunsaturated Fat: .389 g. Cholesterol: 22.9 mg. Trans Fat: 0 g. Total Omega-3 FA: .071 g. Total Omega-6 FA: .231 g. Potassium: 20.1 mg. Sodium: 1.531 mg. Vitamin K: .792 mcg. Folic Acid: 24.1 mcg.

❈ ALMOND SPICE BARS ❈

ORIGIN: GERMANY
NOT DIABETIC ADAPTABLE*

This "cookie" is a popular spice bar in Germany, and no wonder. The flavors tease your palate with just enough almond, lemon, and allspice to make you want more. These make a good dessert as well. Mix according to the directions, and the cakelike batter will rise perfectly.

MAKES THIRTY 3-INCH OR FORTY-EIGHT 2- TO 2½-INCH BARS
SODIUM PER RECIPE: 208 MG
SODIUM PER BAR (30): 6.934 MG
SODIUM PER BAR (48): 4.334 MG

THE SPICE BARS

No-stick cooking spray

2¼ cups unbleached, all-purpose flour (5.625 mg)
½   cup unsalted whole almonds, ground or finely chopped
      (.69 mg)
2   level teaspoons grated lemon zest (.24 mg)
1   teaspoon ground cinnamon (.598 mg)
1   teaspoon ground allspice (1.463 mg)
¼   teaspoon ground cloves (1.276 mg)
2   large eggs (126 mg)
¾   cup white granulated sugar (trace)
¾   cup honey (10.2 mg)
½   cup nonfat milk with added vitamins A & D (51.5 mg)
2   teaspoons Featherweight Baking Powder (9 mg)

THE GLAZE

1   cup confectioners' sugar (1.2 mg)
½   teaspoon almond extract (.189 mg)
1   teaspoon grated lemon zest (.12 mg)
1   tablespoon plus 1 teaspoon low-sodium water (trace)

To make the bars: Preheat the oven to 400°F. Prepare a 17×11-inch baking or jelly-roll pan by spraying the bottom and sides with no-stick cooking spray and then dusting it with flour.

In a small bowl, stir together the flour, almonds, lemon zest, and spices.

In a medium mixing bowl, beat the eggs and sugar until thick and smooth, about 4 minutes. Stir in the honey and milk with a wooden spoon.

When the oven has reached 400°F, gradually stir into the honey mixture, the flour mixture still using the wooden spoon, and beat until smooth. Add the baking powder and beat for about 1 minute, or until well mixed.

Using a rubber spatula, spread the batter quickly and smoothly in the prepared pan. Put the pan into the oven immediately and bake for about 12 to 15 minutes, or until the bars are done; when you press down gently on the top it will spring back.

While the bars are baking, prepare the glaze. Mix all the ingredients in a small mixing bowl and beat until smooth.

Remove the bars from the oven, let stand for 1 or 2 minutes, and then turn out onto a wire rack. If you want the baked top to be the top of the bars, then top with another rack and invert once again.

Spread the hot or warm bars with the glaze. You want them completely covered with a thin glaze. Immediately after glazing, cut into 1×3-inch or 1×2–2½-inch bars.

To store, place the bars on a paper plate or a dish and freeze. Once frozen, transfer to ziplock bags. Or store on the shelf in a ziplock bag for up to 5 days.

Nutrient Data per Spice Bar (30):
Calories: 115.9. Protein: 2.07 g. Carbohydrate: 24.1 g. Dietary Fiber: .631 g. Total Sugars: 16.1 g. Total Fat: 1.659 g. Saturated Fat: .22 g. Monounsaturated Fat: .914 g. Polyunsaturated Fat: .381 g. Cholesterol: 14.2 mg. Trans Fat: 0 g. Total Omega-3 FA: .006 g. Total Omega-6 FA: 0 g. Potassium: 77.9 mg. Sodium: 6.934 mg. Vitamin K: .087 mcg. Folic Acid: 14.4 mcg.

Nutrient Data per Spice Bar (48):
Calories: 72.4. Protein: 1.294 g. Carbohydrate: 15.1 g. Dietary Fiber: .395 g. Total Sugars: 10.1 g. Total Fat: 1.037 g. Saturated Fat: .137 g. Monounsaturated Fat: .571 g. Polyunsaturated Fat: .238 g. Cholesterol: 8.864 mg. Trans Fat: 0 g. Total Omega-3 FA: .003 g. Total Omega-6 FA: 0 g. Potassium: 48.7 mg. Sodium: 4.334 mg. Vitamin K: .054 mcg. Folic Acid: 9.023 mcgcg.

❈ CHOCOLATE COOKIES ❈

ORIGIN: AUSTRIA
DIABETIC ADAPTABLE

If you make these, serve them as occasional treats. If you ever travel to Austria, ask for the real thing and you can be assured, unless they change the original recipe, that there will be no salt, baking powder, or baking soda included. But, always ask.

The Austrians like to put a glaze on these cookies although I prefer them without the glaze. (I also like Baker's German's Baking Chocolate, which may be the reason.) I suggest you try them each way and decide for yourself— it's also more fun that way.

MAKES: TWENTY-FIVE 2-INCH COOKIES
SODIUM PER RECIPE (WITHOUT GLAZE): 80.4 MG
SODIUM PER RECIPE (WITH GLAZE): 96.3 MG
SODIUM PER COOKIE (WITHOUT GLAZE): 3.216 MG
SODIUM PER COOKIE (WITH GLAZE): 3.854 MG

THE COOKIE

2   squares (13 grams) Baker's German's sweet chocolate* (.465 mg)
5   tablespoons unsalted butter (7.81 mg)
1   cup white granulated sugar or Splenda (.084 mg)
1   large egg (63 mg)
1   egg yolk (8.16 mg)
½   teaspoon vanilla extract (.189 mg)
1⅓   cups all-purpose flour (3.325 mg)
⅓   cup unsalted walnuts, finely chopped (.792 mg)

*If you don't care for Baker's German's chocolate, then choose either Baker's brand Bittersweet or Semisweet chocolate.

THE GLAZE

1   square Baker's German's sweet chocolate (.232 mg)
1   tablespoon unsalted butter (1.562 mg)
¼   teaspoon vanilla extract (.094 mg)
1   cup confectioners' sugar, unsifted (1.2 mg)
2   tablespoons nonfat milk with added vitamins A & D
    (12.9 mg)

Preheat oven to 350°F.

To make the cookies: Melt together the chocolate and the unsalted butter in a medium saucepan.

Remove from heat, stir in the sugar, whole egg, egg yolk, and vanilla, and mix together well. Stir in the flour and unsalted walnuts.

Shape into ¾- to 1-inch balls. Place on cookie sheets lined with parchment paper.

Bake at 350°F for 8 to 12 minutes.

To make the glaze: Melt the chocolate and unsalted butter in a small saucepan. Remove from heat. Add the vanilla, confectioners' sugar, and nonfat milk, and blend well.

Dip the cookies into the glaze to cover. Let dry on waxed paper before storing.

Store the cookies in an airtight container between layers of waxed paper.

Serve as treats.

Nutrient Date per Cookie with Glaze:
Calories: 63.7. Protein: .751 g. Carbohydrate: 5.53 g. Dietary Fiber: .117 g. Total Sugars: 5.007 g. Total Fat: 4.564 g. Saturated Fat: 2.217 g. Monounsaturated Fat: 1.166 g. Polyunsaturated Fat: .902 g. Cholesterol: 24.2 mg. Trans Fat: 0 g. Total Omega-3 FA: .165 g. Total Omega-6 FA: .074 g. Potassium: 20.1 mg. Sodium: 3.854 mg. Vitamin K: .291 mcg. Folic Acid: 0 mcg.

Nutrient Date per Cookie Without Glaze:
Calories: 39.1. Protein: .677 g. Carbohydrate: .599 g. Dietary Fiber: .113 g. Total Sugars: .24 g. Total Fat: 3.962 g. Saturated Fat: 1.842 g. Monounsaturated Fat: .993 g. Polyunsaturated Fat: .878 g. Cholesterol: 23 mg. Trans Fat: 0 g. Total Omega-3 FA: .161 g. Total Omega-6 FA: .062 g. Potassium: 15.6 mg. Sodium: 3.216 mg. Vitamin K: .251 mcg. Folic Acid: 0 mcg.

❖ MARZIPAN-STUFFED APPLES ❖

ORIGIN: GERMANY
NOT DIABETIC ADAPTABLE

I've been a baked apple nut since I can remember and that goes before kindergarten. I would eat others' leftovers when a child. It didn't really matter that far back how they were baked, as long as they were baked with something sweet. Germans like baked apples as well, and they know how to make them with many variations including this one. We use a nonalcoholic wine (Fré) to make the glaze. Serve hot, with the glaze ladled over the apples.

MAKES 8 WHOLE-APPLE SERVINGS   MAKES 16 HALF-APPLE SERVINGS*
SODIUM PER RECIPE: 40.6 MG
SODIUM PER SERVING (WHOLE APPLE): 5.074
SODIUM PER SERVING (HALF APPLE): 2.537

THE GLAZE
⅔ cup nonalcoholic wine** or red grape juice (12.2 mg)
⅓ cup white granulated sugar or Splenda (trace)
⅓ cup raw honey (4.515 mg)
1 tablespoon unsalted butter† (1.562 mg)

THE APPLE
8 medium Granny Smith apples, unpeeled but cored (11 mg)
1 lemon, zested and halved (1.16 mg)
1 (7-ounce) package marzipan, at room temperature and chopped or diced (trace)
1 cup fresh or unthawed frozen cranberries, lightly chopped or each berry halved (3.6 mg)
⅓ cup golden raisins (6.534 mg)
2 level tablespoons chopped unsalted almonds‡ (3.408 mg)
2 teaspoons grated lemon zest (from above lemon) (.72 mg)
½ teaspoon ground cinnamon (.299 mg)
¼ teaspoon ground nutmeg (.088 mg)

Prepare the glaze: In a medium or small heavy-bottomed saucepan bring the wine, sugar or Splenda, honey, and butter to a boil. Reduce the heat and let simmer for 10 to 12 minutes. Set the glaze aside.

Preheat oven to 375°F.

Wash and core the apples. Peel only the top half. Brush the top half with the cut side of half the lemon; this will keep the apples from turning brown. Reserve the lemon half.

Set the apples upright in a large baking pan, being careful that the apples are not touching each other or the pan itself.

*These apples are sweet and delicious and high in calories. So, we serve a half apple in a dessert dish and it works out well.
**Fré makes a good nonalcoholic wine. There are others as well.
†You can add one or two more to help with the syrup if you think it's needed.
‡Quick work with a handheld blender mechanism.

Mix together the marzipan, lemon juice from the two lemon halves, the fresh or frozen cranberries, golden raisins, almonds, lemon zest, cinnamon, and nutmeg. Press the mixture into the core of each apple firmly, packing in as much as you can.

Using a turkey baster, baste the apples and the filling with the glazing syrup.

Bake for 50 to 60 minutes, reglazing the apples with the remaining syrup halfway through.

Serve hot. The apples can be covered and chilled and then reheated for serving later. To reheat, set the oven to 300°F and warm the apples for about 20 minutes.

Nutrient Data per Apple:
Calories: 306.1. Protein: 3.312 g. Carbohydrate: 64.5 g. Dietary Fiber: 5.291 g. Total Sugars: 51.3 g. Total Fat: 6.374 g. Saturated Fat: 1.189 g. Monounsaturated Fat: 1.721 g. Polyunsaturated Fat: .662 g. Cholesterol: 3.816 mg. Trans Fat: 0 g. Total Omega-3 FA: .047 g. Total Omega-6 FA: .038 g. Potassium: 262.1 mg. Sodium: 5.074 mg. Vitamin K: 4.013 mcg. Folic Acid: 0 mcg.

Nutrient Data per Half Apple:
Calories: 153. Protein: 1.656 g. Carbohydrate: 32.2 g. Dietary Fiber: 2.646 g. Total Sugars: 25.7 g. Total Fat: 3.187 g. Saturated Fat: .594 g. Monounsaturated Fat: .86 g. Polyunsaturated Fat: .331 g. Cholesterol: 1.908 mg. Trans Fat: 0 g. Total Omega-3 FA: .024 g. Total Omega-6 FA: .019 g. Potassium: 131.1 mg. Sodium: 2.537 mg. Vitamin K: 2.007 mcg. Folic Acid: 0 mcg.

❖ ITALIAN CANNOLI ❖

ORIGIN: SICILY
DIABETIC ADAPTABLE

This is a great treat for your guests and for you when they come to enjoy a dinner party. It's normally a deep-fat-fried item that we have converted to an oven-baked dessert. This cuts out literally scores of fat grams and still tastes great. You will have to get some cannoli tubes, or forms. You can find some at www.megaheart.com under the kitchen section. We suggest you purchase 8 of them. This recipe makes 40 cannoli shells and the oven time for each batch is about 10 minutes. Most any local kitchen store will have the tubes as well; they come in sets of four.

MAKES 40 CANNOLI   SODIUM PER RECIPE (RICOTTA FILLING): 760.2 MG
SODIUM PER CANNOLI (RICOTTA FILLING): 19.0 MG
SODIUM PER RECIPE (WHIPPED CREAM FILLING): 221.1 MG
SODIUM PER CANNOLI (WHIPPED CREAM FILLING): 5.528 MG
SODIUM PER CANNOLI SHELL (EMPTY): 3.521 MG

THE PASTRY*
2 large eggs, beaten (126 mg)
4 tablespoons unsalted butter, softened (6.248 mg)
3 cups all-purpose flour (7.5 mg)
¼ cup granulated sugar or Splenda (trace)
1 teaspoon ground cinnamon (.598 mg)
6 tablespoons cold, low-sodium water (trace)
2 tablespoons white balsamic vinegar (.3 mg)
½ teaspoon vanilla extract (.189 mg)
   No-stick cooking spray

THE RICOTTA FILLING†
3 cups whole-milk ricotta cheese (619.9 mg)
1¼ cups confectioners' sugar (1.5 mg)
   Pinch of cinnamon (trace)
2 teaspoons vanilla extract (.756 mg)
   Pinch of ground ginger (trace)
¼ cup grated Baker's Semisweet chocolate (4.62 mg)

SPECIAL EQUIPMENT NEEDED
4 to, preferably, 8 cannoli tubes
   Pasta maker; a rolling pin isn't enough for success
   Baker's pastry bag and decorating tips
   Baking sheet with parchment or cooking paper
   Cooling rack

Making the cannoli: Place the butter out about an hour before starting.
   In a medium mixing bowl, sift together the flour, sugar, and cinnamon.
   Beat the eggs well in a small bowl and set aside.
   Cut the softened unsalted butter into the flour using a pastry blender until the pieces are the size of small peas. Stir in the beaten eggs.
   Add the water, sugar, and the vinegar a tablespoon at a time, and mix, using a fork or your fingertips. Add the vanilla. If the dough needs more liquid, add another tablespoon of vinegar (.15 mg sodium). If you need still more, add only one more tablespoon of water.
   Knead the mixture in the bowl with your hands until it's almost combined; it will be a crumbly dough. Turn the dough out onto a lightly floured

*You can add ground unsalted pistachios or pine nuts to the dough mix for extra flavor. We don't usually do that but it does offer a different flavor.
†Many fillings are available, including one you might create. See Variations (page 11). We use a no-salt-added brand ricotta named "Precious."

board and knead for about 5 minutes. Shape into a log about 3 inches in diameter.

Wrap the log in waxed paper and place into the refrigerator for about 1 hour, or as long as overnight. If you refrigerate it overnight, let it stand on your countertop for an hour before rolling it out.

Preheat the oven to 400°F with the rack in the center. Place parchment paper on a baking sheet and set aside.

Using Pam or another no-stick cooking spray, oil the cannoli tubes and set aside.

Bring the dough to your floured board and cut off a piece about ½-inch thick. Using a rolling pin, roll it as thinly as your strength permits. Using your pasta maker, roll the dough just slightly thinner than what you started with, and then turn the pasta machine a notch down, rolling it again and again until it's nearly paper-thin. You'll have to handhold the dough during the last few rolls so that the dough doesn't fold over on itself. (If it does, it may not separate again.) The dough could expand to two feet or longer.

Set the dough on a long wooden breadboard. Slice the dough into 4-inch squares or just 4-inch lengths if the dough out of the pasta maker ends up about 4 inches wide. Now, bring a cannoli tube to the dough and set it down on one of the 4-inch pieces. Make sure each end of the tube is open for the first inch. Roll the dough up. Overlap the dough and trim off any excess. Pinch the dough together tightly. Place each cannoli on the baking sheet, keeping a generous space between each of them.

Bake in the preheated oven for 6 minutes. Turn over to the unbaked side, and bake for another 4 minutes. Remove and set on a cooling rack. Grab one end of the tube with a pad, glove, or heavy cloth and slide the cannoli shell off onto the baking sheet. Do that with all eight.

Oil the tubes again and start all over.

Prepare the ricotta filling: Take the ricotta out of the container the night before and put it into a pierced, not wire metal colander and place the colander over a large pan where it will "hang." Cover and put back into the refrigerator overnight. This will allow the excess liquid in the ricotta to drain and help your cannolis stay together longer. Never use ricotta after five days once it's been opened or put into cannoli.

Whisking by hand, or using an electric mixer on medium speed, beat the first three ingredients until smooth. Using a wooden spoon, stir in cinnamon, ginger, and the grated chocolate. Place the mixture in the refrigerator to chill.

When ready to serve the cannoli, fill the with the chilled ricotta filling or one of the whipped cream fillings outlined in the following variations. Use a baker's pastry bag and round tip to squeeze the ricotta mixture into the cannoli (unless using the variation with pressurized whipped cream). Dust with confectioners' sugar* and serve.

An option is to melt 2 cups of semisweet chocolate chips in a double boiler and, using tongs, dip the shells into the chocolate and then set on waxed paper to cool and harden. Once hardened, fill with one of the fillings below, dust with confectioners' sugar and some ground pistachios or other unsalted nut, if desired, and serve. (Add 20 calories per cannoli and .5 mg sodium if you dip them in chocolate.)

VARIATIONS

INSTANT WHIPPED CREAM FILLING

Use this easy filling for a single unit and a quick treat for children or guests.

1 **cannoli shell (3.817 mg)**
3 **tablespoons canned, pressurized, whipped cream (15.6 mg)**
½ **teaspoon confectioners' sugar (trace)**

Dust the inside of shell with the confectioners' sugar and squirt the whipped cream into the shell from each end.

HOMEMADE WHIPPED CREAM FILLING

For several cannoli, try homemade sweetened whipped cream.

SODIUM PER CANNOLI: 4.718 MG

1 **pint heavy whipped cream (84 mg)**
½ **cup confectioners' sugar* (.6 mg)**

Using a pastry bag and decorating tip, fill each shell with the sweetened whipped cream and serve, dusted with a bit of confectioners' sugar.

Nutrient Data per Ricotta-Filled Cannoli:
Protein: 2.451 g. Carbohydrate: 6.361 g. Dietary Fiber: .094 g. Total Sugars: 5.069 g. Total Fat: 4.113 g. Saturated Fat: 2.523 g. Monounsaturated Fat: 1.169 g. Polyunsaturated Fat: .161 g. Cholesterol: 23 mg. Trans Fat: 0 g. Total Omega-3 FA: .031 g. Total Omega-6 FA: .031 g. Potassium: 28.5 mg. Sodium: 19 mg. Vitamin K: .329 mcg. Folic Acid: 0 mcg.

Nutrient Data per Homemade Whipped Cream–Filled Cannoli:
Calories: 69.9. Protein: 1.359 g. Carbohydrate: 10.1 g. Dietary Fiber: .287 g. Total Sugars: 2.801 g. Total Fat: 2.606 g. Saturated Fat: 1.513 g. Monounsaturated Fat: .723 g. Polyunsaturated Fat: .158 g. Cholesterol: 17.7 mg. Trans Fat: 0 g. Total Omega-3 FA: .029 g. Total Omega-6 FA: .031 mg. Iron: .506 mg. Potassium: 16.7 mg. Sodium: 4.688 mg. Vitamin K: .25 mcg. Folic Acid: 14.4 mcg.

*You can also top the cannoli with canned, pressurized, whipped cream and sprinkle that with the ground nuts.

Nutrient Data per Canned Whipped Cream to Filled Cannoli:
Calories: 73.8. Protein: .39 g. Carbohydrate: 6.944 g. Dietary Fiber: .1 mg. Total Sugars: 6.563 g. Total Fat: 1.75 g. Saturated Fat: 1.017 g. Monounsaturated Fat: .493 g. Polyunsaturated Fat: .093 g. Cholesterol: 14.8 mg. Trans Fat: 0 g. Total Omega-3 FA: .011 g. Total Omega-6 FA: .031 g. Iron: .205 mg. Potassium: 38.1 mg. Sodium: 6.624 mg. Vitamin K: .164 mcg. Folic Acid: 0 mcg.

❧ CARAMEL POPCORN ❧

ORIGIN: NEW MEXICO, 3,000 YEARS AGO
DIABETIC ACCEPTABLE*

In 1948 and 1950, anthropologist Herbert Dick and botanist Earle Smith, Harvard graduate students, came out of a bat cave in New Mexico and showed the world where the first "ears of corn" and "popped corn" had originated. Cave dwellers had been enjoying corn centuries earlier.

Today, most of the world's popcorn comes from the midwestern part of the United States, mostly from Nebraska, Indiana, and Iowa. In 1890, popcorn became popular enough for whole farming communities to raise it and make a good income from it. They dubbed their new-found largesse "prairie gold."

Commercially produced, candied popcorn comes with a lot of added salt. Use no-salt organic popcorn available from Healthy Heart Market (www.healthyheartmarket .com) or, if you're lucky, from your local grocer. (This recipe has been adapted from a Splenda recipe.)

MAKES 12 LOOSELY FILLED CUPS   SODIUM PER RECIPE: 74.5 MG
SODIUM PER CUP (SPLENDA): 6.206 MG
SODIUM PER CUP (SUGAR) 6.206 MG

No-stick cooking spray
1   (2 ounces) package Healthy Heart Market organic, microwave popcorn† (trace)
1   egg white (54.8 mg)
2   tablespoons Grandma's molasses (14 mg)
2   teaspoons vanilla extract (.756 mg)
½   teaspoon onion powder (.648 mg)
¾   cup Splenda Granular‡ (trace), or sugar (trace)
½   cup unsalted peanuts (4.29 mg)

*When using Splenda, a serving has low carbohydrates and low sugars.
†Approximately ¼ cup of kernels
‡Sugar ratings are the same as Splenda when counting sodium.

Preheat the oven to 325°F. Lightly spray a 13×11-inch pan with no-stick cooking spray. Set aside.

After popping the corn, place it in a large bowl. In a smaller bowl, stir together the egg white, molasses, vanilla, onion powder, and Splenda or sugar. Whisk it well. Add the peanuts, and stir until the peanuts are well coated. Pour this mixture over the popcorn and, using two large wooden or oiled metal spoons, toss until the popcorn is coated.

Place the popcorn in the oiled baking pan and bake for 25 minutes, stirring occasionally. The popcorn is done when crispy. Remove from oven and spread onto lightly sprayed waxed paper to cool.

Serve at room temperature, or store in sealed ziplock bags in cool place for up to 2 days.

Nutrient Data per Cup, Using Splenda:
Calories: 65.4. Protein: 2.518 g. Carbohydrate: 7.873 g. Dietary Fiber: 1.369 g. Total Sugars: 2.244 g. Total Fat: 3.156 g. Saturated Fat: .378 g. Monounsaturated Fat: 1.503 g. Polyunsaturated Fat: .876 g. Cholesterol: 0 mg. Trans Fat: 0 g. Total Omega-3 FA: .001 g. Total Omega-6 FA: 0 g. Potassium: 94.1 mg. Sodium: 6.206 mg. Vitamin K: .004 mcg. Folic Acid: 0 mcg.

Nutrient Data per Cup, Using Sugar:
Calories: 113.8. Protein: 2.518 g. Carbohydrate: 20.4 g. Dietary Fiber: 1.369 g. Total Sugars: 14.7 g. Total Fat: 3.156 g. Saturated Fat: .378 g. Monounsaturated Fat: 1.503 g. Polyunsaturated Fat: .876 g. Cholesterol: 0 mg. Trans Fat: 0 g. Total Omega-3 FA: .001 g. Total Omega-6 FA: 0 g. Potassium: 94.4 mg. Sodium: 6.206 mg. Vitamin K: .004 mcg. Folic Acid: 0 mcg.

❖ CHOCOLATE MOUSSE ❖

ORIGIN: FRANCE
DIABETIC ADAPTABLE

Chocolate mousse brings back some memories that are at times embarrassing and other times humorous. I had never had a real chocolate mousse until my wife and I went to a small French restaurant in New York while working there and visiting my brother, who recommended the place. Now, this was a while ago. I had just returned from Walla Walla, Washington, and a new restaurant there called the Black Angus. We had dinner for two, drinks for two, and all the trimmings for $11.50 and that was considered stiff at the time, but it was a good meal and a well-known restaurant. So, we were in New York, and we go to a French restaurant and ordered a small meal with chocolate mousse for dessert. Wow, it was the best chocolate anything we'd ever had. We extolled over it and beamed with delight. Then came the bill. Two very small meals came to $60. That would be quite a *bit more today, more than likely over $250. That $60 cash didn't exist in my wallet, so I pulled out a credit card and the French waiter waved his hands at me. No! Cash only. Together, we were able to dig up the sixty, but left without a tip and with cab fare back to our hotel—two kids from a farm hitting the big time! The place? It was called Le Veau d'Or and at this writing it's still at 129 East 60th Street, New York, NY.*

MAKE 8 SERVINGS   SODIUM PER RECIPE: 191.8 MG
SODIUM PER SERVING: 24 MG

1¼-ounce envelope unflavored gelatin (13.7 mg)
¼   cup white granulated sugar or Splenda (trace)
¼   cup Hershey's unsweetened cocoa (trace)
½   cup low-sodium water (trace)
½   cup low-fat or reduced-fat evaporated milk (142.2 mg)
2   tablespoons Hershey's Genuine Chocolate Flavor Syrup
      (25 mg)
2   teaspoons pure vanilla extract* (.756 mg)
      Canned, pressurized, whipped cream for garnish

In a 1½-quart saucepan, combine the gelatin, sugar, cocoa, and water. Bring to a boil over high heat, stirring as you do. Once boiling, pour into a 2-quart pot or metal bowl and stir in the evaporated milk and chocolate syrup. Cover with plastic wrap or a tight-fitting lid and place in the freezer for 1 hour.

When frozen, beat the mixture with an electric mixer on high speed until it's thick enough to hold peaks, about 3 to 4 minutes. Stir in the vanilla. Divide the mousse evenly among four ½-cup serving bowls or ramekins and smooth the tops with a spoon. Cover tightly with plastic wrap so that the wrap doesn't touch the mousse and chill in refrigerator for at least an hour, or up to one day.

Serve cold, topped with a dollop of canned, pressurized, low-fat, whipped cream.

Nutrient Data per Serving:
Calories: 60.9. Protein: 2.45 g. Carbohydrate: 11.1 g. Dietary Fiber: .5 g. Total Sugars: 7.627 g. Total Fat: .582 g. Saturated Fat: .192 g. Monounsaturated Fat: .17 g. Polyunsaturated Fat: .019 g. Cholesterol: 1.27 mg. Trans Fat: 0 g. Total Omega-3 FA: 0 g. Total Omega-6 FA: 0 g. Potassium: 184.4 mg. Sodium: 24 mg. Vitamin K: .004 mcg. Folic Acid: 0 mcg.

*Use pure vanilla extract instead of imitation vanilla flavoring.

❈ CRANBERRY-APPLE PIE ❈

ORIGN: U.S.A.
DIABETIC ADAPTABLE

I confess: Thanksgiving and Christmas parties get to me. No, I don't ingest any salt or high-sodium foods, but I do get into a higher-calorie mode for at least one party. Just to be safe, I make my own party foods no matter where the party may be taking place. And guess what, with all the help I get with eating these treats, I come home with only empty plates and dishes.

This recipe offers you a choice between a pie made with unsalted butter or today's Zero Trans Fat Crisco shortening. To cut your calorie intake, we suggest you slice the pie into 12 or 16 pieces rather than the standard 8, and then you can enjoy it guiltfree. We've done the numbers for 12 and 16 slices. This is a high-calorie treat.

**MAKES ONE 9- TO 10-INCH PIE   SODIUM PER PIE: 57.4 MG
SODIUM PER SLICE (12): 4.787 MG
SODIUM PER SLICE (16): 3.59 MG**

1 **One-Crust No-Trans-Fat Pie Shell (12.2 mg) (See Page 2)**

THE CRUMBLE TOPPING*
¾ **cup all-purpose flour (1.875 mg)**
½ **stick unsalted butter or Crisco's Zero Trans Fat shortening (6.215 mg)**
½ **cup white granulated sugar or Splenda (trace)**
1 **teaspoon ground cinnamon (.598 mg)**

THE FILLING
6 **medium to large apples, peeled, cored, and sliced (8.28 mg)**
1 **cup low-sodium water (trace)**
2 **cups fresh cranberries (23.4 mg)**
1¼ **cup white granulated sugar or Splenda† (trace)**
1 **teaspoon ground cinnamon (.598 mg)**
2 **tablespoons cornstarch or white flour (1.728 mg)**

---

*An alternative to fighting back the calories here is to make this a deep-dish pie and place a light crumble crust on the top. Bake at the same temperature in an 8×8-inch oiled baking dish. That would cut 1,200 calories off the total.
†Want it sweeter? Add another ½ cup sugar or Splenda.

Preheat oven to 425°F.

Prepare the One-Crust Pie Shell.

To make the crumble topping: Mix all ingredients together in a medium mixing bowl using your hands. If using butter, let it be cold. Mix until the ingredients become crumbly. Set aside.

To make the filling: Wash, core, and slice the apples. Pour water into medium-size bowl. Place the slices into the bowl with ½ teaspoon ascorbic acid or a tablespoon of Sure-Jell Ever-Fresh.

Wash the cranberries, discarding any damaged berries. Drain the water from the apples and mix in the cranberries. Add the sugar, cinnamon, and cornstarch and stir together until well mixed.

Pour the filling into the pie shell and even it out. Sprinkle the crumble mixture generously over the top.

Place the pie on a baking sheet or spread out aluminum wrap under the pie pan to catch any juices that may bubble over. Bake for 40 to 50 minutes, or until the top has turned a nice golden color.

Serve hot or warmed.

Nutrient Data per Slice (12):
Calories: 528. Protein: 10.7 g. Carbohydrate: 81.9 g. Dietary Fiber: 10.7 g. Total Sugars: 36.4 g. Total Fat: 18.4 g. Saturated Fat: 8.172 g. Monounsaturated Fat: 6.053 g. Polyunsaturated Fat: 3.351 g. Cholesterol: 25.7 mg. Trans Fat: 0 g. Total Omega-3 FA: .204 g. Total Omega-6 FA: .102 g. Potassium: 543.4 mg. Sodium: 4.787 mg. Vitamin K: 2.022 mcg. Folic Acid: 28.1 mcg.

Nutrient Data per Slice (16):
Calories: 396. Protein: 8.057 g. Carbohydrate: 61.4 g. Dietary Fiber: 8.01 g. Total Sugars: 27.3 g. Total Fat: 13.8 g. Saturated Fat: 6.129 g. Monounsaturated Fat: 4.54 g. Polyunsaturated Fat: 2.513 g. Cholesterol: 19.3 mg. Trans Fat: 0 g. Total Omega-3 FA: .153 g. Total Omega-6 FA: .076 g. Potassium: 407.6 mg. Sodium: 3.59 mg. Vitamin K: 1.516 mcg. Folic Acid: 21.1 mcg.

❖ DATE-WALNUT COOKIES ❖

ORIGIN: GERMANY
DIABETICS, SEE FOOTNOTE*

This recipe is similar to the Iraqi version of date-nut cookies that follows. The Germans don't use butter or oil, however, for this cookie, yet it's as wonderful tasting as the one with butter.

MAKES 48 COOKIES   SODIUM PER RECIPE: 195.3 MG
SODIUM PER COOKIE: 4.07 MG

*There are about 29 grams of sugar in 5 to 6 dates. Or, 117. 6 grams of carbohydrates. Diabetics may want to eliminate the dates and just use the nuts.

3 **large egg whites (164.3 mg)**
1 **teaspoon cream of tartar (1.56 mg)**
1 **cup unbleached, all-purpose flour (2.5 mg)**
1 **cup white granulated sugar or Splenda (trace)**
1 **tablespoon half-and-half (6.15 mg)**
1 **tablespoon Featherweight baking powder (13.5 mg)**
1 **cup chopped dates (about 20 dates) (4.8 mg)**
1 **cup chopped, unsalted walnuts (2.5 mg)**

Preheat oven to 350°F. If you have a double oven, preheat both.

Prepare two cookie sheets or jelly-roll pans by lining with a cooking or parchment paper, or lightly (very lightly) grease the pan.

Beat the egg whites with the cream of tartar until the whites peak.

Gradually add the sugar, still beating the egg whites. Gradually beat in the flour and cream.

Make sure your oven is at temperature. Then, beat in the baking powder and, using a wooden spoon, gently stir in the dates and walnuts.

Place heaping teaspoons of the batter about 1½ inches apart on the lined cookie sheets.

Immediately put the cookie sheet(s) into the preheated oven and bake the cookies for 10 minutes, or until they turn golden brown. (If using double ovens, bake the two sheets at the same time. This recipe won't work well with two sheets in the same oven.) Remove and cool the cookies on a wire rack.

Nutrient Data per Cookie:
Calories: 52.8. Protein: 1.196 g. Carbohydrate: 9.075 g. Dietary Fiber: .538 g. Total Sugars: 4.214 g. Total Fat: 1.618 g. Saturated Fat: .121 g. Monounsaturated Fat: .409 g. Polyunsaturated Fat: .926 g. Cholesterol: .116 mg. Trans Fat: 0 mg. Total Omega-3 FA: .106 g. Total Omega-6 FA: 0 g. Potassium: 83.9 mg. Sodium: 4.07 mg. Vitamin K: .082 mcg. Folic Acid: 4.01 mcg.

❖ WALNUT COOKIES WITH DATES ❖

ORIGIN: IRAQ
DIABETICS, SEE FOOTNOTE*

Nuts and dates, dates and nuts. Who doesn't like them? Mix them together and you've got a cookie that is a treat for all. While growing up, I lived for a while on a ranch in the Southern California desert, where date palms abounded. Fruit stands with dates and nuts were prolific and popular. A date milk shake was my favorite, followed by Stuffed

*There are about 29 grams of sugar in 5 to 6 dates. Or, 117.6 grams of carbohydrates.

Dates (see page 29) and date cookies. This recipe from Iraq makes a great batter and a very tasty cookie.*

MAKES 48 COOKIES   SODIUM PER RECIPE: 239.7 MG
SODIUM PER COOKIE: 4.994 MG

1   **cup unbleached, all-purpose flour (2.5 mg)**
½   **teaspoon ground cardamom (.18 mg)**
4   **tablespoons unsalted butter, softened (6.248 mg)**
1   **cup white granulated sugar or Splenda (trace)**
3   **large eggs (210 mg)**
1   **tablespoon Featherweight baking powder (13.5 mg)**
1   **cup chopped dates (about 20 dates) (4.8 mg)**
1   **cup chopped unsalted walnuts (2.5 mg)**

Preheat the oven to 350°F. If you have a double oven, preheat both. If you have just one, place one rack at the high-middle position and the other at the low-middle position.

Line two cookie sheets or jelly-roll pans with cooking or parchment paper, or lightly (very lightly) grease the pans.

Sift together the flour and cardamom and set aside.

Beat together the unsalted butter, sugar, and eggs until smooth. Gradually add the flour, and mix until a creamy batter has formed. Have the nuts and dates ready, and when the oven is at temperature, beat in the baking powder and quickly stir in the dates and walnuts.

Place heaping teaspoons of the batter about 1½ inches apart on the cookie sheets.

Immediately put the cookie sheets into the preheated oven and bake the cookies for 15 minutes, or until they turn golden brown.

If using a single oven†, place one sheet on the top rack and the other on the bottom rack. Bake for about 15 to 20 minutes. One of the sheets may finish before the other. They will turn a golden brown.

Remove from the oven and cool the cookies on a wire rack.

Nutrient Data per Cookie:
Calories: 64.3. Protein: 1.367 g. Carbohydrate: 9.047 g. Dietary Fiber: .543 g. Total Sugars: 4.223 g. Total Fat: 2.85 g. Saturated Fat: .803 g. Monounsaturated Fat: .767 g. Polyunsaturated Fat: 1.003 g. Cholesterol: 15.8 mg. Trans Fat: 0 g. Total Omega-3 FA: .115 g. Total Omega-6 FA: .026 g. Potassium: 74.5 mg. Sodium: 4.994 mg. Vitamin K: .17 mcg. Folic Acid: 4.01 mcg.

*You can cut the fat down by cutting the unsalted butter in half, or, you can make the Date-Walnut cookies on Page 16—note the similarities. If you want the Middle Eastern flavor (Iraqi in this case), then add the cardamom to the German recipe.
†If you want to bake in a single oven one at a time, that's okay, too. But add a teaspoon of Featherweight baking powder to the remaining batter just before baking, stirring it in quickly and forming and baking the cookies immediately.

❖ French Vanilla Pudding ❖

ORIGIN: FRANCE
DIABETICS, SEE FOOTNOTE*

Remember when? I mean when vanilla pudding was very popular and you could find it in anyone's kitchen or refrigerator? Seems like it fell out of favor for a while, but now we're bringing it back for a dessert or a snack. Our version is low in fat and high in flavor and does not gamble with the uncooked egg white that was usually stirred into the cooked batter and left to sit for a while before chilling, at which time a highly caloric and fattening, rich, whipped cream was stirred in. So, where's the flavor, you ask? It's in the vanilla, where it always was. Give this one a try. We think you'll like it.

**MAKES 6 DESSERT-CUP SIZE SERVINGS   SODIUM PER RECIPE: 260.2 MG
SODIUM PER SERVING: 43.4 MG**

⅓   **cup white granulated sugar or Splenda (trace)**
3   **tablespoons cornstarch (2.304 mg)**
2½   **cups nonfat or 1% milk* with added vitamins A & D
       (257.2 mg)**
1¾   **teaspoons vanilla extract or flavoring (.661 mg)**

In a saucepan, mix the sugar or Splenda and cornstarch together, then stir in the milk gradually until the cornstarch mixture is dissolved and smooth. Put over medium heat, and cook, stirring continuously. Once the ingredients thicken, cook for another 2 to 3 minutes, then add the vanilla.

Pour into 6 dessert cups and chill. You may also pour into molds rinsed with cold water (and left slightly wet), and then chill until firm.

Turn out the molded puddings onto serving dishes.

Nutrient Date per Serving:
Calories: 97.4. Protein: 3.452 g. Carbohydrate: 20.2 g. Dietary Fiber: .038 g. Total Sugars: 16.4 g. Total Fat: .085 g. Saturated Fat: .12 g. Monounsaturated Fat: .049 g. Polyunsaturated Fat: .008 g. Cholesterol: 2.042 mg. Trans Fat: 0 g. Total Omega-3 FA: .001 g. Total Omega-6 FA: 0 g. Potassium: 161.4 mg. Sodium: 43.4 mg. Vitamin K: 0 mcg. Folic Acid: 0 mcg.

*The bulk of the sugars and carbohydrates in this recipe are in the granulated sugar (66.5 g) and the milk (31.2 g).

❖ Favorite British Fruitcake ❖

Origin: Great Britain
Not Adaptable for Diabetics

My mother, Alice Gazzaniga, of Welsh-Irish descent, made the most fantastic fruitcakes during Christmas. Because of her "secret recipe" I never fully understood why others in school would say, "I hate fruitcake." Well, one day I got a bite of one those dry, more-cake-than-fruit, and tasteless cakes. I began to understand the phrase about "hating" fruitcake.

This recipe is more than a fruitcake. It's absolutely delicious and a real treat. It's very British-Welsh-Irish in nature. Maureen now makes it every Christmas for the family, friends, and our favorite cardiologist, Dr. Michael Fowler, who raves over it (just like I do). Make it ahead of time so you can drizzle some brandy on it to keep it moist and flavorful, then wrap it as a gift or store it for the holidays. Wrap in cheesecloth, sprinkle a little brandy or rum over it, and wrap it again in aluminum foil. It will store for up to 6 months. Go gently during the holidays, because of the calories, but do enjoy at least a little of this wonderful fruitcake.

Makes: 2 large loaves or 3 smaller loaves   Equivalent to 32 slices
Sodium per Recipe (Using Real Baking Soda)*: 1095 mg
Sodium per Recipe (Using Ener-G Baking Soda)†: 619.3 mg
Sodium per Slice (32) Using Real Baking Soda*: 34.2 mg
Sodium per Slice (32) Using Ener-G Baking Soda†: 19.4 mg

1   **pound candied pineapple (trace)**
1   **pound candied cherries (trace)**
½   **pound seedless dark raisins (26 mg)**
½   **pound pitted dates (4.272 mg)**
¼   **pound candied citron (60 mg)**
⅛   **pound candied lemon peel (30 mg)**
⅛   **pound candied orange peel (30 mg)**

*You may use 1 tablespoon of Ener-G baking soda, but mix it in just before forming the cake or loaves and putting into the oven. This will subtract the entire amount of sodium listed for baking soda. All other nutrient data except for calcium remains the same when exchanging Ener-G baking soda with regular baking soda. Calcium increases by 10 mg per slice.

†Data based on using Arm & Hammer baking soda. Baking sodas can range from 850 mg to 1,200 mg per teaspoon.

½ **pound golden raisins, packed (23.1 mg)**
½ **pound currants (15.3 mg)**
½ **pound unsalted pecans (2.268 mg)**
½ **cup dark brandy or rum (2.24 mg)**
   Oil or trans-fat-free Crisco for greasing pans (trace)
¼ **pound (1 stick) unsalted butter (12.4 mg)**
1 **cup white granulated sugar (trace)**
1 **cup brown sugar, firmly packed (85.8 mg)**
2 **cups sifted all-purpose flour (5 mg)**
½ **teaspoon ground mace (.68 mg)**
½ **teaspoon ground cinnamon (.299 mg)**
½ **teaspoon baking soda (476 mg) (see Footnotes, Page 20)**
5 **large eggs (315 mg)**
1 **tablespoon nonfat milk (6.426 mg)**
1 **teaspoon almond extract (.378 mg)**

On the first day: Place all the fruits in large mixing bowl. Leave the fruit in whole pieces. Do not cut up. Pour the brandy or rum over the fruit. Cover with plastic wrap and let stand overnight at room temperature.

On the second day: Prepare two 9×5-inch pans or three 8×3⅞-inch baking pans by lightly greasing them with unsalted shortening. You may use aluminum foil pans if giving them as gifts.

Preheat oven to 300°F.

Cream together the butter and the brown sugar, and then the white sugar.

Sift 1½ cups of the flour with the spices and the baking soda onto a sheet of waxed paper. Toss the remaining ½ cup of the flour with the fruits and nuts to keep them from sticking together. Mix well.

In another bowl, beat the eggs slightly. Mix in the milk and almond extract. Add the egg mixture alternately three times with the flour mixture to the creamed sugar mixture. Pour the batter over the fruit and nuts. Mix gently until thoroughly combined.

Pour the batter into the prepared loaf pans. Bake larger pans for about 2 hours, but test after 1½ hours by inserting a thin-bladed knife to see if it comes out clean. Smaller loaves will take about 1½ hours or more. Ovens may vary, and they bake very slowly at such a low temperature. Cool in pan for half an hour before unmolding.

When thoroughly cool, wrap the cake in cheesecloth, dampen lightly with brandy or rum, and store in a covered container or wrap in foil. The cakes need to be checked every week and the cheesecloth probably moistened again.

Nutrient Data per Slice, Using Standard Baking Soda:
Calories: 386.7. Protein: 3.551 g. Carbohydrate: 72.6 g. Dietary Fiber: 3.032 g. Total Sugars: 56.1 g. Total Fat: 9.245 g. Saturated Fat: 2.534 g. Monounsaturated Fat: 4.176 g. Polyunsaturated Fat: 1.879 g. Cholesterol: 40.6 mg. Trans Fat: 0 g. Total Omega-3 FA: .103 g. Total Omega-6 FA: .077 g. Potassium: 272.5 mg. Sodium: 34.2 mg. Vitamin K: 1.153 mcg. Folic Acid: 12 mcg.

Nutrient Values per Slice, Using Ener-G Baking Soda:
Calories: 386.7. Protein: 3.551 g. Carbohydrate: 72.6 g. Dietary Fiber: 3.032 g. Total Sugars: 56.1 g. Total Fat: 9.245 g. Saturated Fat: 2.534 g. Monounsaturated Fat: 4.176 g. Polyunsaturated Fat: 1.879 g. Cholesterol: 40.6 mg. Trans Fat: 0 g. Total Omega-3 FA: .103 g. Total Omega-6 FA: .077 g. Potassium: 272.5 mg. Sodium: 19.4 mg. Vitamin K: 1.153 mcg. Folic Acid: 12 mc.

◈ MANDELBROT ◈

ORIGIN: GERMANY
DIABETIC ADAPTABLE*

This delicious Jewish "bread," when baked and sliced, appears more like a biscotti cookie than bread. It's not a biscotti, though, but a hard-crusted, sweet, and soft centered cookie. We've added dark cocoa for a visual and tasty treat as well as a healthy one. We've kept the almonds to just a third of a cup to help cut calories, and added almond extract to enhance the flavor. If you want more almonds, we suggest adding only up to half a cup total. The German word "mandel" means "almond." "Brot" means "bread" in German.

You will be preparing the dough with substitute baking powder so, once the baking powder is wet, you'll have to work quickly. Have your breadboards ready and your oven hot.

MAKES 24 TO 48 COOKIES   SODIUM PER RECIPE: 265.6 MG
SODIUM PER COOKIE (24): 10.7 MG
SODIUM PER COOKIE (48) 5.369 MG

3   large eggs (189 mg)
1   cup white granulated sugar or Splenda (trace)
½   cup expeller-pressed canola oil (trace)
1   tablespoon almond extract (1.17 mg)
1   tablespoon cider vinegar (.15 mg)
3   cups plus 2 tablespoons unbleached, all-purpose flour (7.655 mg)
2   tablespoons potato flour (7.75 mg)
2   tablespoons Featherweight or Ener-G baking powder (27 mg)
⅓   cup chopped unsalted almonds (.455 mg)
1½   tablespoons cocoa powder†(24.5 mg)

*Diabetics can replace the sugar with ½ to ¾ cup of Splenda. Total carbohydrates are mostly in the sugar (200 g), and the flour (298 g).
†We use Hershey's unsweetened cocoa. Make sure you don't use a chocolate drink mix; most are heavy with salt.

Preheat the oven to 350°F. Set the rack for the middle of oven.

Line a jelly-roll pan or baking sheet with parchment paper.

Prepare two breadboards by lightly flouring them.

Beat the eggs with a rotary beater in a medium mixing bowl. Add the sugar, oil, almond extract, and vinegar and beat until well combined.

In a large bowl, stir together the two flours, the baking powder, and chopped almonds.

Using a wooden spoon, add the egg mixture to the flour mixture gradually. Stir together until well blended.

Work quickly to finish the bread and get it into the hot oven before the baking powder begins to lose its power. Split the dough in half, shape each into a ball, and place each on a floured breadboard. Press one ball down into a rectangular shape until it's about ½ inch thick.

Mix the cocoa into the other ball by kneading with your hands. When ready, set the ball on the floured board and press down into a rectangle shape about ½ inch thick.

Join the two halves together, one on top of the other, and roll up into a log lengthwise. Place the log on the parchment paper and press down with your hands, forming a long rectangle 16–18 inches long and 2–3 inches wide. This should sit nicely on the baking sheet in a diagonal position.

Quickly place into oven. Reduce the heat to 325°F. Bake for about 32 to 38 minutes, or until done. Test with a toothpick. When it comes out dry, the mandelbrot is done. The white surface will just begin to turn a golden brown.

Cool on rack for about 5 to 10 minutes, then slice diagonally into individual servings.

Nutrient Value per Cookie (24):
Calories: 169. Protein: 3.902 g. Carbohydrate: 25.3 g. Dietary Fiber: 2.284 g. Total Sugars: 8.71 g. Total Fat: 7.038 g. Saturated Fat: 1.038 g. Monounsaturated Fat: 3.802 g. Polyunsaturated Fat: 1.763 g. Cholesterol: 26.4 mg. Trans Fat: 0 g. Total Omega-3 FA: .431 g. Total Omega-6 FA: 0 g. Potassium: 317.2 mg. Sodium: 10.7 mg. Vitamin K: 5.736 mcg. Folic Acid: 24.6 mcg.

Nutrient Value per Cookie (48):
Calories: 84.3. Protein: 1.951 g. Carbohydrate: 12.7 g. Dietary Fiber: 1.142 g. Total Sugars: 4.355 g. Total Fat: 3.498 g. Saturated Fat: .66 g. Monounsaturated Fat: 2.226 g. Polyunsaturated Fat: .434 g. Cholesterol: 13.2 mg. Trans Fat: 0 g. Total Omega-3 FA: .022 g. Total Omega-6 FA: 0 g. Potassium: 158.6 mg. Sodium: 5.369 mg. Vitamin K: 1.452 mcg. Folic Acid: 12.3 mcg.

❈ MILANESE PANETTONE ❈

ORIGIN: ITALY
DIABETICS, SEE FOOTNOTE*
BREAD MACHINE KNEAD—OVEN BAKE

Panettone is usually a Christmastime bread in Milan, Italy, where it originated. However, you can make it for guests year-round and they'll love you for it.

MAKES 1 LARGE PANETTONE LOAF, 16 TO 24 SERVINGS
SODIUM PER RECIPE: 280.4 MG
SODIUM PER SLICE (16 SERVINGS): 17.5 MG
SODIUM PER SLICE (24 SERVINGS): 11.7 MG

1   cup low-sodium water less 1 tablespoon, at 110°F (127.4 mg)
1   tablespoon white balsamic vinegar (.15 mg)
2   large eggs (126 mg)
3   tablespoons extra-virgin olive oil (trace mg)
½   cup nonfat plain yogurt (93.7 mg)
1   teaspoon vanilla extract (.378 mg)
2¾   cups unbleached, bread flour (6.875 mg)
¼   cup potato flour (15.5 mg)
1   tablespoons grated lemon zest (.36 mg)
⅓   cup white granulated sugar or Splenda (.666 mg)
¼   teaspoon ascorbic acid (trace)
3   teaspoons vital wheat gluten (6.75 mg)
2½   teaspoons bread machine yeast (4.98 mg)
½   cup Zante currants (5.76 mg)
⅓   cup black raisins, packed, plumped in hot water (6.044 mg)
½   cup dried or candied fruit (13.9 mg)

Place the first 13 ingredients (water through yeast) into the bread machine in the order listed and set for dough.

At the sound of the buzzer, add the currants, raisins, and fruit.

When the dough is ready, transfer it to a lightly floured board and shape for the pan you're going to use. This recipe works best in a panettone pan, but a Bundt cake pan works well, too. The dough will be highly pliable so you can roll it out into a log for the Bundt pan. Lightly grease whichever pan you're going to use.

*The bulk sugars are in candied fruit and in raisins. (Granulated sugar may be replaced by Splenda. Subtract 67 g of carbohydrates when doing so.) The bulk of the carbohydrates are in flour and fruits. Currants are high in sugars (48.4 g).

Let the panettone rise in warm place or proofing oven covered with a tight cloth. After it doubles in size, about an hour, bake at 375°F for about 45 minutes.

Cool on a rack.

Nutrient Data per Slice (16):
Calories: 174.4. Protein: 5.285 g. Carbohydrate: 30.9 g. Dietary Fiber: 1.198 g. Total Sugars: 10.1 g. Total Fat: 3.481 g. Saturated Fat: .59 g. Monounsaturated Fat: 2.151 g. Polyunsaturated Fat: .447 g. Cholesterol: 26.6 mg. Trans Fat: 0 g. Total Omega-3 FA: .03 g. Total Omega-6 FA: 0 g. Potassium: 176.4 mg. Sodium: 17.5 mg. Vitamin K: 1.878 mcg. Folic Acid: 33.1 mcg.

Nutrient Data per Slice (24):
Calories: 116.3. Protein: 3.523 g. Carbohydrate: 20.6 g. Dietary Fiber: .799 g. Total Sugars: 6.762 g. Total Fat: 2.32 g. Saturated Fat: .393 g. Monounsaturated Fat: 1.434 g. Polyunsaturated Fat: .298 g. Cholesterol: 17.7 mg. Trans Fat: 0 g. Total Omega-3 FA: .02 g. Total Omega-6 FA: 0 g. Potassium: 117.6 mg. Sodium: 11.7 mg. Vitamin K: 1.252 mcg. Folic Acid: 22.1 mcg.

◈ PEACH PIE ◈

ORIGIN: U.S.A.
DIABETICS, SEE FOOTNOTE*

We once had Hale peach trees when we lived "on property." When those peaches came in, we were handing them out and eating them as quickly as we could. Peaches don't hang around very long before becoming a bit too ripe to eat or cook with. One of the ways we consumed them was this easy-to-make pie, a dish that became very popular in our neighborhood.

MAKE 8 SERVINGS   SODIUM PER RECIPE: 12.2 MG
SODIUM PER SERVING: 1.531 MG

1   **8- or 9-inch baked pie shell (see page 12) (12.3 mg)**
5   **cups (approximately 7 medium) thinly sliced peaches (trace)**
1   **teaspoon ascorbic acid or lemon juice† (trace)**
1   **cup white granulated sugar or Splenda (trace)**
3   **tablespoons cornstarch (1.89 mg)**
½   **cup low-sodium water (trace)**

*The crust has 96 grams of carbohydrates. The peaches have 81 grams of carbohydrates and 71.3 grams of sugars. You can replace the granulated sugar with Splenda to make this pie.
†You may use Sure-Jell Ever-Fresh Fruit Protector, but the sugar level rises if you do. Use the ascorbic powder you may have purchased for bread making. You can obtain it from King Arthur's Baker's Catalogue, at www.kingarthurflour.com/shop/.

Bake the pie shell. Set aside.

Peel the peaches, slice, and put in a mixing bowl. Mix the ascorbic acid or lemon juice with the peaches to keep them from turning brown.

Mash enough peaches to make 1 cup.

In a medium saucepan, stir the sugar and cornstarch together. Gradually stir in the water and the crushed peaches. Cook the mixture over medium heat, stirring constantly. When the mixture thickens and boils, cook for only 1 minute more, stirring constantly. Remove from heat and let cool.

Fill the baked pie shell with the remaining peaches. Using a rubber spatula, spread the cooked peach mixture over the peaches. The mixture will seep down into the peaches. Chill at least 3 hours before serving or until it sets.

Nutrient Data per Serving:
Calories: 272.9. Protein: 2.672 g. Carbohydrate: 47.1 g. Dietary Fiber: 2.016 g. Total Sugars: 33.9 g. Total Fat: 9.057 g. Saturated Fat: 5.421 g. Monounsaturated Fat: 2.58 g. Polyunsaturated Fat: .476 g. Cholesterol: 23.3 mg. Trans Fat: 0 g. Total Omega-3 FA: .131 g. Total Omega-6 FA: 0 g. Potassium: 222.6 mg. Sodium: 1.531 mg. Vitamin K: 2.762 mcg. Folic Acid: 0 mcg.

◈ PERSIMMON PUDDING ◈

ORIGIN: MULTIPLE
DIABETICS, SEE FOOTNOTE*

The persimmon is one of those food items that some might say, "You either hate them or love them." The first persimmon was apparently "native" to China. It moved through Asia and finally made it to the United States in the 1800s. The word "persimmon" however, came from the Algonquian Indians of the northeastern part of the Americas. There are varieties to consider as well when speaking of persimmons. These include those in the astringent category: Korean and Hachiya, and those in the nonastringent category: Fuyu or Japanese persimmon, Jiro or Hanagosho.

MAKES 2 LOAVES   SODIUM PER RECIPE: 171.2 MG
SODIUM PER SERVING (16): 10.7 MG
SODIUM PER SERVING (32): 5.35 MG

2 cups white granulated sugar or Splenda (trace)
2 cups unbleached, all-purpose flour (5 mg)

*The granulated sugar has 400 grams of carbohydrates and 400 grams of sugar. The flour has 190.8 carbohydrates. The persimmons have 84.2 grams of sugars and 124.9 grams of carbohydrates.

2 **cups nonastringent persimmon pulp (6.72 mg)**
2 **cups dates, chopped (6.64 mg)**
2 **cups unsalted walnuts, chopped (4 mg)**
1 **cup nonfat milk with added vitamins A & D (102.9 mg)**
2 **teaspoons vanilla extract (.756 mg)**
3 **tablespoons melted unsalted butter (4.686 mg)**
3 **level tablespoons Featherweight baking powder (40.5 mg)**
2 **tablespoons Ener-G baking soda (trace)**

Preheat the oven to 350°F. Set the rack in the middle of the oven.

Grease or oil two 8½×4½×2½-inch loaf pans, dust them with flour and set aside.

Sift the sugar and flour together. Add the rest of the ingredients, and stir thoroughly with a wooden spoon. When ready to pour the batter into the loaf pans and just before baking, stir in the baking powder and baking soda and then pour into pans. Get the pans into oven quickly, and bake for 1 to 1½ hours. You can also bake these in a single large loaf pan for 1½ hours, or until done.

Nutrient Data per Serving (16):
Calories: 351.8. Protein: 4.812 g. Carbohydrate: 64.2 g. Dietary Fiber: 4.493 g. Total Sugars: 44.6 g. Total Fat: 10.6 g. Saturated Fat: 2.193 g. Monounsaturated Fat: 1.72 g. Polyunsaturated Fat: 6.069 g. Cholesterol: 6.031 mg. Trans Fat: 0 g. Total Omega-3 FA: 1.158 g. Total Omega-6 FA: .058 g. Potassium: 585.4 mg. Sodium: 10.7 mg. Vitamin K: 2.223 mcg. Folic Acid: 24.1 mcg.

Nutrient Data per Serving (32):
Calories: 175.9. Protein: 2.406 g. Carbohydrate: 32.1 g. Dietary Fiber: 2.247 g. Total Sugars: 22.3 g. Total Fat: 5.324 g. Saturated Fat: 1.096 g. Monounsaturated Fat: .86 g. Polyunsaturated Fat: 3.034 g. Cholesterol: 3.015 mg. Trans Fat: 0 g. Total Omega-3 FA: .579 g. Total Omega-6 FA: .029 g. Potassium: 292.7 mg. Sodium: 5.35 mg. Vitamin K: 1.111 mcg. Folic Acid: 12 mcg.

❖ LEMON POUND CAKE WITH POPPY SEEDS ❖

ORIGIN: GREAT BRITAIN
DIABETIC ADAPTABLE*

The pound cake was created by the British in the early 1700s. Not too surprising is how the cake was named. The original versions contained one pound each of butter, sugar, eggs, and flour, and no leavening. Back in those "good old days," most people couldn't read, so remembering a pound of each made life a lot easier if you wanted a

---

*Three cups of Splenda may prove too costly to make this cake, unless of course you absolutely love pound cake. In that case, go for it. This is a marvelous recipe.

good cake. Today, both baking powder and salt are used for the leavening, although salt is not needed for anything other than extending the shelf life. Try this one for a really special occasion. You and your guests will rave over it.

MAKES 20 SERVINGS*   SODIUM PER RECIPE: 547.5 MG
SODIUM PER SERVING: 27.4 MG

No-stick cooking spray
1 **cup unsalted butter (2 sticks), at room temperature (25 mg)**
3 **cups white granulated sugar (trace)**
6 **large eggs (378 mg)**
1 **cup light or regular sour cream (121.9 mg)**
2 **teaspoons lemon extract or flavoring (.7567 mg)**
1 **tablespoon poppy seeds (.588 mg)**
2 **teaspoons lemon zest (grated peel) (.24 mg)**
3 **cups, unbleached, all-purpose flour (7.5 mg)**
1 **tablespoon Featherweight baking powder (13.5 mg)**

Spray a Bundt pan with no-stick cooking spray and dust lightly with flour.

Preheat the oven to 350°F.

Using a heavy-duty electric mixer, cream together the butter and sugar in a medium to large mixing bowl, adding the sugar 1 cup at a time. Beat until light and fluffy.

Beat in 1 egg at a time until thoroughly mixed. Add the sour cream and lemon extract and beat until smooth. Add the poppy seeds and lemon zest and beat until mixed.

Mix in the flour.

When the oven is at temperature and you're ready to put the batter in the pan, mix in the baking powder. Immediately scrape the batter into the Bundt pan and place into the preheated oven.

Bake at 350°F for 1 hour and 15 to 25 minutes. Test with a long toothpick. When the toothpick comes out dry, cake is done.

Remove the cake from the oven and let stand for 10 or 15 minutes in the pan to cool. When ready, unmold on a serving plate or cake platter, place the platter on top of cake (face down), and invert.

Serve as is or for a nice lemon glaze, stir together 2 cups confectioners' sugar with 5 to 6 tablespoons of freshly squeezed lemon juice. Spread over warm pound cake.

Nutrient Data per Slice (20):
Calories: 315.2. Protein: 4.313 g. Carbohydrate: 45.4 g. Dietary Fiber: .558 g. Total Sugars: 30.2 g. Total Fat: 13.4 g. Saturated Fat: 7.832 g. Monounsaturated Fat: 3.679 g. Polyunsaturated Fat: .761 g. Cholesterol: 92.9 mg. Trans Fat: 0 g. Total Omega-3 FA: .123 g. Total Omega-6 FA: .246 g. Potassium: 137.7 mg. Sodium: 27.4 mg. Vitamin K: 1.011 mcg. Folic Acid: 28.9 mcg.

*The cake will yield 24 to 30 servings if cut into thinner slices.

❧ STUFFED DATES ❧

ORIGIN: MECCA, CALIFORNIA, BASED ON NORTH AFRICAN RECIPE
NOT DIABETIC ADAPTABLE

There are many uses for dates including cookies, cakes, and jams to simply serving them at parties as stuffed treats. And, there is a variety of recipes for these little morsels, but too many of them include of all things, bacon and butter. This easy-to-prepare recipe has been in our family for years and came from our early years living in California's date country.

**MAKES 24 STUFFED DATES   SODIUM PER RECIPE: 9.142 MG
SODIUM PER DATE: .381 MG**

24 **Medjool dates, pitted (5.76 mg)**
2   **tablespoons unsalted, blanched almonds, chopped (2.211 mg)**
2   **tablespoons confectioners' sugar (.15 mg)**
24 **walnut halves (1.021 mg)**

Using a food processor fitted with the metal blade, finely chop the almonds.

Lay the almonds and sugar on a work surface such as waxed paper and mix together.

Cut each date open lengthwise, remove the pit of each date, and insert a walnut half. Roll the date in the sugar-almond mixture, making sure some of the almonds and sugar get into the open split.

Set the dates on a serving dish in a concentric circle and serve.

These can also be stored at room temperature in ziplock bags or an airtight container.

Nutrient Data per Date:
Calories: 87.5. Protein: .904 g. Carbohydrate: 19 g. Dietary Fiber: 1.836 g. Total Sugars: 16.6 g. Total Fat: 1.857 g. Saturated Fat: .172 g. Monounsaturated Fat: .472 g. Polyunsaturated Fat: 1.094 g. Cholesterol: 0 mg. Trans Fat: 0 g. Total Omega-3 FA: .196 g. Total Omega-6 FA: 0 g. Potassium: 181.8 mg. Sodium: .381 mg. Vitamin K: .705 mcg. Folic Acid: 0 mcg.

VANILLA-FLAVORED CUPCAKES WITH
❖ ORANGE ZEST TOPPING ❖

DIABETIC ADAPTABLE*

Cupcakes are just small cakes. Let's face it, if we can make a cake with a batter, why can't we make smaller cupcakes? The answer is: We can and we do. The only difference is the size and the cooking time and of course the pans. There are various shapes we can make as well. For instance, if you put the batter for this cake into "muffin top" pans, you can make six 2-layer, 4-inch-diameter birthday cakes for the kids (and we know from experience that they'll love them). Or, of course, you can make twelve single-layer cakes for them. Just punch a candle or two into them and you've got a winner on your hands for the wee ones.

MAKES 24 CUPCAKES   SODIUM PER RECIPE: 220.9 MG
SODIUM PER CUPCAKE WITH TOPPING (24): 9.206
SODIUM PER 4-INCH MUFFIN TOP SIZE WITH TOPPING (12): 18.4 MG
SODIUM PER CUPCAKE WITHOUT TOPPING (24): 8.646
SODIUM PER 4-INCH MUFFIN TOP SIZE WITHOUT TOPPING (12): 17.3

THE CUPCAKES

2	cups Softasilk cake flour (5.48 mg)
1¼	cups Splenda or white granulated sugar (trace)
⅓	cup softened unsalted butter (8.24 mg)
1	large egg (63 mg)
¼	teaspoon onion powder (trace)
1	cup nonfat milk with added vitamins A & D (102.9 mg)
1½	teaspoons vanilla extract (.567 mg)
2	tablespoons Featherweight baking powder† (27 mg)

*The cupcake is diabetic adaptable, but not the topping. You can make a Splenda-based syrupy, orange zest topping instead. (The cupcakes will taste just as good.) There are two ways to make this topping. The first is to combine 1 cup Splenda Sugar for Baking (0 mg) with ¼ cup orange juice in a small pot and bring to a boil, stirring until Splenda dissolves. Cool completely before spreading on cupcakes. The second is to bring 1 cup of Splenda and 2 tablespoons of orange juice to boil in a small pot, stirring until the Splenda dissolves. Cool completely before spreading on cupcakes.

†Featherweight baking powder should be mixed in just before you pour the batter into the cups and place them in the oven. You will use 1 tablespoon for the first batch of batter and when that portion has baked, then mix the second tablespoon into the second half of the batter and bake. Featherweight contains potassium chloride. You can also make this using Ener-G baking powder. Increase the total measurement to 3 level tablespoons if using Ener-G and subtract the 27 mg of sodium. Ener-G is pure calcium carbonate.

THE TOPPING

1   **cup confectioners' sugar (1.2 mg)**
1½ **tablespoons freshly grated orange zest**
1   **tablespoon unsalted butter, softened (1.562 mg)**
2   **tablespoons nonfat milk with added vitamins A & D (10.3 mg)**
1   **teaspoon vanilla extract (.378 mg)**

Preheat oven to 375°F.

Prepare your pans by placing nonstick paper cups into muffin pan cups or, if making muffin tops, very lightly spray the cups with oil as well as just around the edges where the cakes might overlap after rising. (We use Baker's Advantage Top-Of-Muffin pans by Roshco.)

Sift the flour and sugar into a medium mixing bowl. Using a handheld or countertop electric mixer, mix the unsalted butter and ⅔ cup of the milk into the flour and sugar. Mix for 1 to 2 minutes, or until smooth. Add the egg and vanilla and the remaining milk and beat together for another 2 minutes.

Unless you have a double oven, you will need to bake the muffin pans one after the other. Since items using Featherweight baking powder must be put into the oven within moments of its being introduced into the batter, split the batter into two bowls at this point.

Add 1 tablespoon of the baking powder to one of the bowls of batter and beat for about 30 seconds. Using a ¼-cup measuring cup filled not quite to the top, pour the batter into each cupcake cup. If using a muffin-top pan, pour in ¼ cup plus whatever it takes to half-fill the muffin cup.

Place the pan into the oven immediately and set the timer for 12 minutes. Test a cupcake with a toothpick. If it comes out clean, the cakes are done; they will have browned slightly on the top. If the toothpick is sticky, let them bake for another minute or two.

Cool on a rack. Repeat the procedure with the second bowl of batter.

You can prepare the topping while the cupcake are baking or after they have cooled. We make the topping after the cupcakes have cooled since putting topping on hot or warm cupcakes can easily tear up the cupcake.

Beat together all ingredients for the topping except 1 tablespoon of the milk. If it appears the second tablespoon is needed, then add it and continue beating until the topping is smooth. Spread on the cupcakes with a knife or flat spatula.

Nutrient Data per Cupcake with Topping (24):
Calories: 137.2. Protein: 1.612 g. Carbohydrate: 25.5 g. Dietary Fiber: .223 g. Total Sugars: 16 g. Total Fat: 3.336 g. Saturated Fat: 2.001 g. Monounsaturated Fat: .875 g. Polyunsaturated Fat: .19 g. Cholesterol: 17 mg. Trans Fat: 0 g. Total Omega-3 FA: .028 g. Total Omega-6 FA: .08 g. Potassium: 160.6 mg. Sodium: 9.206 mg. Vitamin K: .301 mcg. Folic Acid: 15.8 mcg.

Nutrient Data per Muffin-Top Cupcake with Topping (12):
Calories: 274.3. Protein: 3.225 g. Carbohydrate: 51.1 g. Dietary Fiber: .446 g. Total Sugars: 32 g. Total Fat: 6.673 g. Saturated Fat: 4.003 g. Monounsaturated Fat: 1.75 g.

Polyunsaturated Fat: .379 g. Cholesterol: 34 mg. Trans Fat: 0 g. Total Omega-3 FA: .056 g. Total Omega-6 FA: .161 g. Potassium: 321.3 mg. Sodium: 18.4 mg. Vitamin K: .603 mcg. Folic Acid: 31.5 mcg.

Nutrient Data per Muffin-Top Cupcake Without Topping (12):
Calories: 225.2. Protein: 3.145 g. Carbohydrate: 41 g. Dietary Fiber: .446 g. Total Sugars: 22 g. Total Fat: 5.701 g. Saturated Fat: 3.391 g. Monounsaturated Fat: 1.498 g. Polyunsaturated Fat: .338 g. Cholesterol: 31.5 mg. Trans Fat: 0 g. Total Omega-3 FA: .048 g. Total Omega-6 FA: .135 g. Potassium: 317.1 mg. Sodium: 17.3 mg. Vitamin K: .52 mcg. Folic Acid: 31.5 mcg.

Nutrient Data per Cupcake Without Topping (24):
Calories: 112.6. Protein: 1.573 g. Carbohydrate: 20.5 g. Dietary Fiber: .223 g. Total Sugars: 11 g. Total Fat: 2.85 g. Saturated Fat: 1.695 g. Monounsaturated Fat: .749 g. Polyunsaturated Fat: .169 g. Cholesterol: 15.7 mg. Trans Fat: 0 g. Total Omega-3 FA: .024 g. Total Omega-6 FA: .068 g. Potassium: 158.5 mg. Sodium: 8.646 mg. Vitamin K: .26 mcg. Folic Acid: 15.8 mcg.

SAUCES AND SPICES

❖ ❖ ❖ ❖ ❖ ❖ ❖ ❖

While filming a French chef in Paris, I asked him why France was credited with so many wonderful sauces. His answer was simple and to the point. "Because France didn't have access to good food, so they buried what they ate in great sauces." And so, it seems, did a lot of other people around the world.

Famous sauces have come out of areas of the world that might surprise you. But the ones we enjoy worldwide often include the same thing: lots of salt.

From America's Cajun country to Asia's soy- and fish-sauce world, sodium ranks high in most sauces because of the salt that's used in them. Mexican sauces, Italian sauces, Chinese, African, and South American sauces along with the well-known European sauces all contain too much sodium for us to enjoy them as originally created.

In this section you'll find substitute recipes for soy sauce, hoisin sauce, dipping sauce, enchilada sauce, and a bunch more. Our soy sauce and hoisin sauce are sure to surprise you, as well as our Texas Barbecue Sauce.

We also think you'll like some of the flavors from other parts of the world, like the Asian satay sauce otherwise known as Peanut Dipping Sauce and Niter Kebbeh, which is not a sauce as much as a spicy olive oil used with the Ethiopian bread.

Sauces can be a lot of fun and perk up your meals, especially since you've already given up using salt. Another way to give your dishes an added zing is to use a squeeze of fresh lemon or lime juice. Spices come in nicely as well. You can find a good collection of spice mixes in *The No-Salt, Lowest-Sodium Light Meals Book* and our favorite spice for meats in this section: Don's Herbes de Provence Spice Mix. Use this mix as a rub for lamb, beef, or fowl. You'll never need that salt shaker again.

❂ AVOCADO CREAM SAUCE ❂

ORIGIN: CALIFORNIA

SERVES: 6 SODIUM PER RECIPE: 420 MG
SODIUM PER SERVING 70 MG

THE SAUCE†
½ **cup dry white nonalcoholic wine, such as Fré (8.12 mg)**
2 **garlic cloves, minced (1.02 mg)**
1 **medium Hass avocado*, skin and pit removed (13.8 mg)**
¼ **cup whole milk (24.4 mg)**
¼ **cup half-and-half (24.8 mg)**
2 **teaspoons fresh lemon juice (trace)**
  Dash of cayenne pepper (trace)

Bring the wine and garlic to a boil into a small pan and cook, uncovered, for 3 to 4 minutes. Transfer to a blender or use a small handheld blender to puree the mixture with the avocado. Add the remaining ingredients. Process for a few seconds and return the mixture to the saucepan. Reheat and serve warm over fish.

Nutrient Data per Tablespoon Sauce:
Calories: 223.6. Protein: 23.1 g. Carbohydrate: 4.314 g. Dietary Fiber: 2.163 g. Total Sugars: .905 g. Total Fat: 12.6 g. Saturated Fat: 2.559 g. Monounsaturated Fat: 5.53 g. Polyunsaturated Fat: 3.044 g. Cholesterol: 72.7 mg. Trans Fat: 0 g. Total Omega-3 FA: 1.912 g. Total Omega-6 FA: .004 g. Potassium: 563.8 mg. Sodium: 70 mg. Vitamin K: 6.768 mcg. Folic Acid: 0 mcg.

❂ FRUIT CHUTNEY ❂

ORIGIN: AFRICA
NOT DIABETIC ACCEPTABLE

Chutney, first created in India in the 1600s, takes on the flavors of the local region where it's made and that's why there are so many different recipes. This recipe from Africa uses a variety of dried fruits and is absolutely delicious served with meat or blended with a little hot water to be used as a glaze while roasting or grilling.

You may preserve chutney by following a standard canning process for jams and jellies, or store in a covered container in your refrigerator.

*Or 173 grams of available variety.
†About 6 servings when used as a sauce for fish.

½ **cup dried apricots (6.5 mg)**
½ **cup dried apples (37.4 mg)**
½ **cup golden raisins (9.9 mg)**
½ **cup pitted dates (about 10) (2.4 mg)**
1 **tablespoon crystallized ginger (trace)**
¾ **cup chopped onion (about ½ onion) (3.6 mg)**
1 **tablespoon minced garlic (about 2 to 4 cloves) (1.428)**
½ **cup plus 1 tablespoon cider vinegar (1.35 mg)**
¼ **cup plus 1 tablespoon low-sodium water (trace)**
⅓ **cup white granulated sugar or Splenda (trace)**
1 **teaspoon mustard powder (trace)**
1 **teaspoon ground ginger (.576 mg)**
1 **teaspoon ground coriander (.63 mg)**
¼ **teaspoon ground cinnamon (.149 mg)**
¼ **teaspoon cayenne pepper (.135 mg)**

Chop all the dried fruits except for the raisins and place all the dried fruits and crystallized ginger into an enameled or stainless-steel pan. Add the onion, garlic, vinegar, water, sugar or Splenda, and the mustard powder and spices. Mix thoroughly and bring to a boil over medium-high heat. Reduce the heat to the lowest temperature, cover partially, and cook for 45 minutes to 1 hour. Stir frequently, especially after the first 30 minutes. If during the last half hour of cooking the mixture needs more liquid, add water a tablespoon at a time. The mixture will be quite firm when done.

Remove from the heat and let cool. You may store it, covered, in your refrigerator for up to 10 days. If you choose to preserve it, follow reliable directions for doing so, and use sterilized jars.

Nutrient Data per Tablespoon:
Calories: 35.7. Protein: .299 g. Carbohydrate: 9.331 g. Dietary Fiber: .683 g. Total Sugars: 6.185 g. Total Fat: .077 g. Saturated Fat: .016 g. Monounsaturated Fat: .026 g. Polyunsaturated Fat: .018 g. Cholesterol: 0 mg. Trans Fat: 0 g. Total Omega-3 FA: .001 g. Total Omega-6 FA: 0 g. Potassium: 78.1 mg. Sodium: 2.002 mg. Vitamin K: .23 mcg. Folic Acid: 0 mcg.

❖ DON'S FLAVOR ENHANCER ❖

When we say "salt substitute," we aren't speaking of salt, but a substitute for flavor. Salt substitutes that don't use or contain salt will not help out as a leavening agent or a preservative. My flavor enhancer replaces salt in many recipes as a "kicker" when a mix of spices is needed. It works well with soups, Italian dishes, barbecued meats, and it even works in some bread recipes. This recipe is for a big batch that you can put into a large shaker or store in a Mason jar. You can also adapt this to your own tastes. Keep testing while putting it together. Like most of my spice mixes, I suggest buying larger containers of ingredient spices from a discount grocery store like Smart and Final, Costco, or a fine restaurant supplier. It's less expensive in the long run. Always store in a tight container and in a dark, cool place. Remember, too, real salt has 2,350 mg of sodium per teaspoon while this flavor enhancer has only 2.76 mg of sodium per teaspoon.

MAKES 13½ TEASPOONS
SODIUM PER RECIPE: 37.7 MG SODIUM PER TEASPOON: 2.793 MG

5	tablespoons unsalted onion powder (17.5mg)
3½	tablespoons unsalted garlic powder (7.644mg)
1	tablespoon paprika (2.346mg)
2	tablespoons dry mustard powder (0mg)
1	tablespoon ground thyme (2.365mg)
1	teaspoon white pepper (.12mg)
2	teaspoons celery seed (6.4mg)
¼	teaspoon ground cloves (1.276mg)

Mix all the ingredients together, shake well, store what you aren't going to use soon in a tight container in a cool, dark place. Taste before storing. If you want one of the flavors above to be increased then add ¼ teaspoon at a time and shake well before testing again.

If you want to kick this up even more, add some lemon zest, pureed to a powder in a food processor. Also, powder some dill weed and add that if you're using this on vegetables.

Nutrient Values per Teaspoon:
Calories: 23.8. Protein: 1.011 g. Carbohydrate: 4.416 g. Dietary Fiber: .672 g. Total Sugars: 0 g. Total Fat: .485 g. Saturated Fat: .081 g. Monounsaturated Fat: .194 g. Polyunsaturated Fat: .169 g. Cholesterol: 0 mg. Calcium: 25.6 mg. Iron: .851 mg. Potassium: 70.8 mg. Sodium: 2.793 mg. Vitamin K: 0 mcg. Folate: 5.538 mcg.

◈ DON'S HERBES DE PROVENCE SPICE MIX ◈

ORIGIN: FRANCE
DIABETIC ACCEPTABLE

My wife brought home a small bag of dried herbs from Provence, France. We tried them and they were out of this world. It was a mix that we found we could use on beef, chicken, turkey, and in soups and stews, and just about anything that had meat or potatoes in it. Give it a try, we're sure you'll like it.

**MAKES: 20 TEASPOONS   SODIUM PER RECIPE: 21.1 MG
SODIUM PER TEASPOON: 1.056 MG**

4 **tablespoons dried thyme (9.46 mg)**
4 **tablespoons dried summer savory (4.224 mg)**
1 **teaspoon lavender (trace)***
1 **tablespoon dried basil (1.53 mg)**
2 **teaspoons dried sage (.154 mg)**
1 **tablespoon dried rosemary (1.65 mg)**
3 **tablespoons dried marjoram (3.927 mg)
   (.168 mg)**

Mix together and shake. Store in a tightly sealed container.
   Use with meats, potatoes, soups, and stews.

Nutrient Data per Teaspoon:
Calories: 6.885. Protein: .22 g. Carbohydrate: 1.619 g. Dietary Fiber: 1.029 g. Total Sugars: .03 g. Total Fat: .179 g. Saturated Fat: .072 g. Monounsaturated Fat: .014 g. Polyunsaturated Fat: .031 g. Cholesterol: 0 mg. Trans Fat: 0 g. Total Omega-3 FA: .02 g. Total Omega-6 FA: 0 g. Potassium: 30.5 mg. Sodium: 1.056 mg. Vitamin K: 21.4 mcg. Folic Acid: 0 mcg.

❖ DON'S SOY SAUCE REPLACEMENT ❖

ORIGIN: ASIA
DIABETICS, SEE FOOTNOTE**

Make and store for future use. This tastes so close to the real thing you won't believe it. The recipe is from The No-Salt, Lowest-Sodium *Cookbook, but with the addition of the garlic. Use in any Asian recipe calling for soy sauce.*

**MAKES 1 CUP   SODIUM PER RECIPE: 28.4 MG
SODIUM PER TABLESPOON: 1.775 MG**

¾ **cup rice vinegar† (1.8 mg)**
1 **garlic clove, crushed in garlic press (.51 mg)**
3 **tablespoons Grandma's molasses (22.2 mg)**
1 **tablespoon onion powder (3.888 mg)**

*Culinary-grade lavender, not the potpourri kind.
**Sugars and carbohydrates are mostly in the molasses. We weren't successful attempting this recipe with any substitutes. It is acceptable as is.
†Not seasoned

Combine all the ingredients in a small jar, tighten the lid, and shake well. Store in the refrigerator. Use as needed.

Nutrient Data per Tablespoon:
Calories: 14.3. Protein: .057 g. Carbohydrate: 3.891 g. Dietary Fiber: .03 g. Total Sugars: 2.906 g. Total Fat: .009 g. Saturated Fat: .002 g. Monounsaturated Fat: .002 g. Polyunsaturated Fat: .004 g. Cholesterol: 0 mg. Trans Fat: 0 g. Total Omega-3 FA: 0 g. Total Omega-6 FA: 0 g. Potassium: 71.1 mg. Sodium: 1.775 mg. Vitamin K: .021 mcg. Folic Acid: 0 mcg.

❧ EASY COCONUT MILK ❧ ❧

ORIGIN: AFRICA
DIABETICS: USE RAW COCONUT

When I filmed in Tahiti, in the '70s, I worked with a local Polynesian named Rene Tupano. Rene could climb a coconut tree barefooted so fast that following him with a movie camera was like following the takeoff of an airplane. He'd get to the top, knock on some coconuts, then drop a few. "There are stages," he said, "about twenty-six of them. Only one is good for the milk." We would then crack open the outer shell and break through the interior (hairy) shell and drink the milk. It was incredible.

When I returned from that trip, I bought a can of coconut milk and, yuk. Tasteless! Canned coconut milk still has very little flavor, so when we need coconut milk for a recipe, we make our own. Maureen came up with this recipe and it works wonderfully. We use lightly sweetened coconut chunks (we get ours at Trader Joe's), and from these we make our own milk. The flavor tastes much better to us.

MAKES: 1 CUP   SODIUM PER RECIPE: 60 MG
SODIUM PER TABLESPOON: 3.75 MG

1 cup diced unsalted/sweet coconut* (the dried-food snack) (60 mg)
1 cup boiling, low-sodium water (trace)

Place both of the above ingredients into a blender and puree. This will equal 1 cup of coconut milk for any recipes calling for it. We found this preferable to canned coconut milk, but you may use the latter if you choose.

---

*A cup of shredded fresh coconut has 16 mg of sodium. Finding fresh coconut may prove challenging since much of what we get in our grocery stores is dried.

Nutrient Data per Tablespoon:
Calories: 37.5. Protein: .188 g. Carbohydrate: 4.5 g. Dietary Fiber: .938 g. Total Sugars: 2.25 g. Total Fat: 2.062 g. Saturated Fat: 1.312 g. Monounsaturated Fat: 0 g. Polyunsaturated Fat: 0 g. Cholesterol: 0 mg. Trans Fat: 0 g. Total Omega-3 FA: 0 g. Total Omega-6 FA: 0 g. Potassium: 0 mg. Sodium: 3.75 mg. Vitamin K: 0 mcg. Folic Acid: 0 mcg.

❈ GUACAMOLE ❈

ORIGIN: MEXICO
DIABETIC ACCEPTABLE

Perhaps you have your own guacamole recipe. If you do, you can still try this original Mexican version. We used to enjoy this recipe at a Mexican restaurant in Burbank, California, where I worked in the film business. It's great with our Carnitas, Fajitas, and on salads or as a dip. Options include adding Grandma's No-Salt chili powder. A very simple but tasty guacamole can be made by just mashing an avocado and adding nothing. Serve it fresh with a squeeze of lemon juice to help retain the color.

**MAKES 2 CUPS OR 32 TABLESPOONS   SODIUM PER RECIPE: 40.8 MG
SODIUM PER TABLESPOON: 1.276 MG**

2   **Hass avocados (27.7 mg)**
½   **cup chopped onion (2.4 mg)**
1   **tablespoon chopped jalapeño pepper (about 1 pepper) (.16 mg)**
2   **garlic cloves, chopped (1.02 mg)**
1   **tomato, seeded and chopped (9.1 mg)**
3   **tablespoons fresh lemon juice (.46 mg)**

Peel, pit, and mash the avocados. A potato masher works fine. Add all the remaining ingredients and mix thoroughly. The guacamole is best eaten the same day, but if you want to save it for the next, sprinkle with fresh lemon juice, cover with plastic wrap, and refrigerate. If the top darkens, you can scrape it off just before serving.

Nutrient Data per Tablespoon:
Calories: 20.9. Protein: .309 g. Carbohydrate: 1.626 g. Dietary Fiber: .862 g. Total Sugars: .343 g. Total Fat: 1.684 g. Saturated Fat: .234 g. Monounsaturated Fat: 1.063 g. Polyunsaturated Fat: .208 g. Cholesterol: 0 mg. Trans Fat: 0 g. Total Omega-3 FA: .026 g. Total Omega-6 FA: .002 g. Potassium: 75.5 mg. Sodium: 1.276 mg. Vitamin K: 2.781 mcg. Folic Acid: 0 mcg.

❧ FRESH SALSA ❧

ORIGIN: MEXICO
DIABETIC ACCEPTABLE

Salsa works with many Mexican dishes, including our Carnitas (see page 70). You can make this and store it in an airtight container for up to 3 days in your refrigerator. It also makes a great dip for parties when using no-salt Mexican-style tortilla chips.

**MAKES 2 CUPS (32 TABLESPOONS)   SODIUM PER RECIPE: 25.1 MG
SODIUM PER TABLESPOON: .784 MG**

2   **cups fresh tomatoes, seeded and chopped (18 mg)**
⅓ **cup onion, chopped (1.588 mg)**
1   **jalapeño pepper, chili, chopped (.14 mg)**
2   **tablespoons cilantro, chopped (5.184 mg)**
⅛ **teaspoon white pepper (.015 mg)**
3   **to 4 tablespoons of fresh-squeezed lemon juice (.61 mg)***

Place all of the ingredients into a small bowl and mix thoroughly. Serve at room temperature with any Mexican dish or as a dip.

Nutrient Data per Tablespoon:
Calories: 3.235. Protein: .13 g. Carbohydrate: .772 g. Dietary Fiber: .183 g. Total Sugars: .408 g. Total Fat: .028 g. Saturated Fat: .006 g. Monounsaturated Fat: .007 g. Polyunsaturated Fat: .017 g. Cholesterol: 0 mg. Trans Fat: 0 g. Total Omega-3 FA: 0 g. Total Omega-6 FA: 0 g. Potassium: 33.2 mg. Sodium: .784 mg. Vitamin K: .936 mcg. Folic Acid: 0 mcg.

❧ ITALIAN MARINARA SAUCE ❧

ORIGIN: ITALY
DIABETIC ACCEPTABLE

Different marinara sauces are found throughout Italy and Sicily. Some are complex in flavor whereas others are simple. This recipe, put together by Maureen after her trip to Italy (searching for great recipes), is one of the best I've ever eaten. You can put this on polenta, pasta, or use it on your low-sodium pizza.

*Data based on 4 tablespoons

1   tablespoon extra-virgin olive oil (trace)
1   cup chopped onion (4.8 mg)
4   large garlic cloves, minced (2.04 mg)
4   ounces (½ cup) sliced mushrooms (.96 mg)
1   teaspoon dried oregano (.27 mg)
2   teaspoons dried basil (.476 mg)
⅛   teaspoon ground white pepper** (.015 mg)
1   (14.5-ounce) can no-salt-added tomatoes† (105 mg)
1   (8-ounce) can no-salt-added tomato sauce (70 mg)
1   (14.5-ounce) can filtered no-sodium low-sodium water‡
     (trace)

Sauté the onion, garlic, and mushrooms in olive oil over medium high heat until transparent, about 5 minutes. Add the herbs and white pepper and stir for 1 minute more. Add the tomatoes, tomato sauce, and water. Simmer for 1 hour, uncovered. If not using the sauce immediately, store it in tightly lidded container in the refrigerator for up to 3 days, or freeze for longer storage.

Nutrient Data per Cup:
Calories: 94.3. Protein: 1.728 g. Carbohydrate: 12.8 g. Dietary Fiber: 1.924 g. Total Sugars: 4.503 g. Total Fat: 3.504 g. Saturated Fat: .483 g. Monounsaturated Fat: 2.509 g. Polyunsaturated Fat: .41 g. Cholesterol: 0 mg. Trans Fat: 0 g. Total Omega-3 FA: .052 g. Total Omega-6 FA: 0 g. Potassium 248.1 mg. Sodium: 45.9 mg. Vitamin K: 11 mcg. Folic Acid: 0 mcg.

Nutrient Data per Tablespoon:
Calories: 5.892. Protein: .108 g. Carbohydrate: .799 g. Dietary Fiber: .12 g. Total Sugars: .281 g. Total Fat: .219 g. Saturated Fat: .03 g. Monounsaturated Fat: .157 g. Polyunsaturated Fat: .026 g. Cholesterol: 0 mg. Trans Fat: 0 g. Total Omega-3 FA: .003 g. Total Omega-6 FA: 0 g. Potassium: 15.5 mg. Sodium: 2.868 mg. Vitamin K: .69 mcg. Folic Acid: 0 mcg.

*Amount depends upon simmer time and how much evaporates.
**May use less.
†USDA Ratings range from 54 mg per can to 100+. We tested this recipe using S&W No-Salt-Added Tomatoes.
‡After pouring the tomatoes into the pan, put the water in the same can and use that.

✺ RED CHILI SAUCE ✺

ORIGIN: MEXICO
DIABETIC ACCEPTABLE

Maureen has made this sauce many times, and each time she does it seems to get tastier. Try it with soup and enchiladas—you'll love it. (For Chicken Enchiladas, see page 79.) The chilies used here are the large dried chilies, often packaged and found in most produce sections of markets.

**MAKES APPROXIMATELY 3 CUPS SODIUM PER RECIPE: 106 MG
SODIUM PER CUP: 35.3 MG
SODIUM PER TABLESPOON: 2.208 MG**

10 **dried New Mexico or California chilies (73.1 mg)**
1 **large onion (4.5 mg)**
3 **garlic cloves (1.53 mg)**
6 **cups low-sodium water (trace)**
2 **(8-ounce) cans no-salt-added tomato sauce (26.8 mg)**

Stem the chilies and place in 3- to 4-quart pan. Quarter the onion and peel the garlic. Add them to the chilies. Cover with water and simmer for about 30 minutes. When the chilies are soft, remove them from the heat and place half of the batch plus ¾ cup of the cooking liquid in a blender, or in a deep bowl if using a handheld blender. Blend thoroughly and then place the mixture in a sieve that has been placed over a small bowl. Stir with a firm spoon until only a thick paste is left in the sieve. Scrape the bottom of the sieve often. Discard the thick paste in the sieve and repeat the process with the remaining chilies plus ¾ cup of cooking liquid. You should have about 2 cups of chili sauce. Mix this with two 8-ounce cans of no-salt-added tomato sauce.

Nutrient Data per Cup:
Calories: 209.1. Protein: 8.429 g. Carbohydrate: 41 g. Dietary Fiber: 14.2 g. Total Sugars: 2.17 g. Total Fat: 4.864 g. Saturated Fat: .497 g. Monounsaturated Fat: .307 g. Polyunsaturated Fat: 2.652 g. Cholesterol: 0 mg. Trans-Fatty Acids: 0 g. Total Omega-3 FA: .095 g. Total Omega-6 FA: 0 g. Iron: 6.966 mg. Potassium: 175.2 mg. Sodium: 35.3 mg. Vitamin K: .242 mcg. Folic Acid: 0 mcg.

Nutrient Data per Tablespoon:
Calories: 13.1. Protein: .527 g. Carbohydrate: 2.565 g. Dietary Fiber: .889 g. Total Sugars: .136 g. Total Fat: .304 g. Saturated Fat: .031 g. Monounsaturated Fat: .019 g. Polyunsaturated Fat: .166 g. Cholesterol: 0 mg. Trans-Fatty Acids: 0 g. Total Omega-3 FA: .006 g. Total Omega-6 FA: 0 g. Iron: .435 mg. Potassium: 109.5 mg. Sodium: 2.208 mg. Vitamin K: .015 mcg. Folic Acid: 0 mcg.

❂ MARINADE FOR VEGETABLES ❂

ORIGIN: VIETNAM
DIABETIC ACCEPTABLE*

You can marinate almost any vegetable with this mix. This recipe has been specifically created for Thai, Japanese, Vietnamese, and Chinese recipes and particularly for as the Vietnamese Bánh Mì Sandwich recipe (see page 127).

MAKES 14 TABLESPOONS   SODIUM PER RECIPE: 1.524 MG
SODIUM PER TABLESPOON: .109 MG

½ **cup white granulated sugar or Splenda (1 mg)**
½ **cup rice vinegar (1.2 mg)**
¼ **teaspoon onion powder (.283 mg)**

Mix together the sugar, rice vinegar, and onion powder in a small bowl and stir vigorously. Add in your choice of raw vegetables and toss until well coated. Cover and place into the refrigerator for at least 20 minutes, or as long as overnight.

Nutrient Data per Tablespoon:
Calories: 29. Protein: .004 g. Carbohydrate: 7.682 g. Dietary Fiber: .002 g. Total Sugars: 7.657 g. Total Fat: 0 g. Saturated Fat: 0 g. Monounsaturated Fat: 0 g. Polyunsaturated Fat: 0 g. Cholesterol: 0 mg. Trans Fat: 0 g. Total Omega-3 FA: 0 g. Total Omega-6 FA: 0 g. Potassium: 9.118 mg. Sodium: .109 mg. Vitamin K: .002 mcg. Folic Acid: 0 mcg.

❂ MAUREEN'S CAJUN SPICE MIX ❂

ORIGIN: SOUTHERN U.S.A.
DIABETIC ACCEPTABLE

"Cajun" usually means it's hot, but this mix has more than just heat. It's got flavors that help fish, fowl, and ribs perk up when baked, boiled, or barbecued. This recipe makes only a teaspoon and a half, but you can double or triple it or increase it even more if you want to put some in a jar for later use. That's how we usually do it.

MAKES 1½ TEASPOONS   SODIUM PER RECIPE: 2.229 MG
SODIUM PER TEASPOON: 1.486 MG

¼ **teaspoon celery seeds (.8 mg)**
¼ **teaspoon mustard powder (trace)**

*Diabetics, exchange the sugar with Splenda.

¼ teaspoon paprika (.178 mg)
⅛ teaspoon cayenne pepper (.067 mg)
⅛ teaspoon ground cloves (.638 mg)
⅛ teaspoon ground allspice (.183 mg)
⅛ teaspoon ground mace (.17 mg)
⅛ teaspoon ground cardamom (.045 mg)
⅛ teaspoon ground ginger (.072 mg)
⅛ teaspoon ground cinnamon (.075 mg)

Measure the spices into a small bowl and mix thoroughly. Use immediately or store for later use.

Nutrient Data per Teaspoon:
Calories: 7.489. Protein: .282 g. Carbohydrate: 1.134 g. Dietary Fiber: .503 g. Total Sugars: .067 g. Total Fat: .376 g. Saturated Fat: .069 g. Monounsaturated Fat: .135 g. Polyunsaturated Fat: .113 g. Cholesterol: 0 mg. Trans Fat: 0 g. Total Omega-3 FA: .013 g. Total Omega-6 FA: 0 g. Potassium: 26.8 mg. Sodium: 1.486 mg. Vitamin K: .711 mcg. Folic Acid: 0 mcg.

◈ EASY ENCHILADA SAUCE ◈

ORIGIN: MEXICO
DIABETIC ADAPTABLE*

This sauce tastes almost exactly like the Red Chili Sauce in this book and The No-Salt, Lowest-Sodium Light Meals Book *(pages 29–30), which uses real red chili peppers and takes longer to prepare. Either one is delicious, but if your time is limited, this one is truly easy. It can be made ahead of time and frozen for future use.*

MAKES: 2½ CUPS   SODIUM PER RECIPE: 94.7 MG
SODIUM PER CUP: 64.4 MG

1   teaspoon extra-virgin olive oil (trace)
1   cup onion, chopped (4.8 mg)
3   garlic cloves (1.53 mg)
1   teaspoon dried oregano (.255 mg)
2½ tablespoons Grandma's or other no-salt chili powder (trace)
2   tablespoons unsalted butter (3.124 mg)
2   tablespoons flour 2 cups (.381 mg)
2   cups Maureen's Easy Chicken Broth (see page 113)
    (75.6 mg) or 2 cups low-sodium water (trace)

*The carbohydrates are mostly in the onion (16.2 g), the flour (14.5 g), and the fresh tomato (7.056 g). A cup of canned, no-salt tomatoes would have 10.5 g of carbohydrates.

1 cup pureed tomatoes (use either fresh peeled and seeded (9 mg), or canned no-salt-added (60 mg))*

Sauté the onion and garlic in olive oil over medium heat until translucent. Sprinkle the oregano and chili powder over the onion mixture and stir for 1 to 2 minutes.

Melt the butter in 3-quart saucepan and add the flour. Cook over medium heat until bubbly, then remove from heat and add the chicken broth or water. Stir until blended and return to the heat. Cook until the roux thickens and then add the onion-garlic-spice mixture. Add the tomato puree and cook for 30 minutes; the sauce will thicken.

Nutrient Values per Cup:
Calories: 260.2. Protein: 6.607 g. Carbohydrate: 25.9 g. Dietary Fiber: 3.02 g. Total Sugars: 6.015 g. Total Fat: 16 g. Saturated Fat: 7.061 g. Monounsaturated Fat: 5.062 g. Polyunsaturated Fat: 1.44 g. Cholesterol: 43.3 g. Trans Fat: 0 g. Total Omega-3 FA: .16 g. Total Omega-6 FA: .246 g. Potassium: 423.2 mg. Sodium: 37.9 mg. Vitamin K: 16.7 mcg. Folic Acid: 11.7 mcg.

❖ MAUREEN'S GARAM MASALA ❖

ORIGIN: INDIA
DIABETIC ACCEPTABLE

Ready-made garam masala is available at some Indian specialty stores in many health and gourmet shops, as well as from some online sources. Check them for salt if you find them. It is also very easy to make your own spice mix and store it in a tightly lidded jar. Don't make too much of it, though; spices that are stored for long periods lose their flavor.

MAKES: 10 TEASPOONS   SODIUM PER RECIPE: 16.09 MG
SODIUM PER TEASPOON: 1.609 MG

1 **cinnamon stick* (.598 mg)**
1 **teaspoon cumin seeds, ground† (3.528 mg)**
½ **teaspoon cloves (2.552 mg)**
½ **teaspoon black peppercorns (.06 mg)**
⅛ **teaspoon freshly grated nutmeg (.044 mg)**
¼ **teaspoon ground mace (.34 mg)**
½ **tablespoon ground cardamom‡ (.522 mg)**

*Use a 2-inch length of cinnamon stick broken into pieces.
†Black cumin seeds are acceptable as well.
‡Although not always available, it's better to find black cardamom seeds.

Heat a heavy skillet or frying pan. Break the cinnamon stick into smaller pieces into the pan after it has heated a few minutes. Add the cumin seeds, cloves, and peppercorns. Shake the pan over the flame while the spices cook. We don't want them to burn.

Let them roll around until their color darkens. When done, set the pan on a cool burner and let the spices cool.

When cooled, grind the spices in a coffee grinder and then blend in the nutmeg, mace, and cardamom.

Store in airtight container in a cool, dark place for up to 3 months. You can double the ingredients.

Nutrients per Teaspoon:
Calories: 3.128. Calories: 7.011. Protein: .212 g. Carbohydrate: 1.383 g. Dietary Fiber: .652 g. Total Sugars: .042 g. Total Fat: .255 g. Saturated Fat: .051 g. Monounsaturated Fat: .087 g. Polyunsaturated Fat: .041 g. Cholesterol: 0 mg. Trans Fat: 0 g. Total Omega-3 FA: .011 g. Total Omega-6 FA: 0 g. Iron: .633 mg. Potassium: 20.4 mg. Sodium: 1.609 mg. Vitamin K: .488 mcg. Folic Acid: 0 mcg.

❖ Maureen's Tarragon Sauce ❖

Origin: U.S.A.
Diabetic Acceptable

This is easy to make but oh so good. Use with chicken and especially with wild game bird dishes.

Makes: 4 tablespoons   Sodium per Recipe: 3.012 mg
Sodium per Tablespoon: .753 mg

1 **tablespoon unsalted butter (1.562 mg)**
3 **tablespoons fresh lemon juice (.458 mg)**
1 **teaspoon dried tarragon (.992 mg)**

Melt the butter over low heat on the stove top or in a microwave oven. Stir in the lemon juice and tarragon. Serve hot with chicken or game birds.

Nutrient Data per Tablespoon:
Calories: 29.5. Protein: .165 g. Carbohydrate: 1.19 g. Dietary Fiber: .075 g. Total Sugars: .277 g. Total Fat: 2.908 g. Saturated Fat: 1.831 g. Monounsaturated Fat: .748 g. Polyunsaturated Fat: .123 g. Cholesterol: 7.633 mg. Trans Fat: 0 g. Total Omega-3 FA: .034 g. Total Omega-6 FA: .077 g. Potassium: 27.1 mg. Sodium: .753 mg. Vitamin K: .249 mcg. Folic Acid: 0 mcg.

❧ MINTY CUCUMBER SAUCE WITH YOGURT ❧

ORIGIN: MIDDLE EAST
DIABETIC ADAPTABLE

This mint-flavored sauce can be used with chicken, pork, or lamb. Simply put a few tablespoons on your plate and dip your meat into the sauce. It's refreshing with a bit of a bite that adds handsomely to the meat flavor.

MAKES 4 TO 6 SERVINGS   SODIUM PER RECIPE: 265 MG
SODIUM PER SERVING (4): 66.2 MG
SODIUM PER SERVING (6): 44.2 MG

½   **teaspoon ground cumin seeds, toasted and ground***
    (1.764 mg)
1½ **cups plain yogurt† (258 mg)**
1   **5- to 6-inch English or standard waxed cucumber, peeled**
    and grated (3.16 mg)
2   **tablespoons fresh mint, finely chopped (1.984 mg)**
⅛   **teaspoon cayenne pepper, or more to taste (.067 mg)**
    White pepper (trace)

Place all the ingredients in a small bowl, adding the white pepper to taste. Stir until smooth. Refrigerate until ready to use, or use right away.

Place two or three tablespoons of the sauce in small bowls for each serving.

Nutrient Data per Serving (4):
Calories: 65.2. Protein: 5.17 g. Carbohydrate: 7.707 g. Dietary Fiber: .447 g. Total Sugars: .557 g. Total Fat: 1.57 g. Saturated Fat: .934 g. Monounsaturated Fat: .431 g. Polyunsaturated Fat: .063 g. Cholesterol: 5.604 mg. Trans Fat: 0 g. Total Omega-3 FA: .009 g. Total Omega-6 FA: 0 g. Potassium: 283.5 mg. Sodium: 66.2 mg. Vitamin K: 2.903 mcg. Folic Acid: 0 mcg.

Nutrient Data per Serving (6):
Calories: 43.4. Protein: 3.447 g. Carbohydrate: 5.138 g. Dietary Fiber: .298 g. Total Sugars: .371 g. Total Fat: 1.047 g. Saturated Fat: .622 g. Monounsaturated Fat: .287 g. Polyunsaturated Fat: .042 g. Cholesterol: 3.736 g. Trans Fat: 0 g. Total Omega-3 FA: .006 g. Total Omega-6 FA: 0 g. Potassium: 189 mg. Sodium: 44.2 mg. Vitamin K: 1.936 mcg. Folic Acid: 0 mcg.

*Roast the cumin seed in a medium-hot and small, dry frying pan and stir until their color either intensifies or turns a slightly darker color. Grind the toasted seeds with a mortar and pestle, or use a coffee grinder.
†All natural. Make sure it doesn't have sugar in it.

❖ NITER KEBBEH ❖

ORIGIN: ETHIOPIA
DIABETIC ACCEPTABLE

Niter kebbeh, *which really means "spiced butter oil," is usually a highly seasoned clarified butter that is used in Ethiopian cooking. Although similar to ghee,* niter kebbeh *is spiced with simmered onions, garlic, ginger, and other spices and then strained. In order to cut down the saturated fat in a true* niter kebbeh, *we've modified it for use in our Ethiopian Spice Bread (see page 180) and use what is considered "the good oil." The original version, of course, hardened after it was prepared and was easy to store in a "block" or solid mass. This version can be stored in a bottle or sealed jar much as you'd store flavored olive oils. We use this oil in this book only in the spiced bread. The bread is delicious, but that, too, we had to cut down in calories and fat, yet were able to keep the wonderful flavors intact. You can also make your own version by adding other favorite spices such as basil or fenugreek.*

MAKES ABOUT 1 CUP OR 16 TABLESPOONS   SODIUM PER CUP: 5.644 MG
SODIUM PER TABLESPOON: .353 MG

1½	**cups extra-virgin olive oil (trace)**
½	**small onion, peeled and coarsely chopped (1.05 mg)**
2	**garlic cloves, finely chopped (1.02 mg)**
2	**teaspoons fresh ginger, peeled and grated (8.52 mg)**
¾	**teaspoon ground turmeric (.836 mg)**
⅛	**teaspoon ground cardamom* (.045 mg)**
1	**(2-inch-long) cinnamon stick (.598 mg)**
2	**whole cloves (1.531 mg)**
⅛	**teaspoon ground nutmeg (.044 mg)**

In a medium, high-sided saucepan over medium heat, bring the olive oil to a near-boil. Stir in all the ingredients, being careful to not splash. Reduce the heat to the lowest setting and simmer the oil, uncovered and undisturbed, for 15 to 20 minutes. If the oil starts to burn (it shouldn't, but might), immediately remove it from the heat to stop the cooking.

Slowly strain the cooked oil into another pan or a bowl through two or three layers of cheesecloth. Discard the seasonings. If there are any solids

---

*Or a small pinch of cardamom seeds.

left in the oil, strain it again. You don't want any solid matter in the oil at all.

Pour your new *kebbeh* into a jar or bottle and seal tightly (I like to use an old red wine vinegar jar, relabeled of course.) Store at room temperature until ready to use. It can be kept at room temperature, for 1 to 2 months.

Nutrient Data per Tablespoon:
Calories: 84.6. Protein: .07 g. Carbohydrate: .637 g. Dietary Fiber: .172 g. Total Sugars: .115 g. Total Fat: 9.289 g. Saturated Fat: 1.342 g. Monounsaturated Fat: 4.448 g. Polyunsaturated Fat: 3.065 g. Cholesterol: 0 mg. Trans Fat: 0 g. Total Omega-3 FA: .043 g. Total Omega-6 FA: 0 g. Potassium: 10.6 mg. Sodium: .353 mg. Vitamin K: 2.076 mcg. Folic Acid: 0 mcg.

❈ PEANUT DIPPING SAUCE ❈

ORIGIN: THAILAND
DIABETIC ADAPTABLE*

This sauce gives a wonderful kick to your chicken dinner.
If you like peanuts or peanut butter, this Thai sauce will excite your palate in ways never before tested. However, if you're already a peanut sauce lover, this one will just make your life a lot more fun, since it has hardly any sodium in it per serving. We don't overdo it when using this recipe. It has lots of calories from fat, so go gently.

MAKES 8 SERVINGS   SODIUM PER RECIPE: 25.2 MG
SODIUM PER TABLESPOON: 3.152

½ **cup unsalted peanut butter (21.9 mg)**
⅓ **cup water low-sodium water (trace)**
3 **tablespoons white granulated sugar or Splenda (.378 mg)**
2 **tablespoons plus 1 teaspoon of sesame chili oil (trace)**
1½ **tablespoons rice vinegar (.225 mg)**
6 **garlic cloves, minced (3.06 mg)**

Mix all the ingredients with handheld immersion blender or in a blender. Heat and serve as a dipping sauce. Heat in the microwave or on the stove top.

Nutrient Data per Serving:
Calories: 146.9. Protein: 4.189 g. Carbohydrate: 8.788 g. Dietary Fiber: 1.015 g. Total Sugars: 6.396 g. Total Fat: 11.5 g. Saturated Fat: 2.144 g. Monounsaturated Fat: 5.174 g. Polyunsaturated Fat: 3.659 g. Cholesterol: 0 mg. Trans Fat: 0 g. Total Omega-3 FA: .023 g. Total Omega-6 FA: 0 g. Potassium: 116.6 mg. Sodium: 3.152 mg. Vitamin K: .591 mcg. Folic Acid: 0 mcg.

*Diabetics, replace sugar with Splenda or stevia. Peanut butter has 25 grams carbohydrates and 11 grams of sugars.

⚛ PESTO FOR CHICKEN SANDWICHES ⚛

ORIGIN: ITALY
DIABETIC ACCEPTABLE

Not the same as our Basic Pesto, this version was created just for our Pesto Chicken Sandwich (see page 141). You may also use it with pasta, but note that it doesn't contain the usual cheese a classic or basic pesto has. When you make the sandwich, you will add melted cheese to the sandwich.

**MAKES ENOUGH FOR 6 SANDWICH SERVINGS   SODIUM PER RECIPE: 4.127 MG
SODIUM PER SERVING: .688 MG**

⅓ **cup unsalted pine nuts, lightly toasted in an oven at 350°F
    for a few minutes (.891 mg)**
1 **cup fresh basil leaves (1.696 mg)**
3 **medium garlic cloves (1.53 mg)**
⅓ **cup extra-virgin (light) olive oil (trace)**
    Pinch of dried tarragon (.1 mg)

Place all the ingredients in a food processor or use a handheld blender to make a coarse paste. Sprinkle with a bit of white pepper to taste after you spread it on the sandwich.

Use immediately or, to store, cover the paste with a little additional olive oil, cover the container, and refrigerate, but no longer than 24 hours. The pesto will quickly begin to turn brown after that.

Nutrients per Serving:
Calories: 159.1. Protein: 1.292 g. Carbohydrate: 1.775 g. Dietary Fiber: .582 g. Total Sugars: .303 g. Total Fat: 17 g. Saturated Fat: 1.966 g. Monounsaturated Fat: 10.2 g. Polyunsaturated Fat: 3.749 g. Cholesterol: 0 mg. Trans Fat: 0 g. Total Omega-3 FA: .137 g. Total Omega-6 FA: .034 g. Potassium: 83.2 mg. Sodium: .688 mg. Vitamin K: 40.5 mcg. Folic Acid: 0 mcg.

⚛ PEPPER DIPPING SAUCE ⚛

ORIGIN: GREECE AND ITALY
DIABETIC ACCEPTABLE

This recipe works well with Greek and Italian white fish dishes. The plus is that you can also serve it with crackers and cream cheese—or your own low-sodium cheese concoction—at parties. Dip your salt-free potato chips into it as well.

1   **teaspoon white granulated sugar or ½ teaspoon Splenda (trace)**
½   **cup diced onion (2.4 mg)**
½   **cup seeded and chopped red bell pepper (1.49 mg)**
2   **tablespoons chopped jalapeño pepper (.14 mg)**
½   **cup apple cider vinegar (1.2 mg)**
1   **teaspoon whole mustard seeds* (.165 mg)**
1   **tablespoon cornstarch (.749 mg)**
1   **tablespoon low-sodium water (trace)**

Place all the ingredients into a saucepan, except the cornstarch and water, and bring to a boil. Lower the heat and simmer for 15 minutes, stirring often.

Puree the mixture, then return the pureed sauce to the pan and place over medium heat.

Mix the cornstarch and water. Add it to the puree and cook, stirring continually, until it thickens; few minutes.

Serve with white fish or chicken, or chill as a sauce for appetizers.

Nutrient Data per Tablespoon:
Calories: 8.588. Protein: .157 g. Carbohydrate: 2.09 g. Dietary Fiber: .223 g. Total Sugars: 1.159 g. Total Fat: .083 g. Saturated Fat: .008 g. Monounsaturated Fat: .043 g. Polyunsaturated Fat: .024 g. Cholesterol: 0 mg. Trans Fat: 0 g. Total Omega-3 FA: .008 g. Total Omega-6 FA: 0 g. Potassium: 27.8 mg. Sodium: .384 mg. Vitamin K: .344 mcg. Folic Acid: 0 mcg.

❖ APPLESAUCE ❖

Origin: U.S.A.
Diabetic Acceptable

You can make this quick and easy applesauce† and refrigerate what you don't use in a canning jar or bowl, as long as you keep it covered.

Makes 4 Cups   Sodium per Recipe: *14.8 mg*
Sodium per Cup: *3.712 mg*

---

*Can use pickling spice instead.
†From *The No Salt, Lowest-Sodium Cookbook.*

5 to 10 medium, unpeeled apples* (13.8 mg)
½ cup low-sodium water (trace)
1 tablespoon fresh lemon juice (.153 mg)
½ cup white granulated sugar or Splenda† (trace)
1½ teaspoon ground cinnamon‡ (.897 mg)

Wash, core, and chop the apples. Combine the water, lemon juice, and chopped apple in a medium cooking pot. Bring to a quick boil over medium-high heat, stirring often. Reduce the heat to medium and continue cooking, stirring occasionally. When the apples soften, add the sugar and cinnamon, and cook and stir for about 5 minutes. Remove the pot from the heat and let it stand for 5 minutes, covered. Serve the applesauce hot or cold, or use it in any recipe in this book when called for.

Nutrient Data per Cup:
Calories: 279.4. Protein: .945 g. Carbohydrate: 73.7 g. Dietary Fiber: 8.764 g. Total Sugars: 60.9 g. Total Fat: .614 g. Saturated Fat: .102 g. Monounsaturated Fat: .028 g. Polyunsaturated Fat: .181 g. Cholesterol: 0 mg. Trans Fat: 0 g. Total Omega-3 FA: .031 g. Total Omega-6 FA: 0 g. Potassium: 378.7 mg. Sodium: 3.712 mg. Vitamin K: 7.859 mcg. Folic Acid: 0 mcg.

❖ SWISS CHEESE SAUCE ❖

ORIGIN: SWITZERLAND
DIABETIC ACCEPTABLE

This recipe came about when we developed the Chicken Braciole with Lemon Sauce (page 75) and wanted to serve it with cauliflower. A tablespoon of this sauce over the cauliflower, and the meal was not only excellent, it was picturesque. Later, we discovered, this sauce also made a great fondue by just adding another ounce of low-sodium, no-salt Swiss cheese.

MAKES 1 CUP   SODIUM PER RECIPE: 112.8 MG
SODIUM PER TABLESPOON: 7.049 MG

1 tablespoon unsalted butter (1.562 mg)
1 tablespoon all-purpose, unbleached flour (.157 mg)
1 cup nonfat milk with added vitamins A & D (102.9 mg)
¼ teaspoon mustard powder (trace)
¼ teaspoon onion powder (.324 mg)
¹⁄₁₆ teaspoon ground white pepper (trace)

*Nutrient Data Based on 10 medium apples. Carbohydrates (190.69)
†More or less according to your taste. If using 10 apples, you may want 2 teaspoons.
‡Using Splenda subtracts 100 g carbohydrates.

2 ounces low-sodium Swiss cheese, grated (about ½ cup) (7.84 mg)*

Melt the butter in a small saucepan over medium heat. Add the flour, stirring constantly, until well blended and bubbling. Remove the pan from the heat and add the milk all at once, stirring until well blended. Return the pan to the heat and stir in the spices. Cook the mixture, stirring constantly, until it thickens and comes to a boil. Continue cooking for 1 minute, reduce the heat to low, and add the grated cheese. Mix until the cheese melts and the sauce is smooth.

This is delicious served over vegetables like cauliflower and broccoli, or it can be used as a Welsh Rabbit, served over toast.

Nutrient Data per Tablespoon:
Calories: 26.8. Protein: 1.581 g. Carbohydrate: 1.295 g. Dietary Fiber: .018 g. Total Sugars: .84 g. Total Fat: 1.706 g. Saturated Fat: 1.097 g. Monounsaturated Fat: .453 g. Polyunsaturated Fat: .067 g. Cholesterol: 5.434 mg. Trans Fat: 0 g. Total Omega-3 FA: .018 g. Total Omega-6 FA: .019 g. Potassium: 29 mg. Sodium: 7.049 mg. Vitamin K: .149 mcg. Folic Acid: .756 mcg.

✦ TEXAS BARBECUE SAUCE ✦

ORIGIN: TEXAS
DIABETIC ACCEPTABLE

True Texas barbecue sauce uses about 7,000 mg of sodium just from the salt. Then more might be added with Worcestershire sauce and Tabasco sauce, each loaded with sodium. We've made this sauce for many a barbecued rib and think you'll like our version of a true Texas barbecue sauce.

MAKES 3 CUPS   SODIUM PER RECIPE: 320.9 MG
SODIUM PER CUP: 88.1 MG
SODIUM PER TABLESPOON: 6.686 MG

1 (6-ounce) can no-salt-added tomato paste[†] (166.6 mg)
2 (8-ounce) cans no-salt-added tomato sauce[‡] (53.7 mg)

*Low-sodium, no-salt Swiss cheese is available throughout the United States and often supplied by local cheesemakers.
[†]The sodium level figure is from latest USDA database. Check your can for serving size level and multiply by servings in cans. Contadina comes to 100 mg a can and Hunt's, for instance, lists 75 mg. We have yet to find a can of no-salt-added tomato paste that matches the USDA figures.
[‡]This sodium level figure is a USDA figure from its latest database. Check your can of no-salt-added tomato sauce for its level. Some go as high as 20 mg per ¼ cup or 80 mg per cup.

½ cup low-sodium water (trace)
½ medium onion, minced (1.65 mg)
⅓ cup fresh lemon juice (.805 mg)
2 tablespoons Grandma's or B'rer Rabbit molasses (19 mg)
1 teaspoon onion powder (1.296 mg)
2 teaspoons mustard powder (trace)
½ teaspoon ground cloves (2.552 mg)
¾ teaspoon cayenne or crushed red pepper (1.193 mg)
½ teaspoon dried thyme (.385 mg)
¼ teaspoon dried sage (trace)
1 tablespoon barley malt (15 mg)
1 tablespoon cider vinegar (.15 mg)
4 garlic cloves, minced (2.04 mg)
¼ cup brown sugar, loosely packed (56.6 mg)

Place all the ingredients into a saucepan and stir over medium-low heat for about 10 minutes or more to get all the flavors mixed together for a great sauce.

Use this sauce to baste meat before and while barbecuing. You may use some of the sauce to marinate meat overnight in the refrigerator. Discard all sauce that the meat was marinating in. Baste with sauce that has been stored separately, away from the raw meat.

Nutrient Data per Tablespoon:
Calories: 23.9. Protein: .357 g. Carbohydrate: 5.951 g. Dietary Fiber: .38 g. Total Sugars: 4.183 g. Total Fat: .086 g. Saturated Fat: .015 g. Monounsaturated Fat: .02 g. Polyunsaturated Fat: .032 g. Cholesterol: 0 mg. Trans Fat: 0 g. Total Omega-3 FA: .002 g. Total Omega-6 FA: 0 g. Potassium: 107.8 mg. Sodium: 6.686 mg. Vitamin K: .824 mcg. Folic Acid: 0 mcg.

❧ TZATZIKI SAUCE ❧

ORIGIN: GREECE
DIABETIC ACCEPTABLE

This cucumber-yogurt sauce works especially well with our Greek Meat Loaf recipe on page 100. You can alter it to a basic sauce of just yogurt, cucumbers, and olive oil, or even add more vegetables like diced tomatoes or sliced green onions.

MAKES 16 TABLESPOONS (1 CUP)   SODIUM PER RECIPE: 91.6 MG
SODIUM PER TABLESPOON: 5.728 MG

¾ cup plain whole-milk yogurt (85.3 mg)
1 tablespoon extra-virgin olive oil (trace)

    Juice of 1 lemon (.47 mg)
2 **garlic cloves, minced (1.02 mg)**
    Pinch of ground white pepper (trace)
1 **small packet Splenda (trace)**
1 **small English cucumber,* peeled and diced (3.16 mg)**
1 **tablespoon finely chopped fresh mint leaves (1.71 mg)**

Mix together the yogurt, olive oil, lemon juice, garlic, pepper, and Splenda. Cover and refrigerate for 1 hour.

Blend the mixture with a whisk until smooth. Add the diced cucumbers and the chopped mint to the mixture.

Serve with gyros in warmed pita bread. You can also add diced tomatoes and diced onions to this mixture when you make it a pocket pita sandwich. (See Don's Pocket Pita Bread, page 176).

Nutrient Data per Tablespoon:
Calories: 17.3. Protein: .507 g. Carbohydrate: 1.18 g. Dietary Fiber: .122 g. Total Sugars: .211 g. Total Fat: 1.238 g. Saturated Fat: .357 g. Monounsaturated Fat: .727 g. Polyunsaturated Fat: .098 g. Cholesterol: 1.459 mg. Trans Fat: 0 g. Total Omega-3 FA: .008 g. Total Omega-6 FA: 0 g. Potassium: 38 mg. Sodium: 5.728 mg. Vitamin K: 1.224 mcg. Folic Acid: 0 mcg.

◆ DON'S HOISIN SAUCE ◆

ORIGIN: ASIA
DIABETICS, SEE FOOTNOTE†

Hoisin sauce, also known as Peking sauce, or "dipping sauce," is often used with Chinese Peking Duck. It is also used extensively in all Asian cooking, although it may have different names such as tương đen *in Vietnam, which translates to "black sauce." Commercially available, hoisin sauce is extremely high in sodium levels. So, we put this sauce together as a replacement, and it works very well.*

**MAKES 9 TABLESPOONS   SODIUM PER RECIPE: 18.8 MG
SODIUM PER TABLESPOON: 2.084 MG**

4 **tablespoons Don's Soy Sauce Replacement (page 37) (6.843 mg)**
2 **tablespoons unsalted peanut butter (10.9 mg)**

---

*If you use an English cucumber, you really don't have to seed it. All other cucumbers should be seeded.
†Diabetics, the peanut butter, honey, and soy sauce replacement all contain sugars and carbohydrates.

1   tablespoon honey* (.84 mg)
2   teaspoons white wine vinegar (.30 mg)
⅛   teaspoon garlic or onion powder (.091 mg)
2   teaspoons Sesame Seed Chili oil or hot pepper oil (trace)
⅛   teaspoon ground white pepper (trace)

Combine all the ingredients and mix together with a handheld blender or a single-blade beater until well mixed. The sauce can be stored in refrigerator, but is better if you use it soon after making it. It works with any recipe calling for hoisin sauce.

Nutrient Data per Tablespoon:
Calories: 63.8. Protein: 1.815 g. Carbohydrate: 4.99 g. Dietary Fiber: .445 g. Total Sugars: 3.647 g. Total Fat: 4.587 g. Saturated Fat: .875 g. Monounsaturated Fat: 2.084 g. Polyunsaturated Fat: 1.405 g. Cholesterol: 0 mg. Trans Fat: 0 g. Total Omega-3 FA: .008 g. Total Omega-6 FA: 0 g. Potassium: 79.9 mg. Sodium: 2.084 mg. Vitamin K: .179 mcg. Folic Acid: 0 mcg.

*Molasses may be used instead. The peanut-butter flavor stands out more when using the honey.

MEAT

Varieties of meat are found worldwide but in some locales there is generally a single popular meat and often that meat is lamb or chicken.

Lamb is big in Arabic countries and along the Mediterranean Sea, while chicken and fish are important in Asian countries.

No single animal holds the honor of being the "world's" favorite meat although you can more than likely hold your own opinions in that regard.

Chicken is definitely a candidate for worldwide popularity while beef would more than likely come in second.

Meat wasn't in the human diet at the beginning of our history. Some early humans probably started eating meat for survival in their own environment. Early competition for food probably led humans to the fire pit where they eventually cooked the meat they ate. How long ago was that? Archaeologists figure about 2.5 million years ago. Stone tools used for butchering first appear in the fossil records about that time.

After all those years, we are still eating meat, although our preparation and cooking is much different from our early ancestor's.

There are concerns today about diseases that meats might bring with them. In most countries, good controls have been put into place to prevent those diseases from reaching us, but things aren't perfect. In our home, we still eat meat, but we do search for organic meats and wild fish. Usually if you have access to organic meat, the farm or meat-market people can tell you exactly where it came from. When we serve turkey on our American Thanksgiving we always get an organic, nonprocessed bird. Otherwise most turkeys are injected with a high-sodium "filler," which we don't want.

Today, chickens are often "brined" or soaked in a salty brine solution. Be on guard for that as well. The normal per-ounce level of sodium for chicken is around 18 mg. If brined, that can climb to between 80 and 100 mg per ounce. The same is true of pork.

Packaged, frozen, or broadly distributed meats often have additives, and those additives are generally high in sodium. Read labels and make sure you understand what you are getting.

Meat can be prepared in many, many different ways. What we have done here is collect the best recipes we've prepared over the years, or those we enjoyed while traveling and adjusted them for our *no-salt, lowest-sodium* lifestyle.

We have created sauces, spice mixes, and dishes to make your no-salt lifestyle enjoyable.

✦ ALBÓNDIGAS CON ARROZ ✦

ORIGIN: MEXICO AND SOUTH AMERICA
DIABETIC ACCEPTABLE

Our grandchildren were visiting when we decided to try these South American meatballs. Sarah, 10, and David, 8, asked if they could help. It's a perfect recipe for children to make. After they had washed their hands and I had cooked the onions and garlic, Sarah beat the egg and David added the spices to the meat. They rolled the meatballs to perfect golf-ball size and then rolled them in the flour. I decided it would be safer if I was the one to put them in the hot frying pan. Sarah wanted to continue by chopping the tomatoes and parsley. Needless to say, they were proud of their culinary endeavors and really enjoyed eating the meal.

**MAKES 24 MEATBALLS; 4 TO 6 SERVINGS   SODIUM PER RECIPE: 396.2 MG
SODIUM PER MEATBALL: 16.5 MG**

2   tablespoons olive oil (trace)
1   cup chopped onions (4.8 mg)
2   garlic cloves, minced (1.02 mg)
1   large egg (63 mg)
1   pound 95 percent lean ground beef (299.4 mg)
½   cup cooked rice (trace)
2   teaspoons Grandma's chili powder* (trace)
¼   teaspoon ground white pepper (.03 mg)
½   cup unbleached, all-purpose flour (1.25 mg)
2   large tomatoes, chopped (18.2 mg)
4   tablespoons chopped fresh parsley (8.512 mg)

Heat 1 tablespoon of the oil in a 12-inch frying pan, add the onions and garlic, and sauté for 5 minutes over medium heat, stirring often so as not to burn them. Remove from the heat and cool.

Beat the egg in a large bowl until its color lightens. Add the ground beef, rice, chili powder, cooled onion-garlic mixture, and pepper to the egg. Mix thoroughly as you would for a meat loaf. Shape the meat mixture into golf-ball size meatballs.

Pour the flour onto a piece of waxed paper on a flat surface and roll the meatballs in the flour until they are covered with the flour.

Heat the remaining tablespoon of oil over medium heat and carefully place the meatballs into the hot oil. Turn frequently while frying. When

*Or a brand that doesn't contain salt with the chili powder.

they are lightly browned, approximately 10 minutes, add the tomatoes and parsley. Mix gently, turn the heat to low, cover, and continue to cook for at least 20 minutes.

We serve this dish with additional rice and a vegetable. Delicious!

Nutrient Data per Meatball:
Calories: 60. Protein: 4.902 g. Carbohydrate: 4.603 g. Dietary Fiber: .39 g. Total Sugars: .715 g. Total Fat: 2.374 g. Saturated Fat: .657 g. Monounsaturated Fat: 1.333 g. Polyunsaturated Fat: .229 g. Cholesterol: 20.5 mg. Trans Fat: .064 g. Total Omega-3 FA: .024 g. Total Omega-6 FA: .002 g. Potassium: 122.2 mg. Sodium: 16.5 mg. Vitamin K: 12.4 mcg. Folic Acid: 6.18 mcg.

❂ BAHAMAS GINGER LAMB CHOPS ❂

ORIGIN: BERMUDA
DIABETIC ADAPTABLE*

While filming in Bermuda, I ran across this recipe at dinner one evening. It reminded me of a large navy reception party during my ROTC midshipmen years while in Havana (pre-Castro). It is flavorful, different, and distinct enough to bring back memories, even after many years.

MAKES 4 SERVINGS   SODIUM PER RECIPE: 272.5 MG
SODIUM PER SERVING: 68.1 MG

4   rib or loin lamb chops (about 4 ounces each) (267.6 mg)
2   garlic cloves, minced (1.02 mg)
½   teaspoon ground, dried rosemary (.3 mg)
     Juice of ½ lemon (.235 mg)
3   tablespoons plus 1 teaspoon extra-virgin olive oil (trace)
     Juice of 1 lime or ½ lemon (.235 mg)
1½ teaspoons brown sugar, loosely packed (2.691 mg)
1   teaspoon ground ginger (.576 mg)
⅛   teaspoon ground white pepper (.015 mg)

Combine the garlic, rosemary, lemon juice, and 1 teaspoon of the olive oil and mix into a paste. Make slashes in the lamb around its outer edges and press the paste into the spaces. Make a few slashes on the top (not too deep) and do the same there.

Combine the remaining oil, lime juice, brown sugar, ground ginger, and white pepper and stir with a whisk. Marinate the lamb in this mixture for 3 hours or overnight. Turn at least once. These chops make a terrific

*Diabetics, the brown sugar has 6.638 g carbohydrates. Or try Brown Twin Sugar as a replacement.

barbecue, but you can also cook them under a hot broiler for up to 15 minutes, turning and basting frequently with the marinade.

Nutrient Data per Serving:
Calories: 257.4. Protein: 21 g. Carbohydrate: 3.148 g. Dietary Fiber: .195 g. Total Sugars: 1.831 g. Total Fat: 17.4 g. Saturated Fat: 7.99 g. Monounsaturated Fat: 7.165 g. Polyunsaturated Fat: 1.087 g. Cholesterol: 74.8 mg. Trans Fat: 0 g. Total Omega-3 FA: .211 g. Total Omega-6 FA: 0 g. Potassium: 376.1 mg. Sodium: 68.1 mg. Vitamin K: .239 mcg. Folic Acid: 0 mcg.

❖ ENGLISH BANGERS ❖

ORIGIN: ENGLAND
DIABETIC ACCEPTABLE

On my first trip to England I was very, very busy. I was there for seven days and I think I worked twenty-four hours each day. We were under a "crunch" from one of America's top TV networks and "crunch" was a good word. The first day we ate out of a large Halliburton case I had filled with granola bars and a few other tidbits. (Not a good low-sodium diet, by the way.) Finally, after eating on the run, we arrived one morning at the scene for another day's shooting. We were to film the Queen's butler. We arrived before sunup and, lo and behold, there before us was a traditional, real British breakfast.

Now, I've been a Horatio Hornblower fan and a C. S. Forester fan for fifty years. I remembered Horatio's wanting pork sausage and eggs on his ship once he became a captain—and he reveled over it. So here it was: A real Horatio Hornblower choice for breakfast. And was it great sausage? You bet! So, naturally, what I did was create this no-salt, lower-fat version. The British, however, may put in a half pound of pork fat for this recipe, but don't look for that here. They will also add salt, but of course we don't. Enjoy! These are terrific!

MAKES EIGHTEEN 2-INCH SAUSAGE PATTIES   SODIUM PER RECIPE: 270.7 MG
SODIUM PER SAUSAGE: 15 MG

¼ teaspoon granulated onion or onion powder (.324 mg)
   Big pinch of ground nutmeg (trace)
   Big pinch of ground cloves (trace)
   Big pinch of ground thyme (trace)
1   **pound lean ground pork* (253.1 mg)**

*Preferably from the shoulder and make sure it's lean.

¾ of a ¾-inch-thick slice of bread from Basic Bread Crumbs
    recipe,* toasted and crumbled into crumbs (see page 161)
    (.851 mg)
2   large egg yolks (16.3 mg)
    Sausage casings, optional

In a medium mixing bowl, mix together the onion powder and other
spices. If you have a grinder or food processor, you can use it to mix the
spices with the meat, or use your hands to knead the meat with the spices
until well mixed. Add the bread crumbs and egg yolks and mix well with
your hands or a wooden spoon.

If you're going to put the mixture into sausage skins, then you should
chill the meat for a while to better handle it. Otherwise it's ready to fry as
patties in a nonstick pan with no added oil.

You may also barbecue the patties or grill them over a hot flame. Serve
hot with breakfast fare.

Nutrient Data per Banger:
*Calories: 77. Protein: 4.686 g. Carbohydrate: 1.008 g. Dietary Fiber: .039 g. Total Sugars:
.06 g. Total Fat: 5.876 g. Saturated Fat: 2.164 g. Monounsaturated Fat: 2.624 g.
Polyunsaturated Fat: .567 g. Cholesterol: 41.4 mg. Trans Fat: 0 g. Total Omega-3 FA: .022 g.
Total Omega-6 FA: 0 g. Potassium: 76.3 mg. Sodium: 15 mg. Vitamin K: .043 mcg. Folic Acid:
0 mcg.*

❖ YUGOSLAVIAN GRILLED SAUSAGES ❖

ORIGIN: SERBIA AND CROATIA
DIABETIC ACCEPTABLE

*A grape grower who lived in the central valley of Califor-
nia, many years ago, first served this delicious treat to
me. Along with other dishes he prepared, this one for
čevapciči stands out and is worth the time. You can cook
these on a barbecue, a charcoal grill, or use a heavy-duty
frying pan with a spritz of oil and turn the sausages
every few minutes until done.*

MAKES 8 SAUSAGES   SODIUM PER RECIPE: 327.4 MG
SODIUM PER SAUSAGE: 40.9 MG

½   pound ground lamb or pork† (113.4 mg)
½   pound ground lean beef (chuck is best) (149.2 mg)
1   large egg, lightly beaten (63 mg)
3   drops Tabasco sauce (.76 mg)

*See Basic Bread Crumbs recipe (page 167) for instructions.
†Or use venison or veal.

½ **teaspoon dried marjoram (.231 mg)**
½ **teaspoon paprika (.357 mg)**
1 **large garlic clove, crushed (.51 mg)**

Using a wooden spoon, combine all the ingredients in a medium mixing bowl and blend well. Form into finger-shaped sausages about ¾ inch thick and 4 inches long. If cooking over a charcoal grill, cook slowly and turn frequently. The Yugoslavians like to brown them on the outside and leave a little pink on the inside. Since they have pork in them, I cook them through but don't burn them. If using a frying pan, lightly coat it with oil, and cook the sausages over medium heat, turning often. Yugoslavian tradition calls for serving these on a bed of chopped onions with diced hot peppers, a variety of mixed vegetables, and your favorite dinner bread.

Nutrient Values Per Sausage:
Calories: 110.4. Protein: 12.1 g. Carbohydrate: .268 g. Dietary Fiber: .072 g. Total Sugars: .067 g. Total Fat: 6.429 g. Saturated Fat: 2.455 g. Monounsaturated Fat: 2.77 g. Polyunsaturated Fat: .404 g. Cholesterol: 64.4 mg. Trans Fat: 0 g. Total Omega-3 FA: .038 g. Total Omega-6 FA: 0 g. Potassium: 197.5 mg. Sodium: 40.9 mg. Vitamin K: .363 mcg. Folic Acid: 0 mcg.

❖ BASQUE CHORIZO ❖

ORIGIN: SPAIN
DIABETIC ACCEPTABLE

This mild chorizo has a different flavor than Don's Authentically Hot Chorizo (see page 95), which is a much hotter version. The contest between the two depends upon what you like—hot or mild. In our opinion, this is another terrific recipe submitted by our friend Dixie Guillen.

MAKES EIGHT 2-OUNCE SERVINGS   SODIUM PER RECIPE: 256.8 MG
SODIUM PER CHORIZO: 32.1 MG

1 **pound lean ground pork (253.1 mg)**
1 **garlic clove, minced (.51 mg)**
2 **tablespoons red wine vinegar (.30 mg)**
1 **tablespoon no-salt-added chili powder* (trace)**
1 **tablespoon dried oregano (.81 mg)**
½ **tablespoon paprika (1.173 mg)**
¼ **teaspoon ground cumin† (.882 mg)**

Mix all the ingredients thoroughly, and cover and chill for at least 30 minutes before cooking.

*We use and recommend Grandma's chili powder.
†If you have cumin seeds, you can grind them down with a mortar and pestle, or if you have a coffee grinder, that will work, too.

Shape however you like, from disks to cylinder-shaped sausages, and fry in nonstick pan or on a griddle.

Nutrient Data per Chorizo:
Calories: 155.1. Protein: 9.711 g. Carbohydrate: 1.425 g. Dietary Fiber: .465 g. Total Sugars: .299 g. Total Fat: 12.2 g. Saturated Fat: 4.475 g. Monounsaturated Fat: 5.353 g. Polyunsaturated Fat: 1.153 g. Cholesterol: 40.7 mg. Trans Fat: 0 g. Total Omega-3 FA: .072 g. Total Omega-6 FA: 0 g. Potassium: 190 mg. Sodium: 32.1 mg. Vitamin K: 4.552 mcg. Folic Acid: 0 mcg.

❋ BEEF AND WALNUTS ❋

ORIGIN: MIDDLE EAST*
DIABETIC ADAPTABLE

There was a period of time when we "extended" meat patties with various fillers to help cut the costs of feeding five children. Many recipes came out of that, but this is one of the best. Although this recipe is an entrée cooked with meat to serve over rice, you can also make a tasty sandwich by creating patties. I fry the patties without the orange juice on a nonstick surface, using no oil, and pressing down on them until they're very thin. This way we can serve just 2 ounces of meat, thereby cutting down on the fat and calories.

MAKES 4 SERVINGS   SODIUM PER RECIPE: 309.7 MG
SODIUM PER SERVING: 77.4 MG

1   **pound lean ground beef† (299.4 mg)**
¼   **cup chopped fresh cilantro leaves (6.21 mg)**
¾   **cup orange juice (1.86 mg)**
   Zest of 1 orange (.72 mg)
⅓   **cup coarsely chopped unsalted walnuts (.772 mg)**
½   **teaspoon ground allspice (.731 mg)**

Brown the beef with the cilantro over medium heat until thoroughly cooked. Add the orange juice, orange zest, walnuts, and allspice and cook for 10 minutes more.

This is an easy and quick meal that is absolutely delicious served over boiled rice.

We particularly liked it served with Fried Tomatoes (see page 227)

Nutrient Data per Serving:
Calories: 290.8. Protein: 24.6 g. Carbohydrate: 7.955 g. Dietary Fiber: 1.508 g. Total Sugars: 4.158 g. Total Fat: 17.8 g. Saturated Fat: 5.212 g. Monounsaturated Fat: 5.825 g.

*In the area of Jordan, Lebanon, and Palestine
†Nutrient Data based on 10 percent fat, 90 percent lean beef

Polyunsaturated Fat: 4.971 g. Cholesterol: 73.7 mg. Trans Fat: .723 g. Total Omega-3 FA: .974 g. Total Omega-6 FA: .011 g. Potassium: 529.4 mg. Sodium: 77.4 mg. Vitamin K: 1.214 mcg. Folic Acid: 0 mcg.

❖ BOBOTIE ❖

ORIGIN: SOUTH AFRICA
DIABETIC ACCEPTABLE

You will find this a delicious meat loaf made either with all beef or half beef and half lamb, depending on your taste. When I served it to my daughter-in-law, Kim, she remarked that it was by far the best meat loaf she had ever eaten. The hot apple jelly or chutney recipe that is also in the book is a delightful accompaniment. You may use any chutney that doesn't include salt. Traditional recipes include an egg custard topping that is cooked during the last 15 minutes, but to cut down on the fat and cholesterol I have omitted it. We found it to be just as pleasing without it.

MAKES 8 TO 10 SERVINGS   SODIUM PER RECIPE: **804.5** MG
SODIUM PER SERVING (8): **100.6** MG
SODIUM PER SERVING (10): **80.4** MG

1   cup Basic Bread Crumbs* (see page 161) (4.065 mg)
1   cup nonfat milk with added vitamins A & D† (102.9 mg)
1   tablespoon olive oil (trace)
2   cups chopped onion (9.6 mg)
1   medium tart apple, peeled, cored, and chopped (1.38 mg)
½   cup golden raisins, packed (9.9 mg)
¼   cup unsalted, slivered almonds (.345 mg)
1   teaspoon white granulated sugar or Splenda (trace)
2   tablespoons curry powder (6.552 mg)
1   large egg (70 mg)
2   pounds ground beef, or 1 pound each of ground beef and
      ground lamb (598.8 mg)
2   tablespoons lemon juice (.305 mg)
1   teaspoon lemon zest (.12 mg)
4   bay leaves (.552 mg)
    Ground white pepper (trace)

*Diabetics, make your white bread with Splenda instead of sugar to help lower carbohydrates.
†USDA rates sodium levels in nonfat milk with added vitamin A lower than milk without it.

Preheat the oven to 350°F.

Soak the bread crumbs in milk until soft, 5 to 10 minutes. Drain and reserve any extra milk.

While the bread crumbs are soaking, heat the olive oil in a frying pan, add the onions and apple, and sauté until soft, about 5 minutes. Add the raisins, almonds, sugar, and curry powder and cook for an additional minute.

Lightly beat the egg in large bowl and add any of the reserved milk. Mix until blended. Then, add the ground meat, bread crumbs, onion-apple mixture, lemon juice, and zest. Mix with your hands and shape evenly into a meat loaf.

Place the meat loaf in a buttered or oil-sprayed casserole. Insert the bay leaves vertically in the top of loaf and sprinkle with the white pepper. Bake at 350°F for 1 hour. Remove the bay leaves before serving. Bobotie is traditionally served with boiled rice.

Nutrient Data per Serving (8):
Calories: 335.2. Protein: 29 g. Carbohydrate: 26.2 g. Dietary Fiber: 2.917 g. Total Sugars: 12.5 g. Total Fat: 13 g. Saturated Fat: 4.074 g. Monounsaturated Fat: 5.96 g. Polyunsaturated Fat: 2.07 g. Cholesterol: 99.9 mg. Trans Fat: .387 g. Total Omega-3 FA: .123 g. Total Omega-6 FA: .009 g. Potassium: 681 mg. Sodium: 100.6 mg. Vitamin K: 3.453 mcg. Folic Acid: 0 mcg.

Nutrient Data per Serving (10):
Calories: 268.2. Protein: 23.2 g. Carbohydrate: 21 g. Dietary Fiber: 2.334 g. Total Sugars: 9.981 g. Total Fat: 10.4 g. Saturated Fat: 3.259 g. Monounsaturated Fat: 4.768 g. Polyunsaturated Fat: 1.656 g. Cholesterol: 80 mg. Trans Fat: .309 mg. Total Omega-3 FA: .099 g. Total Omega-6 FA: .007 mg. Potassium: 544.8 mg. Sodium: 80.4 mg. Vitamin K: 2.762 mcg. Folic Acid: 0 mcg.

❖ BOEUF BOURGUIGNON ❖

ORIGIN: FRANCE
DIABETIC ADAPTABLE*

While in France with her teacher friends, Maureen ate many interesting dishes and each had its own flavors that tantalized and treated us to new ideas. The traditional French recipe uses bacon and red wine. Of course, I wanted to make this dish but without the extra fats and sodium from the bacon and without the alcohol content from the wine. So, here it is, just as tasty, and relatively easy to make. A delicious stew made with surprising flavors. We were also able to reproduce the "wine taste" by using alcohol-free wine.

MAKES 6 SERVINGS   SODIUM PER RECIPE: 580 MG
SODIUM PER SERVING: 96.7 MG

*Carbohydrates are in the brown sugar (40.3 g), and the onions (58.8 g).

THE STEW

1½ pounds top round or other top cut of beef (We used cross-rib
     roast cut into 1½-inch chunks) (353.8 mg)
1   tablespoon extra-virgin olive oil (trace)
1   cup chopped onion (4.8 mg)
1   carrot, chopped (42.1 mg)
2   garlic cloves, chopped (1.02 mg)
1   tablespoon unbleached, all-purpose flour (.156 mg)
¼   teaspoon crushed dried rosemary (.15 mg)
¼   teaspoon ground white pepper (.03 mg)
¼   teaspoon crushed dried thyme (.193 mg)
1   cup homemade, unsalted beef or vegetable broth* (18.6 mg)
1   cup alcohol-free red wine† (32.5 mg)
3   tablespoons brown sugar, packed (16.1 mg)
2   tablespoons balsamic vinegar (.3 mg)
3   tablespoons no-salt-added tomato paste (47 mg)

THE VEGETABLE GARNITURE

1   tablespoon olive oil (trace)
12   boiling onions, peeled (place onions in boiling water for
     1 to 2 minutes for easy peeling) (12.6 mg)
8   ounces whole mushrooms (7.68 mg)
3   carrots, peeled and cut into 3-inch pieces (boiled for a few
     minutes until just tender) (42.1 mg)

In a Dutch oven or other heavy pan, brown one-half of the meat in the oil over medium-high heat for 5 to 6 minutes. Repeat with the second batch. Transfer the meat to a plate. Lower the heat to medium and add the onions, carrot, and garlic and sauté until the onions become translucent, about 5 minutes.

Return the meat and juices to pan and stir. Sprinkle with the flour, herbs, and pepper and mix thoroughly. Add the broth, wine, sugar, vinegar, and tomato paste. Mix thoroughly. Bring the stew to a boil over medium-high heat, then lower the heat and cover with a lid. Simmer for 1 hour. Remove the lid and continue to cook for an additional hour. Traditional recipes usually bake the stew in a slow oven anywhere from 2 to 4 hours, but we find this method just as delicious.

Meanwhile, heat 2 teaspoons of the olive oil over medium-high heat in a frying pan and sauté the mushrooms until golden brown and just releasing their juices. Remove the mushrooms from the pan and set aside. Add the remaining teaspoon of olive oil to the pan, return it to the heat, and

*Data figured on beef broth from *The No-Salt, Lowest-Sodium Light Meals Book*
†We use a wine called Fré (which means "free").

sauté the onions in the oil until they turn golden, about 5 minutes. Add the boiled carrot to the onions and continue to sauté for another 2 minutes. Incorporate the sautéed vegetables into the stew and cook for an additional 15 minutes. Serve in pasta or shallow soup bowls. Leftovers of this stew are excellent on the following day.

Nutrient Data per Serving:
Calories: 290.3. Protein: 29.4 g. Carbohydrate: 24.4 g. Dietary Fiber: 2.964 g. Total Sugars: 13.4 g. Total Fat: 8.633 g. Saturated Fat: 1.977 g. Monounsaturated Fat: 4.86 g. Polyunsaturated Fat: .781 g. Cholesterol: 65.3 mg. Trans Fat: 0 g. Total Omega-3 FA: .052 g. Total Omega-6 FA: 0 g. Potassium: 949 mg. Sodium: 96.7 mg. Vitamin K: 8.067 mcg. Folic Acid: 2.005 mcg.

❖ CARNE ASADA ❖

ORIGIN: MEXICO
DIABETIC ACCEPTABLE

An easy-to-prepare dish that will become a favorite—its tangy flavor makes it one of ours.

MAKES 6 SERVINGS   SODIUM PER RECIPE: 251.6 MG
SODIUM PER SERVING: 41.9 MG

1   **pound skirt steak or round steak, thinly sliced* (244.9 mg)**
    Juice from 3 limes (about ¼ cup) (2.28 mg)
¼   **teaspoon ground white pepper (.03 mg)**
8   **garlic cloves, crushed in garlic press (4.08 mg)**
1   **teaspoon dried oregano (.27 mg)**

Place the steak in large, flat pan that's at least 13×9 inches. Cover the steak with half the pepper, half the lime juice, and half the crushed garlic and oregano. Turn the meat over and do the same to the other side with the remaining seasonings.

Cover tightly with plastic wrap and refrigerate overnight.

Two ways we like to cook the steak are to grill it on the barbecue or on a nonstick griddle on the stove top.

Cook over medium high heat until done. Serve with Spanish or Mexican Rice (see page 231) and/or Flour Tortillas (see page 182).

Nutrient Data per Serving:
Calories: 151. Protein: 15.9 g. Carbohydrate: 3.184 g. Dietary Fiber: .315 g. Total Sugars: .373 g. Total Fat: 8.14 g. Saturated Fat: 3.189 g. Monounsaturated Fat: 3.497 g. Polyunsaturated Fat: .341 g. Cholesterol: 46.9 mg. Trans Fat: 0 g. Total Omega-3 FA: .106 g. Total Omega-6 FA: 0 g. Potassium: 301.9 mg. Sodium: 41.9 mg. Vitamin K: 2.035 mcg. Folic Acid: 0 mcg g. Folate: 8.383 mcg.

*The steak is cut very thinly from a larger round steak, as though "butterflied" off the larger piece. One pound will be about 5 such slices.

❖ BIRRIA ❖

ORIGIN: MEXICO
DIABETIC ACCEPTABLE

This authentic Mexican recipe for beef with chili sauce came to us from Dixie Guillen, who worked with Maureen during her teaching years. Dixie explained, "This recipe is from Dave's sister, Cecilia Sandoval. It was also served at a wedding, when we cooked 25 pounds of beef at a time in my electric roaster out on the deck. It's very good." We tried it, and she's right. It's excellent!

MAKES 8 SERVINGS   SODIUM PER RECIPE: 1103 MG
SODIUM PER SERVING: 137.9 MG

4   **pounds boneless lean beef (1070 mg)**
⅔   **cup no-salt-added chili powder* (trace)**
4   **cloves, garlic, minced (5.103 mg)**
1   **teaspoon cumin powder (3.528 mg)**
1   **teaspoon thyme (.77 mg)**
1   **teaspoon marjoram (.462 mg)**
1   **tablespoon dried oregano† (.81 mg)**
10 **whole cloves (10 mg)**
1   **tablespoon black peppercorns (trace)**
3   **whole bay leaves (5.103 mg)**
½   **cup red nonalcoholic wine (8.12 mg)**
½   **cup low-sodium water (trace)**

THE GARNISH
2   **tablespoons cilantro, chopped (5.184 mg)**
1   **small onion, chopped (2.1 mg)**
    fresh juice of two limes‡ (1.52 mg)

Place all of the ingredients, except for the meat and garnish items, in a blender and puree.

Rub the roast with the pureed mixture and marinate overnight, covered in a pan in the refrigerator.

Bake with marinade in a Dutch oven at 350°F for 3½ to 4 hours, until very tender. You may also cook in a Crock-Pot set for Low or High.

---

*We use Grandma's chili powder. Dixie Guillen grinds hot red dried chili pods to obtain her unsalted chili powder.
†Preferably freshly dried
‡Use more fresh lime juice if needed.

Serve on warm corn tortillas*. Garnish with cilantro, chopped onion, and fresh lime juice.

Nutrient Data per Serving:
Calories: 347.2. Protein: 49.2 g. Carbohydrate: 5.426 g. Dietary Fiber: .785 g. Total Sugars: .587 g. Total Fat: 13.4 g. Saturated Fat: 4.799 g. Monounsaturated Fat: 5.386 g. Polyunsaturated Fat: .548 g. Cholesterol: 133.8 mg. Trans Fat: 0 g. Total Omega-3 FA: .078 g. Total Omega-6 FA: 0 g. Potassium: 858.4 mg. Sodium: 137.9 mg. Vitamin K: 8.514 mcg. Folic Acid: 0 mcg.

❧ CARNITAS ❧

ORIGIN: MEXICO
DIABETIC ACCEPTABLE

Fun to make and tasty.

MAKES 8 SERVINGS   SODIUM PER RECIPE: 332.5 MG
SODIUM PER SERVING: 41.6 MG

1½ **pounds boneless pork loin or sirloin chops (306.2 mg)**
2 **garlic cloves (1.02 mg)**
½ **cup chopped onion (2.4 mg)**
2 **cups low-sodium water (trace)**
8 **corn tortillas* (22.9 mg)**

Remove any fat from the meat and reserve. Heat the fat in a frying pan and remove when rendered. If there is no fat, substitute 2 teaspoons olive oil.

Cut the pork into 1-inch chunks and brown lightly in the fat over medium heat. Add the garlic and onion and continue to brown. Add the water and reduce to a simmer. Partially cover, and cook the meat for 1 hour, or until tender.

Wrap the meat in the warmed corn tortillas. Suggested additions are a tablespoon or two for each carnita of the Fresh Salsa (see page 40) and Guacamole (see page 39). Serve with refried beans as a side.

Nutrient Data per Carnita:
Calories: 192.3. Protein: 20.2 g. Carbohydrate: 13.4 g. Dietary Fiber: 1.508 g. Total Sugars: .436 g. Total Fat: 6.173 g. Saturated Fat: 1.995 g. Monounsaturated Fat: 2.663 g. Polyunsaturated Fat: .895 g. Cholesterol: 46.8 mg. Trans Fat: 0 g. Total Omega-3 FA: .035 g. Total Omega-6 FA: 0 g. Potassium: 415.5 mg. Sodium: 41.6 mg. Vitamin K: .051 mcg. Folic Acid: 25.7 mcg.

*Make sure your corn torillas have no more than 15 mg per tortilla.

✸ CASSOLITA ✸

ORIGIN: SPAIN
DIABETIC ACCEPTABLE

The Jews from Spain and Portugal brought this uniquely distinctive recipe to other parts of the world. We added oranges, which the Spanish love and which grow abundantly in their country. The original Jewish recipe would not use pork as we do, but we hope you enjoy our version.

MAKES 6 SERVINGS   SODIUM PER RECIPE: 376.6 MG
SODIUM PER SERVING: 62.8 MG

1   **butternut, or other variety of winter squash, peeled***
     (12.9 mg)
1½   **pounds pork loin cut into 1-inch chunks (353.8 mg)**
     Juice of 1 medium orange (trace)
1   **large onion, peeled, halved, and thinly sliced (at least 2 to 3**
     cups) (4.5 mg)
2   **teaspoons olive oil (trace)**
¼   **teaspoon sugar or Splenda (trace)**
1   **tablespoon low-sodium water (trace)**
¼   **cup golden raisins, packed, then plumped in hot water**
     (4.95 mg)
3   **tablespoons unsalted slivered almonds, toasted (trace)**
1   **tablespoon white granulated sugar or Splenda (trace)**
½   **teaspoon ground cinnamon (.299 mg)**

Preheat the oven to 350°F. Cut the peeled squash in half. Place the squash in a casserole dish, add 2 tablespoons of low-sodium water, and bake for 45 minutes.

Trim excess fat from the pork and put it in a large frying pan to render the fat. If there is not enough fat to cover the bottom of the pan, add 1 teaspoon of olive oil.

Add the pork to the pan and brown lightly over medium-high heat. Add the juice of the orange, lower the heat, cover, and cook for 15 minutes. Remove the cover and continue to cook on low heat for 30 minutes. If too much of the liquid evaporates, add more juice.

In a separate frying pan, sauté the onions in 2 teaspoons olive oil over low heat for 30 minutes, or until soft and translucent. Increase the heat to medium and add ¼ teaspoon of the sugar and 1 tablespoon of water and continue cooking until the onions carmelize. Drain the raisins and add to the onions.

Toast the almonds for a few minutes until crunchy.

*Sodium level varies slightly from squash to squash.

Mix the remaining sugar with the cinnamon.

When the squash is cooked, remove it from oven. Cut into chunks and return to casserole dish. Sprinkle with the sugar-cinnamon mixture. Top with the onion and raisins. Pour the pork on top and return the cassolita to the oven to heat through for 10 minutes. Sprinkle with the toasted almonds and serve.

Nutrient Values per Serving:
Calories: 260.6. Protein: 25.8 g. Carbohydrate: 20.1 g. Dietary Fiber: 2.358 g. Total Sugars: 8.982 g. Total Fat: 8.801 g. Saturated Fat: 2.504 g. Monounsaturated Fat: 4.494 g. Polyunsaturated Fat: 1.08 g. Cholesterol: 66.9 mg. Trans Fat: 0 g. Total Omega-3 FA: .057 g. Total Omega-6 FA: 0 g. Potassium: 818.2 mg. Sodium: 62.8 mg. Vitamin K: 1.294 mcg. Folic Acid: 0 mcg.

❖ CERDO ASADO ❖

ORIGIN: SOUTH AMERICA
DIABETIC ADAPTABLE*

Choose a nice lean pork roast. Bake and serve it with the delicious orange pan sauce—you'll be back for more.

MAKES 6 SERVINGS†   SODIUM PER RECIPE: 578 MG
SODIUM PER SERVING: 96.3 MG

1 **(3-pound) boneless pork loin roast (571.5 mg)**
¼ **teaspoon ground white pepper (.03 mg)**
2 **cups fresh orange juice‡ (4.96 mg)**
1 **tablespoon orange zest (.18 mg)**
2 **garlic cloves, minced (1.02 mg)**
¼ **teaspoon dried oregano (.067 mg)**
2 **teaspoons unbleached, all-purpose-flour (.25 mg)**
1 **cup low-sodium water (trace)**

Preheat the oven to 375°F.

Sprinkle the roast with the pepper. Place it in a roasting pan with sides to contain the marinade. (A Pyrex dish works well.) Place it in the oven and roast for 30 minutes.

While the roast is cooking, mix the orange juice, zest, garlic, and oregano in a small bowl. After the 30 minutes, pour the juice over the pork and return it to the oven for an additional 1½ hours of cooking. Baste every 15 minutes.

*Diabetics, 51.6 carbohydrates are in the orange juice. You can use the same amount of water and 1 to 2 teaspoons of orange extract for the flavoring.
†Depending on your serving size, you might get more servings. Figures and data here figured on six 4-ounce pieces of pork (after roasting).
‡Or you may use "Not from Concentrate" orange juice.

At the end of the roasting time, transfer the meat to a warm platter and scrape all the juice and drippings from the bottom of the pan into a 12-inch frying pan. Mix the flour into the cup of water, stir until smooth. Add the flour-water mixture to the drippings in the frying pan and stir continuously while you bring the sauce to a slow boil over medium heat, about 5 minutes, or until sauce is slightly thickened. The sauce should be smooth except for the small bits of garlic and orange zest. Slice the meat and pour the sauce over the slices.

Nutrient Data per Serving:
Calories: 526.3. Protein: 46 g. Carbohydrate: 10.9 g. Dietary Fiber: .407 g. Total Sugars: 6.963 g. Total Fat: 32 g. Saturated Fat: 11 g. Monounsaturated Fat: 14.2 g. Polyunsaturated Fat: 3.451 g. Cholesterol: 136.1 mg. Trans Fat: 0 g. Total Omega-3 FA: .24 g. Total Omega-6 FA: 0 g. Potassium: 1046 mg. Sodium: 96.3 mg. Vitamin K: .569 mcg. Folic Acid: 3.208 mcg.

❖ CHICKEN AND DUMPLINGS ❖

ORIGIN: SOUTHERN U.S.A.
DIABETIC ACCEPTABLE

The dumplings we use here are made from the same recipe that we use for our Chinese Steamed Buns. If you like chicken and dumplings, you'll love this and best yet: it's low in sodium.

MAKES 6 SERVINGS   SODIUM PER RECIPE: **391.3** MG
SODIUM PER SERVING: **65.2** MG

1   tablespoon unsalted butter (1.562 mg)
1   tablespoon olive oil (trace)
½   cup chopped shallots (9.6 mg)
⅛   teaspoon ground white pepper (trace)
1/16 teaspoon cayenne pepper (.097 mg)
3   tablespoons all-purpose flour (.5 mg)
2   cups Maureen's Easy Chicken Broth (see page 113) (41.6 mg)
¼   cup sour cream (30.5 mg)
2   tablespoons fresh lemon juice (.61 mg)
4   boneless, skinless chicken half breasts, cut into bite-size pieces (306.8 mg)
8   Chinese Steamed Buns* (see page 172), unsteamed (60.4 mg)

*The recipe makes 15 steamed buns. Prepare the recipe and bake the balance in the oven if you want rolls or sandwich bread, or follow the recipe for steaming if you want some of those delicate buns to serve later.

Melt the butter with the oil in a deep stockpot. When the butter and oil are bubbling, add the shallots, sprinkle with the white and cayenne pepper, and sauté for 4 to 5 minutes.

Add the flour and stir thoroughly. Remove the pan from the heat and add the chicken broth all at once. Stir until smooth. Return the pot to the heat and continue cooking until the mixture thickens. Add the sour cream and lemon juice. Stir until well blended.

Add the chicken and simmer until cooked through. Shape the bun dough into dumpings about the size of golf balls, and drop on top. Reduce the heat to low, cover, and cook for 20 minutes. Do not remove lid during this time.

Nutrient Data per Serving:
Calories: 187.6. Protein: 20.2 g. Carbohydrate: 7.966 g. Dietary Fiber: .488 g. Total Sugars: .278 g. Total Fat: 8.096 g. Saturated Fat: 3.276 g. Monounsaturated Fat: 2.768 g. Polyunsaturated Fat: 1.357 g. Cholesterol: 58.7 mg. Trans Fat: .02 g. Total Omega-3 FA: .098 g. Total Omega-6 FA: .051 g. Potassium: 317.1 mg. Sodium: 65.2 mg. Vitamin K: 1.616 mcg. Folic Acid: 6.417 mcg.

❋ GREEK CHICKEN WITH SPICY TOMATOES ❋

ORIGIN: GREECE
DIABETIC ACCEPTABLE

We were thrilled to find that Lindsay Olives produces low-sodium pitted black olives in cans. When used in recipes like this, they add flavor and character. A little added lemon juice, olive oil, and rosemary sprigs also help. Try our Greek Olive and Rosemary Bread (see page 187) using the same low-sodium olives.

MAKES 6 SERVINGS   SODIUM PER RECIPE: 732.7 MG
SODIUM PER SERVING: 122.1 MG

4   to 6 (approximately 1½ pounds) boneless, skinless chicken
     half breasts* (460.2 mg)
2   teaspoons extra-virgin olive oil (trace)
¾   medium white onion, finely chopped (3.3 mg)
3   garlic cloves, crushed in a garlic (1.53 mg)
1   (14.5-ounce) can no-salt-added diced tomatoes, with liquid
     (105 mg)
½   teaspoon ground cinnamon (.299 mg)
¼   teaspoon onion powder (.324 mg)

*Make sure your chicken meat supplier has not soaked your purchase in brine. If there's an FDA label it should allow the chicken no more than 20 mg sodium per ounce. Anything higher has been soaked in a salty brine, which will bring the chicken up to about 100 mg sodium per ounce.

⅛ teaspoon Don's Flavor Enhancer (see page 35), optional
20 Lindsay low-sodium pitted olives, dried on a paper towel, 10
   of them cut in half* (160 mg)
¼ teaspoon crushed red pepper or cayenne pepper† (.135 mg)
   Pinch of ground white or black pepper (trace)
¼ cup filtered or no-sodium water (trace)
1 tablespoon dried basil†† (1.428 mg)
   Juice of 1 lemon, or to taste (.47 mg)
   Lemon wedges for serving

In a large frying pan, brown the chicken in the extra-virgin olive oil over medium heat, turning twice. Add the onions and garlic and cook for about 2 minutes, or until the onions turn translucent. Add the tomatoes, cinnamon, cayenne, onion powder, Don's Flavor Enhancer (if using), the olives, and pepper to taste and stir.

Cover and simmer for 15 minutes. Turn the chicken and simmer for another 10 to 15 minutes, or until the chicken is cooked. Don't overcook it.

Remove the chicken, set it on a plate or dish, and put a lid over it to keep it warm. Add the water along with the basil and the lemon juice, and bring to light boil. Simmer for a few minutes until the sauce is thick.

Serve the chicken hot with the sauce and wedges of lemon.

Nutrient Data per Serving:
Calories: 215.6. Protein: 28.3 g. Carbohydrate: 6.739 g. Dietary Fiber: 1.321 g. Total Sugars: 2.797 g. Total Fat: 7.701 g. Saturated Fat: 1.007 g. Monounsaturated Fat: 4.69 g. Polyunsaturated Fat: .819 g. Cholesterol: 68.4 mg. Trans Fat: .03 g. Total Omega-3 FA: .095 g. Total Omega-6 FA: 0 g. Potassium: 464.1 mg. Sodium: 122.1 mg. Vitamin K: 15.2 mcg. Folic Acid: 0 mcg.

CHICKEN BRACIOLE WITH
❋ LEMON SAUCE ❋

ORIGIN: ITALY
DIABETIC ADAPTABLE

Braciole is usually a thin slice of meat that is wrapped around a stuffing. You can find literally hundreds of braciole recipes, most using wine. We pan-sear this one on a nonstick (an All-Clad Teflon smooth griddle) and then

*Available from www.healthyheartmarket.com or 1-888-685-5988.
†We recommend a full ¼ teaspoon, but if you don't like "hot" food, cut it to ⅛ teaspoon.
††Parsley may be exchanged for the basil.

bake it in the oven using Maureen's Tarragon Sauce (see page 46) We think you'll find it truly exciting and easy to make.

MAKES 4 SERVINGS   SODIUM PER RECIPE: 321.2 MG
SODIUM PER SERVING: 80.3 MG

THE FILLING
¼ **cup golden raisins, packed (4.35 mg)**
2 **garlic cloves, minced (1.02 mg)**
1 **tablespoon olive oil (trace)**
   Pinch of ground white pepper (trace)
2 **tablespoons fresh lemon juice (.488 mg)**
¼ **cup unsalted pine nuts, lightly toasted (.675 mg)**
2 **ounces low-sodium Swiss cheese, grated (about ½ cup)**
   (7.84 mg)

THE BRACIOLE
4 **(4-ounce) boneless, skinless chicken half breasts (about**
   1 pound)† (306.8 mg)
1 **teaspoon olive oil (trace)**

Prepare the filling first. Mix all the ingredients for the filling with the exception of the cheese and nuts. Cover the raisins and garlic with olive oil and lemon juice. Sprinkle with the pepper. Lightly toast the pine nuts and set aside. Add the cheese and nuts right before rolling the braciole.

Preheat the oven to 350°F.

Prepare the chicken breasts by covering them with plastic wrap and pounding them with a mallet until thin enough to roll easily. Place ⅓ cup of the filling in the center of each and spread evenly, leaving at least 1 inch around the edges uncovered. Roll and tie the braciole with kitchen string.

Sauté the braciole on a nonstick griddle, using a small amount of olive oil, until golden, 5 to 10 minutes. Turn several times.

Place the braciole in casserole dish. Pour a little of Maureen's Tarragon Sauce on each.

Bake, uncovered, 20 to 25 minutes, or until cooked through.

Serve hot with steamed cauliflower and broccoli, drizzled with Swiss Cheese Sauce (see page 52) for flavor and presentation.

---

†Nutrient Data figure based on four 4-ounce half breasts, or one pound. The recipe may work better for you with a few more ounces per serving (calculate before it is cooked), but don't exceed 6-ounce portions.

Nutrient Data per Serving:
Calories: 311.7. Protein: 32.8 g. Carbohydrate: 10.4 g. Dietary Fiber: .762 g. Total Sugars: 5.975 g. Total Fat: 15.6 g. Saturated Fat: 3.913 g. Monounsaturated Fat: 6.283 g. Polyunsaturated Fat: 3.807 g. Cholesterol: 81.3 mg. Trans Fat: .029 g. Total Omega-3 FA: .109 g. Total Omega-6 FA: .038 g. Potassium: 455.9 mg. Sodium: 80.3 mg. Vitamin K: 7.872 mcg. Folic Acid: 0 mcg.

❖ CHICKEN CORDON BLEU ❖

ORIGIN: FRANCE
DIABETIC ACCEPTABLE

You might know Cordon Bleu simply as chicken stuffed with ham and cheese and maybe fried or baked in a breaded coating. But, "cordon bleu" is French for "blue ribbon." In France, a blue ribbon was often given to women as a reward for culinary excellence.

The original chicken cordon bleu was (and still is) made using either veal or chicken stuffed with prosciutto or another ham and Gruyère or Swiss cheese. Sure sounds good, right? Since we can't eat the ham or the salty cheese anymore, we came up with our own version of this delectable French dish. We decided to save a few calories by not rolling the chicken breasts in bread crumbs, and of course we can't use the ham because of the excessive sodium levels, so we tried unsalted frozen artichoke hearts, which the French are fond of. We also added chopped scallions for flavor, and of course, we use low-sodium Swiss cheese. Please try it, we're sure you'll enjoy this great entrée.

MAKES 4 SERVINGS   SODIUM PER RECIPE: 502.4 MG
SODIUM PER SERVING: 125.6 MG

4   **(4-ounce) boneless, skinless chicken half breasts (about 1 pound) (306.8 mg)**
2   **ounces low-sodium Swiss cheese, grated (about ½ cup), for the chicken (17.2 mg)**
1   **tablespoon olive oil (trace)**
½   **cup chopped shallots (about 2 large) (9 mg)**
1   **cup frozen artichoke hearts (can be thawed in the microwave for a couple of minutes) (89 mg)**
1   **tablespoon plus 1 teaspoon fresh lemon juice (.203 mg)**
¼   **teaspoon ground white pepper (.03 mg)**
1   **cup Maureen's Easy Chicken Broth (see page 113) (37.8 mg)**
⅛   **teaspoon Don's Herbes de Provence (see page 36) (1.56 mg)**

1   tablespoon cornstarch (.315 mg)
1   tablespoon low-sodium water (trace)
1   tablespoon chopped fresh parsley (2.128 mg)
¼   cup sour cream (30.5 mg)
1   ounce grated low-sodium Swiss cheese for the sauce
      (8.61 mg)

Prepare the chicken breasts by covering both sides with plastic wrap and pounding them with a mallet until they can be stuffed and rolled easily. Be careful not to make them too thin as you might tear through the meat.

Preheat the oven to 350°F.

Meanwhile, fix the filling. Heat 2 teaspoons of the olive oil in a frying pan large enough to accommodate the chicken. Add the shallots and the artichoke hearts and sauté for 3 to 5 minutes. Then sprinkle with 1 tablespoon of the lemon juice and ⅛ teaspoon of the white pepper and stir thoroughly.

Place ¼ cup of the scallion-artichoke mixture in the center of each breast. Sprinkle one-fourth of the cheese over the mixture and roll up the breast. Secure each breast with kitchen string.

Reheat the frying pan over medium heat and add the remaining olive oil. Gently place each stuffed chicken breast into the pan and brown lightly for 5 minutes on each side. Transfer the chicken to a small casserole (an 8×8-inch baking dish works well). Place the casserole in the oven and bake the chicken for 10 minutes while you prepare the sauce.

Pour the broth into same frying pan and turn the heat up to medium-high. Scrape any bits of meat off the bottom of the pan. Mix in the Herbes de Provence and the remaining ⅛ teaspoon of white pepper. Add the cornstarch to the remaining teaspoon of lemon juice plus 1 tablespoon low-sodium water in a small cup, lower the heat to medium, and add the mixture to the pan, stirring constantly while it thickens, about 2 minutes. After it has thickened, add the parsley and sour cream. Stir until well blended and pour over the chicken.

Return the chicken to the oven and bake for another 5 to 10 minutes, or until the sauce is bubbling.

Nutritional Data per Serving:
Calories: 290.1. Protein: 34.8 g. Carbohydrate: 10.6 g. Dietary Fiber: 2.281 g. Total Sugars: .905 g. Total Fat: 11.9 g. Saturated Fat: 5.433 g. Monounsaturated Fat: 4.411 g. Polyunsaturated Fat: 1.083 g. Cholesterol: 94 mg. Trans Fat: .029 g. Total Omega-3 FA: .146 g. Total Omega-6 FA: 0 g. Potassium: 84.6 mg. Sodium: 125.6 mg. Vitamin K: 23.9 mcg. Folic Acid: 0 mcg.

❖ CHICKEN ENCHILADAS ❖

ORIGIN: MEXICO
DIABETIC ACCEPTABLE

A dear friend, Dixie Guillen, gave us the Easy Enchilada Sauce recipe we recommend for these enchiladas.* She explained that the recipe was from her sister-in-law, Cecilia Sandoval. It is an amazingly easy sauce to prepare.

MAKES 12 ENCHILADAS   SODIUM PER RECIPE: *600.7 MG*
SODIUM PER ENCHILADA: *50.1 MG*

1   **medium onion, chopped (3.3 mg)**
1   **tablespoon olive oil (trace)**
4   **garlic cloves, chopped (2.04 mg)**
4   **(4-ounce) boneless, skinless chicken half breasts (about 1 pound) (306.8 mg)**
8   **ounces of low-sodium Cheddar cheese, or 2 cups grated† (80 mg)**
12   **low-sodium corn tortillas‡ (82.6 mg)**
2½   **cups enchilada sauce**

Sauté the onion and garlic in the olive oil for 5 minutes. Add the chicken breasts and cook over medium heat until tender, 15 to 20 minutes. Remove the chicken and let rest a few minutes. Cut in ¼-inch slices, or shred. Place it back into the pan with the onion and garlic mixture, add 1 cup enchilada sauce, and turn heat to low just to keep the filling warm.

Prepare a 13×9-inch casserole dish by spraying with no-stick cooking oil, or use a nonstick pan. Spread 1 cup of sauce over the bottom of the prepared dish. Reserve the remaining sauce to pour over the enchiladas.

Prepare the enchiladas by warming the tortillas on both sides and filling them with 1/12 of the chicken mixture and a small amount of the cheese. Roll up the enchiladas and place in the casserole, seam side down. Cover with the remaining sauce and cheese.

Bake the enchiladas at 350°F, covered with aluminum foil, for 25 minutes, then uncover and bake for 10 minutes more.

*Use either Dixie's Easy Enchilada Sauce on (see page 44) or Red Chili Sauce (see page 42).

†Currently, there are two we know of: Heluva Good and Rumiano cheese. Visit www .megaheart.com/wheretobuy.html to locate these two companies and their online purchase pages.

‡Most commercial corn tortillas are low sodium and without salt. Check the FDA label to make sure.

Nutrient Data per Enchilada:
*Calories: 113.2. Protein: 15.8 g. Carbohydrate: 12.3 g. Dietary Fiber: 3.038 g. Total
Sugars: .764 g. Total Fat: 8.649 g. Saturated Fat: 4.395 g. Monounsaturated Fat: 1.056 g.
Polyunsaturated Fat: .767 g. Cholesterol: 22.8 mg. Trans Fat: .01 g. Total Omega-3 FA:
.041 g. Total Omega-6 FA: 0 g. Potassium: 540.3 mg. Sodium: 50.1 mg. Vitamin K: .847
mcg. Folic Acid: 0 mcg.*

CHICKEN HEKKA

ORIGIN: JAPAN
DIABETICS, SEE FOOTNOTE*

*This recipe works best as a stir-fry, but you can use a non-
stick pan and it will come out just as tasty as if you were
using oil in a standard wok or pan. You can also bake this
one if you like, but we do prefer the stir-fry. Follow the instructions to make a great meal!*

MAKES 2 SERVINGS   SODIUM PER RECIPE: 146 MG**
SODIUM PER SERVING: 73 MG

1   large, boneless, skinless chicken half breast† (76.7 mg)
1   tablespoon white granulated sugar (trace)
1   tablespoon low-sodium molasses†† (7 mg)
2   tablespoons white wine vinegar (.30 mg)
½   teaspoon ground ginger (.288 mg)
½   tablespoon onion powder (1.863 mg)
1   teaspoon extra-virgin olive oil‡ (trace)
1   medium carrot, julienned (42.1 mg)
½   medium onion, chopped (3.3 mg)
6   fresh mushrooms, thinly sliced (1.68 mg)
8   snow peas (.816 mg)
2   ounces rice noodles, soaked and cut into 2-inch-long pieces
    (12 mg)

Cut the chicken into bite-size pieces.

In a small bowl, stir together the sugar, molasses, vinegar, ginger, and
onion powder. Set aside.

*Carbohydrates are in the noodles (40.59) and sugar and molasses. Use Splenda instead.
**May be doubled or quadrupled. Per-serving nutrient data remains the same.
†Or two boneless, skinless chicken thighs
††B'rer Rabbit or Grandma's molasses are low in sodium.
‡If you don't have a nonstick pan, you'll have to increase the olive oil to 2 tablespoons.

Heat a nonstick wok or skillet over high heat, put in oil and the chicken. Pour in the liquid mixture, and stir and cook for about 3 minutes.

Add the vegetables one variety at a time, stirring a half minute to a minute after each addition: add the carrots, stir, add the onions, stir, add the mushrooms, snow peas, and rice noodles last. Then stir and cook for another 3 to 4 minutes, or until the snow peas are bright green and still crisp.

Nutrient Data per Serving:
Calories: 298.5. Protein: 19.6 g. Carbohydrate: 47.1 g. Dietary Fiber: 3.065 g. Total Sugars: 18.5 g. Total Fat: 4.445 g. Saturated Fat: .802 g. Monounsaturated Fat: 2.219 g. Polyunsaturated Fat: .85 g. Cholesterol: 61.3 mg. Trans Fat: .015 g. Total Omega-3 FA: .062 g. Total Omega-6 FA: 0 g. Potassium: 664.1 mg. Sodium: 73 mg. Vitamin K: 5.899 mcg. Folic Acid: 61.6 mcg.

❖ CHICKEN KATSU WITH TONKATSU SAUCE ❖

ORIGIN: JAPAN
DIABETICS, SEE FOOTNOTE*

I spent nearly a year in Japan and learned much about their food and even brought back a few recipes. This one was a favorite; however, it normally uses soy sauce and Worcestershire sauce. Both are too high in sodium for us. So, I've invented a Worcestershire sauce replacement. Like my soy sauce replacement, my Worcestershire sauce replacement receipe (included below) works very well.

The recipe also calls for Japanese panko bread crumbs. To make panko, a light and airy bread is dried and only the center is crumbled into crumbs. It's great for frying, which this recipe calls for in its original form (we bake it). You can also use any no-salt bread you have, including commercial. Simply toast it, crumble it, and you've got what you need. I prefer to use a no-salt whole wheat bread for this recipe. By the way, the original recipe contains about 2400 mg sodium per serving.

MAKES 4 SERVINGS   SODIUM PER RECIPE: 242.6 MG
SODIUM PER SERVING: 60.7 MG

THE SAUCE
¼ **cup no-salt-added ketchup (12 mg)**
¼ **teaspoon mustard powder (trace)**

---

*Diabetics, most of the carbohydrates are in the molasses (16 g) and ketchup (16.4 g) and bread (41.9 g).

Pinch of cayenne pepper* (.043 mg)
1 teaspoon onion powder (1.134 mg)
1 tablespoon red or white wine vinegar (.15 mg)
1 tablespoon Grandma's or B'rer Rabbit molasses† (7 mg)

THE OVEN-BAKED CHICKEN (SEE NOTE BELOW)
1 tablespoon olive oil (trace)
¾ cup Ciabatta bread crumbs‡ (5.751 mg)
1 large egg, beaten (63 mg)
2 skinless, boneless chicken half breasts, butterflied (118.7 mg), or breasts†† (153.4 mg)
 Flour, if deep-frying

Preheat oven to 350°F.

To make the sauce: Stir together all the ingredients and set aside.

Prepare a baking dish large enough to hold the two pieces of chicken, by lightly coating the bottom with olive oil.

Place the crumbs into a small bowl. Beat the egg in a small mixing bowl.

Pound the chicken breasts to a thickness of about ¼ inch. Dip a chicken breast into the egg and then the bread crumbs, pressing the coating onto both sides. Put the chicken into the oiled baking dish. Repeat the procedure with the second piece.

Bake the chicken for 30 minutes. Turn the chicken over carefully, increase the heat to 375°F, and bake for another 20 minutes.

Serve hot on rice or with potato or another vegetable of your choice. Spread the sauce over each chicken piece or place it in a bowl on the table and use as a dipping sauce.

Note: If you are going to deep-fry this chicken, then add ½ cup unbleached, all-purpose flour to the recipe (1.25 mg) After wetting the chicken with the egg batter, dip it into the flour, and then the bread crumbs.

Nutrient Data per Serving:
Calories: 198.9. Protein: 17.2 g. Carbohydrate: 19.4 g. Dietary Fiber: .637 g. Total Sugars: 7.283 g. Total Fat: 5.92 g. Saturated Fat: 1.119 g. Monounsaturated Fat: 3.429 g. Polyunsaturated Fat: .803 g. Cholesterol: 87.1 mg. Trans Fat: .015 g. Total Omega-3 FA: .066 g. Total Omega-6 FA: 0 g. Potassium: 354 mg. Sodium: 60.7 mg. Vitamin K: 2.937 mcg. Folic Acid: 19.7 mcg.

*Or white pepper
†Or other no-salt molasses
‡See page 173 for Ciabatta recipe, and Basic Bread Crumbs recipe, page 167, for instructions.
††Nutrient Data based on higher value

❊ CUMIN SEED CHICKEN ❊

ORIGIN: INDIA
DIABETIC ACCEPTABLE

Cumin, it is said in India, has curative properties. This recipe will take you to a new level of flavor, one we believe you'll truly enjoy. It's easy to prepare and a real treat. Serve hot right off the stove.

MAKES 4 SERVINGS   SODIUM PER RECIPE: 550.8 MG
SODIUM PER SERVING: 137.7 MG

3 **tablespoons whole cumin seeds* (30.2 mg)**
3 **tablespoons expeller-pressed canola oil (trace)**
2 **teaspoons whole black peppercorns (1 mg)**
1 **teaspoon ground coriander (.63 mg)**
2 **level teaspoons ground cardamom† (.72 mg)**
1 **fresh jalapeño pepper, chopped (3.15 mg)**
3 **garlic cloves, minced (1.53 mg)**
1 **(1-inch) piece fresh ginger, grated (about 1 tablespoon) (.78 mg)**
2 **teaspoons ground cumin (7.056 mg)**
4 **skinless chicken legs (268.3 mg)**
4 **boneless, skinless chicken thighs (237.4 mg)**

Toast 1 tablespoon of the cumin seeds in a small frying pan without oil over medium to medium-high heat, stirring frequently, for about 2 minutes. The color will intensify to a darker shade of brown. Set aside.

Grind the remaining 2 tablespoons of cumin seeds and the black peppercorns, using a mortar and pestle. In a large pan or wok, heat the oil over medium to medium-high heat and fry this mixture for about 2 minutes.†

Add the finely chopped jalapeño pepper, minced garlic, and grated ginger, and cook for about 2 minutes.

Add the coriander, cardamom, and ground cumin. Stir while cooking for about 2 minutes.

When the spice paste is sizzling, add the chicken pieces and, using tongs, turn them over until each side is well coated with the spices. Cook, covered over medium-low heat, for about 20 to 25 minutes. After 25 minutes, check

---

*You may find the best deals at a local Indian store or online at www.megaheart.com/wheretobuy.htm. For this recipe, toast/dry-fry 1 tablespoon and grind down 2 tablespoons with your mortar and pestle.
†Or use 3 to 4 cardamom pods and toast these with the cumin seeds and peppercorns.

for doneness; the chicken should be just nearly done. Lift the lid and sprinkle the toasted cumin seeds on the top of each piece of chicken, cover, and simmer for another 5 minutes.

Serve hot. You might want to serve this with our Minty Cucumber Sauce (see page 46).

A vegetable side serving could be: an ear of corn, summer squash, or fresh green beans.

Nutrient Values per Serving:
Calories: 304.3. Protein: 30.9 g. Carbohydrate: 5.836 g. Dietary Fiber: 1.45 g. Total Sugars: .75 g. Total Fat: 17.6 g. Saturated Fat: 2.309 g. Monounsaturated Fat: 8.798 g. Polyunsaturated Fat: 4.739 g. Cholesterol: 119.7 mg. Trans Fat: .154 g. Total Omega-3 FA: 1.137 g. Total Omega-6 FA: 0 g. Potassium: 514.9 mg. Sodium: 137.7 mg. Vitamin K: 20 mcg. Folic Acid: 0 mcg.

CHICKEN WITH HONEY

❖ MURGHI MADI ❖

ORIGIN: INDIA
DIABETIC ACCEPTABLE

This is a dish we were served in a local Indian restaurant. We think you'll find it delicious, especially if you enjoy the spices in this recipe. Give it a try. It also barbecues wonderfully if you use convection heat.

MAKES 4 SERVINGS   SODIUM PER RECIPE: 243.9 MG
SODIUM PER SERVING: 61 MG

THE PASTE
2 **garlic cloves, minced (1.02 mg)**
1 **tablespoon finely peeled, grated fresh ginger or 1½ teaspoons ground ginger (.864 mg)**
2 **tablespoons fresh lemon or lime juice (.984 mg)**
5 **tablespoons honey (4.2 mg)**
2 **teaspoons Grandma's chili powder* (trace)**
1 **tablespoon paprika (2.346 mg)**
1 **tablespoon cornstarch (1.152 mg)**

THE CHICKEN
3 **skinless chicken half breasts (230.1 mg)**
1 **lemon, quartered (3.254 mg)**
2 **sprigs fresh cilantro for garnish (trace)**

*Or other no-salt-added chili powder. Most commercial chili powder has a lot of salt in it.

Put the paste ingredients in a blender or food processor. Blend until a smooth paste forms. Set aside.

Wash the chicken and make small shallow incisions all over with the tip of a sharp knife.

Rub the chicken with the spice paste and let sit for at least 20 minutes and up to 30 minutes in the refrigerator.

If using a barbecue, lay the chicken on a rack away from heat and cover. Cook with convection heat. Barbecue until the juices run clear.

If using an oven, preheat to 400°F and bake the chicken for 45 to 50 minutes, or until it is cooked through.

Serve hot with a lemon quarter and garnish with the cilantro sprigs.

Nutrient Data per Serving:
Calories: 209.9. Protein: 21.3 g. Carbohydrate: 30.9 g. Dietary Fiber: 2.161 g. Total Sugars: 21.4 g. Total Fat: 1.585 g. Saturated Fat: .355 g. Monounsaturated Fat: .298 g. Polyunsaturated Fat: .432 g. Cholesterol: 51.3 mg. Trans Fat: .022 g. Total Omega-3 FA: .061 g. Total Omega-6 FA: 0 g. Potassium: 348.5 mg. Sodium: 61 mg. Vitamin K: 1.662 mcg. Folic Acid: 0 mcg.

❖ CHICKEN WITH NUTS ❖

ORIGIN: AFRICA
DIABETIC ADAPTABLE

We offer this recipe from Africa with options for the nuts. However, we do prefer the cashews not only for their compatibility with the chicken, but also because they have fewer calories per serving than either peanuts or almonds. But, we've had this recipe with each, and each offers its own unique flavor. The choice is yours.

We hope you're able to make the coconut milk fresh according to the instructions for Easy Coconut Milk (see page 38).*

MAKE 4 SERVINGS   SODIUM PER RECIPE: 366.4 MG
SODIUM PER SERVING: 91.6 MG

4   (4-ounce) chicken half breasts (about 1 pound) (306.8 mg)
2   tablespoons olive oil (trace)
1½ cups chopped onions (7.2 mg)
½   cup Maureen's Easy Chicken Broth (see page 113)
        (10.4 mg)
½   cup coconut milk (30 mg)
2   tablespoons fresh lime or lemon juice (.984 mg)

*You may also use canned coconut milk (with no salt added).

¼ **teaspoon ground white pepper (.03 mg)**
½ **cup unsalted nuts (cashews, peanuts, or almonds)* (11 mg)**

Heat the oil in a large frying pan over medium-high heat. Pat the chicken dry and place in the hot oil. Brown the chicken on both sides, 6 to 8 minutes per side. Transfer to a plate and keep warm.

Lower the heat to medium and add the onions to the frying pan. Cook for about 5 minutes, or until they begin to soften, scraping up any meat particles that are stuck to the bottom of the pan. Stir in the chicken broth and coconut milk and bring to a simmer. Return the chicken to the pan, partially cover with lid, and cook for 20 minutes.

Once again, transfer the chicken to the plate and cover to keep warm. Strain the liquid through a sieve into a small bowl. Press the onions through the sieve several times. You should have at least 1 cup of liquid. Pour the sauce back into the pan and stir in the lime juice and white pepper. Return the chicken to the pan, sprinkle with the cashews, and reheat for a few minutes. Serve hot over boiled rice.

Nutrient Data per Serving:
Calories: 396.8. Protein: 31.2 g. Carbohydrate: 22.3 g. Dietary Fiber: 3.432 g. Total Sugars: 8.134 g. Total Fat: 20.6 g. Saturated Fat: 5.578 g. Monounsaturated Fat: 10.1 g. Polyunsaturated Fat: 2.444 g. Cholesterol: 69.9 mg. Trans Fat: .029 g. Total Omega-3 FA: .134 g. Total Omega-6 FA: 0 g. Potassium: 513.4 mg. Sodium: 91.6 mg. Vitamin K: 10.8 mcg. Folic Acid: 0 mcg.

CHICKEN WITH MASALA
❖ CHANA AND RICE ❖

ORIGIN: INDIA
DIABETIC ACCEPTABLE

One of the exciting things about traveling around the world is that you run into a variety of foods that you are not completely familiar with in your own country. Yet, when you return and serve them, everyone loves the flavor and the presentation and assumes you created it. This recipe for chicken with spiced chickpeas will serve you well, both for guests and yourself. If you are going to serve rice, then steam a cup of basmati rice in your steamer and set it aside for serving.

†We like unsalted cashews, which are also lower in calories than unsalted peanuts or unsalted almonds.

THE RICE

3 cups steamed basmati rice* (.733 mg)

THE BEAN MIXTURE

1   tablespoon expeller-pressed canola or olive oil
       (trace)
2   garlic cloves, chopped (1.02 mg)
1½ teaspoons ground cumin (5.292 mg)
1   teaspoon ground coriander (1.266 mg)
1   teaspoon Grandma's chili powder† (trace)
1   medium white onion, chopped (3.3 mg)
1   (15-ounce) can Eden Organic unsalted garbanzo beans
       (chickpeas) (35 mg)
1   (14.5-ounce) cans no-salt-added diced, stewed, or whole
       tomatoes (105 mg)
¼   teaspoon Maureen's Garam Masala (see page 45)
       (.179 mg)
     Ground white pepper (trace)
2   tablespoons chopped fresh cilantro (trace)

THE CHICKEN

3   boneless, skinless chicken half breasts (230.1 mg)
⅛   teaspoon ground white pepper (.015 mg)
½   teaspoon curry powder (.52 mg)
½   cup reduced-fat sour cream (49.6 mg)

Prepare the rice according to package directions (30 to 35 minutes).

To prepare the chickpeas: Heat the oil in a large pan. Stir in the garlic, cumin, coriander, chili powder, and onions and cook for 5 minutes over medium heat. Stir in the garbanzo beans and the tomatoes. Cook for another 5 to 10 minutes, stirring frequently. Add the garam masala (if you don't have garam marsala and don't want to make it, then skip this step) and season to taste with white pepper, or use black pepper if you prefer. Cook for another another 10 minutes or so. Stir in the cilantro, set the bean mixture aside, and keep it warm.

Prepare the chicken: Mix the white pepper and curry powder together and rub into the chicken breasts. Grill the chicken on a barbecue grill or

---

*1 cup of rice has 2 mg of sodium and about 716 calories. Divide by four when serving to obtain total figures.
†Or other no-salt chili powder

under the broiler, turning as needed. Cook until the meat is tender and not pink. This may take 20 to 25 minutes.

Let the chicken rest for 5 to 10 minutes.

Slice the chicken breasts. On a serving plate, spoon the bean mixture over a mound of basmati rice and top with the sliced chicken breast.

Pass around the sour cream for garnish, and top with a few fresh cilantro leaves.

Nutrient Data per Serving
Calories: 318.6. Protein: 29 g. Carbohydrate: 26 g. Dietary Fiber: 5.884 g. Total Sugars: 3.901 g. Total Fat: 9.857 g. Saturated Fat: 2.828 g. Monounsaturated Fat: 3.513 g. Polyunsaturated Fat: 1.474 g. Cholesterol: 63.1 mg. Trans Fat: .022 g. Total Omega-3 FA: .417 g. Total Omega-6 FA: 0 g. Potassium: 475.5 mg. Sodium: 107.8 mg. Vitamin K: 7.091 mcg. Folic Acid: 0 mcg.

❄ CHINESE CHICKEN WING APPETIZERS ❄

ORIGIN: CHINA
DIABETIC ACCEPTABLE

While raising our five youngsters, eating at our table was sometimes a challenge. Actually the challenge was making sure you got your "fair share of the fare." Our youngest seemed always to end up with the chicken wings since those were kicked aside by the others before she got the platter.

Many years later while serving them (guests now with their own children) I made the mistake of serving her the wings first. She handled it with as much grace as you can imagine without the sound effects or the walls tumbling down. Dumb me; I had thought all those years she really liked the wings. Guess who ate them that night. After that, I had to come up with a new recipe and serve them only as appetizers.

My friend Scott Leysath, "the Sporting Chef," passed this recipe along to us. I've made some changes over the years, including eliminating the salt and changing the soy or hoisin sauce to my own designed replacement. Serve as appetizers or as a main course for a light meal.

MAKES 4 SERVINGS (3 WINGS PER SERVING)   SODIUM PER RECIPE: 176.1 MG
SODIUM PER SERVING: 34 MG
SODIUM PER CHICKEN WING: 14.7 MG

12	chicken wings, skin removed (165.2 mg)*
¼	cup warm low-sodium water (trace)
2½	teaspoons honey (.697 mg)
3	tablespoons Don's Soy Sauce Replacement (see page 37) (5.325 mg)
4	garlic cloves, finely minced (2.04 mg)
¼	teaspoon granulated onion or salt-free onion powder (.324 mg)
1	small onion†, finely minced (2.1 mg)
½	teaspoon ground ginger (.288 mg)
¼	teaspoon ground white pepper (.03 mg)

Mix together the water, honey, soy sauce replacement, garlic, granulated and minced onion, ginger, and white pepper to taste, and marinate the chicken in this mixture in refrigerator for about 30 minutes.

Preheat the oven to 350°F.

Place the chicken wings on a baking or cookie sheet lined with cooking or parchment paper. Bake for 30 minutes, brushing every 10 minutes with the marinade.

Set the oven to broil, and broil the chicken wings for about 4 minutes, brushing with the marinade just before broiling. Turn the wings at the 2-minute mark so they don't burn. Serve hot. You can also store these in an airtight container in refrigerator for later use.

Nutrient Data per Serving of 4:
Calories: 102. Protein: 11.7 g. Carbohydrate: 9.703 g. Dietary Fiber: .434 g. Total Sugars: 6.506 g. Total Fat: 1.861 g. Saturated Fat: .494 g. Monounsaturated Fat: .444 g. Polyunsaturated Fat: .435 g. Cholesterol: 29.1 mg. Trans Fat: .036 g. Total Omega-3 FA: .058 g. Total Omega-6 FA: 0 g. Potassium: 196.4 mg. Sodium: 44 mg. Vitamin K: .136 mcg. Folic Acid: 0 mcg..

Nutrient Data per Wing:
Calories: 34. Protein: 3.89 g. Carbohydrate: 3.234 g. Dietary Fiber: .145 g. Total Sugars: 2.169 g. Total Fat: .62 g. Saturated Fat: .165 g. Monounsaturated Fat: .148 g. Polyunsaturated Fat: .145 g. Cholesterol: 9.69 mg. Trans Fat: .012 g. Total Omega-3 FA: .019 g. Total Omega-6 FA: 0 g. Potassium: 65.5 mg. Sodium: 14.7 mg. Vitamin K: .045 mcg. Folic Acid: 0 mcg.

*12 wings with skin have 254 mg sodium.
†Scallions or green onions also work very well.

◈ CHINESE CHOW MEIN CHICKEN SALAD ◈

ORIGIN: CHINA
DIABETIC ADAPTABLE

This salad normally calls for chow mein noodles; however, the sodium level of commercially available chow mein noodles is high (a cup has 197 mg of sodium). So, we recommend for the noodles that you fry are cooked, regular, durum wheat pasta noodles in a dry nonstick pan. We have included those instructions at the end of this recipe.

You may cook the chicken your favorite way, or you may want to try the method used in China (we guarantee it's tasty). This recipe is a complete dinner.

MAKES 4 SERVINGS   SODIUM PER RECIPE: 497.9 MG
SODIUM PER SERVING: 124.5 MG

¾   **pound boneless, skinless, nonbrined chicken breasts, cooked (230.1 mg)**
½   **cup rice vinegar (1.2 mg)**
½   **cup Don's Soy Sauce Replacement (see page 37) (13.7 mg)**
6   **tablespoons Don's Hoisin Sauce (see page 55) (32.3 mg)**
1½ **tablespoons peeled and grated fresh ginger (1.43 mg)**
3   **tablespoons sesame oil (trace)**
4   **cups chopped napa cabbage* (197 mg)**
½   **medium to large red bell pepper, seeded and chopped (1.65 mg)**
½   **medium to large yellow bell pepper, seeded and chopped (1.86 mg)**
1   **small sweet onion, chopped† (2.1 mg)**
2   **ounces standard durum wheat (not whole wheat) thin spaghetti (16 mg)***
2   **tablespoons expeller-pressed canola extra-virgin olive oil (trace)**

Whisk together the vinegar, half of the soy sauce replacement, all the hoisin sauce, and the ginger and sesame oil in a small bowl. Put the chicken breasts into a Dutch oven or other heavy-bottomed pot. Pour half of the vinegar mixture over the chicken and reserve the rest to use as the dressing. Add the remaining soy sauce replacement and 3 cups of low-sodium water to the chicken. Bring to a boil over high heat, cover, reduce

*54.1 g carbohydrates
†Also known as Chinese cabbage
‡Or use scallions, thinly sliced.

the heat, and over low heat until the chicken is cooked. This should take no longer than 10 minutes.

When chicken is done, transfer it to a platter or plate and cover loosely with aluminum foil or plastic wrap or waxed paper and refrigerate until cool.

To make the chow mein noodles: While the chicken is cooling, cook the 2 ounces of spaghetti per package instructions. (You want a cup of noodles after cooking.) Drain, rinse, and dry them on paper towels.

Heat about 2 tablespoons of canola oil on a nonstick griddle over medium heat. Cook the noodles in small batches, stirring frequently. Cook until they turn a golden brown, then turn over and cook the other side. Remove and set aside on paper towels to drain and cool. These should be a bit crispy now, and perfect for your salad.

When it has cooled, about 20 minutes, shred the chicken or slice it into long, thin strips. We use a couple of forks to shred it roughly into long strips—this works well with the salad.

Put the chicken into a medium to large salad bowl and toss with 2 or 3 tablespoons of the reserved dressing. Season with white pepper to taste. Add the vegetables, starting with the napa cabbage, and toss with any remaining dressing. Sprinkle with your homemade chow mein noodles.

Nutrient Data per Salad:
Calories: 416.7. Protein: 27.7 g. Carbohydrate: 36.5 g. Dietary Fiber: 2.91 g. Total Sugars: 13.8 g. Total Fat: 19.3 g. Saturated Fat: 3.274 g. Monounsaturated Fat: 7.7 g. Polyunsaturated Fat: 6.961 g. Cholesterol: 69.4 mg. Trans Fat: .022 g. Total Omega-3 FA: .103 g. Total Omega-6 FA: 0 g. Potassium: 881.5 mg. Sodium: 124.5 mg. Vitamin K: 2.966 mcg. Folic Acid: 41 mcg.

CURRIED CHICKEN WITH STEAMED
❖ BASMATI RICE ❖

ORIGIN: INDIA
DIABETIC ADAPTABLE

This easy-to-prepare entrée will excite your palate and make you want to try the recipe with lamb, chicken, white shellfish such as scallops, and even with sodium-free fresh shrimp.

**MAKES 6 SERVINGS   SODIUM PER RECIPE: 456.8 MG
SODIUM PER SERVING: 76.1 MG**

3 **boneless, skinless, chicken half-breasts, cooked, cut into bite-size pieces (230.1 mg)**
1 **cup raw basmati rice (makes about 3 cups, steamed) (2 mg)**
1 **tablespoon extra-virgin olive oil (trace)**
1 **medium onion, chopped (3.3 mg)**

2   garlic cloves, minced (1.02 mg)
1¼   tablespoons curry powder (4.095 mg)
1½   tablespoons cornstarch (.945 mg)
2   cups 1% milk with added vitamins A & D (214.7 mg)
1   to 2 tablespoons fresh lemon juice (.39 mg)
2   teaspoons white balsamic vinegar (.099 mg)
1   tablespoon finely chopped fresh chives (.09 mg)

Cook the chicken and set aside. You may use leftover chicken if you have it, or even cooked lamb.

Steam the basmati rice according to package directions, and set aside.

Heat the oil in a medium saucepan, over medium heat. Add the onion and garlic and sauté until soft and translucent. Add the curry powder and cook and stir for another minute or so until well mixed. Dissolve the cornstarch in the milk.

Move the saucepan off the heat and stir in the milk, mixing until smooth. Put the pan back on the heat and stir steadily until the sauce has thickened. Stir in the chicken and continue to cook over medium heat for a few more minutes, or until hot enough to serve. Stir in the lemon juice, balsamic vinegar, and chives.

Serve on a bed of steamed basmati rice.

Nutrient Data per Serving:
Calories: 260.4. Protein: 19 g. Carbohydrate: 35.7 g. Dietary Fiber: 1.701 g. Total Sugars: 5.323 g. Total Fat: 4.149 g. Saturated Fat: 1.095 g. Monounsaturated Fat: 2.197 g. Polyunsaturated Fat: .514 g. Cholesterol: 38.3 mg. Trans Fat: .015 g. Total Omega-3 FA: .062 g. Total Omega-6 FA: .022 g. Potassium: 359.7 mg. Sodium: 76.1 mg. Vitamin K: 4.015 mcg. Folic Acid: 75 mcg.

❖ CURRIED MEAT ❖

ORIGIN: INDIA
DIABETIC ADAPTABLE

India seems to be the home of curry and curry-based recipes. This is an especially tasty recipe and one worth attempting.

MAKES 8 SERVINGS   SODIUM PER RECIPE: 797.6 MG
SODIUM PER SERVING: 99.7 MG

1 cup basmati rice (makes about 3 cups, steamed)* (2 mg)
2 pounds lamb sirloin chops (580.6 mg) or beef sirloin
   (526.2 mg), cut into bite-size pieces†

*Double the rice if serving all the curry in the same evening. Rice has 158.3 g carbohydrates.
†We used the lamb sodium for our nutrient data.

3 tablespoons extra-virgin olive oil (trace)
2 large onions, finely chopped (9 mg)
1 (14-ounce) can no-salt-added tomatoes, chopped (105 mg)
1 teaspoon ginger paste, or ½ teaspoon ground ginger (.288 mg)
1 teaspoon unsalted garlic paste, or 3 garlic cloves, pressed or (1.53 mg)
2 teaspoons ground coriander (1.26 mg)
½ teaspoon ground turmeric (.418 mg)
½ teaspoon cayenne pepper or red chili powder (.27 mg)
2 to 3 cups low-sodium water as needed (trace)
2 tablespoons no-salt-added tomato paste (31.4 mg)
5 medium Yukon gold or red potatoes, halved (63.9 mg)
  Juice of 1 lemon, or to taste (.75 mg)
  Leaves from 2 sprigs fresh cilantro, chopped (3.798 mg)

Using your steamer, prepare the rice first and set aside.

Heat the oil in a saucepan. Add the chopped onions and sauté until golden. Add the tomatoes, ginger, garlic, coriander, turmeric, and cayenne or red chili powder and continue to cook on low heat for about 10 minutes.

Add the tomato paste and low-sodium water and simmer until the sauce begins to thicken. Add the lamb or beef and raise the temperature to medium heat, stirring often, until the meat juices are nearly evaporated.

When the meat is tender, add the potatoes, and cook until the potatoes are done, about an hour. Stir in the lemon juice and cilantro.

Serve hot over the rice.

Nutrient Data per Serving:
Calories: 322.9. Protein: 26.6 g. Carbohydrate: 28.3 g. Dietary Fiber: 4.65 g. Total Sugars: 5.008 g. Total Fat: 10.9 g. Saturated Fat: 2.954 g. Monounsaturated Fat: 6.135 g. Polyunsaturated Fat: .925 g. Cholesterol: 72.6 mg. Trans Fat: 0 g. Total Omega-3 FA: .138 g. Total Omega-6 FA: 0 g. Potassium: 1124 mg. Sodium: 99.7 mg. Vitamin K: 8.968 mcg. Folic Acid: 0 mcg.

❖ DON'S CHICKEN PROVENÇAL ❖

ORIGIN: FRANCE
DIABETIC ACCEPTABLE

*This tasty treat may be barbecued as well as oven baked.
It's worth the trip to learn just how tasty a chicken can get.*
MAKES 4 SERVINGS   SODIUM PER RECIPE (366.1 MG)
SODIUM PER SERVING: (93.8 MG)

1 whole fryer chicken, cleaned and rinsed* (366.1 mg)
  Grated zest of 1 lemon, (approximately 2 tablespoons)
    (.72 mg)
  Juice of 1 lemon (.47 mg)
2 tablespoons extra-virgin olive oil (trace)
1 teaspoon dried thyme (.77 mg)
1 teaspoon dried basil (.476 mg)
½ teaspoon fennel seed (.88 mg)
½ teaspoon dried savory (.168 mg)
½ teaspoon lavender** (trace)
½ teaspoon Don's Flavor Enhancer† (.43 mg)
1 tablespoon Oregon Flavor Rack Garlic Lover's Garlic‡
    (4.368 mg)
1 teaspoon ground black pepper (.924 mg)

Preheat oven to 350°F.

In medium bowl combine the lemon zest, the lemon juice (the more juice from the lemon the better), and the olive oil. Add the herbs and stir together the remaining ingredients except the chicken.

Place your chicken in a lightly oiled roaster pan, fitted with a roasting rack. (This allows for better roasting.)

Using your fingers, pull the breast skin of the chicken up on each side and spoon some of the herb mix between skin and meat.

Spread the remaining herb mixture over the whole chicken, making sure to coat the entire bird.

Roast for 50 to 60 minutes, depending on your oven and the size of the chicken. When the leg moves freely, and the juices run clear when the thigh area is pierced with the tip of a sharp knife, the bird is done. Use a meat thermometer for accurate temperature.

Nutrient Data per Serving (8)
Calories: 361.9. Protein: 25 g. Carbohydrate: 5.916 g. Dietary Fiber: 1.397 g. Total Sugars: 1.443 g. Total Fat: 26.3 g. Saturated Fat: 6.484 g. Monounsaturated Fat: 13 g. Polyunsaturated Fat: 4.893 g. Cholesterol: 117.7 mg. Trans Fat: 0 g. Total Omega-3 FA: .3 g. Total Omega-6 FA: 0 g. Potassium: 343.1 mg. Sodium: 93.8 mg. Vitamin K: 16.9 mcg. Folic Acid: 0 mcg.

*Nutrient data from edible part only
**Lavender is available from most natural food stores. This delicious herb (the lavender flower) hasn't quite caught on in supermarkets yet. Buy only *culinary* grade, not the potpourri kind.
†From *The No-Salt, Lowest-Sodium Light Meals Book.*
‡From Oregon Flavor Rack, www.spiceman.com. If you don't have this wonderful mix in stock, use 3 minced garlic cloves, 1 teaspoon parsley flakes, and ½ teaspoon onion flakes instead.

◈ DON'S AUTHENTICALLY HOT CHORIZO ◈

ORIGIN: OLD MEXICO
DIABETIC ACCEPTABLE*

We first ran into chorizo on Don's father's ranch in the hot desert of Coachella Valley in the '50s. Now, we thought the desert was hot, but chorizo is hotter. Originally a Basque and Spanish sausage the Mexicans made their version by using their favorite chilies and spices. Today it is considered to be the "greatest sausage" you can eat in the American Southwest as well as in Mexico. But be careful—it's hot, and when enjoying it for breakfast you won't need too much of it. Chorizo helps add flavor to stews, soups, tacos, and anything requiring that good old Mexican food heat.

The standard chorizo has 700 mg sodium per 2 ounces. As you can see, this one has only 32.6 mg. The flavors are hardly different. It also freezes well.

Chorizo is great for a winter breakfast. Make some of it into 3- or 4-ounce packages, and freeze.

**MAKES: EIGHT 2-OUNCE SERVINGS   SODIUM PER RECIPE: 260.6 MG
SODIUM PER 2-OUNCE SAUSAGE: 32.6 MG**

1	**pound lean ground pork (253.1 mg)**
³⁄₄	**teaspoon onion powder (.972 mg)**
3	**tablespoons Grandma's chili powder† (trace)**
½	**teaspoon McCormick's crushed red pepper‡ (12.2 mg)**
3	**garlic cloves, minced (1.53 mg)**
1	**tablespoon dried oregano (.81 mg)**
1	**teaspoon whole cumin seeds, crushed with a mortar and pestle (3.528 mg)**
½	**teaspoon ground white pepper (.06 mg)**
³⁄₄	**teaspoon white granulated sugar or Splenda (trace)**
2	**tablespoons apple cider or white wine vinegar (.3 mg)**
1¼	**tablespoons low-sodium water (trace)**

*Diabetics, the peppers would contain 11.9 g carbohydrates and 7.1 grams of sugars.
†You may want to start with 3 tablespoons and work your way up. If you can't get Grandma's, find a brand that does not add salt to the chili.
‡McCormick Spices has a great crushed red pepper. If you prefer to chop up whole dried red peppers, use 6 small peppers. (These are very thin peppers about 3 inches in length.)

Break up the meat, add the rest of the ingredients, and knead with your hands until well mixed. At this point the chorizo will keep for at least a few days in your refrigerator (remember to check the "use by" date on the meat package). Or let it season for a couple days in the refrigerator, then tuck 4-ounces each into separate small ziplock bags. Then tuck those bags into a large freezer ziplock bag. Frozen chorizo should keeps well for up to 3 months.

Cook as patties, links, or break up when adding to omelets, soups, or other dishes to help add flavor.

Nutrient Data per Serving (8)
Calories: 160.7. Protein: 9.782 g. Carbohydrate: 2.636 g. Dietary Fiber: .423 g. Total Sugars: .751 g. Total Fat: 12.3 g. Saturated Fat: 4.475 g. Monounsaturated Fat: 5.38 g. Polyunsaturated Fat: 1.137 g. Cholesterol: 40.7 mg. Trans-Fatty Acids: 0 g. Total Omega-3 FA: .069 g. Total Omega-6 FA: 0 g. Iron: 1.046 mg. Potassium: 190.9 mg. Sodium: 32.6 mg. Vitamin K: 4.326 mcg. Folic Acid: 0 mcg.

❂ APPLE-STUFFED PORK CHOPS ❂

ORIGIN: FRANCE
DIABETIC ACCEPTABLE

I'm not sure if this is French or Basque. I first enjoyed this stuffed pork chop one evening in a Basque restaurant across from the Cousteau film editing studio where I was working. I would suspect it's a combination of both French tastes and those of the Basques. At any rate, it's worth the try, because the flavors are uniquely juxtaposed.

MAKES 4 SERVINGS SODIUM PER RECIPE: 276.2 MG
SODIUM PER SERVING WITHOUT RAISINS: 69.1 MG
SODIUM PER SERVING WITH RAISINS: 71.5 MG

THE PORK CHOPS
4 **boneless pork chops about 1½ inch thick, trimmed of fat (231.3 mg)**

THE STUFFING
1 **tablespoon olive oil (trace)**
1 **cup fresh bread crumbs (see page 167) (1.137 mg)**
1 **medium onion, chopped (3.3 mg)**
1 **celery stalk (about 8 inches long), chopped (32 mg)**
2 **small tart apples, cored and chopped (2.12 mg)**
2 **tablespoons chopped parsley (4.256 mg)**
⅛ **teaspoon ground ginger (.072 mg)**
4 **teaspoons melted unsalted butter (2.082 mg)**

Ground white pepper (trace)

½ **cup seedless golden raisins (9.9 mg), optional**

THE RUB

1 **teaspoon ground sage (.077 mg)**

½ **teaspoon ginger (.288 mg)**

⅛ **teaspoon ground cloves (.638 mg)**

Using a sharp knife, cut pockets into sides of thick pork chops. Insert a sharp knife into the side of the chop and slide the knife toward the upper bone and then curve downward to make the pocket. It helps to use your other hand to press on the meat while making the slice. The opening should be large enough to insert 2 tablespoons of dressing. Don't butterfly the entire chop.

In a nonstick pan over medium heat, sauté the onion, celery, and apple in half of the olive oil until translucent, 5 to 8 minutes. Remove from the heat, add the bread crumbs, ginger, parsley, unsalted butter, and white pepper to taste. Stir and press together until it binds. Place approximately 2 tablespoons of the dressing in each pocket.

Mix together the rub ingredients in a small bowl. Rub the chops with the spice rub. Hold chops together with toothpicks while cooking.

Preheat oven to 350°F.

Heat remaining oil over medium high heat in a large nonstick skillet and sear the chops for approximately 3 minutes on each side until they are brown. Meanwhile, lightly grease a casserole dish. Place the chops in the prepared dish and the rest of the stuffing around the chops.

Bake for about 45 minutes to an hour. If using the optional raisins, sprinkle them over and around the chops during the last 5 to 10 minutes of baking.

Serve hot.

Nutrient Data per Serving Without Raisins:
Calories: 266.1. Protein: 25.3 g. Carbohydrate: 12.7 g. Dietary Fiber: 1.595 g. Total Sugars: 4.422 g. Total Fat: 12.4 g. Saturated Fat: 4.618 g. Monounsaturated Fat: 5.766 g. Polyunsaturated Fat: 1.125 g. Cholesterol: 81.6 mg. Trans Fat: 0 g. Total Omega-3 FA: .09 g. Total Omega-6 FA: .102 g. Potassium: 542.9 mg. Sodium: 69.1 mg. Vitamin K: 40.3 mcg. Folic Acid: 10.3 mcg.

Nutrient Data per Serving with Raisins:
Calories: 328.4. Protein: 26 g. Carbohydrate: 29.1 g. Dietary Fiber: 2.42 g. Total Sugars: 16.6 g. Total Fat: 12.5 g. Saturated Fat: 4.649 g. Monounsaturated Fat: 5.769 g. Polyunsaturated Fat: 1.152 g. Cholesterol: 81.6 mg. Trans Fat: 0 g. Total Omega-3 FA: .097 g. Total Omega-6 FA: .102 mg. Potassium: 696.8 mg. Sodium: 71.5 mg. Vitamin K: 41 mcg. Folic Acid: 10.3 mcg.

ORIGIN: INDIA
DIABETIC ACCEPTABLE

Chinggis Raan (also known as Mughlai style) was used as the title for this leg of lamb recipe only because the warrior Genghis Khan (1162–1227) is the first known human to roast a whole leg of lamb. (I can't envision him doing this in a kitchen like we have. Instead, I picture that lamb leg at the end of a sword over a nighttime campfire with a few hundred soldiers standing guard.) In India this same roast recipe with some variations is also known as shahi raan *and* peshawari raan.

My particular reason for liking the title we use here is my own history. I studied Genghis Khan in college (mostly his battle history) and later while in the marines, used some of his tactics in training others, which proved highly successful. The old guy was as mean as they come, but he was a smart battlefield tactician.

By the way, garam masala is not one specific recipe in Indian food. Many versions exist. The one you'll find in this book is from Maureen, who spent a lot of time in an Indian food store coming to terms with what tasted best for our recipes.

MAKES 6 TO 8 SERVINGS   SODIUM PER RECIPE: 664 MG
SODIUM PER SERVING (6): 110.7 MG
SODIUM PER SERVING (8): 83 MG

1   large onion, chopped (4.5 mg)
3   garlic cloves, minced (1.53 mg)
1   (1-inch) piece fresh ginger, peeled and chopped (.78 mg)
1   teaspoon ground coriander (.63 mg)
2   tablespoons blanched almonds, ground in processor[†]
     (3.402 mg)
1   teaspoon ground turmeric (.836 mg)
1   teaspoon Maureen's Garam Masala (see page 45) (.714 mg)
1   teaspoon crushed red pepper or cayenne pepper (.54 mg)
     Juice of 1 lemon (.47 mg)
½   cup low-fat plain yogurt, whisked or beaten (86 mg)

[†]Use your processor and grind down unsalted almonds whole or halves.

2 **pound leg of lamb (553.4 mg)**
18 **whole cloves (10.2 mg)**
2 **garlic cloves, slivered (1.02 mg)**

Preheat your oven to 375°F.

Put the onion, spices, and lemon juice in the bowl of your food processor and process until you have a paste. Add the yogurt a few tablespoons at a time and blend.

Remove excess fat from the leg and cut an incision, about an inch or more deep, diagonally from one end of the meat to the other. You can make this cut on both sides if you like. Fill this cut with the paste. Then make small incisions about ¾ inch deep evenly around meat. Push some of the paste into some of them and whole cloves in others, and push in a sliver of garlic in others. Use this pattern completely around the leg. You may use more cloves, depending on the size of the lamb leg. This also works well with a boneless leg of lamb*.

Lightly grease a baking pan with oil. Place the leg of lamb in the center of the pan; do not use a rack. Slather the paste on the lamb and then put the rest around the lamb on the pan bottom.

Cover with aluminum foil, without touching the lamb, and roast for 1¾ to 2½ hours. You can punch a meat thermometer through the foil as long as the foil remains tight around the hole. Remove the foil when the internal temperature reaches about 168°F. Then let it roast for about 10 minutes more, or until the thermometer registers 170°F.

Place the meat on a nice serving platter and let it rest for a few minutes before carving and serving. Cover loosely with foil and let rest.

Nutrient Data per Serving (6)
Calories: 253.8. Protein: 33.6 g. Carbohydrate: 7.594 g. Dietary Fiber: 1.553 g. Total Sugars: 1.359 g. Total Fat: 9.661 g. Saturated Fat: 2.802 g. Monounsaturated Fat: 4.456 g. Polyunsaturated Fat: 1.258 g. Cholesterol: 98 mg. Trans Fat: 0 g. Total Omega-3 FA: .146 g. Total Omega-6 FA: 0 g. Potassium: 607.1 mg. Sodium: 110.7 mg. Vitamin K: 1.419 mcg. Folic Acid: 0 mcg.

Nutrient Data per Serving (8)
Calories: 190.3. Protein: 25.2 g. Carbohydrate: 5.695 g. Dietary Fiber: 1.165 g. Total Sugars: 1.02 g. Total Fat: 7.246 g. Saturated Fat: 2.101 g. Monounsaturated Fat: 3.342 g. Polyunsaturated Fat: .944 g. Cholesterol: 73.5 mg. Trans Fat: 0 g. Total Omega-3 FA: .109 g. Total Omega-6 FA: 0 g. Potassium: 455.3 mg. Sodium: 83 mg. Vitamin K: 1.064 mcg. Folic Acid: 0 mcg.

*If using a boneless leg, you might not need to cut the slash. Put the paste into the folded areas.

❖ GREEK MEAT LOAF ❖

ORIGIN: GREECE
DIABETIC ACCEPTABLE

This recipe is made like a meat loaf, but the meat can be used in pita sandwiches, in regular bread sandwiches, or rolled in a pita-style bread or Greek flatbread. It works well with the Greek Tzatziki Sauce (see page 54).

MAKES 10 SERVINGS (ONE ¾- TO 1-INCH-THICK SLICE PER SERVING)
SODIUM PER RECIPE: 831.3 MG
SODIUM PER SERVING: 83.1 MG

1½ pounds lean ground lamb (400 mg)
1   pound lean ground beef (298.3 mg)
½   cup whole-milk plain yogurt (56.8 mg)
1   cup finely chopped onion (4.8 mg)
4   garlic cloves, finely crushed in a garlic press (2.04 mg)
1   cup dry Basic Bread Crumbs (see page 167) (4.065 mg)
2   large eggs, lightly beaten (63 mg)
3   tablespoons finely chopped fresh mint leaves, or 1
        tablespoon dried mint, crumbled (1.488 mg)
½   teaspoon ground white pepper (.06 mg)
1   teaspoon dried basil, roughly crushed (.476 mg)
1½ teaspoons dried oregano, roughly crushed (.255 mg)
     Olive oil spray

Preheat the oven to 350°F.

Put the lamb, beef, yogurt, onion, garlic, bread crumbs, and eggs into a large mixing bowl and mix together with your hands or a wooden spoon until well combined. Mix in the remaining ingredients and turn out onto board.

Spray a 9×5-inch loaf pan with olive oil spray. Pack the mixture firmly into loaf pan.

Bake the meat loaf for 1½ hours.†

Remove the meat loaf from the oven. Pour out the liquid (fat and water). Let the meat loaf cool in the pan for about 20 minutes. Serve in pita pocket bread (see Don's Pocket Pita Bread, page 176), in sandwiches or, as you wish, on a plate with our Tzatziki Sauce drizzled over the meat.

---

†The meat mixture can be fried in patties, but we like to avoid the extra oil.

This also freezes well, or refrigerate overnight if you want to slice this for sandwiches or other uses. If you refrigerate it, slice and reheat in your microwave. Serve with sauce, sliced red onion, and tomatoes if you like.

Nutrient Data per Serving:
Calories: 356.2. Protein: 21.8 g. Carbohydrate: 8.822 g. Dietary Fiber: .743 g. Total Sugars: 1.187 g. Total Fat: 25.4 g. Saturated Fat: 10.9 g. Monounsaturated Fat: 10.4 g. Polyunsaturated Fat: 1.74 g. Cholesterol: 105.5 mg. Trans Fat: 0 g. Total Omega-3 FA: .358 g. Total Omega-6 FA: 0 g. Potassium: 355.5 mg. Sodium: 83.1 mg. Vitamin K: 5.869 mcg. Folic Acid: 0 mcg.

❂ HUNGARIAN CHICKEN PAPRIKA ❂

ORIGIN: HUNGARY
DIABETICS, SEE FOOTNOTE*

Soon after the Hungarian revolution of 1956 collapsed under Soviet power, our mother hired a new immigrant from Hungary as a housecleaner. She worked very hard and eventually obtained her U.S. citizenship. She could also cook, and sometimes when Mother was gone, Anna would prepare chicken paprika for our family's dinner. Maureen has taken that recipe and adapted it for our low-sodium use, and wow! What a job she did! You'll really love this one.

MAKES 6 SERVINGS SODIUM PER RECIPE: 640.2 MG
SODIUM PER SERVING: 106.7 MG

1½   **pounds boneless, skinless, chicken (breasts and thighs mixed) (485.4 mg)**
1   **tablespoon plus 1 teaspoon olive oil (trace)**
1   **cup chopped onion (4.8 mg)**
2   **garlic cloves, chopped (1.02 mg)**
1   **tablespoon paprika (2.346 mg)**
1   **cup Maureen's Easy Chicken Broth (see page 113) (37.8 mg)**
1   **teaspoon unbleached, all-purpose flour (.051 mg)**
½   **cup sour cream (60.9 mg), or whole-milk plain yogurt (56.8 mg)†**
8   **ounces wide egg noodles (47.9 mg)**

*Most of the carbohydrates are in the onions (16.2 g) and noodles (162.2 g).
†See Nutrient Data if using plain yogurt instead of sour cream; the fat is lower when using yogurt.

Heat the olive oil in a large frying pan over medium-high heat. Sauté the onion and garlic in the oil until translucent, about 5 minutes; do not brown.

Add the paprika and stir until the onion and garlic are coated. Push the onion mixture to the side of the pan. Reduce the heat to medium and add the chicken pieces. Brown lightly on both sides, 10 to 15 minutes.

Add the chicken broth, bring to a boil, turn down the heat, cover, and simmer for 30 minutes. Remove the lid and continue simmering for 30 minutes more.

When the chicken is almost done, put the water on for the noodles and cook the noodles according to package directions. Mix the flour into the sour cream so it is ready when the chicken is done.

While the noodles are cooking, transfer the chicken to a plate and cover with foil to keep warm. Pour the sour cream mixture into the pan sauce and stir well. Reheat using low heat for 5 minutes. The sauce will thicken somewhat.

Drain the noodles, place them in a serving dish, place the chicken on top, and cover with the sauce.

Nutrient Data per Serving (with Sour Cream):
Calories: 366.3. Protein: 29.8 g. Carbohydrate: 32.4 g. Dietary Fiber: 1.997 g. Total Sugars: 1.931 g. Total Fat: 12.7 g. Saturated Fat: 4.291 g. Monounsaturated Fat: 5.073 g. Polyunsaturated Fat: 1.942 g. Cholesterol: 122 mg. Trans Fat: 0 g. Total Omega-3 FA: .209 g. Total Omega-6 FA: 0 g. Potassium: 452.4 mg. Sodium: 106.7 mg. Vitamin K: 5.95 mcg. Folic Acid: 82.5 mcg.

Nutrient Data per Serving (with Whole Milk Yogurt):
Calories: 337.8. Protein: 29.9 g. Carbohydrate: 32.5 g. Dietary Fiber: 1.997 g. Total Sugars: 1.901 g. Total Fat: 9.328 g. Saturated Fat: 2.218 g. Monounsaturated Fat: 4.095 g. Polyunsaturated Fat: 1.812 g. Cholesterol: 116.2 mg. Trans Fat: 0 g. Total Omega-3 FA: .15 g. Total Omega-6 FA: 0 g. Potassium: 456.4 mg. Sodium: 106 mg. Vitamin K: 5.758 mcg. Folic Acid: 82.5 mcg.

❈ HUNGARIAN GOULASH ❈

ORIGIN: HUNGARY
DIABETICS, SEE FOOTNOTE*

When we think of Hungarian cuisine, paprika and garlic come to mind. We've included two recipes: Chicken Paprika and the well-known Hungarian Goulash, which is a stew flavored with onions. We've added plenty of onions and garlic to enhance flavor and heart-healthy vitamins. Hope you enjoy them.

*Carbohydrates are highest in noodles (16.2 g).

1   pound top round or other lean cut of beef, cut into 1-inch
     cubes (272.2 mg)
1   tablespoon olive oil (trace)
1   cup chopped onion (4.8 mg)
3   garlic cloves, chopped (1.53 mg)
2   tablespoons all-purpose flour (.312 mg)
1   tablespoon paprika (2.346 mg)
⅛   teaspoon ground white pepper (.015 mg)
1   (14.5-ounce) can no-salt-added tomatoes, pureed (105 mg)
¼   cup low-sodium water (trace)
     8 ounces wide egg noodles (47.9 mg)

Heat the olive oil in a Dutch oven. Add the beef and brown, stirring
often.

When the meat is browned, add the onion and garlic and cook until
translucent, approximately 5 minutes, stirring often. Sprinkle the mixture
with the flour, paprika, and white pepper and stir until blended. Immediately add the tomatoes, stir, and add the water. Bring the mixture to a boil.
Then turn down the heat, cover, and simmer for 1½ hours.

Meanwhile, boil the noodles according to the package directions.

When the goulash and noodles are done, add the sour cream to the
meat mixture and reheat gently for an additional 5 minutes. Serve hot over
the boiled noodles.

Accompany with string beans or cauliflower and broccoli. For a bread
to go along with this meal, try our Russian Black Bread (page 199) or
Flaxseed Meal and Raisin Bread (page 181).

Nutrient Data per Serving:
*Calories: 331.1. Protein: 23.4 g. Carbohydrate: 35.2 g. Dietary Fiber: 2.527 g. Total
Sugars: 3.393 g. Total Fat: 10 g. Saturated Fat: 3.038 g. Monounsaturated Fat: 4.746 g.
Polyunsaturated Fat: 1.026 g. Cholesterol: 66.3 mg. Trans-Fatty Acids: 0 g. Total Omega-3
FA: .121 g. Total Omega-6 FA: 0 g. Iron: 3.614 mg. Potassium: 520.3 mg. Sodium: 72.3 mg.
Vitamin K: 3.51 mcg. Folic Acid: 86.1 mcg.*

ORIGIN: ITALIAN
DIABETIC ACCEPTABLE

Our best lasagne ever, updated from our earlier version created five years ago just for the no-salt, low-sodium lifestyle. This one uses low-sodium Swiss cheese, real ricotta, and best of all, noodles you don't have to boil beforehand. I guarantee your friends will not know that this lasagne is without added salt. It's also only 329 calories. Serve with a cucumber-tomato salad.

MAKES 12 SERVINGS   SODIUM PER RECIPE: 1116 MG
SODIUM PER SERVING: 93 MG

THE SAUCE
1   teaspoon extra-virgin olive oil (trace)
4   garlic cloves, chopped (2.04 mg)
1   cup chopped onion (4.8 mg)
4   ounces sliced mushrooms (about 1½ to 2 cups) (4.536 mg)
2   teaspoons dried basil (.952 mg)
⅛   teaspoon ground white pepper (trace)
1   teaspoon dried oregano (.27 mg)
¾   pound cooked homemade Don's Sweet Italian Sausage (see
      page 107) (204.3 mg)
1   (14-ounce) can no-salt-added tomatoes (54.6 mg)
½   (6-ounce) can no-salt-added tomato paste (50 mg)
⅛   teaspoon ground white pepper (trace)
1   (14-ounce) can (from tomatoes) low-sodium water
      (trace)
2   tablespoons fresh lemon juice (.61 mg)
8   ounces low-sodium Swiss cheese*, grated (about 3 cups)
      (93 mg)

*No-salt-added, low-sodium Swiss cheese ranges from 5 mg per ounce up to 15. We have used the USDA rating for this recipe since we were able to find Swiss in the USDA category coast to coast during our May 2004 travels across the country.

THE RICOTTA
3 cups Precious brand whole-milk ricotta cheese or other ricotta (619.9 mg)
1 teaspoon ground cinnamon (.598 mg)

THE NOODLES
12 Barilla Oven-Ready, No-Boil Lasagna noodles (80 mg)

For the Sauce: Sauté the vegetables in the oil in a 3-quart pan until translucent and the mushrooms begin to release their juices, about 5 minutes. Sprinkle with the herbs and pepper and sauté 1 minute more. Add the tomatoes, tomato paste, white pepper, and water.

Bring the sauce to a boil over medium heat, reduce the heat, and simmer for about 1 hour, stirring occasionally.

While the sauce is cooking, mix together the ricotta and cinnamon and set aside.

Preheat oven to 350°F.

To assemble: Spray a 13×9-inch Pyrex-style baking dish or a baking pan with olive oil spray and spread one cup of the sauce from the 3-quart pan over the bottom of the dish/pan. Set 4 of the noodles on top of the sauce, overlapping slightly. Place 1 cup of the ricotta-cinnamon mixture on top and spread evenly. Layer with one-third of the sausage and 1 cup of the Swiss cheese. Repeat building two more layers starting with noodles, then the sauce, ricotta, sausage, and grated Swiss.

Cover the lasagne with aluminum foil, bake at 350°F for 45 minutes. Remove the foil and bake for another 10 to 15 minutes, or until the cheese turns golden. Serve hot. The lasagne may be cut into serving portions and frozen in aluminum foil up to 3 months, or store the lasagne, covered, in the refrigerator for up to 4 days. Reheat to serve.

Nutrient Data per Serving:
Calories: 339. Protein: 20.4 g. Carbohydrate: 20 g. Dietary Fiber: 2.176 g. Total Sugars: 1.684 g. Total Fat: 19.3 g. Saturated Fat: 10.7 g. Monounsaturated Fat: 6.437 g. Polyunsaturated Fat: 1.005 g. Cholesterol: 69.1 mg. Trans Fat: 0 g. Total Omega-3 FA: .1 g. Total Omega-6 FA: 0 g. Potassium: 343 mg. Sodium: 93 mg. Vitamin K: 5.746 mcg. Folic Acid: 0 mcg.

❖ DON'S MOCK SAUSAGE ❖

ORIGIN: WORLDWIDE
DIABETIC ACCEPTABLE

Not everyone eats pork, but those who do love a good pork sausage. Unfortunately for us, most commercial sausage is loaded with salt, nitrates, and other high-sodium ingredients. It also has a lot of saturated fat. We can change all that in our kitchens with some clever mixing of spices and very lean ground pork, turkey, or chicken. I personally like the very lean ground turkey for cutting down on the fats and because it's always available in our area. I hope the same is true for you. You can make these and serve them in two-ounce size patties. They'll taste just like the real thing.

MAKES 6   SODIUM PER RECIPE: 191.3 MG
SODIUM PER PATTY (TURKEY): 31.9 MG

6   **ounces lean ground turkey (142 mg)**
2   **ounces lean ground pork (47.6 mg)**
¼   **teaspoon ground pepper (.231 mg)**
    Pinch of ground cloves (.612 mg)
½   **teaspoon ground sage (trace)**
½   **teaspoon minced fresh or powdered garlic (.369 mg)**
⅛   **teaspoon onion powder (.141 mg)**
    Large pinch of mace (.136 mg)
⅛   **teaspoon allspice (.183 mg)**
1   **teaspoon extra-virgin olive oil (trace)**

In a medium bowl, mix together all ingredients except for the oil.

Shape into 4 evenly sized patties and cook in a nonstick pan with the olive oil over medium heat. Cook each side for 5 to 8 minutes, or until browned.

Serve hot with eggs, or as dinner with freshly steamed broccoli, asparagus, or squash, and sliced tomatoes.

Nutrient Data per Sausage Patty:
Calories: 78.7. Protein: 6.855 g. Carbohydrate: .371 g. Dietary Fiber: .101 g. Total Sugars: .077 g. Total Fat: 5.364 g. Saturated Fat: 1.727 g. Monounsaturated Fat: 2.308 g. Polyunsaturated Fat: .807 g. Cholesterol: 30.1 mg. Trans Fat: .069 g. Total Omega-3 FA: .042 g. Total Omega-6 FA: 0 g. Iron: .501 mg. Potassium: 105.1 mg. Sodium: 31.9 mg. Vitamin K: 1.505 mcg. Folic Acid: 0 mcg.

✸ DON'S SWEET ITALIAN SAUSAGE ✸

ORIGIN: ITALY
DIABETIC ACCEPTABLE

You can actually make this sausage and put it into casings that you can purchase online* or in your local specialty shop if you're lucky enough to have one. Otherwise just cook my favorite Italian sausage on a griddle and use in our Italian Lasagne (see page 104) or in any other recipe you like. This is an old family recipe.

**MAKES: FIFTEEN 2½-INCH SAUSAGES†   SODIUM PER RECIPE: 258 MG
SODIUM PER SAUSAGE: 17.2 MG**

½ **teaspoon onion powder (.648 mg)**
1   **teaspoon fennel seed (1.76 mg)**
½ **teaspoon freshly ground black pepper (.462 mg)**
1   **pound lean ground pork (254 mg)**
½ **tablespoon chopped, fresh parsley (1.064 mg)**

Grind the onion powder, black pepper, and fennel seed together with a mortar and pestle until a fine powder. (The fresh aroma of the fennel serves to please while doing this.) Add to the meat along with the parsley and mix thoroughly.

Spread out on a board and, using a large, flat spatula, flatten it to a thickness of ½ inch. Using a 2- to 2½-inch cookie cutter, cut out patties and place on a nonstick griddle, using no oil. For the last few patties you'll have to pull together the scraps, reshape, and cut again.

Fry the patties on the griddle over medium to medium-low heat. Turn when half done and finish cooking on the other side. You can store the sausages in ziplock bags or serve immediately. Serve with breakfast or mix into a marinara sauce for a tasty pasta dinner.

Nutrient Data per Sausage:
Calories: 80.5. Protein: 5.145 g. Carbohydrate: .188 g. Dietary Fiber: .08 g. Total Sugars: .03 g. Total Fat: 6.432 g. Saturated Fat: 2.382 g. Monounsaturated Fat: 2.869 g. Polyunsaturated Fat: .581 g. Cholesterol: 21.8 mg. Trans Fat: 0 g. Total Omega-3 FA: .021 g. Total Omega-6 FA: 0 g. Potassium: 91.4 mg. Sodium: 17.2 mg. Vitamin K: 2.195 mcg. Folic Acid: 0 mcg.

*Visit www.sausagemania.com/casings.html or www.megaheart.com/sausagemania.html.
†You may double the recipe to increase the number of sausages.

❖ JAPANESE SPICY CHICKEN ❖

ORIGIN: JAPAN
DIABETIC ADAPTABLE*

*When I first arrived in Japan for my six-month stint there,
I thought they had only fried rice to offer. Fried rice was
the only meal offered to us in the northern part of Japan
where we were stationed. I truly enjoyed the rice, but after a few trips into Tokyo I quickly discovered a whole new
world of Japanese gourmet cooking. Chicken was popular
there and this recipe surprised me for its simplicity and the
use of hot chili peppers. I have replaced the soy sauce with
my own mixture, but the rest is authentic. Enjoy!*

MAKES 4 SERVINGS   SODIUM PER RECIPE: 326.6 MG
SODIUM PER SERVING: 81.7 MG

1 cup basmati rice (makes 3 cups, steamed) (9.25 mg)
4 (4-ounce) boneless, skinless, chicken half breasts†
   (306.8 mg)
1 tablespoon cornstarch (.63 mg)
1 cup low-sodium water (trace)
½ cup white balsamic vinegar (1.2 mg)
¼ cup Don's Soy Sauce Replacement (see page 37)
   (7.099 mg)
1½ tablespoons white granulated sugar or Splenda (1.89 mg)
3 garlic cloves, peeled and crushed in a garlic press (1.53 mg)
1 fresh small hot chili pepper or jalapeño, seeded and
   chopped (3.15 mg)

Steam the rice in 1¼ cups water in a rice steamer and keep warm.

Dissolve the cornstarch in the water in a large saucepan.

Place all the remaining ingredients in the saucepan over high heat and
bring to boil. Cover, reduce the heat, and simmer for about 20 minutes.
Remove any fat or foam that rises to the surface.

Uncover and increase the heat, turning the meat often in the sauce.
Cook until the liquid has reduced to a nice glaze but enough remains to
serve with the chicken.

To serve place a scoop of rice on each serving plate, top with the
chicken, and spoon the sauce with or without (your choice) the garlic
and pepper chunks over the chicken. Let the sauce drizzle down into
the rice.

*Diabetics, the rice has 147.9g of carbohydrates.
†Or four large thighs or three large half breasts.

Nutrient Data per Serving:
Calories: 346.5. Protein: 30.8 g. Carbohydrate: 49.9 g. Dietary Fiber: .792 g. Total Sugars: 9.596 g. Total Fat: 1.812 g. Saturated Fat: .479 g. Monounsaturated Fat: .453 g. Polyunsaturated Fat: .434 g. Cholesterol: 68.4 mg. Trans Fat: .029 g. Total Omega-3 FA: .063 g. Total Omega-6 FA: 0 g. Potassium: 471.9 mg. Sodium: 81.7 mg. Vitamin K: .674 mcg. Folic Acid: 103.1 mcgg.

❂ LIGHT SUMMER CHICKEN SALAD ❂

ORIGIN: FRANCE
DIABETIC ACCEPTABLE

I made a trip to Paris, then down to Cannes and Nice, and at the hot time of year. In Nice I entered a small "Le Sandwich" shop and asked for something very light. This is pretty much what they served me, but on a highly salted French bread. Use our French Baguette recipe (see page 165) for a very delightful hot afternoon lunch. When making it now, I use leftover barbecued chicken—my favorite way of cooking nearly all our meals during the hot summers.

MAKES 2 SERVINGS   SODIUM PER RECIPE: 152.1 MG
SODIUM PER SERVING: 76 MG

THE SALAD FIXINGS

1   grilled or baked chicken half breast (about 5 to 6 ounces of meat), cut into bite-size pieces (76.7 mg)
2   large leaves of romaine lettuce (11.3 mg)
10 or 12 Sun Gold cherry tomatoes (10.2 mg)
1   small chilled cucumber (3.16 mg)
1   medium peeled and grated carrot (42.1 mg)
12   red or green seedless grapes† (.40 mg)
2   ounces low-sodium Cheddar or Swiss cheese, grated (a little over ½ cup) (7.84 mg)

THE DRESSING

1   tablespoon extra-virgin olive oil (trace)
2   tablespoons Red Star Raspberry vinegar (.30 mg)
½ to 1 .035-ounce packet Splenda sweetener‡ (trace)

*Diabetics, each sandwich has 14.8 grams of carbohydrates.
†You may leave out or exchange for other light seasonal fruit like mandarins, raspberries, blackberries, or strawberries.
‡The dressing is from *The No-Salt, Lowest-Sodium Light Meals Book*. If you use sugar instead of Splenda, then use about ⅛ to ¼ teaspoon. (Each splenda packet contains ¼ teaspoon Splenda)

Cut the chicken into small pieces.

Cut off the bottom of the romaine, pull the leaves apart, wash thoroughly, and spin dry. (We advise using packaged romaine.) Make a chiffonade by rolling up each leaf one at a time and cutting the roll crosswise in thin ribbons. (You will need about 3 cups of shredded lettuce for the salad.) Put the romaine into a salad bowl.

Wash and slice the tomatoes in half. Peel, wash, and thinly slice the cucumber. Wash, peel and grate the carrots. Wash the grapes.

Combine the ingredients for the salad dressing.

Toss the salad with the dressing and serve.

Nutrient Values per Serving:
Calories: 291.8. Protein: 24.2 g. Carbohydrate: 14.8 g. Dietary Fiber: 4.195 g. Total Sugars: 7.248 g. Total Fat: 15.8 g. Saturated Fat: 6.181 g. Monounsaturated Fat: 7.265 g. Polyunsaturated Fat: 1.412 g. Cholesterol: 60 mg. Trans Fat: .015 g. Total Omega-3 FA: .26 g. Total Omega-6 FA: 0 g. Potassium: 840.4 mg. Sodium: 76.2 mg. Vitamin K: 132.5 mcg. Folic Acid: 0 mcg.

❂ MARINATED PORK TENDERLOIN ❂

ORIGIN: SOUTHWEST U.S.A.
DIABETIC ACCEPTABLE*

Cerdo Adobado, or marinated pork, may be one of the best meals you'll ever serve yourself or your friends. The flavor of this dish is exciting. You can serve the pork as a meal over steamed Mexican rice or in a rolled corn tortilla or a homemade flour tortilla or even shredded over a salad entrée. The sauce is what will catch you— and you'll want to make it over and over again. If you don't eat pork, try it with lean beef tenderloin or other beef roast.

MAKES 4 SERVINGS   SODIUM PER RECIPE: 259.3 MG
SODIUM PER SERVING: 64.8 MG

1 **tablespoon olive oil (trace)**
1 **pound pork roast (204.1 mg)**
2 **cups chopped onion (9.6 mg)**
2 **tablespoons chopped garlic (2.856 mg)**
2 **cups Maureen's Easy Chicken Broth (see page 113) (39.6 mg)**

*Diabetics, the bulk of carbohydrates are in the (32.4g) and the honey (34.6g).

2   tablespoons honey (1.68 mg)
2   tablespoons red wine vinegar (.30 mg)
½   cup Grandma's chili powder (trace)
1   tablespoon plus 1 teaspoon dried oregano (1.08 mg)

Preheat the oven to 325°F.

Heat the tablespoon of oil in a 3- to 4-quart Dutch oven. Brown the pork roast in the oil on all sides over medium heat, 10 to 12 minutes. Transfer the roast to a plate and put the onions and garlic in the same pan. Sauté until translucent, about 5 minutes, stirring frequently to scrape up any browned meat particles on the bottom of the pot.

Add the chicken broth, honey, vinegar, and spices to the onion mixture and stir well. Bring to a boil, then reduce the heat, and simmer for 15 minutes.

Puree the mixture in a blender, or use a handheld blender, and process until well combined. You will have about 2½ cups of marinade.

Return the roast to the Dutch oven. Pour the marinade over the roast, cover, and place in oven. Bake 2 to 2½ hours.

To serve, shred or slice the pork and spread the sauce, which will now be thick, over it.

This is traditionally served with flour tortillas. We found it delicious served on warm white corn tortillas, topped with our Fresh Salsa (see page 40).

Nutrient Data per Serving:
Calories: 340.4. Protein: 27.8 g. Carbohydrate: 27.4 g. Dietary Fiber: 2.401 g. Total Sugars: 12.4 g. Total Fat: 14.3 g. Saturated Fat: 3.608 g. Monounsaturated Fat: 6.698 g. Polyunsaturated Fat: 1.559 g. Cholesterol: 74.2 mg. Trans Fat: 0 g. Total Omega-3 FA: .163 g. Total Omega-6 FA: 0 g. Potassium: 710.4 mg. Sodium: 64.8 mg. Vitamin K: 22.4 mcg. Folic Acid: 0 mcg.

MAUREEN'S UNIQUELY AMERICAN
❖ MEAT LOAF ❖

ORIGIN: U.S.A.
DIABETIC ACCEPTABLE

School days, school days, let's have another meat loaf sandwich on school days. Just kidding. But maybe not. During WWII when I was attending grammar school, my mother had to come up with a lot of lunches for her four children and meat loaf was the most "stretchable" dish she could create. The slices were relatively thin but thick enough. She extended the loaf with potatoes, bread crumbs, and even fresh bread. After about four years of

that I never wanted to see one again. But my wife, ahh,
yes, the lovely Maureen, has a much better recipe—one
that just might knock your socks off. It's worth the try and
very easy to make.

MAKES 10 SERVINGS (ONE ¾-INCH SLICE IS A SERVING)

SODIUM PER RECIPE: 879.7 MG SODIUM PER SERVING: 88 MG

1 tablespoon olive oil (trace)
1 onion, chopped (4.5 mg)
3 garlic cloves, chopped (1.53 mg)
½ cup yellow and red bell peppers, cored, seeded, and chopped
    (1.49 mg)
½ cup carrots, chopped (22.4 mg)
¼ teaspoon ground white pepper (trace)
    Don's Herbes de Provence (see page 36) (trace)
¼ cup chopped parsley (8.4 mg)
1 pound ground beef (298.3 mg)
½ pound ground pork (126.6 mg)
½ pound ground turkey (213.2 mg)
2 large eggs, slightly beaten (126 mg)
½ cup nonfat milk with added vitamins A & D (51.5 mg)
1 cup Basic Bread Crumbs (see page 167) (4.065 mg)

Heat the oil in a large frying pan, over medium heat and sauté the vegetables until translucent, about 10 minutes. Reduce the heat if they start to brown. Sprinkle with pepper and Don's Herbes de Provence to taste and cook 1 minute more. You want at least 1 cup of mixture when cooked. Add the fresh parsley and remove from the heat.

Preheat the oven to 350°F.

Mix together the beef, pork, turkey, eggs, milk, and bread crumbs, and 1 cup of the sautéed vegetables.

Shape into a loaf and place in lightly oiled loaf pan.

Bake for 1½ hours.

Nutrient Data per Serving:
Calories: 276.9. Protein: 19.1 g. Carbohydrate: 9.519 g. Dietary Fiber: .909 g. Total Sugars: 2.411 g. Total Fat: 17.6 g. Saturated Fat: 6.382 g. Monounsaturated Fat: 7.812 g. Polyunsaturated Fat: 1.57 g. Cholesterol: 110 mg. Trans Fat: .062 g. Total Omega-3 FA: .123 g. Total Omega-6 FA: 0 g. Potassium: 361.3 mg. Sodium: 88 mg. Vitamin K: 26.9 mcg. Folic Acid: 0 mcg.

◈ MAUREEN'S EASY CHICKEN BROTH ◈

ORIGN: WORLDWIDE
DIABETIC ACCEPTABLE

We wanted a chicken broth that tasted just like the real thing but one that didn't use salt or any of the chemical-based additives, including those using a high level of potassium chloride. When we wrote The No-Salt, Lowest-Sodium Light Meals Book, *Maureen came up with a great chemical-free broth. She doesn't refer to this new recipe as a replacement for that one but instead as another way to make a great-tasting chicken broth.*

MAKES 2 QUARTS   SODIUM PER RECIPE: *302.3* MG
SODIUM PER CUP: *37.8* MG

3 **pounds nonbrined chicken† whole or parts (146.4 mg)‡**
3 **quarts low-sodium water (trace)**
2 **carrots, peeled and sliced (42.7 mg)**
1 **onion, quartered (4.5 mg)**
1 **cup chopped celery (104.4 mg)**
3 **whole garlic cloves (1.53 mg)**
6 **whole peppercorns (trace)**

Put the chicken in a large stockpot and cover with water. Bring the water and chicken to a boil and then reduce to a simmer. Skim off any scum that forms on the top until it stops forming. Add the vegetables and peppercorns and simmer, partially covered, for 3 hours.

Remove the chicken and strain the broth into a bowl. Cool down, cover, and refrigerate overnight. Let the chicken cool and remove the fat and bones. When removing bones, do so carefully as it is easy to miss a small bone. Store in the refrigerator until ready to use.

The next day, remove the broth from refrigerator and skim any fat that has accumulated on top. Now, the broth is ready to use. You should have at least 1½ to 2 quarts of broth. (You will need 2 cups of broth and 2 cups of chicken for the Chicken Enchilada recipe on page 79).

---

†Read the packages or ask your butcher. Many chicken processors are now brining their chickens, which could put chicken out of reach for low-sodium diets.
‡Not all the sodium will make it into the broth. We estimate about one-third of this figure is more accurate; however, we are sticking to FDA and USDA rules here by listing the total amount in the three pounds of chicken.

Nutrient Values per Cup:
Calories: 72.1. Protein: 5.241 g. Carbohydrate: 3.874 g. Dietary Fiber: .838 g. Total Sugars: 1.612 g. Total Fat: 3.95 g. Saturated Fat: 1.125 g. Monounsaturated Fat: 1.6 g. Polyunsaturated Fat: .873 g. Cholesterol: 23.5 mg. Trans Fat: 0 g. Total Omega-3 FA: .048 g. Total Omega-6 FA: 0 g. Potassium: 153.8 mg. Sodium: 37.8 mg. Vitamin K: 5.44 mcg. Folic Acid: 0 mcg.

❖ MOROCCAN LAMB CHOPS ❖

ORIGIN: MOROCCO
DIABETIC ACCEPTABLE

Moroccans love tangy spices and these lamb chops will demonstrate their favorite flavors. Go ahead, try them, you'll be pleasantly surprised.

MAKES 4 SERVINGS   SODIUM PER RECIPE: 296.6 MG
SODIUM PER SERVING: 74.1 MG

1   teaspoon ground cumin (3.528 mg)
1   teaspoon paprika (.714 mg)
1   teaspoon ground coriander (.63 mg)
¼   teaspoon ground cloves (.744 mg)
¼   teaspoon crushed red pepper (.135 mg)
8   lean rib lamb chops, with about 2 ounces of meat each*
     (435.5 mg)

Mix the dry ingredients together and rub on the chops. Let stand for a few minutes.

Either grill the chops on barbecue or bake them at 425°F on a broiler pan, sprayed with no-stick cooking spray, for 25 minutes.

Nutrient Values per Serving:
Calories: 155.3. Protein: 23.4 g. Carbohydrate: .916 g. Dietary Fiber: .516 g. Total Sugars: .081 g. Total Fat: 5.879 g. Saturated Fat: 2.243 g. Monounsaturated Fat: 2.453 g. Polyunsaturated Fat: .39 g. Cholesterol: 72.6 mg. Trans Fat: 0 g. Total Omega-3 FA: .094 g. Total Omega-6 FA: 0 g. Potassium: 418.9 mg. Sodium: 74.1 mg. Vitamin K: .726 mcg. Folic Acid: 0 mcg.

*The chops will weigh more because of the bone.

❈ PERUVIAN SPICY CHICKEN ❈

ORIGIN: PERU
DIABETIC ACCEPTABLE

I enjoy trying recipes out on family members, particularly our grandchildren. I thought this one might be a bit too spicy for our three-year-old Alexander, but his comment was, "Boy, Grandma, this is delicious! Can I have some more?"

MAKES 4 TO 5 SERVINGS   SODIUM PER RECIPE: 396.9 MG
SODIUM PER SERVING (4): 99.2 MG
SODIUM PER SERVING (5): 79.4 MG)

½ teaspoon crushed red pepper (.27 mg)
¼ cup nonfat milk with added vitamins A & D, or enough to
       saturate the bread (25.7 mg)
2   slices low-sodium White Bread (see page 203) (1.967 mg)
1   tablespoon plus 1 teaspoon olive oil (trace)
1   pound boneless, skinless chicken breasts (about 4), cut into
       chunks (306.8 mg)
1   cup chopped onion (4.8 mg)
2   garlic cloves, minced (1.02 mg)
2   cups chopped, peeled, and seeded tomatoes (about 2 medium
       tomatoes) (18 mg)
1   cup Maureen's Easy Chicken Broth (see page 113) (37.8 mg)
¼ teaspoon ground white pepper (.03 mg)
1   hard-boiled egg, peeled and sliced, optional (63 mg)

Soak the crushed pepper in a small amount of hot water. Pour the milk into a shallow pan (a pie pan works well) and soak the bread until all the milk is absorbed. Shred it and leave it in the pan while you prepare the rest of the ingredients.

Heat 1 teaspoon of oil in a 4- to 5-quart Dutch oven. Cook the chicken over medium-high heat until lightly browned, about 10 minutes, stirring frequently. Transfer the chicken to a plate and keep warm. Heat 1 tablespoon of oil in the Dutch oven, add the onions and garlic, and cook them until they soften and brown lightly; do not burn. Stir in the tomatoes, the drained, crushed pepper, the white pepper, and the bread. Stir constantly for 2 minutes and add the broth. Mix thoroughly, and add the cooked chicken. Lower the heat, cover, and cook for an additional 20 to 30 minutes, until the chicken is tender.

This dish is usually topped with sliced hard-boiled eggs and olives. We omitted the olives, but one or two egg slices makes it authentically South American.

Traditionally served with sweet potatoes.

Nutrient Data per Serving (4):
Calories: 288.4. Protein: 31.9 g. Carbohydrate: 20 g. Dietary Fiber: 2.366 g. Total Sugars: 6.167 g. Total Fat: 8.624 g. Saturated Fat: 1.546 g. Monounsaturated Fat: 5.103 g. Polyunsaturated Fat: 1.345 g. Cholesterol: 74.6 mg. Trans Fat: .029 g. Total Omega-3 FA: .113 g. Total Omega-6 FA: 0 g. Potassium: 664.6 mg. Sodium: 99.1 mg. Vitamin K: 12.6 mcg. Folic Acid: 18 mcg..

Nutrient Data per Serving (5):
Calories: 230.7. Protein: 25.5 g. Carbohydrate: 16 g. Dietary Fiber: 1.893 g. Total Sugars: 4.934 g. Total Fat: 6.899 g. Saturated Fat: 1.237 g. Monounsaturated Fat: 4.082 g. Polyunsaturated Fat: 1.076 g. Cholesterol: 59.7 mg. Trans Fat: .024 g. Total Omega-3 FA: .09 g. Total Omega-6 FA: 0 g. Potassium: 531.7 mg. Sodium: 79.4 mg. Vitamin K: 10.1 mcg. Folic Acid: 14.4 mcg.

❖ POLYNESIAN CHICKEN OR PORK ❖

ORIGIN: TAHITI
DIABETICS, SEE FOOTNOTE*

I spent a few weeks in Papeete, Tahiti, filming, and experienced some good meals and some not-so-good meals. There is a heavy French influence in the Tahiti Islands, still a French Protectorate (ca. 1842–43). We filmed Tahitians roasting a pig underground, netting fish for their food, and more. We lived on the outer part of the island, not in a motel or hotel or vacation lodge. We resided, instead, in the open-air home of Rene Tupano. Lizards would crawl across us at night and mosquitoes were everywhere, although I'd pretty much figured out how to stop that harassment. The roasted pig meat was stored in an open-air upright stand with screens wrapped around it to keep flies and other varmints from it. Needless to say, after a few days of that diet, I took the film crew into Papeete to find a restaurant for a more conventional meal. That's when we were introduced to chicken with a Polynesian sauce that reminded me of a sauce I might find in Japan or China. This recipe is as close as I can come to that meal. It works well with a lean pork roast, too.

*The bulk of the carbohydrates and sugars are in the honey, which has 34.6 grams of carbohydrates and 33.6 grams of sugars. The soy sauce replacement has 8.7 grams of sugars and 11.7 grams of carbohydrates. You can make a honey substitute by mixing 2 tablespoons of Splenda with 2¼ tablespoons of low-sodium water.

THE CHICKEN

3 boneless, skinless chicken half breasts, cut into bite-size
    pieces* (230.1 mg)
3 tablespoons Don's Soy Sauce Replacement (see page 37)
    (6.843 mg)
1 teaspoon Don's Hoisin Sauce (see page 55) (.694 mg)
2 tablespoons honey (1.68 mg)
2 teaspoons grated fresh ginger (.52 mg)
½ teaspoon Chinese five-spice powder (trace)

THE GARNISH

3 green onions, cut crosswise in ¼-inch slices (7.2 mg)
¼ cup chopped fresh cilantro (6.21 mg)

Preheat oven to 375°F.

Toss the chicken with the soy sauce, hoisin sauce, honey, ginger, and Chinese five-spice powder.

Place into a lightly greased baking dish and bake for 35 to 45 minutes, or until chicken is a golden brown.

Serve hot, sprinkled with the garnish of cilantro and onions. If you want more five-spice powder, sprinkle a bit more of that on as well, to suit your taste.

Nutrient Data per Serving:
Calories: 150.4. Protein: 20.9 g. Carbohydrate: 13.1 g. Dietary Fiber: .451 g. Total Sugars: 10.9 g. Total Fat: 1.529 g. Saturated Fat: .372 g. Monounsaturated Fat: .451 g. Polyunsaturated Fat: .379 g. Cholesterol: 51.3 mg. Trans Fat: .022 g. Total Omega-3 FA: .037 g. Total Omega-6 FA: 0 g. Potassium: 341 mg. Sodium: 62.9 mg. Vitamin K: .209 mcg. Folic Acid: 0 mcg.

❖ GREEK LAMB ROAST ❖

ORIGIN: GREECE
DIABETIC ACCEPTABLE

When I was in the film business, I worked on a project for a large corporation owned by a Greek gentleman, well known for his work. I worked on film projects for that company off and on for nearly four years. During that time we ate well. They would often have large parties for

---

*Boneless, skinless thighs work very well with this recipe. About 6 thighs will make 4 servings. Sodium level would be: 356 mg

friends and use giant spits and pits for roasting whole lambs. The "sauce" on the lamb made the special events even more special when the meat touched the palate. Here's the closest I've been able to come to what I remember as wonderful meals.

MAKES 8 SERVINGS   SODIUM PER RECIPE: 534.8 MG
SODIUM PER SERVING: 66.8 MG

2 pounds boneless lamb roast* (526.2 mg)
4 garlic cloves, thinly sliced (3.06 mg)
1 teaspoon onion powder (1.296 mg)
½ teaspoon black or white pepper (.06 mg)
1 tablespoon dried oregano (.81 mg)
   Juice of 1 medium lemon (.47 mg)
2 tablespoons unsalted butter, melted (3.124 mg)
2 tablespoons extra-virgin olive oil (trace)

Wash the meat and pat dry. Set the meat in a roasting pan with a rack. Preheat the oven to 325°F.

Combine the garlic, onion powder, pepper, oregano, butter, lemon juice, and oil in a small bowl.

Make 1-inch incisions in the lamb with a sharp knife. Insert the seasoned garlic into the incisions.

Once the garlic has been inserted, baste the meat with the rest of the oil-butter mixture.

Place the lamb in the oven and roast until meat thermometer shows 175°F to 180°F.

If the juices begin to drip into the pan during roasting, use them to baste the meat.

You may add quartered red potatoes to the pan at about the halfway point or about 45 minutes before the roast is done.

Nutrient Values per Serving:
Calories: 272.3. Protein: 21.8 g. Carbohydrate: 1.785 g. Dietary Fiber: .4 g. Total Sugars: .292 g. Total Fat: 19.4 g. Saturated Fat: 7.832 g. Monounsaturated Fat: 8.577 g. Polyunsaturated Fat: 1.542 g. Cholesterol: 83.6 mg. Trans Fat: 0 g. Total Omega-3 FA: .304 g. Total Omega-6 FA: .077 g. Potassium: 331.2 mg. Sodium: 66.8 mg. Vitamin K: 6.51 mcg. Folic Acid: 0 mcg.

*Works well with leg of lamb.

❧ GERMAN SAUERBRATEN ❧

ORIGIN: GERMANY
DIABETIC ADAPTABLE

Maureen made this recipe more than our usual number of times for tests to get it to the level of flavors it's at now. Then Megaheart member LeeAnn Sutherland offered to test it away from our kitchens. She even translated it into German and presented it to her German class. It was a "big hit," according to LeeAnn, "and in our house, it's a big hit as well." Thank you, LeeAnn, for your great help. We think everyone will find it a big hit. Remember to marinate this for 3 to 4 days.

NOTE: When purchasing beef, put it in a plastic bag in the store (many supermarket meat departments offer plastic bags near the displays). This prevents leakage of meat juices into and onto other foods. Take beef home immediately and refrigerate it at 40°F or lower. Use within 3 to 5 days, including time for marinating.

MAKES 8 SERVINGS   SODIUM PER RECIPE: 1140 MG
SODIUM PER SERVING: 142.5 MG

THE MARINADE
1   cup red wine vinegar (2.4 mg)
2   cups low-sodium water (trace)
2   bay leaves (.414 mg)
1   medium onion, chopped (3.3 mg)
10 whole black peppercorns (10 mg)
4   whole cloves (5.103 mg)

THE MEAT
4   pounds lean beef round or chuck roast (1070 mg)
¼   cup all-purpose flour (2.5 mg)
¼   teaspoon ground white pepper (8.03 mg)
1   tablespoon olive oil (.405 mg)
1   tablespoon unsalted butter (1.562 mg)
1   large onions, cut into eighths (4.5 mg)
1   tomato, cut into eighths (6.15 mg)
½   cup alcohol-free wine, such as Fré (8.68 mg)
½   cup golden raisins (9.9 mg)
3   tablespoons brown sugar (16.1 mg)

To marinate the meat: Mix all the ingredients for the marinade and bring to a boil over medium-high heat. Reduce the heat to a simmer and continue cooking for 15 minutes. Remove from heat and let cool.

Place the meat in a nonreactive pot or casserole dish and pour the marinade over the meat. Cover and place it in the refrigerator for 3 to 4 days, turning it 2 to 3 times a day.

On the day you wish to cook the sauerbraten, remove the meat from the pot and reserve the marinade. Strain the marinade, dry the meat with a paper towel, and sprinkle the meat with flour and pepper.

Heat the oil and the butter in a Dutch oven or other suitable pot with a lid, add the floured meat and brown on all sides.

Add the onion, tomato, and strained marinade. Bring the mixture to a boil, cover, reduce the heat to a simmer and cook for 1½ hours.

Remove the cover, add the alcohol-free wine, raisins, and brown sugar, and cook for an additional 1½ hours, turning the meat every half hour. Add more wine if the liquid reduces too much.

Remove the meat. Degrease the gravy and slice the meat. Then return both the meat and the gravy to the pot and reheat. Serve hot with mashed potatoes or dumplings and red cabbage (see page 230) Delicious!

Nutrient Data per Serving:
Calories: 701.4. Protein: 44.5 g. Carbohydrate: 31.4 g. Dietary Fiber: 1.642 g. Total Sugars: 14.7 g. Total Fat: 43.7 g. Saturated Fat: 17.2 g. Monounsaturated Fat: 19 g. Polyunsaturated Fat: 1.923 g. Cholesterol: 154.2 mg. Trans Fat: 0 g. Total Omega-3 FA: .579 g. Total Omega-6 FA: 0 g. Potassium: 941.1 mg. Sodium: 142.5 mg. Vitamin K: 3.141 mcg. Folic Acid: 24.1 mcg.

Sesame Seed
❈ Sweet-and-Sour Chicken ❈

Origin: China
Not Diabetic Adaptable

You can go into any Chinese restaurant and get your fill of sweet-and-sour chicken with sesame seeds. Most is fried in a wok in deep oil. I filmed the kitchen of a well-known Chinese restaurant once and was astonished to watch the cooks work as hard as they did in the heat they generated with flames dancing around each wok. Prep chefs would build each recipe into piles or small bowls. If you wanted fried rice with chicken, or sweet-and-sour chicken with sesame seeds, it was ready for quick frying. The cooks would pour up to a cup of oil into a wok, dump a container of someone's upcoming dinner into the boiling oil, shake it around for about a minute, and then pour it out on to a serving dish. No liquid came with it, but the cup of oil was gone—ostensibly to the diners awaiting their rather high-calorie meal.

We cut those calories a lot here, as well as the trans-fatty acids, simply by baking the chicken. Do this one right and your taste buds won't notice the difference, but your heart will. If you like Chinese food, this one is for you.

MAKES 6 TO 8 SERVINGS*   SODIUM PER RECIPE: 499.9 MG
SODIUM PER SERVING (6): 83.3 MG
SODIUM PER SERVING: (8) 62.5 MG

2   **tablespoons cold low-sodium water (trace)**
2   **tablespoons cornstarch (1.44 mg)**
¾   **cup white granulated sugar (trace)**
2   **tablespoons brown sugar (10.8 mg)**
6   **tablespoons Grandma's, B'rer Rabbit, or other no-salt molasses (21 mg)**
½   **cup distilled, cider, or other vinegar (1.2 mg)**
½   **teaspoon ground ginger (.288 mg)**
6   **garlic cloves, minced† (3.06 mg)**
6   **(4-ounce) pieces skinless or boneless chicken† (about 1⅓ pounds) (460.2 mg)**
2   **tablespoons sesame seeds (1.98 mg)**

Mix the water and cornstarch and set aside.

Place all the other ingredients, except the chicken and sesame seeds, into a medium saucepan. Stir thoroughly and add the water and cornstarch mixture. Over medium heat, bring the mixture to a boil, lower the heat, and let simmer, stirring frequently, until the sauce thickens. Continue cooking for a few minutes more.

Preheat the oven to 425°F. Place the chicken into a baking dish and spread half the sauce over chicken. Sprinkle with half the sesame seeds. Bake for half an hour, turn over the chicken and pour over the remaining sauce. Sprinkle with the remaining sesame seeds. Serve hot. Sweet-and-Sour Chicken can be reheated. Store it in ziplock bags in refrigerator for up to 4 days.

Nutrient Data per Serving (6):
Calories: 305.6. Protein: 28 g. Carbohydrate: 42.9 g. Dietary Fiber: .46 g. Total Sugars: 35.7 g. Total Fat: 2.989 g. Saturated Fat: .604 g. Monounsaturated Fat: .92 g. Polyunsaturated

*You may halve this recipe, if desired.
†I like to put the cornstarch and water, vinegar, and sugar into my Braun handheld processor along with the garlic and really give it a whirl.
‡You may use small chicken strips or bites that equal a total of 24 ounces for 6 to 8 servings. Boneless, skinless chicken works very well with this recipe.

Fat: .999 g. Cholesterol: 68.4 mg. Trans Fat: .03 g. Total Omega-3 FA: .06 g. Total Omega-6
FA: 0 g. Potassium: 511.9 mg. Sodium: 83.3 mg. Vitamin K: .279 mcg. Folic Acid: 0 mcg.

Nutrient Data per Serving (8):
Calories: 229.2. Protein: 21 g. Carbohydrate: 32.2 g. Dietary Fiber: .345 g. Total Sugars:
26.8 g. Total Fat: 2.241 g. Saturated Fat: .453 g. Monounsaturated Fat: .69 g.
Polyunsaturated Fat: .749 g. Cholesterol: 51.3 mg. Trans Fat: .022 g. Total Omega-3 FA:
.045 g. Total Omega-6 FA: 0 g. Potassium: 383.9 mg. Sodium: 62.5 mg. Vitamin K: .209
mcg. Folic Acid: 0 mcg.

❖ STUFFED FLANK STEAK ❖

ORIGIN: SWITZERLAND
DIABETIC ACCEPTABLE

Our friends the Wingers (Marlene and Jack) visit Marlene's relatives in Switzerland often. So, when we had them over for dinner one night, the low-sodium test we made in Marlene's presence was this Swiss flank steak stuffed with Swiss cheese and spinach. Marlene used to be the home economist for Southern California Gas Company, so we felt like we were really undergoing a tough test here. But Maureen's recipe passed with flying colors.

MAKES 6 SERVINGS SODIUM PER RECIPE: 480.4 MG
SODIUM PER SERVING: 80.1 MG

2   tablespoons extra-virgin olive oil (trace)
1   cup chopped onion (4.8 mg)
5   garlic cloves, chopped or minced (2.55 mg)
4   ounces sliced mushrooms (5.04 mg)
3   cups spinach, cut into 1-inch pieces (71.1 mg)
2   ounces low-sodium Swiss cheese, grated (about ½ cup)
       (7.84 mg)*
1   tablespoon balsamic vinegar (.15 mg)
¼   teaspoon mustard powder (trace)
1½   pounds flank steak (387.8 mg)
½   cup homemade dried Basic Bread Crumbs (see page 167)
       (1,137 mg)

Prepare six 14- to 16-inch strands of kitchen string for tying the rolled
flank steak.

Heat 2 teaspoons of oil in a medium-size frying pan over medium-high
heat. Sauté the onion, garlic, and mushrooms for about 5 minutes, or until

*Check the cheese package and add whatever sodium your brand might have that increases the level.

onions are translucent and mushrooms begin to lose their juices. Drain and set aside.

In the same pan, sauté the spinach about 2 minutes, or until it begins to wilt. Drain and add to mushroom mixture.

Mix the balsamic vinegar, 1 tablespoon of the olive oil, and mustard powder. Whisk until thoroughly blended. Set aside.

Pound meat between 2 pieces of plastic wrap until it is thin enough to roll easily. Spread 1 tablespoon of the vinegar mixture over the surface of the flank steak. Mix the spinach and mushroom mixture with the remaining vinegar mixture add the bread crumbs, and mix everything together.

Place the spinach mixture on top of the flank steak. Sprinkle with grated cheese. Roll up and secure the flank steak by tying it together with the cotton strings.

Preheat the oven to 375°F.

Heat a nonstick grill or large frying pan with the remaining teaspoon of olive oil and sear the flank steak on all sides in the oil over medium-high heat. When browned, place it into a casserole dish that has been sprayed with oil.

Bake the flank steak roll for 20 to 30 minutes, or until the internal temperature reaches the desired level of doneness.*

Allow the meat to rest for a few minutes before slicing and serving.

Serve with potatoes cooked alongside the meat, or with any green vegetable.

Nutrient Values per Serving:
Calories: 286.3. Protein: 29.4 g. Carbohydrate: 8.873 g. Dietary Fiber: 1.154 g. Total Sugars: 1.951 g. Total Fat: 14.5 g. Saturated Fat: 5.282 g. Monounsaturated Fat: 6.892 g. Polyunsaturated Fat: .957 g. Cholesterol: 56.2 mg. Trans Fat: 0 g. Total Omega-3 FA: .126 g. Total Omega-6 FA: 0 g. Potassium: 604.5 mg. Sodium: 80.1 mg. Vitamin K: 76.7 mcg. Folate: 6.875 mcg.

◈ SWEET-AND-SOUR PORK BITES ◈

ORIGIN: CHINA
DIABETIC ADAPTABLE†

What do Chinese restaurants around the world feature most? That's right, sweet-and-sour pork and sweet-and-sour chicken. The flavors and textures of this recipe are straight out of China. Serve with hot steamed rice and fresh-cut vegetables or pineapple chunks.

---

*In our tests 135°F is rare. 145°F is medium. 160°F is well-done.
†If you make your soy sauce replacement with Splenda or Sugar Twin brown sugar.

THE PORK AND VEGETABLES

2   pounds lean, boneless pork (453.6 mg)
1½   tablespoons extra-virgin olive oil (trace)
½   medium green bell pepper, seeded and diced (1.785 mg)
½   medium onion, diced (1.65 mg)
8   snow peas (1.088 mg)
3   medium plum tomatoes, cut into wedges for garnish (9.3 mg)
1   tablespoon lightly toasted sesame seeds for garnish (.99 mg)
1   cup pineapple chunks, optional (9.9 mg)

THE SWEET-AND-SOUR SAUCE

¾   cup low-sodium water (trace)
2   tablespoons cornstarch (1.44 mg)
4   tablespoons Don's Soy Sauce Replacement (see page 37)
       (6.843 mg)
3   tablespoons rice vinegar (.45 mg)
⅔   cup white granulated sugar or Splenda (trace)

Cut the pork into bite-size pieces. Heat 1 tablespoon of the olive oil in a wok or large frying pan over medium-high heat. Sear the meat on all sides, then reduce the heat and cook, stirring frequently for about 5 minutes more until cooked through. Remove from heat while you prepare the vegetables and sauce.

Heat ½ tablespoon of the olive oil in a nonstick pan over medium heat and sauté the vegetables (except the tomatoes) over medium-high heat for 2 minutes; they will still be crisp. Set aside.

Make the sauce: Stir the cornstarch and water together until the cornstarch dissolves. Place all the sauce ingredients into a pan large enough to hold both the meat and the vegetables. Stir in the cornstarch mixture. Bring the sauce to a boil, stirring continually. When the sauce thickens, add the meat and turn down the heat to low. Just before serving, stir in the vegetables and reheat. Add the pineapple chunks, if using.

Serve hot by itself or over steamed rice. Garnish with the tomato wedges and the toasted sesame seeds.

Nutrient Data per Serving:
Calories: 341. Protein: 32.6 g. Carbohydrate: 30.5 g. Dietary Fiber: 1.003 g. Total Sugars: 25.4 g. Total Fat: 9.703 g. Saturated Fat: 2.445 g. Monounsaturated Fat: 4.408 g. Polyunsaturated Fat: 2.169 g. Cholesterol: 98.3 mg. Trans Fat: 0 g. Total Omega-3 FA: .039 g. Total Omega-6 FA: 0 g. Potassium: 728.1 mg. Sodium: 79.5 mg. Vitamin K: 3.997 mcg. Folic Acid: 0 mcg.

LIGHT MEALS

Some of us like to graze during the day. That means we don't sit and eat a full meal on those days. Grazing is just what it sounds like: a little of this and that now and then that gets you through the day with proper nutrition and calories without feeling "stuffed" from a full meal. It's not random, though. My grazing is pretty much controlled ahead of time. Planning makes grazing easier.

Sometimes I just don't feel like having a big meal, so I'll have a bowl of soup, a salad, or a light sandwich. Of course, we prepare some of these recipes ahead of time and store them in the refrigerator.

In this section, we introduce light-meal eating from around the world. Beginning with Alexander's Caesar Salad, this section contains recipes from Vietnam, Italy, Mexico, Japan, and other countries, including a few from the United States. Choose from sandwiches and salads and a great Chicken Noodle Soup as well as Gazpacho and Minestrone. You can use our panini sandwich as a base to build your own version of a panini. Nearly anything works with this exciting Italian invention. Even unsalted peanut butter and jam.

Not only will you keep your calories down, you'll cut deeply into your dietary sodium intake and you won't go hungry.

ORIGIN: MEXICO*
DIABETIC ACCEPTABLE

This salad is named "Alexander's Caesar Salad" because of our three-year-old grandson, Alexander, who took one bite of the salad, kneeled on his chair to get closer to his plate, and devoured the entire plate with gusto. Afterward, he announced, "This is the best salad I ever ate. It's delicious!"

MAKES 12 TABLESPOONS OF DRESSING, OR 6 SERVINGS†
SODIUM PER RECIPE: 113.7 MG
SODIUM PER TABLESPOON: 18.7 MG

THE DRESSING
4 tablespoons extra-virgin olive oil (trace)
2 tablespoons fresh lemon juice (.372 mg)
4 garlic cloves (2.04 mg)
  Pinch of ground white pepper (trace)
½ cup sour cream (60.9 mg)
2 ounces low-sodium Swiss cheese, grated (about ½ cup)
  (8.4 mg)‡

THE SALAD
18 ounces loosely chopped romaine (49.3 mg)

Place the oil, lemon juice, cloves, and pepper into a processor and puree until smooth.

Pour into a bowl, add the sour cream and grated cheese, and stir with wooden spoon until well mixed.

Toss with the romaine in a large salad bowl.

---

*Many culinary historians claim that the Caesar salad originated in a Tijuana, Mexico, restaurant by Caesar Cardini, an Italian restaurateur, circa 1924. Cardini's original salad contained lots of salt, egg yolks, grated Parmesan, Worcestershire sauce, and anchovies. We've enjoyed the recipe as presented here for years, and we think you'll like it, too. And no, it wasn't named after Julius Caesar.
†We figure 2 tablespoons per serving when tossed in loosely chopped romaine. You can make the entire dressing recipe and store it in an airtight container in your refrigerator for up to a week.
‡The USDA rates low-sodium Swiss cheese 4.2 mg per ounce. Packages may show 5 mg. Not all low-sodium Swiss cheese is this low.

Nutrient Data per Serving:
Calories: 177. Protein: 4.63 g. Carbohydrate: 5.121 g. Dietary Fiber: 1.832 g. Total Sugars: 1.33 g. Total Fat: 16 g. Saturated Fat: 5.52 g. Monounsaturated Fat: 8.547 g. Polyunsaturated Fat: 1.286 g. Cholesterol: 17.6 mg. Trans Fat: 0 g. Total Omega-3 FA: .26 g. Total Omega-6 FA: 0 g. Potassium: 262 mg. Sodium: 18.7 mg. Vitamin K: 92 mcg. Folic Acid: 0 mcg.

❈ VIETNAMESE BÁNH MÌ ❈

ORIGIN: VIETNAM
NOT DIABETIC RECOMMENDED*

This is a huge favorite in Saigon, with street vendors selling thousands of sandwiches just like this one—every day. It's like a hoagie, and so easy to make that you just might end up doing it more than a few times. The Vietnamese, of course, use their version of Thailand's nam plah, which is called nuoc mam. as well as soy sauce. We've fixed that so that you can enjoy the same flavors without the high sodium. Also, they sometimes use mayonnaise for the spread. We've changed that by using a sour cream/yogurt mix. Note: One half of this sandwich may prove filling and that's a good thing, because it will cut the calories in half.

MAKES 4 SANDWICHES   SODIUM PER RECIPE: 341.6 MG
SODIUM PER SANDWICH: 85.4 MG

THE MARINADE RUB
3   tablespoons chopped shallots or green onions† (3.6 mg)
4   garlic cloves, crushed in garlic press (2.04 mg)
2   tablespoons Don's Soy Sauce Replacement (see page 37) (3.422 mg)
1   and ½ teaspoons sugar or Splenda (trace)
½   teaspoon Chinese five-spice powder‡ (trace)
¼   teaspoon aniseed, ground (.084 mg)
¾   pound boneless, skinless, chicken thighs or boneless, skinless, chicken breast meat, no fat (230.1 mg)
1   tablespoon olive oil (trace)

*Most of the carbohydrates in this recipe come from the bread and the marinated radishes and carrots.
†Shallots look more like garlic, being composed of multiple cloves with each clove covered by a thin skin. If you can't find shallots, use green onions.
‡You may also use McCormick's or another commercial Chinese five-spice powder.

THE SANDWICH

4 6-inch-long homemade French Baguette rolls (see page 165)
  (17.5 mg) or Ciabatta (page 173)
2 tablespoons light sour cream (25 mg)
2 tablespoons plain yogurt (12.7 mg)
1 cup Marinated Radishes and Carrots, drained (see page 229)
  (43.3 mg)
⅓ red onion, thinly sliced (1.09 mg)
4 sprigs cilantro, or 1 teaspoon ground coriander (.63 mg)
½ English cucumber, peeled and cut into long thin strips
  (2.01 mg)
  Black or white pepper (trace)

Bring together the shallots or chopped onions, garlic, Soy Sauce Replacement, sugar, Chinese five-spice powder, olive oil, and the aniseed in a shallow baking dish and stir until well combined into a paste. Cut shallow slits into the meat and rub in the mixture paste. Refrigerate for 1 hour.

For the following step we use an All-Clad nonstick plain-top griddle (one of our favorite cooking utensils). Preheat your griddle over medium high heat then cook the chicken on each side until done. (If not using nonstick, rub your grill with additional olive oil before cooking chicken.)

Remove the chicken when done and keep warm.

Cut out or pull out a little of the center bread from the baguette buns, then toast the baguettes on the same griddle until crispy but not burned. Cut the chicken into thin strips.

Mix the yogurt and sour cream together. Spoon it into the cavity of each bun and then layer with the marinated radish and carrots. On top of that, place the thinly sliced chicken strips, onion slices, a cilantro sprig, and cucumber and sprinkle the sandwich with Don's Soy Sauce Replacement. Season with black or white pepper to taste.

Nutrient Data per Serving:
Calories: 745.4. Protein: 36.2 g. Carbohydrate: 134.7 g. Dietary Fiber: 5.729 g. Total Sugars: 32.3 g. Total Fat: 6.726 g. Saturated Fat: 1.409 g. Monounsaturated Fat: 3.083 g. Polyunsaturated Fat: 1.175 g. Cholesterol: 59.9 mg. Trans Fat: .022 g. Total Omega-3 FA: .96 g. Total Omega-6 FA: 0 g. Potassium: 702 mg. Sodium: 85.4 mg. Vitamin K: 5.304 mcg. Folic Acid: 0 mcg.

❖ Black Bean Dip ❖

Origin: South America
Diabetic Acceptable

Set this one out at a party with some unsalted tortilla chips and watch it fly away. Tangy without salt, this is an amazing dip from South America.

Makes 24 tablespoons   Sodium per Recipe: 60.6 mg
Sodium per Tablespoon: 2.526 mg

1   teaspoon olive oil (trace)
½   medium onion, chopped (3.3 mg)
2   garlic cloves (1.01 mg)
¼   large green bell pepper, seeded and chopped (1.23 mg)
½   jalapeño pepper, seeded and chopped (.07 mg)
½   teaspoon ground cumin (1.764 mg)
¼   teaspoon cayenne pepper (.135 mg)
1   (14.5-ounce) can Eden Organic no-salt black beans, drained
     (52.5 mg)
2   tablespoons fresh lemon or lime juice (.615 mg)
1   tablespoon low-sodium water (trace)
2   tablespoons chopped fresh cilantro (trace)

Heat the oil in a frying pan and add the onion, garlic, green pepper, and jalapeño. Sauté on low heat about 5 minutes, or until the vegetables become soft and the onions translucent; do not brown. Sprinkle the spices on the vegetables and cook for an additional minute.

Place the beans, lemon juice, water, cilantro, and the cooked vegetables in a food processor or blender. Process the mixture until it is smooth. Remove and place the dip in a serving bowl, cover, and chill for at least an hour. Serve with unsalted tortilla chips.

Nutrient Data per Tablespoon:
Calories: 20. Protein: 1.138 g. Carbohydrate: 3.48 g. Dietary Fiber: .121 g. Total Sugars: .274 g. Total Fat: .211 g. Saturated Fat: .029 g. Monounsaturated Fat: .147 g. Polyunsaturated Fat: .028 g. Cholesterol: 0 mg. Trans Fat: 0 g. Total Omega-3 FA: .002 g. Total Omega-6 FA: 0 g. Potassium: 54.7 mg. Sodium: 2.526 mg. Vitamin K: .315 mcg. Folic Acid: 0 mcg.

✪ BRUSCHETTA ✪

Origin: Italy
Diabetic Acceptable

Truly Italian, this toasted treat can be used for a snack, an appetizer, or just your lunch. Easy to make, all you need is a loaf of our Tuscan bread handy and, voilà! Bruschetta.

Makes 4 to 8 servings · Sodium per Recipe: 14 mg
Sodium per Serving (4): 3.491 mg
Sodium per Serving (8): 1.746 mg

4 **six-inch-thick slices Tuscan Bread (see page 192) (4.224 mg)**
2 **garlic cloves, peeled, cut (1.02 mg)**
1 **medium ripe red tomato (6.15 mg)**
1 **teaspoon dried basil (.476 mg)**
4 **teaspoons extra-virgin olive oil (trace)**

Toast the bread; or set on a hot barbecue grill until toasted, then turn and lightly toast the other side.

Gently rub hot toasted pieces with garlic. Then lay very thin slices of the tomato on the toast, sprinkle with a light touch of fresh or dried basil, and add pepper to taste. Then drizzle a ½ tablespoon of olive oil on each piece.

VARIATIONS

Use fresh basil instead of dried. Add thinly sliced onion, bell pepper, or any other vegetable you like thinly sliced.

Nutrient Data per Serving (4):
Calories: 135.6. Protein: 3.228 g. Carbohydrate: 18.3 g. Dietary Fiber: 1.43 g. Total Sugars: 1.221 g. Total Fat: 5.768 g. Saturated Fat: .84 g. Monounsaturated Fat: 2.476 g. Polyunsaturated Fat: 1.999 g. Cholesterol: 0 mg. Trans Fat: 0 g. Total Omega-3 FA: .033 g. Total Omega-6 FA: 0 g. Potassium: 156.7 mg. Sodium: 3.491 mg. Vitamin K: 9.59 mcg. Folic Acid: 25.6 mcg.

Nutrient Data per Serving (8):
Calories: 67.8. Protein: 1.614 g. Carbohydrate: 9.173 g. Dietary Fiber: .715 g. Total Sugars: .611 g. Total Fat: 2.884 g. Saturated Fat: .42 g. Monounsaturated Fat: 1.238 g. Polyunsaturated Fat: 1 g. Cholesterol: 0 mg. Trans Fat: 0 g. Total Omega-3 FA: .016 g. Total Omega-6 FA: 0 g. Potassium: 78.4 mg. Sodium: 1.746 mg. Vitamin K: 4.795 mcg. Folic Acid: 12.8 mcg.

*Diabetics, most of the carbohydrates come from the bread.

❖ OUR BEST BURRITO ❖

ORIGIN: MEXICO
DIABETIC ADAPTABLE*

Who needs fast-food burritos when you can make your own delicious burritos, and with no salt, salted products, or added sodium. These are made with our own Flour Tortillas (see page 182) and no-salt-added, fat-free canned beans from Eden Organic. You can purchase Eden Organic from www.healthyheartmarket.com *or visit* www .megaheart.com/wheretobuy.html.

MAKES 4 BURRITOS   SODIUM PER RECIPE: 112.1 MG
SODIUM PER BURRITO: 28 MG

1   **(15-ounce) can Eden Organic Pinto Beans; do not drain (52.5 mg)**
½   **medium onion, chopped (1.65 mg)**
3   **garlic cloves, minced or chopped (1.53 mg)**
½   **(4-ounce) can Ortega brand diced green chilies (50 mg)**
2   **ounces low-sodium Cheddar cheese, grated† (20 mg)**
    Juice of 1 lime (.76 mg)
4   **homemade flour tortillas (5.617 mg)**

In a nonstick frying pan, "refry" the beans over medium heat. Smash half of the beans with a wooden spoon while cooking. Add onion, garlic, and chilies and cook until onions are cooked. Stir often. If you like spicy beans, add a little chili powder or cayenne pepper.

Spread the beans on the four tortillas. Squeeze lime juice over top and sprinkle ½ ounce of grated cheese over each one. Heat in a microwave or on a grill just until cheese melts; the tortilla will roll up easily when warmed.

Nutrient Values per Serving:
Calories: 351.8. Protein: 10.1 g. Carbohydrate: 55.4 g. Dietary Fiber: 6.719 g. Total Sugars: .79 g. Total Fat: 9.457 g. Saturated Fat: 1.289 g. Monounsaturated Fat: 6.677 g. Polyunsaturated Fat: .949 g. Cholesterol: 0 mg. Trans Fat: 0 g. Total Omega-3 FA: .064 g. Total Omega-6 FA: 0 g. Potassium: 451 mg. Sodium: 28 mg. Vitamin K: 4.554 mcg. Folic Acid: 0 mcg.

*Diabetics, most of the carbohydrates come from the tortillas. Some are in the beans.
†Heluva Good cheese; Rumiano, or a low-sodium Swiss all work well.

✦ CHICKEN NOODLE SOUP ✦

ORIGIN: WORLDWIDE
DIABETIC ACCEPTABLE

MAKES 4 SERVINGS   SODIUM PER RECIPE: 447.2 MG
SODIUM PER SERVING: 111.8 MG

1 teaspoon olive oil (trace)
1 cup chopped onion (4.8 mg)
3 garlic cloves, minced (1.53 mg)
1 cup chopped celery (80.8 mg)
2 medium carrots, peeled and sliced (about 1 cup) (84.2 mg)
2 tablespoons chopped fresh parsley (4.256 mg)
4 cups Maureen's Easy Chicken Broth (see page 113) (151.1 mg)
4 ounces (¼ package) linguini, cooked to directions (23.9 mg)
1 cup cooked nonbrined chicken breast, cut into desired size
   (skin and bones removed) (92.3 mg)

Heat the olive oil over medium heat and sauté the onion and garlic until translucent. Add the celery and carrots and continue to sauté for another 3 minutes.

Add the chicken broth, bring to a boil, turn down the heat, and simmer for 15 minutes.

Meanwhile, prepare the linguini according to the package directions.

Add the cooked chicken, chopped parsley, and drained, cooked noodles to the broth.

Bring the soup to a boil. Serve hot.

Nutritional Data per Serving (4):
Calories: 260.6. Protein: 18.5 g. Carbohydrate: 32.9 g. Dietary Fiber: 3.578 g. Total Sugars: 5.549 g. Total Fat: 6.143 g. Saturated Fat: 1.583 g. Monounsaturated Fat: 2.362 g. Polyunsaturated Fat: 1.435 g. Cholesterol: 71.2 mg. Trans Fat: .009 g. Total Omega-3 FA: .084 g. Total Omega-6 FA: 0 g. Potassium: 556.2 g. Sodium: 111.8 mg. Vitamin K: 48.8 mcg. Folic Acid: 61.6 mcg.

✦ CHILI RELLENO CASSEROLE ✦

ORIGIN: MEXICO
DIABETIC ACCEPTABLE

Using fresh chilies gives you the real chili relleno flavor. There is a bite to the chilies unlike those that are canned, which are also higher in sodium.

MAKES 2 SERVINGS   SODIUM PER RECIPE: 168.7 MG
SODIUM PER SERVING: 84.3 MG

4   **large, thick, whole Anaheim or poblano chilies (12.6 mg)**
4   **ounces of low-sodium Swiss cheese, half grated, half cut into
      fingers* (15.7 mg)**
2   **large eggs (140 mg)**
¾   **cup nonfat milk with added vitamins A & D (77.2 mg)**
2   **teaspoons unbleached, all-purpose flour (.225 mg)**
⅛   **teaspoon ground white pepper (trace)**

Roast the chilies under the broiler or on a barbecue grill until the skins darken and the chilies begins to soften. The skin will blister, which it needs to do in order to be removed.

Place the chilies into a ziplock bag and seal. Set aside to steam and cool for at least 30 minutes. Another technique, perhaps less time consuming, is to place them in a paper bag and shake them until the skins loosen.

Scrape off all the charred skins from the chilies and discard the stems. Make a slit in the side of each and deseed them.

Preheat the oven to 400°F.

Place a finger of cheese in each chili and place in an 8×8-inch casserole dish that has been sprayed with oil.

Beat the eggs in a small bowl until light and frothy. Add the milk, flour, and pepper and mix until the flour is well incorporated. Pour the mixture over the chilies.

Sprinkle the grated cheese over the top and place the casserole in the oven, and bake the casserole for 25 minutes; it will be lightly browned around the edges.

Nutrient Data per Serving:
Calories: 335.5. Protein: 24.5 g. Carbohydrate: 19.6 g. Dietary Fiber: 1.541 g. Total Sugars: 10.2 g. Total Fat: 18.1 g. Saturated Fat: 10.8 g. Monounsaturated Fat: 5.075 g. Polyunsaturated Fat: 1.012 g. Cholesterol: 159.1 mg. Trans Fat: 0 g. Total Omega-3 FA: .221 g. Total Omega-6 FA: 0 g. Potassium: 551.1 mg. Sodium: 84.3 mg. Vitamin K: 14.3 mcg. Folic Acid: 8.663 mcg.

*Varieties of low-sodium Swiss cheese can be found throughout the world. Ask your grocer if he can get it for you. If you find a brand locally, please let us know at http:// www.megaheart.com (e-mail: don@megaheart.com) and we'll post it to help others locate it as well.

ORIGIN:AFRICA
DIABETIC ACCEPTABLE*

Our first book, The *No-Salt Lowest-Sodium* Cookbook, *has a few paella recipes that came to us from a close friend who lived in Spain at the time. Spain (Valencia) is where the paella pan was first created and it was made out of iron. The word "paella" comes from the Latin "patella," shallow. A paella pan is circular, shallow, and flat. Usually it has round handles on opposite sides. Paellas are usually made with rice ("arroz"), but in North Africa they prefer to use couscous—a wheat dish first made popular in Morocco. Couscous was first created in the Arab world.*

**MAKES 2 SERVINGS   SODIUM PER RECIPE: 119.3 MG
SODIUM PER SERVING: 59.6 MG**

1   tablespoons olive oil (trace)
½   cup each seeded and chopped red and green bell pepper
     (1 to 2) (4.47 mg), and 1 bunch scallions, some green
     parts, chopped 8 (8 mg)
4   garlic cloves, minced (2.04 mg)
2   small tomatoes, seeded and chopped (9.1 mg)
1   tablespoon chopped fresh cilantro (trace)
½   teaspoon ground turmeric (.836 mg)
1/16 teaspoon cayenne pepper (trace)
1⅓   cups low-sodium water (trace)
8   shelled large salt-free and nonbrined shrimp (83.9 mg)
1   cup snow peas (or substitute green peas) (2.52 mg)
⅔   cup couscous (11.14 mg)
     White pepper (trace)
¼   cup toasted slivered almonds (.03 mg)
2   tablespoons chopped fresh parsley (4.256 mg)
½   lemon, cut into wedges (1.62 mg)

Heat the olive oil in a 3-quart saucepan or deep-fry pan.

Sauté the peppers, scallions, and garlic over medium heat for 5 minutes until the peppers are soft. Add the tomatoes, cilantro, turmeric, and cayenne and cook for an additional minute.

Stir in the water and bring to a boil. Add the shrimp, turn down the heat, and simmer for another 3 to 4 minutes, or until the shrimp is pink.

*Most of the carbohydrates are in the couscous grain (88.4 mg), the bell peppers (7 g), and the tomatoes (7.1 g) have the balance.

Stir in the snow peas and cook for another minute.

Mix in the couscous. Cover, remove from heat, and let the mixture steam for 5 minutes.

Uncover the pan and, using a fork, fluff up the couscous. Add white pepper to taste.

Stir in toasted silvered almonds and chopped parsley, or sprinkle them on top; whichever you prefer. Serve the dish accompanied with the lemon wedges.

Nutrient Data per Serving:
Calories: 380.9. Protein: 16.9 g. Carbohydrate: 62.2 g. Dietary Fiber: 8.488 g. Total Sugars: 4.324 g. Total Fat: 8.368 g. Saturated Fat: 1.24 g. Monounsaturated Fat: 5.26 g. Polyunsaturated Fat: 1.318 g. Cholesterol: 42.6 mg. Trans Fat: 0 g. Total Omega-3 FA: .236 g. Total Omega-6 FA: 0 g. Iron: 3.888 mg. Potassium: 740.6 mg. Sodium: 63.6 mg. Vitamin K: 79.4 mcg. Folic Acid: 0 mcg.

❖ CURRIED CHICKEN SALAD ❖

ORIGIN: INDIA
DIABETIC ADAPTABLE*

This recipe makes for interesting variations when serving it. You can make a lunch salad out of it, serve it in a pita pocket bread, or serve as a side dish. It's tasty, loaded with good nutrients, and easy to make.

MAKES 4 SERVINGS   SODIUM PER RECIPE: 285.2 MG
SODIUM PER SERVING: 71.3 MG

THE SALAD
4   cups low-sodium water
1   teaspoon dried dill (2.08 mg)
½   small onion, thinly sliced (1.05 mg)
10   ounces chicken tenders or boneless, skinless chicken breast
       cut into strips (184.1 mg)
¼   cup plain regular yogurt† (28.4 mg)
¼   cup sour cream (25.4 mg)
1   tablespoon fresh lemon juice (.153 mg)
1   tablespoon curry powder (3.276 mg)
¼   cup golden raisins (4.95 mg)
¼   cup chutney (7.357 mg)
2   medium unpeeled apples, cored and chopped finely

*Diabetics may exchange raisins with unsalted peanuts or leave them out altogether.
†You may exchange ¼ cup sour cream for the yogurt, making recipe total for sour cream ½ cup. This will make the mixture thicker.

THE PITA OR SALAD

4   **Don's Pocket Pita Bread (see page 176) (24.4 mg), optional**
¼   **small red onion, diced or chopped (.5 mg)**
2   **cups favorite lettuce or mixed greens (27.9 mg)**
     White pepper (trace)

Boil 4 cups of low-sodium water in a pan with the dill and onion. When the water boils, add the chicken strips and cook for about 5 minutes, or until thoroughly cooked.

When the chicken is cooked, drain, place in a small bowl, and let cool. Cover and refrigerate for 1 hour, or until cold.

Place the yogurt, sour cream, lemon juice, curry powder, raisins, and chutney into a small bowl and mix the dressing thoroughly.

Put the chopped apples and the cold chicken in a medium bowl. Pour the dressing over and mix well.

Serve the salad on lettuce of your choice or in pita bread. Make available chopped lettuce, thinly sliced red onion, and lemon wedge for the sandwiches. Provide white pepper to use per taste.

Nutrient Data per Serving with Pita Bread:
Calories: 304.2. Protein: 23.1 g. Carbohydrate: 40.7 g. Dietary Fiber: 3.874 g. Total Sugars: 6.82 g. Total Fat: 5.882 g. Saturated Fat: 2.417 g. Monounsaturated Fat: 2.085 g. Polyunsaturated Fat: .682 g. Cholesterol: 48.3 mg. Trans-Fatty Acids: .018 g. Total Omega-3 FA: .091 g. Total Omega-6 FA: 0 g. Iron: 7.533 mg. Potassium: 540.3 mg. Sodium: 71.3 mg. Vitamin K: 2.798 mcg. Folic Acid: 0 mcg.

Nutrient Data Per Serving Without Pita Bread:
Calories: 161.1. Protein: 18.5 g. Carbohydrate: 13 g. Dietary Fiber: 1.636 g. Total Sugars: 6.82 g. Total Fat: 4.246 g. Saturated Fat: 2.184 g. Monounsaturated Fat: 1.171 g. Polyunsaturated Fat: .402 g. Cholesterol: 48.3 mg. Trans-Fatty Acids: .018 g. Total Omega-3 FA: .075 g. Total Omega-6 FA: 0 g. Iron: 1.684 mg. Potassium: 441.9 mg. Sodium: 69.5 mg. Vitamin K: 2.247 mcg. Folic Acid: 0 mcg.

❖ FAJITAS ❖

ORIGIN: MEXICO
DIABETIC ACCEPTABLE*

Here's another recipe from Dixie Guillen. This authentic Mexican recipe will truly delight your tastebuds.

MAKES 16 FAJITAS   SODIUM PER RECIPE: 673.4 MG
SODIUM PER FAJITA: 42.1 MG†

*Sugars and carbohydrates are in the onions (6.99 mg), green pepper (2.856 g), granulated sugar (4.196 g), and lime juice (1.384 g). Figures are for sugars listed for total recipe.
†Add sodium for any additions you make to your fajitas.

THE MARINADE

½ **cup extra-virgin olive oil (trace)**
¼ **cup red wine vinegar (.60 mg)**
⅓ **cup fresh lime juice (1.638 mg)**
⅓ **cup chopped onion (1.598 mg)**
1 **jalapeño pepper, seeded and chopped (.14 mg)**
1 **teaspoon white granulated sugar or Splenda (trace)**
1 **teaspoon dried oregano (.27 mg)**
½ **teaspoon ground black pepper (.462 mg)**
¼ **teaspoon ground cumin (.882 mg)**
3 **cloves garlic, minced (1.53 mg)**

THE FAJITAS

2 **pounds nonbrined, boneless, skinless chicken breast, cut into strips (613.6 mg)**
16 **corn tortillas‡ (45.8 mg)**
1 **teaspoon olive oil (trace)**
1 **medium green bell pepper, seeded and cut into strips (trace)**
1 **medium onion, cut in half and sliced (3.3 mg)**

Mix the marinade ingredients together. Place the chicken strips in a glass dish and cover with marinade. Cover the dish. Marinate the chicken for 8 hours in the refrigerator.

When ready to cook and serve the fajitas, heat the 1 teaspoon of olive oil on a nonstick grill or frying pan and cook the pepper and onion slices until they soften and turn slightly brown. Transfer to a plate and keep warm.

Remove the chicken from the marinade. Grill the chicken for 6 to 7 minutes on each side. Transfer to a plate and keep warm.

Warm the corn tortillas one at a time in a dry, nonstick frying pan. When soft enough to roll, place a small amount of the chicken and pepper and onion strips in the center of each and roll. As they are prepared, keep them warm on the grill while fixing the others. Serve all at once. The recipe may be cut in half if necessary.

Delicious served with Fresh Salsa (see page 39), sour cream, and Guacamole (see page 38).

Nutrient Data per Fajita:
Calories: 176.3. Protein: 15.4 g. Carbohydrate: 14.8 g. Dietary Fiber: 1.747 g. Total Sugars: 1.227 g. Total Fat: 6.341 g. Saturated Fat: .996 g. Monounsaturated Fat: 2.785 g. Polyunsaturated Fat: 2.037 g. Cholesterol: 34.2 mg. Trans Fat: .015 g. Total Omega-3 FA: .061 g. Total Omega-6 FA: 0 g. Potassium: 235.4 mg. Sodium: 42.1 mg. Vitamin K: 2.782 mcg. Folate: 36 mcg. Folic Acid: 25.7 mcg.

‡Most commercial corn tortillas will list sodium between 0 and 10 mg sodium per tortilla. Packages with zero (0) will actually have about 2.14 mg sodium per tortilla.

❖ GAZPACHO ❖

ORIGIN: SPAIN
DIABETICS, SEE FOOTNOTE*

This wonderful Spanish soup is good any time of year. It's most delicious when juicy, vine-ripened tomatoes are in season.

—Maureen

MAKES 6 CUPS   SODIUM PER RECIPE: 194.8 MG
SODIUM PER CUP: 32.5 MG

4 **large tomatoes (about 1½ pounds), chopped (36.4 mg)**
6 **garlic cloves, chopped (3.06 mg)**
1 **large cucumber or 2 small, peeled, seeded, and chopped
     (5.6 mg)**
1 **cup chopped celery (80.8 mg)**
1 **cup red onion, chopped (4.8 mg)**
1 **large red bell pepper, seeded and chopped (3.28 mg)**
1 **cup canned, diced, no-salt-added tomatoes, with their juice†
     (60 mg)**
¼ **cup red wine vinegar (.60 mg)**
¼ **teaspoon tarragon (.248 mg)**

Place all the ingredients in a large bowl and toss. Pour into a blender or food processor and process 2 cups at a time until pureed. If possible, continue by adding the unprocessed vegetables as well. If the blender is too small, remove some of the soup and then add the vegetables. Be sure to use some of the liquid as you blend each batch. Chill well before serving. If you plan to serve it immediately, chill the canned tomatoes before using.

This recipe makes up to 6 servings. It is especially nice served with a few toppings. Here are some suggestions: chopped green onion, cucumber, green pepper, and avocado. Accompany with unsalted tortilla chips.

Nutrient Data per Cup:
Calories: 62.5. Protein: 2.514 g. Carbohydrate: 13.6 g. Dietary Fiber: 3.373 g. Total Sugars: 8.052 g. Total Fat: .469 g. Saturated Fat: .096 g. Monounsaturated Fat: .077 g. Polyunsaturated Fat: .248 g. Cholesterol: 0 mg. Trans Fat: 0 g. Total Omega-3 FA: .023 g. Total Omega-6 FA: 0 g. Potassium: 568.2 mg. Sodium: 32.5 mg. Vitamin K: 19.4 mcg. Folic Acid: 0 mcg.

*The carbohydrates in this recipe come mostly from the vegetables. You can refer to the Nutrient Tables in the back of the book for all vegetables and the levels of carbohydrates they contain. (See pages 339–345).
†Fill the cup with the tomatoes and the liquid that comes with them.

◈ MINESTRONE SOUP ◈

ORIGIN: ITALY
DIABETIC ACCEPTABLE

With a smile, I tell you this is our best minestrone recipe yet. Minestrone has so many variations that each time we make it we do it differently and this is the best no-salt version we've ever come up with. Hope you enjoy it.

MAKES 8 TO 10 SERVINGS   SODIUM PER RECIPE: 607.5 MG
SODIUM PER SERVING: 60.8 MG

2   cups dried white beans (32.3 mg)
1   tablespoon extra-virgin olive oil (trace)
1   cup chopped onion (4.8 mg)
3   cloves garlic, minced (1.53 mg)
½   cup green bell pepper, chopped (1.49 mg)
1   cup celery, chopped (80 mg)
2   (14.5 ounce) cans no-salt-added tomatoes (210 mg)
2   small red potatoes, chopped (20.4 mg)
     Low-sodium or distilled water: fill each tomato can, plus one
         cup (trace)
1   large carrot, sliced (49.7 mg)
1½   cups cooked Don's Mock Sausage (page 106)*
         (223.2 mg)
½   teaspoon onion powder (1.863 mg)
½   teaspoon oregano (.112 mg)
1   teaspoon basil (.476 mg)
1   cup green string beans, sliced to 1" lengths (6.6 mg)

Prepare white beans per package instructions, except for any suggested use of salt or fat.

In a 12-quart saucepan, sauté the onion and the garlic until the onion is translucent. Add the green peppers and the celery and continue cooking for about 3 to 5 minutes.

Add the tomatoes and the water. Bring to a boil, turn down to a simmer, and add the rest of the vegetables and spices except for the green beans.

After 20 minutes, add the green beans, cooked white beans, and cooked sausage and continue to cook for an additional 15 minutes.

Add white pepper to taste. Serve hot.

*Crumble and cook the 10 ounces of sausage. There is no need to make patties. (You'll have some left over. You can cook it as patties for another meal.)

Nutrient Data per Serving:
Calories: 175.7. Protein: 10.2 g. Carbohydrate: 21.5 g. Dietary Fiber: 4.225 g. Total Sugars: 3.927 g. Total Fat: 5.368 g. Saturated Fat: 1.453 g. Monounsaturated Fat: 2.635 g. Polyunsaturated Fat: .816 g. Cholesterol: 21.1 mg. Trans Fat: .048 g. Total Omega-3 FA: .052 g. Total Omega-6 FA: 0 g. Iron: 2.224 mg. Potassium: 654.9 mg. Sodium: 60.8 mg. Vitamin K: 10.4 mcg. Folic Acid: 0 mcg.

◈ ITALIAN DELIGHT SANDWICH ◈

ORIGIN: ITALY
DIABETIC ADAPTABLE*

Use your homemade Ciabatta bread for this exciting sandwich that bursts with flavor and freshness.

I first came up with this while in Italy visiting with an IBM executive in Milan. He had a table spread with so much food he could have fed half the country. (I exaggerate of course.) I chose what I wanted and found myself enjoying this so much it has remained in my portfolio of recipes since. I think you'll enjoy it, too.

MAKES 1 SANDWICH   SODIUM PER RECIPE: 31.7 MG

1 **homemade Ciabatta (see page 173)† (1.982 mg)**
2 **slices ripe avocado (1.73 mg)**
2 **tablespoons fresh whole-milk ricotta (26 mg)**
2 **thin slices tomato (1.35 mg)**
5 **fresh basil leaves (.1 mg)**
1 **teaspoon extra-virgin olive oil (trace)**
1 **teaspoon balsamic vinegar (.05 mg)**
3 **thin slices English cucumber (.42 mg)**

Very lightly toast the inside of the bun.

Using a fork, mix the avocado and ricotta together until spreadable. Spread on the lower half of the sandwich bun. Lay the tomato slices on the spread and then the basil leaves.

Stir together the olive oil and vinegar and sprinkle the basil leaves with about half of it. Lay the cucumber on top of that and then sprinkle the remaining olive oil mix on the inside of the top sandwich bread. Join and enjoy!

*The bread has 24 grams of carbohydrates.
†Make your Ciabatta recipe into sandwich buns per our recipe (see page 173) and freeze those you want to save in ziplock bags.

Nutrient Data per Sandwich:
Calories: 236.7. Protein: 8.169 g. Carbohydrate: 29.1 g. Dietary Fiber: 3.006 g. Total Sugars: 1.448 g. Total Fat: 10 g. Saturated Fat: 3.402 g. Monounsaturated Fat: 4.952 g. Polyunsaturated Fat: .9 g. Cholesterol: 15.8 mg. Trans Fat: 0 g. Total Omega-3 FA: .118 g. Total Omega-6 FA: .003 g. Potassium: 300.5 mg. Sodium: 31.7 mg. Vitamin K: 20.2 mcg. Folic Acid: 0 mcg.

❖ PESTO CHICKEN SANDWICH ❖

ORIGIN: ITALY
DIABETIC ADAPTABLE

Searching for something really different yet tasty and nutritious? Try this one. Make our basic pesto and our buttermilk bread buns. Then grill a juicy boneless, skinless chicken breast, use a bit of low-sodium Swiss or low-sodium mozzarella with it, and, Wow! Spectacular flavors burst in your mouth.

MAKES 6 SANDWICHES   SODIUM PER RECIPE: 267.6 MG
SODIUM PER SANDWICH: 44.6 MG

3 **chicken half breasts, butterflied and pounded lightly to an even thickness (230.1 mg)**
6 **buns made from Ciabatta Bread recipe (see page 173) (11.9 mg)**
1 **recipe (6 servings) Pesto for Chicken Sandwiches (see page 50) (4.128 mg)**
6 **medium slices tomato (8.1)**
6 **thin slices onion (1.62 mg)**
3 **ounces low-sodium Swiss cheese, thinly sliced or grated (11.8 mg)**
6 **leaves lettuce (your choice) (1.26 mg)†**

Grill or broil the chicken on a nonstick griddle or in a nonstick pan. If using a standard pan, use a light spritz of olive oil spray.

Lightly toast the opened buns, melt the cheese on the top bun.

Spread the pesto generously across the bottom bun. Lay each chicken piece on the sandwich bun. Layer with the tomato, onion, and lettuce and bring together. Serve hot or warm.

†Data figured on inner leaves of Butterhead (Bibb) lettuce. Iceberg inner leaves would be (11.4 mg) per 6 leaves. Romaine inner leaves would be (2.88 mg) sodium for 6 leaves.

Nutrient Data per Sandwich
Calories: 410.1. Protein: 23 g. Carbohydrate: 28.6 g. Dietary Fiber: 1.999 g. Total Sugars: 1.581 g. Total Fat: 22.7 g. Saturated Fat: 4.815 g. Monounsaturated Fat: 12 g. Polyunsaturated Fat: 4.285 g. Cholesterol: 47.1 mg. Trans Fat: .015 g. Total Omega-3 FA: .222 g. Total Omega-6 FA: .034 g. Potassium: 375.4 mg. Sodium: 44.6 mg. Vitamin K: 43.5 mcg. Folic Acid: 0 mcg.

◈ JAMBALAYA ◈

ORIGIN: SOUTHERN U.S.A.
DIABETICS SEE FOOTNOTE*

Whether you're a Hank Williams fan or not, the word "jambalaya" most likely entered your vocabulary through his song "Jambalaya." This version is as authentic as you can get (without added salt), and with a brand-new Cajun spice mix from the creative spice girl herself, Maureen. And by the way, this is a surprisingly easy one-pot meal.

MAKES 6 SERVINGS   SODIUM PER RECIPE: 612.7 MG
SODIUM PER SERVING: 102.1 MG

½   **pound ground pork (126.6 mg)**
1½   **teaspoons Maureen's Cajun Spice Mix (see page 43)**
        (2.229 mg)
½   **pound boneless, skinless chicken half breasts cut into**
        1½-inch chunks (153.4 mg)
½   **pound (about 12) nonbrined, unsalted shrimp† (124.3 mg)**
2   **tablespoons olive oil (trace)**
1½   **cups chopped onion (7.2 mg)**
1   **green bell pepper, seeded and chopped (about 1 cup) (4.47**
        mg)
6   **garlic cloves minced (3.06 mg)**
1   **(14.5-ounce) can no-salt-added tomatoes (105 mg)**
3   **ounces no-salt-added tomato paste (83.3 mg)**
2½   **cups low-sodium water‡ (trace)**

*Diabetics, 193.4 grams of carbohydrates are in the rice.
†Ask your fish dealer where it came from. If it's from outside the United States, then it may have been salted or brined and the sodium is too high. (Some imported shrimp is not brined or salted, but these are generally difficult to find, and may be from Malaysia or Mexico.) Gulf shrimp are usually what you'll find in the nonbrined, unsalted category. In our area we are able to find these in one supermarket chain and at Whole Foods.
‡You can use Maureen's Easy Chicken Broth (page 113) for more flavor. If you do, add 94.5 mg of sodium to recipe total.

2 whole bay leaves (.276 mg)
¼ teaspoon cayenne pepper (.135 mg)
1¼ cups uncooked long-grain or basmati white rice (2.438 mg)

Spray a Dutch oven or 4-quart pot with olive oil spray and place over medium heat. Put the ground pork in the pot and sprinkle with the Cajun spice mix.

Cook until lightly brown and crumbly, 6 to 8 minutes. Transfer to a small bowl and set aside.

Place 1 tablespoon of the olive oil in the same pot and turn up the heat to medium-high. Add the chunks of chicken and brown, stirring frequently, 8 to 10 minutes. Remove the chicken from the pot and set aside.

Turn down the heat to medium, add the remaining olive oil and add the vegetables to the same pot. Sauté for about 4 minutes, stirring frequently. Do not let them burn.

Add the tomato paste, the tomatoes, and the water and mix well. Stir in the cayenne and the bay leaves. Return the cooked pork and chicken to the pot and bring the mixture to a boil. When the mixture is boiling, add the rice, cover, and reduce the heat to low. Simmer for 25 to 30 minutes, until the rice is tender. Add the shrimp and cook for an additional 10 minutes.

Serve hot with a salad of your choice.

Nutrient Data per Serving:
Calories: 371.9. Protein: 23 g. Carbohydrate: 44 g. Dietary Fiber: 3.033 g. Total Sugars: 5.587 g. Total Fat: 10.7 g. Saturated Fat: 3.472 g. Monounsaturated Fat: 4.951 g. Polyunsaturated Fat: 1.246 g. Cholesterol: 71.2 mg. Trans Fat: .01 g. Total Omega-3 FA: .151 g. Total Omega-6 FA: 0 g. Potassium: 628.6 mg. Sodium: 102.1 mg. Vitamin K: 4.874 mcg. Folate: 110.5 mcg. Folic Acid: 90.2 mcg.

❂ OPEN-FACE CHICKEN SANDWICH ❂

ORIGIN: U.S.A.
DIABETIC ADAPTABLE*

Use homemade French sandwich rolls for this one. You'll enjoy this open-face sandwich, especially if you're on a diet. Make the French Baguette recipe days before, cut them into sandwich lengths, and freeze them in ziplock bags. Then anytime you want a quick, tasty low-calorie and very low-sodium lunch, this one will be there for you.

*Diabetics, the bulk of carbohydrates are in the bun (31 g) and the onion (22.2 g).

¼ teaspoon ground ginger (.144 mg)
2 tablespoons Don's Soy Sauce Replacement (see page 37)
   (3.422 mg)
¾ cup romaine lettuce (3.76 mg) or Savoy cabbage (14.7 mg)
1 (6-ounce) boneless, skinless, chicken half breast (76.7 mg)
1 ounce low-sodium Swiss cheese, grated or thinly sliced
   (3.92 mg)
1 sandwich-size roll from French Baguette recipe (see page
   165) (1.456 mg)
1 medium plum tomato, thinly sliced (3.1 mg)
2 thin slices red onion (6.6 mg)
   White pepper (trace)

Mix the ground ginger with the soy replacement sauce. Shred the lettuce or cabbage and place in a small bowl. Drizzle the soy replacement and ginger over the greens, and set aside in the refrigerator.

Butterfly the chicken breast into 2 pieces. Pound them until they are evenly thin and the right size to fit your roll. Cook the chicken over medium-high heat in nonstick pan that has been sprayed with olive oil. Cook the chicken for 3 to 4 minutes. Turn and cook for 3 to 4 minutes more. When the chicken is nearly done, place half the cheese on top of each chicken breast and cover the pan. Continue cooking until the cheese has melted.

Lightly toast the buns. Arrange the lettuce or cabbage on top of each bun. Pour any extra sauce over the greens and into the bun. Layer the tomato, onion slices, and chicken with the cheese side up on top of the greens. Add white pepper to taste.

Nutritional Data per Sandwich:
Calories: 261.7. Protein: 21.5 g. Carbohydrate: 32.8 g. Dietary Fiber: 3.172 g. Total Sugars: 8.173 g. Total Fat: 5.046 g. Saturated Fat: 2.778 g. Monounsaturated Fat: 1.28 g. Polyunsaturated Fat: .544 g. Cholesterol: 47.1 mg. Trans Fat: .015 g. Total Omega-3 FA: .059 g. Total Omega-6 FA: 0 g. Potassium: 563.5 mg. Sodium: 49.6 mg. Vitamin K: 27.1 mcg. Folic Acid: 0 mcg.

❖ Orange-Glazed Chicken Wraps ❖

Origin: U.S.A.
Diabetic Adaptable*

Once you learn how to make a chicken wrap, you'll probably make up your own flavors and wraps with your own concepts of what should go inside. You can stuff rolled chicken breasts with just about anything, from apples to cranberries to cheese to vegetables or fruit. This recipe is one of my favorites. It can be halved or doubled. The sauce can be made with orange juice, apple juice, or a tasty honey glaze. It's easy to make, and a delight to serve.

**Makes 4 Servings   Sodium per Recipe: 319.9 mg
Sodium per Serving: 80 mg**

THE CHICKEN WRAP
4   (4-to 6-ounce) boneless, skinless chicken half breasts (306.8 mg)
¼   cup scallions, chopped or thinly sliced† (.862 mg)
1   cup dried Basic Bread Crumbs (see page 167) (1.362 mg)
½   cup frozen or fresh cranberries (5.85 mg)
¼   cup homemade Applesauce‡ (see page 51) (.095 mg)
½   cup low-sodium water (trace)
1   level tablespoon orange zest (.18 mg)
1   tablespoon Splenda (or sugar or honey) (trace)
⅛   teaspoon white pepper (.015 mg)
     Freshly ground black pepper

THE GLAZE
1   cup low-sodium water (trace)
1½   tablespoons cornstarch (.945 mg)
     Juice of 4 oranges (approximately 8 tablespoons) (32.44 mg)
2   tablespoons orange zest (grated from above oranges) (.36 mg)
1   tablespoon Splenda (or sugar or honey) (trace)

---

*Diabetics, the orange juice also has 35.8 g of the carbohydrates and bread crumbs have 26.3 g of carbohydrates. Figures are for recipe total.
†May use onion instead
‡Or 1 thinly sliced fresh apple sprinkled with a cinnamon-sugar mix and the juice of half a lemon

Preheat the oven to 350°F.

Pound the chicken breasts to a ¼-inch thickness, taking care not to tear the meat. Set aside.

Prepare the stuffing. If your bread isn't dry, toast it lightly. Remove and break into small cubes. Set aside in a medium mixing bowl. Add the cranberries.

Sauté the scallions over medium-high heat in a small nonstick pan sprayed with oil spray, until translucent. Add to the bread and cranberries.

In a small saucepan, combine the applesauce and water and heat to nearly a boil. Stir in the orange zest just before removing from the heat. Pour this into the bread and cranberry mixture. Stir in the Splenda and white pepper.

Sprinkle the pounded chicken breasts lightly with some black pepper. Place one-quarter of the stuffing on each chicken breast. Roll the breasts and fasten each with two toothpicks.

Place into an 8×8-inch baking dish lightly oiled with olive oil spray. Bake, uncovered, on the middle rack of the oven for 30 to 35 minutes. Some ovens may take longer. Test the meat so that it doesn't overcook and remains soft and moist.

About halfway through the baking time, prepare the glaze.

Mix the water and cornstarch in a small or medium saucepan until smooth. Add the orange juice and zest and bring to a boil over medium heat, stirring steadily, until thickened. Remove and add the Splenda (or honey or sugar) and stir. Add pepper to taste.

Serve the chicken hot with glaze poured over each chicken piece.

Nutrient Data per Serving:
Calories: 314.1. Protein: 34.7 g. Carbohydrate: 37.5 g. Dietary Fiber: 7.476 g. Total Sugars: 8.683 g. Total Fat: 2.385 g. Saturated Fat: .552 g. Monounsaturated Fat: .643 g. Polyunsaturated Fat: .573 g. Cholesterol: 68.4 mg. Trans Fat: .029 g. Total Omega-3 FA: .122 g. Total Omega-6 FA: 0 g. Potassium: 847.6 mg. Sodium: 80 mg. Vitamin K: .492 mcg. Folic Acid: 0 mcg.

❖ NEW LOW-SODIUM PIZZA ❖

ORIGIN: ITALY
DIABETICS, SEE FOOTNOTE*

BREAD MACHINE DOUGH / HAND MADE / OVEN BAKED

Crunchy crust, soft pizza dough, lots of fillings, and plenty of flavor—this one's easy to make if you use bottled,

---

*Carbohydrates are low enough to exchange. Most of the carbohydrates are in the flour (429.2 g).

no-salt-added Ener-G Spaghetti Sauce (www.healthyheart market.com), or Eden Organic No-Salt-Added Spaghetti Sauce. Also available at Healthy Heart Market, this brand has no preservatives, additives, or added chemicals like potassium chloride. This recipe takes about 2½ hours to prepare, including the dough prep time.

MAKES: 14 SLICES   SODIUM PER RECIPE: 109.6 MG
SODIUM PER SLICE: (10): 11
SODIUM PER SLICE (14): 7.83 MG

THE PIZZA DOUGH*

1¼ cups plus 2 tablespoons low-sodium water, or more as needed (trace)
3   tablespoons extra-virgin olive oil (trace)
1   tablespoon cider vinegar (.15 mg)
4½ cups unbleached, all-purpose or bread flour** (11.2 mg)
2   teaspoons chopped fresh basil (.07 mg)
2   garlic cloves, minced (1.02 mg)
1   teaspoon onion powder (1.296 mg)
1   teaspoon sugar or Splenda (.042 mg)
1   teaspoon vital wheat gluten (.72 mg)
⅛   teaspoon ascorbic acid (trace)
2   teaspoons bread machine yeast (3.96 mg)

THE TOPPING

3   garlic cloves, minced (1.53 mg)
1½ tablespoons basil, dried or fresh (2.295 mg)
     Eden Organic No-Salt-Added Spaghetti Sauce† (30 mg)
¼   teaspoon ground cloves (1.276 mg)
3   tablespoons extra-virgin olive oil (trace)
2   cups sliced mushrooms (5.6 mg)
1   cup thinly sliced zucchini (11.3 mg)
1   medium white onion, chopped (3.3 mg)
2   medium tomatoes or 2 large plum tomatoes, thinly sliced (12.3 mg)

*You may use half unbleached white flour and half whole wheat pastry flour.
**Available from www.healthyheartmarket.com or www.edenfoods.com.
†See Heluva Good Cheese online for low-sodium Cheddar. Some brands of low-sodium Swiss may be higher in sodium.
‡You can find other delicious and easy-to-make pizza dough recipes in *The No-Salt, Lowest-Sodium Cookbook* on pages 261 and 262. Also, an excellent pizza dough can be found in *The No-Salt, Lowest-Sodium Baking Book* on page 97.

6 ounces low-sodium white Cheddar, or low-sodium Swiss, grated* (23.5 mg)
½ diced green bell pepper, optional (1.49 mg)

Place the dough ingredients in bread machine and set for Dough. If it needs more water after about 5 or 7 minutes of kneading, then add more as needed one tablespoon at a time. The dough will rise in the machine, but we don't allow a second rise.

While the dough is rising, prepare the topping. Mix the garlic and basil with the Eden Organic No-Salt-Added Spaghetti Sauce in a saucepan. Add ground cloves and any other spices you favor for a good pizza sauce. Place the pan over medium heat and cook the sauce, stirring frequently, until hot. Reduce to a simmer and continue cooking for about 10 minutes, stirring occasionally. (There's no oil in this sauce.)

When the dough is ready, preheat the oven to 375°F. Transfer the dough to a flour-dusted breadboard and press down flat, directing the dough into a circle. If you know how to toss pizza dough, go ahead and do so until the dough is the correct size. If you don't know, then pull dough out into a circle with your hands until it's the shape of your pizza pan. (A pizza pan with holes in the bottom of it is best.)

The dough will be a bit thicker than a thin-crust pizza, but not as thick as a thick-crust pizza.

Spread the sauce on the dough. Then layer the pizza with the veggies and cheese.

Bake in the preheated oven for 25 to 30 minutes.

Note: This recipe was designed as a pan pizza. However, you can cut the dough in half after taking it out of your bread machine and roll it out with a rolling pin to make two large, thin pizza crusts. Bake these for a shorter period of time, around 20 minutes.

Nutrient Data per Slice (14):
Calories: 251.3. Protein: 9.347 g. Carbohydrate: 37.1 g. Dietary Fiber: 2.623 g. Total Sugars: 3.119 g. Total Fat: 6.728 g. Saturated Fat: 2.606 g. Monounsaturated Fat: 3.074 g. Polyunsaturated Fat: .637 g. Cholesterol: 11 mg. Trans Fat: 0 g. Total Omega-3 FA: .088 g. Total Omega-6 FA: 0 g. Potassium: 311.4 mg. Sodium: 7.83 mg. Vitamin K: 12.8 mcg. Folic Acid: 61.9 mcg.

Nutrient Data per Slice (10):
Calories: 351.8. Protein: 13.1 g. Carbohydrate: 52 g. Dietary Fiber: 3.672 g. Total Sugars: 4.367 g. Total Fat: 9.42 g. Saturated Fat: 3.649 g. Monounsaturated Fat: 4.303 g. Polyunsaturated Fat: .892 g. Cholesterol: 15.5 mg. Trans Fat: 0 g. Total Omega-3 FA: .123 g. Total Omega-6 FA: 0 g. Potassium: 435.9 mg. Sodium: 11 mg. Vitamin K: 17.9 mcg. Folic Acid: 86.6 mcg.

*If you want to add meat, here is a serving suggestion: add ½ pound sautéed ground beef or turkey (149.2 mg sodium) (528 calories).

❂ RATATOUILLE ❂

ORIGIN: FRANCE
DIABETICS, SEE FOOTNOTE*

This is one of the healthiest dishes you can make. We like to eat a cup of it as a full dinner entrée, although we admit to cooking up some of Don's Sweet Italian Sausage (see page 107) and adding that, too. With just a small amount, and the ratatouille takes on a whole new flavor. But don't feel you have to, one of the marvels of this sweet-tasting dish is that it's great no matter how you serve it.

MAKES 4 SERVINGS   SODIUM PER RECIPE: 186.9 MG
SODIUM PER SERVING: 46.7 MG

1   **tablespoon extra-virgin olive oil (trace)**
2   **cups chopped onion (9.6 mg)**
2   **medium zucchini, cubed (39.2 mg)**
4   **garlic cloves, minced (2.04 mg)**
1   **small sweet red bell pepper, seeded and cubed (1.48 mg)**
1   **small sweet green bell pepper, seeded and cubed (2.22 mg)**
2   **Japanese eggplants, peeled and cubed† (18.3 mg)**
1   **(14.5-ounce) can no-salt-added tomatoes, with their juice (105 mg)**
½   **teaspoon onion powder (.648 mg)**
⅛   **teaspoon white pepper (.015 mg)**
¼   **cup chopped fresh parsley plus extra for garnish (8.4 mg)**

Heat the olive oil in a medium saucepan. Add the onion, zucchini, garlic, and bell peppers and sauté for 5 to 10 minutes. Stir in the eggplant and the tomatoes with their juice. Simmer for 1 hour. Stir in the onion powder and white pepper and chopped parsley. You may sprinkle any extra parsley over top of each dish as a nice garnish. Serve hot.

Nutrient Data per Serving:
Calories: 171.5. Protein: 5.792 g. Carbohydrate: 31.4 g. Dietary Fiber: 11.8 g. Total Sugars: 14.5 g. Total Fat: 4.187 g. Saturated Fat: .619 g. Monounsaturated Fat: 2.578 g. Polyunsaturated Fat: .69 g. Cholesterol: 0 mg. Trans Fat: 0 g. Total Omega-3 FA: .117 g. Total Omega-6 FA: 0 g. Potassium: 1146 mg. Sodium: 46.7 mg. Vitamin K: 78.4 mcg. Folic Acid: 0 mcg.

*Diabetics, onions have 32.4 grams of carbohydrates. Eggplant has 52.2 grams carbohydrates. The balance of carbohydrates are spread among the rest of the ingredients.
†Japanese eggplant is long, slender, and somewhat lighter in color than regular eggplant. If you can't find Japanese eggplant, use a medium-size regular eggplant.

SOUTHWEST PINTO BEAN
❖ CHORIZO SOUP ❖

ORIGIN: AMERICAN SOUTHWEST
DIABETIC ACCEPTABLE*

When we visited Santa Fe, New Mexico, a few years ago, we dined in an old restaurant that served truly authentic southwestern food. The chorizo soup we had was incredible so we promised ourselves to come up with one very similar. We think this one will delight you, especially if you like a good hot and spicy soup.

MAKES 6 SERVINGS   SODIUM PER RECIPE: 687.6 MG
SODIUM PER SERVING: 114.6 MG

1   tablespoon unsalted butter (1.562 mg)
1   tablespoon all-purpose flour (.225 mg)
3   cups Maureen's Easy Chicken Broth (see page 113)
      (113.4 mg)
1   tablespoon extra-virgin olive oil (trace)
1   cup chopped onion (4.8 mg)
4   garlic cloves, minced (2.04 mg)
1   red bell pepper, seeded and chopped (2.38 mg)
2   tablespoons Grandma's chili powder† (trace)
1   teaspoon ground cumin (3.528 mg)
½   teaspoon dried oregano (.135 mg)
1   (14.5-ounce) can no-salt-added tomatoes (105 mg)
1   (8-ounce) can no-salt-added tomato sauce (26.8 mg)
1   cup frozen unsalted corn (6.816 mg)
2   (14.5-ounce) cans no-salt-added Eden Organic pinto beans
      (105 mg)
1   pound cooked Basque Chorizo‡ (see page 63) (256.8 mg)
4   tablespoons chopped fresh cilantro leaves (trace)
6   dollops sour cream, for garnish (36.9 mg)
1   cup low-fat, unsalted tortilla chips as an accompaniment
      (21.9 mg)

*Most of the carbohydrates in this recipe come from the tortilla chips (116.9 g), corn (47.3 g), tomato sauce (18 g) and onions (16.2 g).
†Or another no-salt chili powder.
‡You can cut the amount of chorizo in half and reduce the soup by 126 mg of sodium or nearly 23 mg per serving.

In a 2-quart saucepan, melt the butter and then add the flour and stir until well blended and bubbling. Remove from the heat and add the chicken broth all at once. Continue cooking over medium heat for about 10 minutes or until slightly thickened.

In a 5-quart soup kettle or Dutch oven, heat the olive oil over medium-high heat. Add the onions, garlic, and bell pepper and sauté for about 5 minutes, or until translucent. Add the chili powder, cumin, and oregano and cook for an additional minute. Add the slightly thickened broth, the canned tomatoes, tomato sauce, corn, and pinto beans to the sautéed vegetables and bring to a simmer.

While the soup is simmering, prepare the chorizo. Add the cooked chorizo to the soup.

Serve with the chopped cilantro leaves, a dollop of sour cream per bowl, and no-salt tortilla chips.

Nutrient Data per Serving:
Calories: 617.7. Protein: 28.8 g. Carbohydrate: 66.2 g. Dietary Fiber: 12.4 g. Total Sugars: 6.923 g. Total Fat: 26.7 g. Saturated Fat: 9.463 g. Monounsaturated Fat: 11.2 g. Polyunsaturated Fat: 3.285 g. Cholesterol: 76.9 mg. Trans Fat: 0 g. Total Omega-3 FA: .222 g. Total Omega-6 FA: .051 g. Potassium: 1247 mg. Sodium: 114.6 mg. Vitamin K: 18.7 mcg. Folic Acid: 2.021 mcg.

❧ CALIFORNIA SUSHI ROLLS ❧

ORIGIN: JAPAN
DIABETIC ACCEPTABLE*

Sushi is the one recipe that everyone told us we wouldn't be able to work out. On the contrary, after you try this one you'll agree that our sushi is as good as "theirs." You can make variations of this as well. What we couldn't do was make a crab sushi, but you can find unsalted tuna (albacore) in fresh fish markets and use that, or you can just go vegetarian. We offer this "California-style" sushi roll that uses avocado and a dash of red and yellow sweet bell peppers with a string of julienned carrots. The combination with the dipping sauce is excellent. See "More About Sushi," page 154.

You will need a bamboo mat for this recipe. (See: Sushi Kit at www.megaheart.com/kit_cabinet.html.)

**MAKES ABOUT 25 TO 30 PIECES   SODIUM PER RECIPE: 55.5 MG
SODIUM PER SERVING (25): 2.2 MG**

*Diabetic, rice has 154.7 g carbohydrates.

THE SUSHI ROLLS

1¼ cups low-sodium water (trace)
1   cup Japanese sticky rice* (1.95 mg)
½   Hass avocado (10.4 mg)
1   tablespoon fresh lemon juice (.153 mg)
1   medium carrot (42.1 mg)
½   medium English cucumber (2.01 mg)
1   piece crystallized ginger (trace)
2   tablespoons rice vinegar (.3 mg)
1   teaspoon Splenda or white granulated sugar (trace)
1   teaspoon white wine vinegar (.05 mg)
¼   teaspoon onion powder (.324 mg)
5   (8×7-inch) pieces toasted nori† (15 mg)

THE DIPPING SAUCE

½   cup white wine vinegar (1.2 mg)
¼   cup rice vinegar (.6 mg)
2   tablespoons Grandma's or B'rer Rabbit molasses‡ (21 mg)
3   teaspoons onion powder (3.88 mg)
1   teaspoon ground ginger (.576 mg)

Cook the rice according to the package directions or in equal amounts of water (one cup of rice to one cup of water). (If you wash the rice you will wash away a lot of its nutrients. Washing the rice is not recommended.)

While rice is cooking, peel and pit the avocado. Spray or gently rub it with the lemon juice. Cut it into ¼-inch-thick strips. Sprinkle lightly with lemon juice to maintain color and freshness.

Clean and peel the carrot. Slice off four sides of the carrot to create a square. Cut the carrot lengthwise into approximately ⅛-inch slices. Stack the slices and then cut lengthwise into approximately ⅛-inch strips.

Peel the English cucumber. If the cucumber is long, cut it in 6-inch lengths, ¼ inch thick, and make the same size slices as the carrot. (You won't need to seed an English cucumber but do seed other types before slicing.)

*Nishiki Sushi Rice (medium grain), Hinode short or medium grain, or Cal Rose are three sushi-type rices you might find in your market. Try to get Nishiki Sushi Rice brand. It's known as a "sticky rice," which is what you really need when making a successful sushi.
†This seaweed product is unsalted and often found in specialty stores or the Asian food aisle of your market. Make sure the sodium level is very low before purchasing. The brand we found was Urishima Yaki Nori No. 1. It's a toasted seaweed. You'll also need a bamboo roller. If you try to roll and press these sushi rolls with your just your fingers, the seaweed with tear quickly.
‡Or other no-salt molasses

Mince the crystallized ginger and set aside for serving.

When the rice is ready, remove it from the pan or steamer and transfer it to a bowl to cool. Cover with a clean kitchen towel, but don't refrigerate it.

While the rice is cooling, whisk together the rice vinegar, white vinegar, the sugar, and the onion powder in a saucepan and simmer the mixture until the sugar is dissolved. Remove from the heat and let it cool. Preheat the oven to 350°F.

Toss the rice with the cooled vinegar mixture to moisten it lightly. Be careful not to smash the rice. The rice may be made 3 hours in advance and kept covered with a dampened cloth at room temperature. I like to use it right away, however, since I think it sticks to the nori much better if used soon after cooking.

Heat the nori in the preheated oven on a baking sheet for 5 to 8 minutes, or until it has softened slightly. Keep it warm by covering it with a cloth until ready to use.

Work on a clean board with one sheet of nori at a time. Place the nori with the lengthwise side toward you. Using your hands, ball up about ¾ cup of the rice without smashing it; then spread it evenly in a layer on the nori sheet, leaving a ½-inch border on the long sides. Sprinkle a pinch of the ground ginger across the rice with each roll you make. The rice should stick to the nori. Turn over the nori-rice layers so that rice is on bottom.

Starting just inside the far edge of the nori, arrange some of the avocado strips horizontally across. Then lay down some of the carrot and cucumber strips alongside, working your way toward the edge nearest you. You'll pretty much cover the nori but leave a good ¾-inch at each edge.

Now roll into a sushi roll, using your hands. The rice should stick well enough for you to do this.

Set the bamboo mat over the roll and squeeze gently to form the log and tighten it up a bit. After forming, remove the bamboo mat and continue the process until all the rolls are assembled.

Cut each roll with a sharp knife into six ¾-inch-thick slices and serve the rolls with the dipping sauce and the crystallized ginger.

Serve freshly made or slightly chilled. The rolls can be stored in the refrigerator up to but not longer than 24 hours, tightly covered.

To prepare the dipping sauce: place all ingredients into a saucepan and simmer over medium heat for about 5 minutes stirring often. Then lower heat to and simmer for another 5 minutes. Cool or chill before serving.

More About Sushi

In Japan, sushi is associated with the sushi bar or shop. Sushi bars play a role in Japan similar to that of the pubs in England—where I once filmed a show. The pub was in Nottingham and the experience was worth a lifetime of trips. Essentially, the sushi "pub" in Japan is a relaxed and informal place where patrons enjoy their food and beverage (often sake) at tables or booths. However, the recognized sushi aficionados sit on a stool at the sushi bar. The sushi choices are usually in a refrigerated display case the master sushi maker works right there in front of the patron.

Sushi is often thought of by Americans as raw seafood. That's not really what sushi is; not all seafood that comes with sushi is served raw. Actually raw seafood is known as *sashimi*. There are various types of sushi, but each one includes the rice and most all are handmade. Another type is the one in this recipe, which is really a sushi roll, or *maki*. *Maki* is made with the sheets of seaweed, or nori. This type is cut into about six bite-size pieces (or slightly larger). Another type of sushi you can make is the pressed sushi known as *oshi*. *Oshi* is cut into bite-size squares. There are other types including the bean curd rolls (*inarizushi*), but the above are the most popular.

You can watch sushi being made on the Web at: www.eatsushi.com/demos.asp, or visit their homepage at www.eatsushi.com.

Nutrient Data per Serving (25):
Calories: 45.4. Protein: .668 g. Carbohydrate: 9.656 g. Dietary Fiber: .421 g. Total Sugars: 2.381 g. Total Fat: .599 g. Saturated Fat: .089 g. Monounsaturated Fat: .355 g. Polyunsaturated Fat: .079 g. Cholesterol: 0 mg. Trans Fat: 0 g. Total Omega-3 FA: .011 g. Total Omega-6 FA: .001 g. Potassium: 82.5 mg. Sodium: 2.2 mg. Vitamin K: 1.029 mcg. Folic Acid: 17.3 mcg.

✷ Thai Sweet and Hot Chili Sandwich ✷

Origin: Bangkok, Thailand
Diabetic*

My close friend in Bangkok, Picha Srisansansee, sent this recipe along to us. Picha worked as a camera assistant for me for a few years and then returned to Bangkok, where he now produces commercials for Thai television. As you will taste here, Picha loves chili-hot food! This "hot," though, is very pleasant and will excite your palate with a wonderful burst of energy.

**Makes 2 sandwiches   Sodium per Recipe: 121 mg
Sodium per Sandwich: 60.5 mg**

THE SAUCE

1   teaspoon white granulated sugar or Splenda (trace)
¼   teaspoon ground ginger (.144 mg)
1   tablespoon sesame chili oil (trace)
4   tablespoons Don's Soy Sauce Replacement (see page 37) (6.843 mg)

THE SANDWICH

1   boneless, skinless, nonbrined chicken half breast (76.7 mg)
2   ounces, no-salt-added Swiss or low-sodium Cheddar cheese (23.7 mg)
8   medium mushrooms, sliced and lightly sautéed without oil in a nonstick pan (5.76 mg)
2   lightly toasted sandwich-size slices or buns from homemade Ciabatta bread (see page 173) (3.964 mg)
1   tablespoons no-salt-added ketchup (3 mg), optional
2   inner leaves of romaine lettuce, cut to sandwich size, optional (.96 mg)

Mix together the sugar, ginger, sesame chili oil, and soy sauce replacement. Set aside.

Butterfly the chicken breast into two pieces. Using a kitchen mallet, pound out the chicken pieces to "sandwich size" and an even thickness. Broil, barbecue, or sauté the chicken over medium heat until done.

Place one-half of the cheese on the inner side of the top piece of the sandwich-size bread or bun and lightly toast until the cheese has melted.

*Diabetics: Most of the carbohydrates are in the Ciabatta bread.

Place the mushrooms on the bottom half and then the cooked chicken. Spread an equal share of the sauce over each piece of chicken and close the sandwich. Slice in half and serve immediately.

If using the ketchup and romaine, spread a very thin layer of the ketchup on the bottom side before laying in the mushrooms. Then lay in the romaine.

Serve with hot or iced tea.

Nutrient Data per Sandwich:
Calories: 405.6. Protein: 27.1 g. Carbohydrate: 38.9 g. Dietary Fiber: 2.127 g. Total Sugars: 9.955 g. Total Fat: 16.2 g. Saturated Fat: 5.993 g. Monounsaturated Fat: 5.522 g. Polyunsaturated Fat: 3.503 g. Cholesterol: 58.8 mg. Trans Fat: .015 g. Total Omega-3 FA: .064 g. Total Omega-6 FA: 0 g. Potassium: 681.8 mg. Sodium: 60.5 mg. Vitamin K: 7.867 mcg. Folic Acid: 0 mcg.

❖ ⬧ SPANISH TORTILLA ⬧ ❖

ORIGIN: SPAIN
DIABETIC ACCEPTABLE

This traditional dish has nothing to do with the Mexican flatbread that we use for tacos or burritos. It is simply a potato omelet, but can have many versions depending on what you add to it. The one we offer here is basic and is made with less oil and fewer potatoes than the Spanish use. Use a nonstick frying pan for this to help cut unnecessary fat. Use two less egg yolks, if you wish.

MAKES 8 SERVINGS   SODIUM PER RECIPE:* 425.8 MG
SODIUM PER SERVING: 53.1 MG

2   **pounds russet potatoes peeled, and thinly sliced (about 2 large or 4 medium) (42.6 mg)**
¼   **cup olive oil (trace)**
1   **large onion, thinly sliced (about 1½ cups) (4.5 mg)**
6   **large eggs (378 mg)**
¼   **teaspoon white pepper (.03 mg)**

After preparing the potatoes, press them between two clean cotton tea towels to remove excess moisture.

Heat the oil in a 12-inch nonstick frying pan over medium-to-low heat and add enough potatoes to cover the bottom of the pan. Then layer with half the onions and repeat with another layer of potatoes, then the balance of onions.

*We use an average rating here for sodium levels, based on our bread recipes.

Cook them slowly for about 20 minutes, continually lifting and turning them with a nonstick spatula, allowing those on top to move to the bottom of the pan. The potatoes will lose their opaqueness and become translucent, but they should not stick together.

Beat the eggs in a large bowl until frothy.

Pour the potato mixture into a colander over a bowl to catch any extra oil. Reserve the oil.

Add the potatoes and onions to the eggs and make sure the eggs cover all of the potato-onion mixture. Return the reserved oil to the frying pan and increase the heat to medium-high.

Add the potato-onion-egg mixture and reduce the heat to medium.

Sprinkle with the white pepper and cook for about 10 minutes, or until the bottom of the tortilla is a golden brown. Shake the pan often to make sure the potatoes aren't sticking. As the tortilla cooks, you should be able to shake the pan and the tortilla will move as one large omelet. Then place a large flat plate (we use a stainless-steel serving platter) over the frying pan and turn the tortilla upside down onto the plate.

Return the frying pan to the stove and slide the tortilla uncooked side down into the frying pan. Continue to cook for another 10 minutes, or until it the bottom is golden brown. Slide the finished tortilla onto a warm serving plate and cut into 8 serving pieces. This makes a delicious supper when served with a green salad.

If preparing in advance, store in an airtight container in the refrigerator and use for lunch or dinner the next day. Reheat in the microwave, covered with a paper towel or waxed paper. It will still be an excellent dish.

Nutrient Data per Serving:
Calories: 207. Protein: 7.177 g. Carbohydrate: 21.5 g. Dietary Fiber: 1.667 g. Total Sugars: 1.752 g. Total Fat: 10.6 g. Saturated Fat: 2.097 g. Monounsaturated Fat: 6.424 g. Polyunsaturated Fat: 1.235 g. Cholesterol: 158.6 mg. Trans Fat: 0 g. Total Omega-3 FA: .092 g. Total Omega-6 FA: 0 g. Potassium: 521.5 mg. Sodium: 53.1 mg. Vitamin K: 6.168 mcg. Folic Acid: 0 mcg.

Nutrient Data per Serving (Removing 2 Yolks):
Calories: 192.9. Protein: 6.504 g. Carbohydrate: 21.4 g. Dietary Fiber: 1.667 g. Total Sugars: 1.714 g. Total Fat: 9.351 g. Saturated Fat: 1.71 g. Monounsaturated Fat: 5.948 g. Polyunsaturated Fat: 1.064 g. Cholesterol: 105.8 mg. Trans Fat: 0 g. Total Omega-3 FA: .083 g. Total Omega-6 FA: 0 g. Potassium: 518.2 mg. Sodium: 51.1 mg. Vitamin K: 6.13 mcg. Folic Acid: 0 mcg.

✺ PANINI PESTO SANDWICH ✺

ORIGIN: AN ITALIAN FAVORITE
DIABETIC ADAPTABLE

DEVELOPED FOR PANINI MAKERS

Use fresh basil for this sandwich, and your favorite home-made, no-salt bread. The breads that work best include baguettes, sourdough, and most of our bun recipes.

**MAKES 2 SANDWICHES   SODIUM PER RECIPE: 111.6 MG
SODIUM PER SANDWICH: 55.8 MG**

4   **slices no-salt bread or 2 no-salt buns, split (20 mg)**
¼   **cup pesto* (.902 mg)**
2   **ounces no-salt, low-sodium Swiss cheese (7.84 mg)**
4   **thin slices ripe tomato (4 mg)**
2   **thin slices (about 2 ounces each) cooked chicken or turkey
     breast meat (76.7 mg)**

Prepare some pesto and keep in airtight container in refrigerator. It will store for up to 2 days if kept sealed after each use.

Preheat the panini maker. Defrost the bread, if frozen, in a microwave on Defrost setting, or use fresh bread. Slice for sandwich use.

Place the low-sodium Swiss cheese on top half of the sandwich bread or bun.

Spread the pesto on the bottom half of the sandwich bread or bun. Lay the cooked chicken on top of the pesto, layer on the tomato slices, and close the sandwich.

If using a panini maker, place both sandwiches on the preheated surface and bring down the lid. Cook for 3 to 5 minutes, or until the bread is golden or crisp and the cheese is melting. You can raise a panini maker's lid to check the progress during cooking and return it to the sandwich if you need to.

Nutrient Data per Panini:
Calories: 424.4. Protein: 27 g. Carbohydrate: 27.3 g. Dietary Fiber: 2.711 g. Total Sugars: 3.944 g. Total Fat: 23.7 g. Saturated Fat: 7.148 g. Monounsaturated Fat: 11.2 g. Polyunsaturated Fat: 3.648 g. Cholesterol: 69.8 mg. Trans Fat: .015 g. Total Omega-3 FA: .15 g. Total Omega-6 FA: .025 g. Calcium: 310.4 mg Potassium: 444.8 mg. Sodium: 55.8 mg. Vitamin K: 34.9 mcg. Folic Acid: 24.1 mcg.

*You can use the pesto in our Pesto Chicken Sandwich (see page 141).

◈ PESTO PASTA ◈

ORIGIN: ITALIAN (GENOVESE)
DIABETIC, SEE FOOTNOTE*

Pesto as we know it, that is, the original pesto, is made in the authentic Genovese style. Ingredients are basic and never change (except in your local market's canned or bottled version). These include basil (basilico); *garlic* (aglio); *pine nuts* (pinoli *or* pignolia); *extra-virgin olive oil; and either a* pecorino *or* Parmigiano) *cheese. It's the world's favorite pasta dish—pasta with pesto. You can also use pesto as a crostini or bruschetta topping or as we do with our Pesto Chicken Sandwich (see page 141). It also makes a great topping for fish.*

**MAKES 6 SERVINGS   SODIUM PER RECIPE: 242.1 MG
SODIUM PER SERVING: 40.4 MG**

⅔ **cup unsalted pine nuts (1.782 mg)**
2 **cups fresh basil leaves (3.392 mg)**
⅓ **cup extra-virgin olive oil† (trace)**
6 **garlic cloves, crushed in a garlic press (3.06 mg)**
1 **cup grated low-sodium Swiss cheese‡ (15.1 mg)**
12 **ounces enriched dry noodles (71.8 mg)**

Roast the pine nuts until golden brown in a toaster oven at 325°F for about 5 minutes, stirring after 3 minutes. Take care not to burn them.

Blend the roasted nuts, basil, oil, and garlic in your processor until it is a smooth paste.

Boil the whole wheat pasta or regular pasta according to the packge directions and drain in a colander. Put in a large bowl and stir the pesto into the hot pasta. Serve immediately.

Nutrient Data per Serving:
Calories: 635.6. Protein: 26.8 g. Carbohydrate: 89.9 g. Dietary Fiber: 5.561 g. Total Sugars: 2.885 g. Total Fat: 21.5 g. Saturated Fat: 6.264 g. Monounsaturated Fat: 6.03 g. Polyunsaturated Fat: 6.461 g. Cholesterol: 79 mg. Trans-Fatty Acids: 0 g. Total Omega-3 FA: .154 g. Total Omega-6 FA: .068 g. Iron: 6.249 mg. Potassium: 873.5 mg. Sodium: 40.4 mg. Vitamin K: 69.2 mcg. Folic Acid: 123.1 mcg

*Most of the carbohydrates are in the noodles (243.3 mg)
†If you want more, you can use up to a ½ cup. If you increase the olive oil, the sodium level doesn't change but total fats do. Add 13.5 grams of total fats per tablespoon, 1.816 grams of which are saturated.
‡If you can't find low-sodium Swiss, you might try the white Cheddar from Heluva Good cheese, www.heluvagood.com.

BREAD

❖　❖　❖　❖　❖　❖　❖　❖

Bread and grains that make bread have served as the principal food for humans since the beginning of time. Historians have written that the first important trade of early man was that of the baker. Archaeologists have even found loaves and rolls in ancient Egyptian tombs. (No jokes about freshness, please.) In Egyptian galleries of the British Museum you can find loaves that were made and baked over 5,000 years ago. The gallery also displays some of the grains of the wheat used to make that bread.

Wheat has also been found in pits where human settlements flourished 8,000 years ago. Bread, both with and without salt (and leavened) is mentioned in the Bible many times. Here's a point that hits home. The ancient Greeks and Romans adopted bread as a staple food from their beginnings. What's interesting is that, even in those days, they argued whether white or brown (whole wheat) bread was better for them.

Predating the Romans and Greeks with findings as far back as the Stone Age (7,500 years ago), archaeologists have found a millstone that was used for grinding corn, wheat, and barley. Some archaeologists and historians feel that man's ability to sow and reap grains and cereals may be a chief reason for humans' developing communities.

Anthropologists believe hunters, referred to at times as "gatherers," first stockpiled the grain as a storable food source. However, when it got wet, due usually to weather and poor storage facilities, it sprouted. The gatherers soon discovered that if the grain was planted, it yielded more seeds and of course, more grain.

The first recorded grains were from Mesopotamia and Egypt, where wheat was most likely chewed. Not much later, it was learned that wheat could be pulverized and made into a paste. Set over a fire, the paste hardened into a flatbread that kept for several days.

Around 1000 B.C., inquiring Egyptians isolated yeast, but didn't combine it in bread right away. At the same time, a new strain of wheat was produced that allowed for refined white bread. Modern bread was now on the table. It didn't take much time for them to discover leavened (raised) bread when yeast was accidentally introduced to the paste. Before yeast arrived, however, many bakers had learned that they could save a piece of dough from a batch of bread to put into the next day's dough. This was the origin of sourdough, a truly flavorful process still used today. Even with all that knowledge about the history of bread, according to botanists, nobody has yet found the wild form of grass from which wheat as we know it was developed.

Today, the generally "commercial" beliefs that you can't make bread without salt have been shelved. With today's knowledge we can make excellent bread by adding a few ingredients to make up for the lost freshness and leavening action offered by salt.

Nearly every country has a signature bread recipe; some have more than a few. Africa has some wonderful bread recipes while in China they don't eat "bread," but do have a wonderful Chinese Steamed Bun, a version of which you can find in this book.

You'll find a variety of bread recipes in this book, and each is worth making at least once. The Russian Black Bread is wonderful as is the Ethiopian Spice Bread, and if you make only one bread recipe in this book, make the Ethiopian Spice Bread. It's worth the effort and will prove to be a popular favorite among your family and friends. We have tried to make most of these bread recipes simple. Some seem to have a lot of ingredients, but after lining them up on your countertop you'll see that each is necessary for the recipe and each is relatively easy to come by. If you can't find ingredients locally, you can find them at www.megaheart.com/wheretobuy.html. Links on that page will take you to suppliers who will sell you the items online. These include Healthy Heart Market, Baker's Catalogue, Bob's Red Mill, and quite a few others. Amazon.com also sells the same products in most cases and if you are buying more than $25 of goods, they often ship free of charge.

We use a bread machine in many of our recipes so that you won't have to expend energy you may not have doing the kneading. Some are bread-machine-only all the way; others, you'll pull the dough out of the machine and shape or form and bake it in your oven. You can also use a standing mixer like a KitchenAid to knead dough. If doing so, you'll have to make a yeast sponge before mixing. When using a bread machine, you don't have to do this.

We recommend Fleischmann's BreadMachine yeast since Fleischmann's adds a bit of ascorbic acid (vitamin C) to their yeast to help with the rising process. You'll add a bit more in each of our recipes. We buy ascorbic acid at Baker's Catalogue (you can find that link at www.megaheart.com/wheretobuy.html as well). We buy about four bags at a time and store the powder in a small re-cycled jam jar that is clearly marked "Ascorbic Acid."

In our first and second books we recommended the Breadman TR810 and the Breadman TR2200 bread machines. We were right about the machines, but probably not wise about naming them, since Breadman (now owned by Salton) discontinued those machines. So, instead, we are going to tell you that you can find our current recom-mended (and tested) machines at www.megaheart.com/kit_cabinet .html

If you already own a machine and you're happy with it, then read your manufacturer's instructions for the order of ingredients and follow those rather than our instructions. Remember that bread machines do wear out. The motors will last longer than the ther-mostats. If you begin to feel your bread is not rising correctly, or you have two or three failures in a row, you've probably worn out that machine and will have to get another—they cost more to repair than they do to purchase new.

Bread flour (also called "strong" or "hard" flour) has a higher gluten content than all-purpose and pastry flours do. Gluten gives a greater elasticity to the dough, which helps to keep the bread light and high during its risings and baking. Please do not substitute all-purpose flour if you are out of bread flour, or vice versa, for the greatest success with our recipes.

❖ AUSTRIAN RYE BREAD ❖

ORIGIN: AUSTRIA
DIABETICS, SEE FOOTNOTE*

BREAD MACHINE RECIPE

When I served as a ski patrolman, I met many skiers who were from Austria. It seems they liked our slopes and ended up running many of them. Jurgen Wetstein was one of those, along with Werner Schuster, his half brother. One ran one ski resort in our area and the other managed another. They each had a food service area, and Austrian recipes abounded. Here's a terrific bread recipe based on one they served and it's straight from the Alps.

MAKES 16 SLICES (1 LOAF)   SODIUM PER RECIPE: 23.9 MG
SODIUM PER SERVING: 1.492 MG

1	cup warm no-sodium or low-sodium water, 100°F to 105°F† (trace)
1½	teaspoons extra-virgin olive oil (trace)
1	tablespoon cider vinegar (.15 mg)
1⅓	cups white, unbleached, bread flour (3.332 mg)
⅔	cup dark rye flour (.852 mg)
¼	teaspoon ascorbic acid (trace)
⅓	cup wheat germ (4.554 mg)
2	tablespoons vital wheat gluten (4.5 mg)
¼	teaspoon ground allspice (.366 mg)
¼	teaspoon ground dried rosemary (.15 mg)
3	tablespoons honey (2.52 mg)
2½	teaspoons active dry yeast (5 mg)

Place all the ingredients in the bread machine pan, set the machine for Light Crust, 1½-Pound Loaf, White Bread.

Cool the bread on a rack. Store in ziplock bags. This bread freezes well.

Nutrient Data per Serving:
Calories: 87.2. Protein: 3.345 g. Carbohydrate: 17.4 g. Dietary Fiber: 1.952 g. Total Sugars: 4.119 g. Total Fat: .948 g. Saturated Fat: .135 g. Monounsaturated Fat: .387 g. Polyunsaturated Fat: .293 g. Cholesterol: 0 mg. Trans Fat: 0 g. Total Omega-3 FA: .032 g. Total Omega-6 FA: 0 g. Potassium: 101.2 mg. Sodium: 1.492 mg. Vitamin K: .6 mcg. Folic Acid: 16 mcg.

*Diabetics, exchange honey with Splenda, and add 2 tablespoons water.
†Add one tablespoon of water if making this at high altitude.

❖ FRENCH BAGUETTE ❖

ORIGIN: FRANCE
DIABETIC ADAPTABLE

BREAD MACHINE KNEAD—OVEN BAKE

This is the true basic French baguette recipe but with the salt left out and our special replacement mixed in. We also recommend you use a bread machine if you don't have the "heart strength" to knead for about 10 to 15 minutes.

Some declare that no matter how hard you try, you can't replicate the real thing found on every street corner in Paris. Try this one, though, and see if it isn't darned close. We think you'll really enjoy it.

MAKES 3 BAGUETTES   SODIUM PER RECIPE: 39.3 MG
SODIUM PER BAGUETTE: 13.1 MG
SODIUM PER ESTIMATED 1-INCH SLICE: .819

2	cups warm low-sodium water, 100°F to 105°F (trace)
1	tablespoon cider vinegar (.15 mg)
5	cups unbleached, all-purpose flour (12.5 mg)
1	teaspoon granulated or soy lecithin (trace)
1	teaspoon granulated sugar or Splenda (.042 mg)
1	teaspoons onion powder 1.296 mg
⅛	teaspoon ascorbic acid (trace)
½	teaspoon vital wheat gluten (1.125 mg)
2¼	teaspoons bread machine yeast* (4.5 mg)
1	egg, beaten and mixed with 1 tablespoon cold water, you will use about a fourth of the mix (17.5 mg)

BREAD MACHINE INSTRUCTIONS

Place the ingredients, except for the egg and water mixture, into bread machine in the order listed. Set on Dough. After the dough is ready, follow the instructions that follow in section titled "After Dough Has Risen."

BY HAND

You may prepare this recipe in your food processor using bread tongs (beaters), or mix by hand using a good wooden spoon.

First, make a yeast sponge. Place the yeast in about ½ cup of warmed

*If making from scratch by hand, use regular active dry yeast or rapid-rise yeast.

water in a small bowl to dissolve. Let it sit for about 5 minutes or so, until it "sponges."

Mix the flour, sugar, gluten, and yeast (either active dry or rapid). Add the water and vinegar and mix for 1 minute. Add the onion powder, ascorbic acid, and mix for another 15 minutes.

Put the dough in a lightly greased bowl, roll it over once, cover with a clean kitchen towel, and leave it to rise in a warm place for 30 minutes for rapid rise yeast and 45 minutes to 1 hour for standard active dry yeast.

AFTER THE DOUGH HAS RISEN

After the dough has risen, turn it out onto a lightly floured surface. Separate the dough into 3 even pieces. Make sure they are equal since that will help the bread cook evenly.

A baguette needs to be rolled tightly for best rise. Flatten each dough ball with the palm of your hands to force out excess gas. Roll the dough away from you while forming a short but bulky log, tucking it in with your fingers as you roll. The outside of the dough will stretch, but not tear, as you roll.

A seam will appear when the dough piece is completely rolled up. Seal this tightly by pinching both sides together, or the roll may unwind during baking. If the dough doesn't seal, moisten the seam slightly with water and pinch the sides together again.

Now stretch the dough by placing your hands on either side of the loaf's center. Apply gentle downward and outward pressure while rolling the dough back and forth on the lightly floured work surface. The loaf should lengthen and you should feel the dough stretch, but not tear. You will be shaping your baguette. Make the log as long as you have a pan for, but no longer than 14 to 16 inches.

When you have 3 such rolls from your 3 balls of dough, place the loaves on trays or baguette pans that have been sprinkled with the cornmeal. With a very sharp knife, slice 3 to 6 diagonal slashes on the top of each loaf, about a ¼ inch deep.

Brush the baguettes with the egg wash. You won't use much of this, but what you do use counts.

Cover the loaves with lightly oiled waxed paper; let rise in warm place for about 45 minutes. If you have a proofing option with your oven, use that for a good rise. Otherwise you can zap your oven to the perfect heat level by turning it on to 350°F and waiting 60 to 70 seconds before turning it off. The heat inside should be just right for rising.

Once the dough has risen it will be nearly double in size. If not handled gently between the rise and the baking, the dough can fall, creating a tough, flat baguette. So don't bump it, drop it, or move it. Leave it in the oven since you'll start baking from zero.

Put a small pan of boiling water in the bottom of oven. Spray (mist) the loaves with warm water if you have a mister.

A trick to making good baguettes is to steam the oven at the beginning of the bake. Spritzing water on the surface of the loaves before you put them in the oven (if you don't want to use the egg wash) is one way to create steam. Placing a baking tray full of ice cubes or water on the bottom of the oven will also cause a steaming effect.

Bake the baguettes at 450°F for at least 35 minutes in a standard oven. If using a convection oven, bake at 425°F for the same period. The baking time may extend to as much as 40 minutes. When the loaves are done, they should be golden brown and their bottoms should sound hollow when tapped.

Allow a minimum of 1 hour for the baguettes to cool before eating.

Nutrient Values per Loaf:
Calories: 816.2. Protein: 24.2 g. Carbohydrate: 166.7 g. Dietary Fiber: 6.301 g. Total Sugars: 6.531 g. Total Fat: 5.29 g. Saturated Fat: .871 g. Monounsaturated Fat: .711 g. Polyunsaturated Fat: 2.13 g. Cholesterol: 17.6 mg. Trans Fat: 0 g. Total Omega-3 FA: .049 g. Total Omega-6 FA: 0 g. Potassium: 376.1 mg. Sodium: 13.1 mg. Vitamin K: .67 mcg. Folic Acid: 320.8 mcg.

Nutrient Data per Estimated 1-inch Slice:
Calories: 51. Protein: 1.515 g. Carbohydrate: 10.4 g. Dietary Fiber: .394 g. Total Sugars: .408 g. Total Fat: .331 g. Saturated Fat: .054 g. Monounsaturated Fat: .044 g. Polyunsaturated Fat: .133 g. Cholesterol: 1.102 mg. Trans Fat: 0 g. Total Omega-3 FA: .003 g. Total Omega-6 FA: 0 g. Potassium: 23.5 mg. Sodium: .819 mg. Vitamin K: .042 mcg. Folic Acid: 20.1 mcg.

❈ BASIC BREAD CRUMBS ❈

FOR RECIPES CALLING FOR WHITE BREAD CRUMBS
DIABETIC ADAPTABLE
BREAD MACHINE RECIPE

Some of our recipes in this book call for white bread crumbs. This recipe will work well when you need bread crumbs. Simply make the bread and then slice and toast it. Or let the bread stand out overnight and then crumble to make the crumbs.

**MAKES 1 LOAF (14 THICK SLICES)   SODIUM PER RECIPE: 15.9 MG
SODIUM PER SLICE: 1.138 MG**

1   **cup warm low-sodium water, 100°F to 110°F (trace)**
1   **tablespoon extra-virgin olive oil (trace)**
1   **tablespoon cider vinegar (.15 mg)**
1   **teaspoon vanilla extract or flavoring (.378 mg)**
3   **cups unbleached bread flour (7.5 mg)**
1   **tablespoon white granulated sugar or Splenda (trace)**
1   **tablespoon vital wheat gluten (2.25 mg)**

¼   **teaspoon ascorbic acid (trace)**
½   **teaspoon salt-free onion powder or granulated onion**
     (.648 mg)
2½ **teaspoons bread machine yeast (5 mg)**

Place all ingredients into the bread machine pan in the order listed and set for White Bread, 2-Pound Loaf, Medium Crust.

When done, cool on a rack. Slice about ¾ inch to 1 inch thick.

To make the crumbs, let slices sit out for a day or toast lightly and then crumble.

You may also use this bread for sandwiches, or store in the freezer for later use. Always keep salt-free bread closed tightly in airtight, ziplock bags or containers.

Nutrient Data per Slice:
Calories: 112.2. Protein: 3.46 g. Carbohydrate: 21.9 g. Dietary Fiber: .878 g. Total Sugars: 1.103 g. Total Fat: .94 g. Saturated Fat: .137 g. Monounsaturated Fat: .346 g. Polyunsaturated Fat: .321 g. Cholesterol: 0 mg. Trans Fat: 0 g. Total Omega-3 FA: .009 g. Total Omega-6 FA: 0 g. Potassium: 45.3 mg. Sodium: 1.138 mg. Vitamin K: .217 mcg. Folic Acid: 41.2 mcg.

❈ SEASONED BREAD CRUMBS ❈

ORIGIN: WORLDWIDE
DIABETIC ADAPTABLE

Can be used for croutons for recipes in this book
MAKES 3 CUPS   SODIUM PER RECIPE: 14.7 MG
SODIUM PER CUP: 4.897 MG

2   **tablespoons unsalted butter* (3.124 mg)**
8   **slices of Basic Bread Crumbs bread† (see page 167)**
     (9.079 mg)
2   **teaspoons Don's Herbes de Provence Spice Mix (see page 36)**
     (2.488 mg)

Preheat the oven to 300°F.

Soften the unsalted butter and spread on both sides of the bread and sprinkle with the herbs. Place on a baking sheet in the oven for 30 minutes. Turn the bread over after the first 15 minutes.

The bread should be dry and lightly toasted when done. Chop into

---

*If butter is not on your diet, you can spray the bread lightly with a spray-type olive oil (trace sodium).
†Nutrient data based on Italian Milano Bread (See *No-Salt, Lowest-Sodium Baking Book*). You can use any low-sodium bread. We also like to use the 7-grain bread in our *No-Salt, Lowest-Sodium Cookbook*.

small pieces. Use as croutons for soups and salads as well as for recipes requiring bread crumbs, such as our meat loaf and gyros recipes.

Nutrient Data per Cup:
Calories: 380.3. Protein: 9.471 g. Carbohydrate: 59.7 g. Dietary Fiber: 3.202 g. Total Sugars: 2.381 g. Total Fat: 11.2 g. Saturated Fat: 5.397 g. Monounsaturated Fat: 4.006 g. Polyunsaturated Fat: .821 g. Cholesterol: 20.4 mg. Trans Fat: 0 g. Total Omega-3 FA: .104 g. Total Omega-6 FA: .205 g. Potassium: 147.3 mg. Sodium: 4.897 mg. Vitamin K: 1.923 mcg. Folic Acid: 0 mcg.

BEST SESAME SEED
❖ BURGER BUNS EVER ❖

ORIGIN: U.S.A.
DIABETIC ADAPTABLE

BREAD MACHINE KNEAD—HAND SHAPE—OVEN BAKE

Who doesn't like hamburgers? Lots of lettuce, onion slices, tomato slices, even sautéed mushrooms, and some of that great low-sodium Cheddar or Swiss cheese. To carry all those delicious and healthy vegetables, we need a great bun. Here it is! Our best yet and easy to make. Enjoy!

MAKES 12 TO 18 BUNS   SODIUM PER RECIPE: 134.6 MG
SODIUM PER BUN (12): 11.2 MG
SODIUM PER BUN (18): 7.478 MG

THE BREAD

1½	cups warmed orange juice, not from concentrate, lots of pulp, about 100°F to 110°F (trace)
½	cup warmed nonfat milk with vitamins A and D, 100°F to 110°F (51.5 mg)
3	tablespoons extra-virgin olive oil (trace)
1	tablespoon apple cider vinegar (.15 mg)
5	cups unbleached bread flour (12.5 mg)
2	tablespoons sugar or Splenda substitute (trace)
1	teaspoon vanilla extract (.378 mg)
½	teaspoon onion powder (.648 mg)
1	tablespoon vital wheat gluten (2.25 mg)
1	tablespoon potato flour (3.1 mg)
¼	teaspoon ascorbic acid (trace)
1	teaspoon granular or soy lecithin (trace)
1	tablespoon bread machine yeast (6 mg)

THE SESAME SEED TOPPING

1 egg white (54.8 mg)
1 tablespoon water (trace)
2 tablespoons sesame seeds (1.98 mg)

Place the bread ingredients, except for the sesame seed topping, in the bread machine pan in order listed. Set the machine to Dough.

Turn the oven to proof temperature with the two racks set so that they can hold two baking sheets. If you don't have a proof button on your oven, turn it on to 300°F for 1 minute, and then turn it off.

Cover 2 baking sheets with parchment paper.

When the dough is nearly done, stir the tablespoon of water into the egg and whisk briskly. Set aside.

Place the dough on a lightly floured board and press or gently roll it out with a rolling pin to a thickness of 1 to 1½ inches. To shape buns, you have a few choices. I like to cut the dough into 12 to 18 rectangular sandwich shapes or use large muffin rings to cut out round buns. Divide the buns between the baking sheets. You should get between 12 and 18 buns for the whole recipe. Baste buns all over, including the sides, with the egg wash and sprinkle generously with the sesame seeds.

Place into the warmed or proof-temperature oven for 45 minutes to 1 hour, uncovered. Or place in a warm spot in your home, lightly covered with a light, flour-dusted cloth. Let rise for about 1 hour.

Preheat the oven to 375°F and bake the buns for 15 to 20 minutes, or until golden brown. Cool on rack. Store in ziplock bags. These travel well if they are stored correctly. Freshness will last for up to 10 days.

Nutrient Date per Bun (12):
Calories: 263.5. Protein: 7.348 g. Carbohydrate: 46.7 g. Dietary Fiber: 1.799 g. Total Sugars: 5.461 g. Total Fat: 4.929 g. Saturated Fat: .692 g. Monounsaturated Fat: 2.876 g. Polyunsaturated Fat: .984 g. Cholesterol: .204 mg. Trans Fat : 0 g. Total Omega-3 FA: .044 g. Total Omega-6 FA: 0 g. Potassium: 119.1 mg. Sodium: 11.2 mg. Vitamin K: 2.192 mcg. Folic Acid: 80.2 mcg.

Nutrient Data per Bun (18):
Calories: 175.6. Protein: 4.898 g. Carbohydrate: 31.1 g. Dietary Fiber: 1.199 g. Total Sugars: 3.64 g. Total Fat: 3.286 g. Saturated Fat: .461 g. Monounsaturated Fat: 1.917 g. Polyunsaturated Fat: .656 g. Cholesterol: .136 mg. Trans Fat: 0 g. Total Omega-3 FA: .029 g. Total Omega-6 FA: 0 g. Potassium: 79.4 mg. Sodium: 7.478 mg. Vitamin K: 1.461 mcg. Folic Acid: 53.5 mcg.

❖ CHALLAH ❖

ORIGIN: JEWISH BREAD
DIABETIC ADAPTABLE

BREAD MACHINE KNEAD—HAND SHAPE—OVEN BAKE

This is traditional Jewish bread eaten on the Sabbath and all Jewish holidays except for Passover. There are many different recipes for challah with most of them using many eggs and lots of butter (instead of olive oil like we do). The large amount of eggs is why it is often referred to as an "egg bread."

Enjoy this bread at breakfast with your favorite jam or preserves or slice it into the Texas-size strips as we do for French toast. Children love this bread for its light sweet flavor. You may double this recipe to bake in a larger braided style on a baking sheet in your oven, but if you do, use only 4 teaspoons of yeast instead of doubling what we have here.

MAKES 1 BRAIDED LOAF (24 SLICES)   SODIUM PER RECIPE: 151.7 MG
SODIUM PER SLICE: 7.268 MG

THE BREAD

½   **cup plus 9 tablespoons warm low-sodium water, 100°F to 110°F (trace)**
2   **large eggs taken out of refrigerator 10 minutes before using (126 mg)**
1   **tablespoon white wine vinegar (.15 mg)**
3   **tablespoons extra-virgin olive oil (trace)**
2   **tablespoons white sugar or Splenda (trace)**
½   **teaspoon onion powder (.648 mg)**
¼   **teaspoon ascorbic acid (trace)**
1   **tablespoon vital wheat gluten (2.25 mg)**
3   **cups less 1 tablespoon unbleached bread flour (7.275 mg)**
2   **tablespoons potato flour (7.75 mg)**
2½ **teaspoons bread machine yeast (4.5 mg)**

THE TOPPING

1 **egg yolk (8.16 mg)**
1 **tablespoon low-sodium water (trace)**
1 **tablespoon poppy seeds (1.848 mg)*, or sesame seeds (.99 mg)**

Place the bread ingredients into the bread machine and set for Dough.

Heat your oven for the rise either using your proof button or by bringing it to 100°F or just under.

Prepare a baking sheet by spraying it with oil and dusting with flour.

Just before the dough is ready, lightly beat the egg yolk with the water and set the egg wash aside.

When the dough is ready, roll it out on a lightly floured board. Break into 2 equal pieces. Form logs by rolling the dough with both hands. This dough will be very pliable so have fun. Braid these on the baking sheet.

*Recipe data lists poppy seeds for the totals.

(If you don't like the braid, pick up the whole thing and twist it until it's even from end to end.)

Baste with the egg wash. Sprinkle poppy seeds or sesame seeds over the top. Cover with lightly oiled waxed paper or very light cloth dusted with flour and let rise for about 1 hour in a warm place such as your proofing oven.

Preheat the oven to 375°F. Bake the challah for 30 to 40 minutes, or until golden brown.

Nutrient Data per Slice:
Calories: 90.6. Protein: 2.737 g. Carbohydrate: 13.8 g. Dietary Fiber: .53 g. Total Sugars: 1.249 g. Total Fat: 2.633 g. Saturated Fat: .47 g. Monounsaturated Fat: 1.535 g. Polyunsaturated Fat: .435 g. Cholesterol: 26.4 mg. Trans Fat: 0 g. Total Omega-3 FA: .023 g. Total Omega-6 FA: 0 g. Potassium: 49.1 mg. Sodium: 7.268 mg. Vitamin K: 1.083 mcg. Folic Acid: 23.3 mcg.

❋ CHINESE STEAMED BUNS ❋

ORIGIN: NORTHERN CHINA
DIABETIC ADAPTABLE

BREAD MACHINE KNEAD—STEAM

I asked my friend, Ken Chung, in China about Chinese bread and he replied, "We don't have bread like the West does. We only have the Chinese Steamed Buns in the north." So he e-mailed me even more info about true Chinese cuisine, and these Chinese steamed buns were a part of his coming to the rescue.

These are excellent. Steam them and serve them hot. They are truly delightful served with a barbecued meal or with a stew. I make them using the bread machine to knead the dough. You can make them by hand, if you prefer, by simply starting with the usual yeast sponge.

MAKES: 16 BUNS   SODIUM PER RECIPE: 120.7 MG
SODIUM PER SERVING: 7.544 MG

THE DOUGH
1   cup warmed, nonfat milk with vitamins A and D, 100°F to 110°F (102.9 mg)
3½ cups unbleached bread flour (8.75 mg)
1   tablespoon vital wheat gluten (2.25 mg)
¼   teaspoon ascorbic acid (trace)
½   cup white granulated sugar or Splenda (trace)
1   tablespoon rice vinegar (.15 mg)
½   teaspoon onion powder (.648 mg)
1   tablespoon bread machine yeast (6 mg)

Place all ingredients in bread machine pan and set for Dough.*

Once your machine has made the dough, roll it out on a lightly floured breadboard and form it into a ball. Place into a lightly greased bowl, cover the top tightly with plastic wrap, and let rise in a proofing oven or other warm place for about 45 minutes, or until it's at least double. Press down to deflate and transfer it to your breadboard. Cut it into 16 even pieces.

Roll each piece in your hands until it is about 2 inches in diameter. If you want to fill the bun with a cooked meat mixture,** or even a treat like jam, prior to steaming, then roll out the ball to a 4-inch disk and place the filling into the center. Roll the dough up and form the ball again. After forming the balls, let them stand for about 5 minutes in a warm place, covered lightly with oiled waxed paper.

To cook the buns, you can use either a wooden steamer† or a metal steamer but you will need to cover them while they steam. Set the buns on the steamer rack about 2 inches apart to allow for expansion.

Steam for 15 to 18 minutes, covered with a high lid to allow the buns to rise.

Serve hot or store covered in refrigerator, and reheat to serve later.

Nutrient Data per Bun:
Calories: 133.4. Protein: 3.995 g. Carbohydrate: 28.4 g. Dietary Fiber: .9 g. Total Sugars: 7.18 g. Total Fat: .323 g. Saturated Fat: .065 g. Monounsaturated Fat: .05 g. Polyunsaturated Fat: .114 g. Cholesterol: .306 mg. Trans Fat: 0 g. Total Omega-3 FA: .006 g. Total Omega-6 FA: 0 g. Potassium: 69.9 mg. Sodium: 7.544 mg. Vitamin K: .085 mcg. Folic Acid: 42.1 mcg.

❖ CIABATTA ❖

ORIGIN: ITALY
DIABETIC ACCEPTABLE‡

BREAD MACHINE KNEAD—HAND SHAPE—OVEN BAKE

This is known as the "slipper" bread since that's that's how it looks and about how high it sits after being baked. (Actually it rises higher than that.) The flavor is terrific, but be forewarned. It takes time to make a good ciabatta. This Italian bread is popular throughout Europe and has

---

*You can prepare the dough for this in your bread machine or by hand. Kneading by hand takes about 10 minutes or so. You have to make a sponge with the yeast first, so use ⅓ cup of water and the remaining liquid should be ¾ cup of warm nonfat milk. When the dough is ready, follow the steps above where the dough is cut into 16 to 18 even pieces.
**You may use chicken or pork or wild game bird.
†A wooden steamer, used generally in a wok, can be found at www.megaheart.com/kit_cabinet.html This is a standard Chinese steamer.
‡Most of the carbohydrates are in the flour mixture (435.3 grams).

reached the United States, where its acceptance is as eager as it was in Europe. You will love this bread and your friends and family will be amazed. You might even get a "wow" out of them. This may be made with a bread machine

**MAKES 4 LOAVES   SODIUM PER RECIPE: 61.3 MG
SODIUM PER SLICE (32): 1.93 MG**

THE SPONGE

1   teaspoon active dry yeast (2 mg)
1   cup warm, low-sodium water, 100° F to 110° F (trace)
1½ cups sifted unbleached bread flour (3.75 mg)

THE DOUGH

1½ teaspoons active dry yeast (3 mg)
5   tablespoons nonfat warm milk (34 mg)
1   cup warm water (trace)
1   tablespoon white wine vinegar (.15 mg)
1   tablespoon olive oil (trace)
3   cups unsifted bread flour (7.5 mg)
¼   teaspoon ascorbic acid (trace)
1   teaspoon onion powder (1.296 mg)
1   tablespoon vital wheat gluten (2.25 mg)

To make the sponge, add the yeast to the water in a medium mixing bowl and let stand for 5 minutes, stirring gently until the yeast dissolves and begins to act.

When proofed, sift the flour into the yeast and stir together, using a wooden spoon. Cover tightly with plastic wrap or a lid and set the sponge in a room-temperature atmosphere overnight. It's best if it sits for 12 to 16 hours.

To make the bread: Mix the yeast into the warmed milk in a small bowl and stir until it's evenly distributed. Let is stand for 5 minutes so that it begins to act. When proofed, put the yeast mixture, the water, vinegar, and olive oil into a large bowl or the bowl of your mixer. Stir the sponge with a wooden spoon. Once combined you can use your dough hook if you have a stand mixer, to mix it for another minute, or until it's thoroughly combined.

Add 2 cups of the flour, the ascorbic acid, onion powder, and gluten and machine-knead for 2 minutes at low speed then increase the speed a notch or two and knead for about 3 minutes more. Add the remaining flour slowly, adding more water if needed, until the dough begins to pull from the sides of the bowl. The dough should be soft to the touch, but not sticky. You may need 2 to 4 tablespoons additional warm water. (Set it aside ahead of time in case you need it during the kneading process.) However, we have never needed it with this recipe. We have used Stone-Buhr's bread flour and King Arthur bread flour with this recipe. Each seems to behave like the other.

Cover or place in a large, oiled bowl and let rise in a warm or slightly warmer than room temperature place to three times its size. This rise is important. About 1 hour is needed. It will triple in size and get a bit bubbly, which is what you want.

Place the dough on a floured board or other generously floured work surface and divide into 2 pieces. Do not punch the dough down. Instead, gently form it into 2 loaves about 10 to 12 inches long and about 3 inches wide. You really need parchment paper under the loaves while they're baking. So place the paper on a baking sheet, flour the paper more than usual, and place each loaf on the flour. Turn each loaf over once so that flour shows on the top. Cover the dough with lightly oiled waxed paper and let rise for 90 minutes in a warm place. If using a proofing oven or other warmer-than-room-temperature spot, there is no need to cover it. The dough will rise only slightly.

The flour on the surface when the bread makes its final rise is what remains on the top of the loaf after baking. After your first baking you'll get the hang of it and know how much flour to use next time if you miss the mark this time around. You can also form the dough into 8 to 10 sandwich rolls, which make incredible sandwiches.

Preheat the oven to 400°F, or if using a convection oven, to 375°F.

Bake the bread for 25 to 30 minutes, or until it just begins to turn golden. During the first 10 minutes, spray (mist) the bread with water 3 times.

Store for up to 4 days in ziplock bags or freeze for up to 1 month.

Nutrient Data per Slice (33):
Calories: 71.4. Protein: 2.214 g. Carbohydrate: 14 g. Dietary Fiber: .531 g. Total Sugars: .229 g. Total Fat: .616 g. Saturated Fat: .09 g. Monounsaturated Fat: .336 g. Polyunsaturated Fat: .116 g. Cholesterol: .051 mg. Trans Fat: 0 g. Total Omega-3 FA: .007 g. Total Omega-6 FA: 0 g. Potassium: 40.8 mg. Sodium: 1.93 mg. Vitamin K: .308 mcg. Folic Acid: 26.3 mcg.

✧ DON'S POCKET PITA BREAD ✧

ORIGIN: MIDDLE EASTERN, POSSIBLY ORIGINATED IN SYRIA
DIABETIC ACCEPTABLE

BREAD MACHINE KNEAD—HAND SHAPE—OVEN BAKE

Use this Middle Eastern recipe for making terrific noontime sandwiches, especially with our Greek Meat Loaf recipe (see page 100). Fill with 1 serving portion of meat loaf and our Tzatziki Sauce (see page 54). Add diced tomatoes and red onion, or make your own sandwich with your favorite mix of lettuce, tomatoes, avocados, etc. Pitas are great for hummus sandwiches as well.

This dough may be made in bread machine or by hand. The bread is best if cooked on tiles or stones, but a heavy-duty, nonstick baking sheet will also work.

**MAKES 12 SIX-INCH PITAS   SODIUM PER RECIPE: 73.5 MG
SODIUM PER SERVING: 6.125 MG**

1¼ cups plus 2 tablespoons warm low-sodium water, 100° F to 110° F (trace)
1   egg white (54.8 mg)
1   tablespoon extra-virgin olive oil (trace)
1   tablespoon white wine vinegar (.15 mg)
1   cup whole wheat or white whole wheat flour (6 mg)
2½ cups unbleached bread flour (6.25 mg)
1   teaspoon onion powder (1.134 mg)
2   garlic cloves, well crushed (1.02 mg)
1   teaspoon white granulated sugar or Splenda (trace)
2   teaspoons bread machine yeast (4 mg)
    Cornmeal for dusting the pan

Place the ingredients in the bread machine according to manufacturer's directions or in the order listed above. Set the machine for Dough.

Preheat the oven to 500°F.

After rising, place the dough on a floured surface and roll it into a log 12 to 14 inch long. Cut into 12 sections. Roll each section into a ball about the size of a tennis ball by pulling the dough down and under a half-dozen times to form the ball. Pinch the ends together each time you pull down and around.

When each ball is completed, put it on a floured surface. Repeat to make the other balls. Cover with a light kitchen towel or waxed paper. The balls should rest for at least 10 minutes.

After this rising period, roll each ball with a rolling pin, flattening it to a

6-inch disk. Rolling these out will take some pressure. Keep plenty of flour on the breadboard so the dough doesn't stick to the board or the rolling pin.

Preheat the oven to 500°F.

Place each pita-shaped disk on a baking pan, sprinkled lightly with either a fine polenta (such as Golden Pheasant brand) or with Albers Cornmeal or another ungerminated corn flour or very low-sodium cornmeal. You should fit about 4 per baking sheet, but don't let them touch one another. Let rest in a warm spot under a light cloth for 20 to 30 minutes.

Slip the baking sheet into the oven.

Close the oven door quickly and bake for 4 to 5 minutes at 500°F. Remove the pitas one at a time with a pancake turner or paddle. Cool on a solid wood surface or on a rack while you bake the remaining disks. They will deflate while cooling.

To use, break the pitas open while still warm and stuff with your favorite sandwich filling. The pitas may be refrigerated in tightly sealed ziplock bags or frozen for future use.

Nutrient Data for one Pocket Pita:
Calories: 145. Protein: 4.667 g. Carbohydrate: 28.2 g. Dietary Fiber: 2.085 g. Total Sugars: .63 g. Total Fat: 1.607 g. Saturated Fat: .229 g.

❧ DUTCH CRUNCH BREAD ❧

ORIGIN: CALIFORNIA
DIABETIC ADAPTABLE*

BREAD MACHINE KNEAD—HAND SHAPE—OVEN BAKE

One of my favorite sandwich breads is easy to make. This tasty sandwich bread will impress your friends as well. Freeze for up to 3 months or serve right out of the oven. Bake until the tops brown. The crisp Dutch crunch topping was popular in the 1960s and '70s.

MAKES 12 SANDWICH ROLLS OR 18 SMALLER BUNS
SODIUM PER RECIPE: 68 MG
SODIUM PER BUN (18): 3.778 MG
SODIUM PER LONG SANDWICH ROLL (12): 5.667 MG

THE BREAD
1¾ cups less 1 tablespoon warmed (90°F to 110°F) distilled or sodium-free water (trace)
3 tablespoons extra-virgin olive oil (trace)
2 tablespoons nonfat milk with added vitamins A & D, slightly warmed (12.9 mg)

*Diabetics, replace sugar with Splenda.

1   teaspoon vanilla extract (.378 mg)
2   tablespoons cider vinegar (.30 mg)
4¾ cups unbleached bread flour (11.9 mg)
¼   cup potato flour (15.5 mg)
1   teaspoon onion powder (1.134 mg)
¼   teaspoon ascorbic acid (trace)
1   tablespoon vital wheat gluten (2.683 mg)
2   teaspoons white granulated sugar (trace)
1   tablespoon bread machine yeast (6 mg)

THE DUTCH CRUNCH TOPPING
4   teaspoons white granulated sugar (trace)
3   tablespoons active dry yeast (18 mg)
¾   cup white rice flour (trace)
2   teaspoons extra-virgin olive oil (trace)
⅔   cups plus two tablespoons filtered low-sodium water,
    warmed to about 80° to 90°F (trace)

Place the ingredients for the dough into the bread machine pan in the order listed. Set the machine for Dough.

Forty minutes before the dough is ready to roll out of the machine,
prepare the topping. Place the rice flour in a large mixing bowl and make
a well. Place the yeast into the well.

Add the remaining topping ingredients and stir together. Cover and let
rest for 35 to 40 minutes at room temperature.

Stir well just before applying to the baked bread.

When the bread dough is ready, knead it slightly on a lightly floured
board and shape it into 12 elongated or rolled sandwich buns. Or shape it
into 3 baguette-size logs for baking on your baguette pan (you'll slice
these into sandwich buns later).

Place the buns on parchment paper on a cooking sheet or, if baguette
shaped, on lightly greased baguette pans. Generously and evenly spread
the topping over each bun or loaf, working this with your hands and making sure the entire top of the bun or roll is covered smoothly. (The topping cannot be colder than the dough.)

Let rise, uncovered, in a warm spot or in an oven preheated to about
90°F to 100°F until they double or more in size. This will take about 45
minutes to 1 hour and 15 minutes.

Preheat the oven to 375°F. and set the rack in the middle position. Bake
the buns until the tops are a deep golden brown, 18 to 25 minutes. (The
Dutch Crunch part should get pretty dark.)

Cool on rack.

Nutrient Data per Hamburger Bun (18):
Calories: 195.8. Protein: 5.45 g. Carbohydrate: 35.6 g. Dietary Fiber: 1.613 g. Total Sugars: 1.762 g. Total Fat: 3.321 g. Saturated Fat: .472 g. Monounsaturated Fat: 2.156 g. Polyunsaturated Fat: .455 g. Cholesterol: .034 mg. Trans Fat: 0 g. Total Omega-3 FA: .034 g. Total Omega-6 FA: 0 g. Potassium: 136.6 mg. Sodium: 3.778 mg. Vitamin K: 1.772 mcg. Folic Acid: 50.8 mcg.

Nutrient Data per Long Sandwich Roll (12):
Calories: 293.6. Protein: 8.176 g. Carbohydrate: 53.4 g. Dietary Fiber: 2.419 g. Total Sugars: 2.643 g. Total Fat: 4.982 g. Saturated Fat: .709 g. Monounsaturated Fat: 3.234 g. Polyunsaturated Fat: .683 g. Cholesterol: .051 mg. Trans Fat: 0 g. Total Omega-3 FA: .051 g. Total Omega-6 FA: 0 g. Potassium: 205 mg. Sodium: 5.667 mg. Vitamin K: 2.658 mcg. Folic Acid: 76.2 mcg.

❈ ETHIOPIAN HONEY BREAD ❈

ORIGIN: ETHIOPIA
DIABETIC ADAPTABLE*

BREAD MACHINE RECIPE

This bread is also known as Ymarina Yewotet Dabo. *You won't find many variations of it if you search elsewhere. Its five primary flavors are honey, cinnamon, cloves, coriander, and, not for our tastes, salt. This recipe was developed from an original Ethiopian recipe tucked away in our files many years ago. It's a marvelous treat and one you'll probably make again.*

MAKES 1 LOAF   SODIUM PER RECIPE: 202.2 MG
SODIUM PER SLICE (18): 11.2 MG

1   **cup warmed nonfat milk with vitamins A and D, 100°F to 110°F (102.9 mg)**

1   **large egg (70 mg)**

½   **cup honey (6.78 mg)**

1   **tablespoon cider vinegar (.15 mg)**

3   **tablespoons extra-virgin olive oil (trace)**

3½   **cups plus 2 tablespoons unbleached bread flour (9.062 mg)**

¼   **teaspoon ascorbic acid (trace)**

1   **teaspoon onion powder (1.296 mg)**

2   **tablespoons potato flour (7.75 mg)**

1   **tablespoon granular lecithin (trace)**

1   **tablespoon vital wheat gluten (2.25 mg)**

1   **teaspoon sugar or Splenda substitute (.084 mg)**

1   **tablespoon ground coriander (1.75 mg)**

*Most of the carbohydrates are in the flour (333.9 g) and honey (139.7 g).

¾ teaspoon ground cinnamon (.448 mg)
¼ teaspoon ground cloves (1.276 mg)
2¾ teaspoons bread machine yeast (5.5 mg)

Place the ingredients in the order listed into your bread pan. Set the bread machine for White Bread, 2½-Pound Loaf, Light Crust; or 2-Pound Loaf, Medium Crust.

When the bread is done, roll out onto rack and let cool. Serve hot straight out of the bread machine or at room temperature.

Nutrient Data per Slice:
Calories: 157.4. Protein: 4.144 g. Carbohydrate: 29.6 g. Dietary Fiber: 1.013 g. Total Sugars: 8.648 g. Total Fat: 2.727 g. Saturated Fat: .456 g. Monounsaturated Fat: 1.027 g. Polyunsaturated Fat: .9 g. Cholesterol: 12 mg. Trans Fat: 0 g. Total Omega-3 FA: .016 g. Total Omega-6 FA: 0 g. Potassium: 95.3 mg. Sodium: 11.2 mg. Vitamin K: .506 mcg. Folic Acid: 38.8 mcg.

❧ ETHIOPIAN SPICE BREAD ❧

ORIGIN: ETHIOPIA
DIABETIC ADAPTABLE*

BREAD MACHINE RECIPE

This recipe uses maple extract instead of fenugreek seeds, which are hard to find. Fenugreek seeds, after toasting, taste a bit like maple so we exchanged the seeds with the extract and the bread fulfilled our expectations. This is a tasty bread with a true Ethiopian flavor.

MAKES 1 LOAF (16 SLICES)   SODIUM PER RECIPE: 217.6 MG
SODIUM PER SLICE: 13.6 MG

1   cup plus 1 tablespoon warmed nonfat milk with added
    vitamins A & D, 100°F to 110°F (110.1 mg)
1   teaspoon sugar (trace)
⅛   teaspoon scant ground dried ginger (.072 mg)
1   large egg (63 mg)
½   cup scant honey, or ⅓ cup Splenda (6.78 mg)
1   tablespoon cider vinegar (.15 mg)
3   tablespoons Niter Kebbeh (see page 48) (1.058 mg)
1   teaspoon maple extract (.378 mg)
3¾ cups unbleached bread flour (9.375 mg)

*Most of the carbohydrates are in the flour (357.7 g) and honey (139.7 g).

¼	cup potato flour (15.5 mg)
1	tablespoon vital wheat gluten (2.25 mg)
¼	teaspoon ascorbic acid (trace)
1	tablespoon ground coriander (1.75 mg)
½	teaspoon ground cinnamon (.299 mg)
¼	teaspoon ground cloves (1.276 mg)
1	tablespoon bread machine yeast (6 mg)

Place all the ingredients into a bread machine pan in the order listed (or according to your manufacturer's directions). Set for White Bread, Medium Crust, 2½-Pound Loaf.

When done transfer to a rack and let cool before slicing.

Nutrient Data per Slice:
Calories: 181.2. Protein: 4.933 g. Carbohydrate: 35.2 g. Dietary Fiber: 1.185 g. Total Sugars: 9.754 g. Total Fat: 2.482 g. Saturated Fat: .429 g. Monounsaturated Fat: 1.049 g. Polyunsaturated Fat: .757 g. Cholesterol: 13.5 mg. Trans Fat: 0 g. Total Omega-3 FA: .018 g. Total Omega-6 FA: 0 g. Potassium: 134.1 mg. Sodium: 13.6 mg. Vitamin K: .556 mcg. Folic Acid: 45.1 mcg.

❈ FLAXSEED MEAL AND RAISIN BREAD ❈

ORIGIN: U.S.A.
DIABETIC ADAPTABLE*

BREAD MACHINE RECIPE

This all-white-flour bread has added fiber from the flaxseed meal and excellent flavor from the raisins and other ingredients. It's easy to put together for your bread machine.

**MAKES 1 LOAF (16 SLICES)   SODIUM PER RECIPE: 43.6 MG
SODIUM PER SLICE (16): 2.724 MG**

1	cup plus 1 tablespoon warm low-sodium water, 100°F to 110°F.
1	tablespoon cider vinegar (.15 mg)
1	tablespoon extra-virgin olive oil (trace)
1	teaspoon vanilla extract (.378 mg)
2¾	cups unbleached bread flour (7.5 mg)

*You may want to reduce or remove the raisins (48.8 g sugars and 65.3 g carbohydrates). If you do, just replace with a teaspoon of ground cinnamon and 3 tablespoons of flaxseed meal for color and and a nutty flavor. When exchanging, you may need to add 1 to 2 tablespoons of filtered, low-sodium water.

¼	cup potato flour (15.5 mg)
2	level tablespoons granular lecithin (trace)
3	tablespoons flaxseed meal (trace)
1	tablespoon vital wheat gluten flour (2.25 mg)
¼	teaspoon ascorbic acid (trace)
1	teaspoon granulated onion* (1.134)
⅓	tablespoon white granulated sugar or Splenda (trace)
2½	teaspoons bread machine yeast (5 mg)
½	cup black seedless raisins, packed† (9.075 mg)

Place all ingredients into the bread machine pan in the order listed, except for the raisins. Keep the yeast dry on top of the dry ingredients.

Set the machine for 2-Pound Loaf, Medium Crust, White Bread, or if you have it, set on Fruits & Nuts. At the sound of the Add-Fruit-Buzzer, add the ½ cup of raisins.

When the bread is done, transfer to a rack and cool. Store in a tightly sealed plastic ziplock bag. This bread freezes well.

Nutrient Data per Slice:
Calories: 140.5. Protein: 3.728 g. Carbohydrate: 26.1 g. Dietary Fiber: 1.354 g. Total Sugars: 4.144 g. Total Fat: 2.582 g. Saturated Fat: .314 g. Monounsaturated Fat: .773 g. Polyunsaturated Fat: .648 g. Cholesterol: 0 mg. Trans Fat: 0 g. Total Omega-3 FA: .012 g. Total Omega-6 FA: 0 g. Potassium: 126.3 mg. Sodium: 2.724 mg. Vitamin K: .776 mcg. Folic Acid: 36.1 mcg.

❈ FLOUR TORTILLAS ❈

ORIGIN: MEXICO
DIABETIC ACCEPTABLE

You can purchase corn tortillas in most local markets, and generally they are very low in sodium or use no salt. But low-sodium, no-salt flour tortillas generally aren't available in stores.

This recipe is a bit of a change from our flour tortilla in The No-Salt, Lowest-Sodium Baking Book. *Either one is a very good recipe, but for this book we made some minor improvements.*

*McCormick or other or no-salt onion powder.
†I prefer to add the raisins at the buzzer for the wonderful speckled appearance the bread has with the flaxseed and raisins. Or you can put them in with all ingredients, which will give you a darker but very flavorful bread. I often make this one with dried cranberries.

MAKES 12 EIGHT-INCH FLOUR TORTILLAS   SODIUM PER RECIPE: 20.5 MG
SODIUM PER TORTILLA: 1.708 MG

4   cups unbleached bread flour (10 mg)
1   teaspoon onion powder (1.134 mg)
½   cup extra-virgin olive oil (trace)
1   tablespoon white wine vinegar (.15 mg)
2   teaspoons freshly squeezed lime juice (.19 mg)
1½   cups low-sodium water (trace)
2   teaspoons Featherweight baking powder (9 mg)

Combine the flour and onion powder in a medium bowl. Add the olive oil
and vinegar and stir with a wooden spoon. Add the lime juice. Then add the
water slowly, mixing it together while doing so. When the dough cleans the
side of the bowl, stop adding the water. Too much water can make a tortilla
tough.

Add in the Featherweight baking powder and knead, using your fingers
to work the dough, for about 8 turns to mix the Featherweight into the
dough.

Form the dough into a ball and cover with plastic or cloth.

Let sit for about 30 minutes to 2 hours in a room-temperature location.

Heat a nonstick flat-surface griddle or a large nonstick frying pan over
medium to medium-high heat. If you use the nonstick, you won't need oil
or butter to "fry" these.

Form 12 evenly sized balls with your hands. Press to form a disk and
place on lightly floured board and place a piece of waxed paper over the
tortilla, roll out to an even thinner disk. If using a tortilla press, follow
manufacturer's instructions. (You can find a tortilla press at a discount
price at www.megaheart.com/kit_cabinet.html.)

If not using a press, lightly flour the board. Press a ball of dough over
your forefinger to create a hole. Set the ball on the breadboard, hole side
down, and roll out the dough with a pin and waxed paper as described
above. To make a circle, roll it once, then turn the dough 90 degrees,
and roll again. Continue doing this until you've rolled it out thinly. Each
ball should make an 8- to 12-inch tortilla.

When a splash of water bounces on the griddle or frying pan, you are
ready to cook the tortillas. You can prepare all the tortillas and then cook
them, or prepare and cook, prepare and cook, and so on. Each tortilla
should cook in about 20 to 30 seconds. Turn the tortilla when it bubbles
and cook the opposite side for 5 to 10 seconds.

You can store the tortillas in the refrigerator overnight in ziplock bags.
Or stack with waxed paper between each tortilla, put into ziplock bag,
and freeze for future use.

Nutrient Values per Tortilla:
Calories: 233. Protein: 4.326 g. Carbohydrate: 32.4 g. Dietary Fiber: 1.156 g. Total Sugars: .261 g. Total Fat: 9.414 g. Saturated Fat: 1.276 g. Monounsaturated Fat: 6.688 g. Polyunsaturated Fat: 1.074 g. Cholesterol: 0 mg. Trans Fat: 0 g. Total Omega-3 FA: .081 g. Total Omega-6 FA: 0 g. Potassium: 132.2 mg. Sodium: 1.708 mg. Vitamin K: 5.552 mcg. Folic Acid: 64.2 mcg.

❈ FRENCH OLIVE BREAD ❈

ORIGIN: FRANCE
DIABETIC ADAPTABLE*

HAND KNEAD—OVEN BAKE

Europeans seem to love olives as much as they love olive oil. We have three olive breads in this book and each is different from the other. Italy, Greece, and France all have terrific breads that contain olives. The nice thing about these recipes is that you can also add other flavors, such as herbs, with the olives if you like, but I find the olives and their juice are flavor enough.

MAKES 1 LOAF   SODIUM PER RECIPE: *152* MG
SODIUM PER SLICE (*16*): *9.5* MG

2⅞ cups unbleached bread flour† (7.188 mg)
2   tablespoons potato flour (7.75 mg)
1   tablespoon vital wheat gluten (2.25 mg)
2   tablespoons granular lecithin (trace)
¼   teaspoon ascorbic acid (trace)
2   tablespoons sugar or Splenda‡ (trace)
2   tablespoons active dry yeast (12 mg)
1   teaspoon granulated onion or salt free onion powder
      (1.134 mg)
15   chopped Lindsay No-Salt-Added black California olives
      (120 mg)
2   tablespoons white balsamic vinegar (.3 mg)
3   tablespoons extra-virgin olive oil (trace)
1   cup warm low-sodium water, 100°F to 110°F (trace)
      Cornmeal for dusting the pan (trace)

*The sugars and carbohydrates are in the granulated sugar each element at (25.2 g). The flour contains 274.2 g carbohydrates.
†Use a few more tablespoons for kneading.
‡You can deduct 100 calories from the total if you use Splenda instead of sugar.

Mix all the ingredients except the cornmeal in a large bowl. Turn out the dough to a lightly floured board.

Using your hands, knead until the dough is smooth and elastic (approximately 5 to 10 minutes).

Lightly oil the sides of the bowl and let rise, tightly covered with plastic wrap, for about 45 minutes to an hour, or until it doubles in size. Press down and knead for 5 to 10 minutes. Return to the same slightly oiled bowl and let rise for about 30 minutes (loosely covered with light flour-dusted cloth), until it doubles in size.

Put a pan of water in the bottom of the oven and preheat the oven to 500°F. On a board, round the dough into a ball, pinching the bottom shut. Place bottom side down onto a sheet pan that has been lightly oiled and dusted with cornmeal, and make a few cross-cuts on top with a very sharp knife. Let rise for about a 30 minutes.

Gently move the bread to the oven and bake at 500°F for 15 minutes. Reduce the heat to 375°F and bake for 30 more minutes, or until done.

Cool on a rack.

Nutrient Data per Slice:
Calories: 135.7 g. Protein: 3.407 g. Carbohydrate: 21.2 g. Dietary Fiber: .955 g. Total Sugars: 1.798 g. Total Fat: 4.316 g. Saturated Fat: .538 g. Monounsaturated Fat: 2.32 g. Polyunsaturated Fat: .805 g. Cholesterol: 0 mg. Trans Fat: 0 g. Total Omega-3 FA: .025 g. Total Omega-6 FA: 0 g. Potassium: 79.7 mg. Sodium: 9.5 mg. Vitamin K: 1.597 mcg. Folic Acid: 34.6 mcg.

❖ CHRISTMAS STOLLEN ❖

ORIGIN: GERMANY
DIABETICS*

BREAD MACHINE KNEAD—HAND ROLL—OVEN BAKE

This recipe is based on the Vienna, or Hamburg, stollen you may occasionally see.

You can leave out the brandy if you like. Good rum makes a tasty exchange. Add some candied fruit like you use for a fruitcake at the end and let the green and red cherries show through the top. If you like your stollen with a white glaze, then make one by mixing confectioners' sugar with a bit of nonfat milk or orange juice.

MAKES 32 SERVINGS   SODIUM PER RECIPE: 404.3 MG
SODIUM PER SERVING: 12.6 MG

*Serving size will have 26.7 g carbohydrates when exchanging Splenda for sugar.

THE STOLLEN

2   cups warmed nonfat or 2% fat milk* with added vitamins A
      & D, 100°F to 110°F (205.8 mg)
1   large egg (63 mg)
4   tablespoons extra-virgin olive oil (trace)
1   teaspoon brandy† (.28 mg)
1   tablespoon cider vinegar (.15 mg)
5¼ cups unbleached bread flour (13.1 mg)
¼   cup potato flour (15.5 mg)
2   tablespoons vital wheat gluten (4.5 mg)
2   tablespoons granular or soy or soy lecithin (trace)
¼   teaspoon ascorbic acid (trace)
3   tablespoons white granulated sugar or Splenda (trace)
1¼ tablespoons bread machine yeast (7.5 mg)
1   cup currants (11.5 mg)
¾   cup slivered or chopped unsalted almonds (1.035 mg)
½   cup diced citron, candied (60 mg)
1   tablespoon grated lemon zest (.36 mg)
1   tablespoon unsalted butter, melted for brushing the dough
      (1.562 mg)

THE GLAZE

2 cups confectioners' sugar (2.4 mg)
1 teaspoon to 1 tablespoon orange juice (.31 mg)

Place the stollen ingredients from the milk through the yeast into the bread machine pan in the order listed. Set the machine for Dough. About 5 to 8 minutes before the machine is finished with the kneading, put the currants, almonds, and citron into the machine and let them knead into the dough.

When finished, place onto lightly flour-dusted breadboard.

Press the dough down, shape into a ball, and let stand for 20 minutes.

Heat your oven to about 100°F. If you have an oven proof setting, turn that on.

Using a flour-dusted rolling pin, roll the ball into a circle about ½ to ¾ inch thick. Lightly brush the center the disk with the melted unsalted butter. If you want to add some dried candied fruit, this is the time to sprinkle the dough with it.

Take up one edge and fold it halfway across to the middle of the dough. Take the opposite side and bring it to meet the first side and seal with your

*Or low-sodium buttermilk (120 mg per cup)
†You may omit or exchange with rum. If omitting, replace with ½ teaspoon vanilla extract.

fingers by pinching it together. Place the log on a lightly greased or parchment-lined baking sheet and pull the ends around to form a crescent shape. Cover, and let rise in a warm spot for 1 to 1½ hours.

Preheat the oven to 375°F just before the rise is finished. Bake the stollen for about 35 to 40 minutes. Cool on a rack.

Brush with melted unsalted butter. When the stollen has cooled for about 1 hour, mix the glaze until smooth and spread over the stollen. Plunk some cherries on the top or sprinkle more currants over the topping.

Nutrient Data per Serving:
Calories: 209.8. Protein: 4.669 g. Carbohydrate: 38 g. Dietary Fiber: 1.946 g. Total Sugars: 11 g. Total Fat: 4.705 g. Saturated Fat: .77 g. Monounsaturated Fat: 2.589 g. Polyunsaturated Fat: .954 g. Cholesterol: 7.87 mg. Trans Fat: 0 g. Total Omega-3 FA: .022 g. Total Omega-6 FA: .01 g. Potassium: 207.1 mg. Sodium: 12.6 mg. Vitamin K: 1.114 mcg. Folic Acid: 31.6 mcg.

❖ GREEK OLIVE AND ROSEMARY BREAD ❖

ORIGIN: GREECE
DIABETIC ADAPTABLE*

BREAD MACHINE KNEAD—HAND SHAPE—OVEN BAKE

You can also make this with white flour. But, don't use ordinary, heavier whole wheat flour if following the recipe exactly; the recipe was designed for use with whole wheat pastry flour. Some brands may call their flour "white wholewheat," which is useable here.

**MAKES 1 LOAF (16 SLICES)   SODIUM PER RECIPE: 270.6 MG
SODIUM PER SLICE: 16.9 MG**

FOR THE BREAD MACHINE
½   cup extra-virgin olive oil (trace)
¾   cup warm low-sodium water, minus 1 tablespoon, 100°F to
       110°F (trace)
¼   cup olive juice from a can of Lindsay Low-Sodium Pitted
       Black Olives (trace)
1   large egg (63 mg)
1   teaspoon honey (.277 mg)
1   tablespoon white wine vinegar (.15 mg)
1½ cups whole wheat pastry flour† (9 mg)

*Leave the honey out and add 1 teaspoon Splenda.
†We use whole wheat pastry flour from Bob's Red Mill (www.bobsredmill.com).

1   cup plus 1 tablespoon unbleached bread flour* (2.567 mg)
2   tablespoons potato flour (7.75 mg)
½   teaspoon onion powder (1.134 mg)
¼   teaspoon ascorbic acid (trace)
1   tablespoon vital wheat gluten (2.25 mg)
2   teaspoons white sugar or Splenda (trace)
2   teaspoons bread machine yeast (3.96 mg)

AFTER THE FIRST RISE
20 Lindsay Low-Sodium pitted black olives, halved (160 mg)
1   tablespoon dried rosemary (1.65 mg)

FOR GLAZING
1   egg yolk, beaten (8.168 mg)
2   teaspoons olive oil (trace)

Place the olive oil through the yeast into the bread machine pan and set for Dough.

While the dough is rising in the machine, towel-dry the olives, place 15 halved olives in a small bowl, and mix with the rosemary. Set the other 5 halved olives aside.

Just before the dough is ready to come out of the machine, beat the egg yolk and water and set the egg wash aside.

Prepare a baking sheet by lining with parchment paper and sprinkling with a generous amount of cornmeal or light polenta. (If you have a Silpat or other silicone baking mat, you can use that instead.)

After the dough has risen, roll it out onto a lightly floured breadboard and press down gently until it's flat and about 12 inches square. Spread the olive-rosemary mixture over it and then pull the sides up and over, and then crosswise again. Knead the bread just a few times, then form a ball by tucking the layers down toward the same point. Set the ball on the baking sheet and press down gently until you have a 12- to 14-inch flat piece about 2 to 2½ inches thick. Shape this into a round. Now press the remaining olives into the dough, evenly around the top but all the way into the dough. Brush with the egg wash. (You won't use all of it.)

If you have a proof setting for your oven, set that for 1½ hours. Cover the dough with lightly floured waxed paper (this is a sticky dough).

If you don't have a proof setting you can preheat the oven to 100°F (no more) and then place the dough, covered, in the oven for the necessary time. (We turn our oven on for 1 minute at 200°F, then turn it off. This seems to work very well.) Or you can cover with waxed paper and place

*For a bread that will stay fresh longer, add 2 tablespoons of granular lecithin (trace) and exchange 3 tablespoons of white flour for 3 tablespoons of potato flour (13.6 mg).

in another warm spot for about 1½ hours. This bread won't rise much. It's more like a flatbread, but it is delicious.

Preheat your oven to 375°F, or if using a convection oven, 350°F.

For the glaze, beat together the egg yolk and oil. Brush over the top of the bread.

Bake the bread for 30 minutes, or until golden brown. Serve hot or warm.

Nutrient Data per Slice:
Calories: 169.9. Protein: 3.643 g. Carbohydrate: 17.4 g. Dietary Fiber: 1.795 g. Total Sugars: 1.052 g. Total Fat: 10 g. Saturated Fat: 1.404 g. Monounsaturated Fat: 6.907 g. Polyunsaturated Fat: 1.063 g. Cholesterol: 26.3 mg. Trans Fat: 0 g. Total Omega-3 FA: .08 g. Total Omega-6 FA: 0 g. Potassium: 96.1 mg. Sodium: 16.9 mg. Vitamin K: 5.338 mcg. Folic Acid: 12.8 mcg.

❖ INDIAN NAAN ❖

ORIGIN: INDIA
DIABETIC ADAPTABLE*

BREAD MACHINE KNEAD—OVEN GRILL (BAKE)

This is as close as our no-salt lifestyle can get to naan. A standard naan recipe, which this was based on, has about 450 mg sodium per serving and more calories. This one has only 19.8 mg sodium per serving. A serving is one naan. Like many other countries that have their own flat-breads, India has produced this jewel and they serve it practically every day. You can find commercial naan in specialty stores.

MAKES 6 NAAN   SODIUM PER RECIPE: 117.3 MG
SODIUM PER SERVING (6): 19.8 MG

¾ **cup no-sodium water† (trace)**
1 **tablespoon apple cider vinegar (.15 mg)**
3 **level tablespoons plain yogurt (37.5 mg)**
1 **egg white (54.8 mg)**
2 **tablespoons ghee (clarified, unsalted butter) (3.124 mg)**
2 **cups whole wheat pastry flour‡ (12 mg)**
2 **teaspoons vital wheat gluten (1.125 mg)**
2 **teaspoons cornstarch (.387 mg)**

*You can exchange sugar with Splenda. Onion powder has 1.703 grams sugars. The bulk of carbohydrates is in the flour.
†Check halfway through the kneading. If the dough doesn't ball up, add water 1 tablespoon at a time. You shouldn't have to do this, but flour varies and sometimes it is necessary.
‡Bob's Red Mill makes a very good whole wheat pastry flour.

1   teaspoon white granulated sugar or Splenda (trace)
¼   teaspoon ascorbic acid (trace)
2   teaspoons onion seeds* (2.592 mg)
1½   teaspoons bread machine yeast (3 mg)
2   tablespoons unsalted butter for brushing the dough
      (1.562 mg)

Place all the ingredients except for the last 2 tablespoons of butter into your bread machine pan as listed or per your manufacturer's instructions. Set the machine for Dough.

When the dough is ready, roll out onto a lightly floured breadboard and break into 6 even pieces. This dough should have elasticity. Push each ball or piece down, then grab an end and pull the other end until it forms a tear shape about 6 to 8 inches long but no longer. Set 3 naans on each on lightly greased baking sheets and smooth out flat to about ¼ to ⅜ inch thick.

Melt the 2 tablespoons of butter and brush the dough. Reserve some of the butter for later.

Put the naan in the proofing oven or in warm area to rise for 15 to 20 minutes, covered with waxed paper or a light cloth.

Set the rack in the lower to middle position of the oven. Preheat the oven to 475°F.

When the oven is to temperature and the dough has risen, place one of the baking sheets into the oven and set your timer for 8 minutes. At 4 minutes, open the oven door and lift each naan with a pancake turner and butter the pan. Set the naan back down onto the butter. Bake for another 8 minutes, but check at 7 minutes. Raise the naan and if the bottom has turned golden brown, then butter the top again and use the turner to flip the naan over to the topside. Bake for 1 minute.

Remove the naan from oven and cool on a rack. Repeat baking the naan with the second baking sheet of dough.

Nutrient Data per Naan:
Calories: 233.3. Protein: 7.674 g. Carbohydrate: 38.3 g. Dietary Fiber: 5.27 g. Total Sugars: 1.338 g. Total Fat: 6.614 g. Saturated Fat: 3.795 g. Monounsaturated Fat: 1.626 g. Polyunsaturated Fat: .533 g. Cholesterol: 15.4 mg. Trans Fat: 0 g. Total Omega-3 FA: .06 g. Total Omega-6 FA: .154 g. Potassium: 229.4 mg. Sodium: 19.8 mg. Vitamin K: 1.29 mcg. Folic Acid: 0 mcg.

*You may replace with 1 level tablespoon onion powder, but we suggest you try to find the onion seeds.

❖ ITALIAN CRUSTY BREAD ❖

ORIGIN: ITALY.
DIABETIC ADAPTABLE*

BREAD MACHINE KNEAD—HAND SHAPE—OVEN BAKE

This delicious bread serves well with any pasta or fish dish. Slice about 1 inch thick for serving. Accompany with olive oil or unsalted butter, or serve plain; either way it's a pleasure. Great for sopping up spaghetti sauce, we think, and you'll really enjoy it!

MAKES 2 LOAVES (TWENTY-EIGHT 1-INCH-THICK SLICES)
SODIUM PER RECIPE: 239.2 MG
SODIUM PER LOAF: 119.6 MG
SODIUM PER SLICE: 8.542 MG

1¾ cups low-sodium water (trace)
2   cups whole wheat pastry flour (12 mg)
1¾ cups white whole wheat flour (12 mg)
1   cup unbleached bread flour (2.5 mg)
¼   cup potato flour (15.5 mg)
½   cup regular or light sour cream (60.9 mg)
2   tablespoons cider vinegar (.30 mg)
2   tablespoons extra-virgin olive oil (trace)
2   large eggs (126 mg)
¼   teaspoon ascorbic acid (trace)
3   tablespoons vital wheat gluten (6.75 mg)
3   tablespoons sugar or Splenda (trace)
1   teaspoon onion powder (1.134 mg)
1   tablespoon bread machine yeast (6 mg)

Place all the ingredients into bread machine in the order listed. Set for Dough.

When the dough is ready, roll it out onto a breadboard, lightly floured with whole wheat flour. Press down. Cut into 2 equal pieces and roll into loaf size. Place into 2 loaf pans that have been lightly oiled and flour dusted.

Let rise, covered with light cloth or waxed paper, in the proofing oven or in warm spot for about 1 hour.

Preheat the oven to 375°F. Bake both loaves at the same time, separated in the oven by about 3 inches, for 30 to 50 minutes.

Cool on a rack. Freeze to store, or store in airtight ziplock bags or an airtight container.

---

*Diabetics, exchange sugar with Splenda to lower carbohydrates to 13.4 g per slice.

Nutritional Data per Slice:
Calories: 114.7. Protein: 4.065 g. Carbohydrate: 18.6 g. Dietary Fiber: 1.874 g. Total Sugars: 1.55 g. Total Fat: 3.115 g. Saturated Fat: .922 g. Monounsaturated Fat: 1.208 g. Polyunsaturated Fat: .574 g. Cholesterol: 16.9 mg. Trans Fat: 0 g. Total Omega-3 FA: .029 g. Total Omega-6 FA: 0 g. Potassium: 107.1 mg. Sodium: 8.542 mg. Vitamin K: .904 mcg. Folic Acid: 12 mcg.

❖ TUSCAN BREAD ❖

ORIGIN: ITALY
DIABETIC ACCEPTABLE

**MAKES 1 LOAF* SODIUM PER RECIPE: 14.8 MG
SODIUM PER HALF SLICE†: .825 MG**

1   ounce active dry yeast, or 5 teaspoons (2 packs) (7 mg)
1¼   cups warm low-sodium water, 100°F to 110°F (trace)
2¼   cups unbleached bread flour (5.625 mg)
¼   cup whole wheat flour (1.5 mg)
1   teaspoon vital wheat gluten (.72 mg)

In a large bowl dissolve the yeast in the water. Once it's dissolved, mix in the flours and stir to make a soft dough.

Knead 10 minutes by hand, or 4 to 5 minutes with a dough hook. Clean and oil the bowl and set the dough back into it.

Cover tightly with plastic wrap and let rise in a warm place, until double in bulk, about two hours. You can press dough down and get a second rise, if you like. (Never "punch" dough down.)

When dough has risen, roll out onto a lightly floured breadboard and flatten it into an oblong, about 8 inches wide and 10 inches long. It will be about a ¼ inch thick. Dough will be soft, so try to use a minimum of extra flour while working it.

Beginning at the long end, roll the dough up into a log, press down to 1 inch thick, and then roll up again. This will activate the gluten in the bread. Tuck both ends of the log under and pinch shut. Roll on the breadboard or in your hands until you have a circular shape (about 10 to 12 inches in diameter).

Place the dough on a flour-dusted baking sheet. Cover with a light flour-dusted cloth and let rise for another hour in a warm place.

---

*This loaf will make 16 half slices for the Bruschetta on page 130.
†A half slice is a pie-shaped slice, butterfly cut. You will get the same number of slices in a different shape from a standard loaf size. We recommend you bake the cylindrical loaf on a baking sheet.

Preheat the oven to 400°F.

Set a small heatproof cereal bowl of water into the oven at the edge or where your baking pan won't touch it.

When the bread has risen and the oven is at the correct temperature, slowly and gently remove the cloth and place the pan into the oven.

Lightly spray the dough with water before beginning to bake and then twice more, at even intervals, during baking cycle.

Bake for 50 minutes. (Check at 40 minutes for darkness.) This is a "crispy" bread. It will be done when you snap the top with a finger and it "rings" hollow. It should come out golden brown.

Nutrient Data per Half Slice:
Calories: 65.4. Protein: 2.243 g. Carbohydrate: 13.5 g. Dietary Fiber: .789 g. Total Sugars: 0 g. Total Fat: .222 g. Saturated Fat: .034 g. Monounsaturated Fat: .037 g. Polyunsaturated Fat: .078 g. Cholesterol: 0 mg. Calcium: 3.408 mg. Iron: .919 mg. Potassium: 39 mg. Sodium: .825 mg. Vitamin K: 0 mcg. Folate: 43 mcg.

❖ ITALIAN OLIVE AND BASIL BREAD ❖

ORIGIN: ITALY
DIABETIC ADAPTABLE

BREAD MACHINE KNEAD—HAND SHAPE—OVEN BAKE

You can add crushed garlic to this recipe for an extra kick. And you might want to experiment after making your first loaf by exchanging 3 tablespoons of flaxseed meal with 1 tablespoon of oil or using 2 tablespoons of granular lecithin in exchange for 1 tablespoon of oil. The flaxseed will darken the bread but provides extra fiber and the moisture that the oil usually provides.

MAKES 1 LOAF (16 SLICES)   SODIUM PER RECIPE: 187.6 MG
SODIUM PER SLICE: 11.7 MG

FOR THE BREAD MACHINE

3   tablespoons extra-virgin olive oil (trace)
1   cup minus 1 tablespoon warm low-sodium or no-sodium water, 100°F to 110°F (trace)
¼   cup liquid from the olive can (trace)
1   large whole egg (63 mg)
1   tablespoon white wine vinegar (.15 mg)
1   cup whole wheat pastry flour (6 mg)
1¾   cups unbleached bread flour (4.375 mg)
¼   cup potato flour* (15.5 mg)
1   teaspoon onion powder (1.296 mg)

¼   teaspoon ascorbic acid (trace)
1   tablespoon vital wheat gluten (2.25 mg)
1   tablespoon white sugar or Splenda (.126 mg)
2¼ teaspoons bread machine yeast (3.96 mg)

AFTER FIRST RISE
10 Lindsay Low-Sodium black, pitted olives, chopped (80 mg)
1   tablespoon dried basil (.476 mg)

FOR GLAZING
1   egg yolk (8.16 mg)
1   teaspoon water (trace)
2   teaspoons olive oil (trace)
1   tablespoon poppy seeds (1.848 mg) or sesame seeds
    (.99 mg)
  Cornmeal for dusting the pan

Place the olive oil through yeast into the bread machine pan and set for Dough.

While the dough is rising in the machine, towel-dry and chop the olives and mix with the dried basil.

Just before the dough is ready to come out of the machine, beat the egg yolk with the water and oil and set the egg wash aside.

Prepare a baking sheet by sprinkling with a generous amount of cornmeal or light polenta.

After the dough has risen, roll out onto a lightly floured breadboard and pat down. Spread the olive-basil mix over the dough and then pull the sides up and over and then crosswise. Knead the dough a few times, then form a ball by tucking the layers down toward the same point. Set the ball on the baking sheet and press down gently until you have a 12-inch-diameter, flat piece of dough about 2 inches thick. Shape this into a flat oval or round shape. Brush lightly with the egg wash.

If you have a proof setting for your oven, set that for 1½ hours. Cover the dough with a very light cloth that is lightly floured, or with waxed paper.

If you don't have a proof setting, you can preheat the oven to about 100°F (no more) and then place the dough, covered, in there for the necessary time. Or you can cover the dough with waxed paper or a lightly floured light cloth and place in another warm spot for about 1½ hours.

Preheat your oven to 375°F, or if using a convection oven, set to 350°F.

*If you don't want the potato flour, exchange it for a ¼ cup of unbleached bread flour. Potato flour will help keep the bread moist and fresh.

Bake the bread for 30 minutes, or until golden brown. Serve hot or warm.

Nutrient Data per Slice:
Calories: 133.9. Protein: 3.928 g. Carbohydrate: 19.8 g. Dietary Fiber: 1.501 g. Total Sugars: 1.07 g. Total Fat: 4.58 g. Saturated Fat: .697 g. Monounsaturated Fat: 2.797 g. Polyunsaturated Fat: .693 g. Cholesterol: 26.3 mg. Trans Fat: 0 g. Total Omega-3 FA: .038 g. Total Omega-6 FA: 0 g. Potassium: 115.5 mg. Sodium: 11.7 mg. Vitamin K: 3.569 mcg. Folic Acid: 21.1 mcg.

❧ KAISER OR KIMELWECK ROLLS ❧

ORIGIN: AUSTRIA
DIABETIC ADAPTABLE*

BREAD MACHINE KNEAD—HAND SHAPE—OVEN BAKE

What exactly is a Kimelweck roll? It's a hard roll, more specifically a crusty kaiser roll, sprinkled with caraway and coarse salt instead of the more familiar poppy seed topping. Shape the dough into a loaf to bake Vienna bread or shape it into thin ropes for salt and pepper sticks, a great snack in lieu of pretzels.

MAKES: 8 ROLLS†   SODIUM PER RECIPE: 74.1 MG
SODIUM PER SANDWICH ROLL: 9.257 MG

THE ROLLS

1   cup warm low-sodium water, 100°F to 110°F (trace)
2   tablespoons extra-virgin olive oil (trace)
1   tablespoon cider vinegar (.15 mg)
1   teaspoon honey (.277 mg)
3   cups unbleached bread flour (7.5 mg)
2   tablespoons vital wheat gluten (4.5 mg)
1   tablespoon white granulated sugar or Splenda (trace)
¼   teaspoon granulated onion or salt-free onion powder (.324 mg)
2½ teaspoons bread machine yeast (5 g)

THE TOPPING

1 tablespoon low-sodium water (trace)
1 large egg white (54.8 mg)
2 teaspoons unsalted caraway seeds (.714 mg)

*You can exchange the sugar with Splenda to lower carbohydrates by 1.5 g per roll. Flour contains 274.2 g.
†To make these rolls softer and give them extended "out-of the-bag" shelf life, add 2 tablespoons of granular lecithin (trace) and replace ¼ cup of flour with ¼ cup of potato flour (15.5 mg)

Place all the ingredients except the egg white and topping ingredients into the bread machine pan in the order listed. Set for Dough.

While the dough is kneading, prepare a large baking sheet by lining with parchment paper.

Just before the dough is ready, whisk together the egg white with the water and set the egg wash aside.

When the dough is ready, roll it out onto a lightly floured board and press down. Shape with your hands to a piece about 8×4 inches and cut into 8 equal pieces. Shape each piece into a smooth round, pinching the bottoms shut. Set on the lined baking sheet and push each down just a bit. Using a sharp knife, cut four radial lines, beginning at the center of the roll and cutting outward, making a curve as you do.

When all the rolls have been cut and have the familiar "kaiser roll" look, use a basting brush to paint each bun with the egg wash. Sprinkle the caraway seeds over each bun.

Using a light cloth dusted with flour or a piece of waxed paper sprayed with olive oil and then dusted with flour, cover the rolls and let rise in a proofing oven or warm spot for 45 minutes to 1 hour.

Preheat the oven to 425°F.

Bake the rolls for 5 minutes, then open the oven door and spritz the rolls with a mist of water. Bake for another 12 to 17 minutes, or until the rolls are brown and crispy.

Cool the rolls on a rack. Store in an airtight container or ziplock bags or freeze. Frozen rolls may be thawed on the countertop in the same bag they were frozen in.

Nutrient Data per Roll:
Calories: 224.8. Protein: 7.322 g. Carbohydrate: 39.4 g. Dietary Fiber: 1.734 g. Total Sugars: 2.563 g. Total Fat: 4.008 g. Saturated Fat: .538 g. Monounsaturated Fat: 2.604 g. Polyunsaturated Fat: .549 g. Cholesterol: 0 mg. Trans Fat: 0 g. Total Omega-3 FA: .038 g. Total Omega-6 FA: 0 g. Potassium: 92.1 mg. Sodium: 9.257 mg. Vitamin K: 2.175 mcg. Folic Acid: 72.2 mcg.

❖ KOLACHE ❖

ORIGIN: SLOVAKIA

DIABETICS, SEE FOOTNOTE*

HAND KNEAD—OVEN BAKE

A sweet bread rich in flavor and history. If you like a sweet bread and you like prunes, then this recipe from Slovakia will please you greatly. Kolache is a Czech word, meaning a wheel-shaped cake. Use any dried fruit

*Diabetics, the bulk of carbohydrates in this recipe are in the prunes (81.4 g), sugar (109 g), milk (12.5 g), and flour (190.8 g).

you like in this recipe, or substitute jam. Festivals are held worldwide, celebrating this bread.

MAKES 30 KOLACHE   SODIUM PER RECIPE: MG
SODIUM PER KOLACHE: 9.973 MG

THE KOLACHE

½   **cup warm, low-sodium water, 100°F to 110°F (trace)**
5   **teaspoons active dry yeast (10 mg)**
½   **cup white granulated sugar or Splenda (trace)**
1   **cup warm nonfat milk warmed to 105°F to 110°F (102.9 mg)**
1   **tablespoon white wine vinegar (.15 mg)**
¼   **teaspoon ascorbic acid (trace)**
1   **level tablespoon vital wheat gluten (2.25 mg)**
½   **cup melted unsalted butter (12.5 mg)**
5¼   **cups unbleached, all-purpose flour (13.125 mg)**
2   **large eggs, beaten (126 mg)**

THE PRUNE FILLING

¾   **cup pitted prunes, chopped (2.55 mg)**
⅓   **teaspoon grated lemon peel (.04 mg)**
1   **tablespoon lemon juice (.177 mg)**
2   **teaspoons sugar or Splenda (.084 mg)**

Warm the water to lukewarm, add the yeast and a pinch of white granulated sugar or Splenda. Stir once and set aside to proof.

In a medium mixing bowl mix together the warmed milk, the white granulated sugar, and the white wine vinegar until well combined. Sift 2 cups of the flour with the gluten and ascorbic acid. Add the melted unsalted butter. Mix well with bread paddles. Add the 2 beaten eggs and proofed yeast mixture and mix well. Set aside, covered, to rest until bubbly and spongy.

Add the remaining 3½ cups of flour and blend well using a wooden spoon or bread beaters on slow. Ball up using your hands and set aside to rise for 1 hour. Press down (don't ever "punch" down) and let rise again for 1 hour.

While the dough is rising the second time, make the filling. (If you don't want a prune filling, you can use a good strawberry, boysenberry, or blackberry jam or preserve.)

Chop the prunes, add water to cover, and bring to a light boil. Reduce to a simmer and cook for about 5 minutes. Add the sugar, grated lemon peel, and lemon juice and let simmer for another 5 minutes. Puree and set aside.

Preheat the oven to 425°F.

When the dough is ready, break off balls of dough about 1 inch in diameter and place on a baking sheet lined with parchment paper or sprayed with a light coating of olive oil. Press a wide indentation in the center of each with your thumb or something just as round. Put the filling in the indentation. Let the Kolache rise for 15 minutes. Bake in the preheated oven for 12 to 18 minutes, or until golden.

Serve hot or warm, plain, or sprinkle with a light dusting of confectioners' sugar.

Nutrient Data per Kolache:
Calories: 147.1. Protein: 3.649 g. Carbohydrate: 25 g. Dietary Fiber: 1.037 g. Total Sugars: 5.778 g. Total Fat: 3.684 g. Saturated Fat: 2.101 g. Monounsaturated Fat: .964 g. Polyunsaturated Fat: .259 g. Cholesterol: 22.4 mg. Trans Fat: 0 g. Total Omega-3 FA: .032 g. Total Omega-6 FA: .082 g. Potassium: 111.1 mg. Sodium: 9.973 mg. Vitamin K: 2.869 mcg. Folic Acid: 33.7 mcg.

❖ PORTUGUESE SWEET BREAD ❖

ORIGIN: PORTUGAL
DIABETIC ADAPTABLE*

BREAD MACHINE RECIPE

You can find this bread throughout Portugal and wherever Portuguese immigrants settled. It's sweet but adaptable for diabetics with the use of Splenda.

MAKES 1 LOAF (16 SLICES)   SODIUM PER RECIPE: 179.7 MG
SODIUM PER SLICE (16 SLICES): 11.2 MG

1   cup nonfat milk with added vitamins A & D, at room temperature (102.9 mg)
1   tablespoon cider vinegar (.15 mg)
1   large egg (63 mg)
3   tablespoons extra-virgin olive oil (trace)
3   cups unbleached bread flour (6.875 mg)
⅓   cup white granulated sugar or Splenda substitute (.666 mg)
¼   teaspoon ascorbic acid (trace)
2   teaspoons vital wheat gluten (1.125 mg)
2½   teaspoons bread machine yeast (5 mg)

Place the ingredients into your bread machine in the order listed. Set for 2-Pound Loaf, Medium Crust, White Bread.

If you have a "Sweet Bread" setting, use that instead.

This bread will balloon in your bread machine and might touch the lid. Don't worry about that, it's expected.

Cool on a rack.

*Diabetics, replace sugar with Splenda. The bulk of carbohydrates are in the flour.

Nutrient Data per Slice:
Calories: 136.5. Protein: 3.749 g. Carbohydrate: 23.2 g. Dietary Fiber: .764 g. Total Sugars: 5.081 g. Total Fat: 3.116 g. Saturated Fat: .495 g. Monounsaturated Fat: 2.033 g. Polyunsaturated Fat: .394 g. Cholesterol: 13.5 mg. Trans Fat: 0 g. Total Omega-3 FA: .028 g. Total Omega-6 FA: 0 g. Potassium: 66.7 mg. Sodium: 11.2 mg. Vitamin K: 1.604 mcg. Folic Acid: 36.1 mcg.

❖ RUSSIAN BLACK BREAD ❖

ORIGIN: RUSSIA
DIABETICS, SEE FOOTNOTE*
BREAD MACHINE RECIPE

We liked this bread a lot after spending time developing it for no-salt lifestyles, and after we were successful in extending its nonsalt shelf life. It uses ginger and fennel seeds as well as decaffinated instant coffee to give it the true Russian black bread flavor. If you don't like the fennel seed flavor, you can leave them out.

MAKES 1 LOAF (16 SLICES)   SODIUM PER RECIPE: 66.1 MG
SODIUM PER SLICE (16): 4.13 MG

1¼ cups plus 2 tablespoons low-sodium water plus more as needed (trace)
½ rounded teaspoon instant decaffinated coffee crystals† (.185 mg)
2 tablespoons cider vinegar (.30 mg)
2¼ cups unbleached bread flour (5.938 mg)
¼ cup potato flour (15.5 mg)
1 cup dark or light rye flour (1.28 mg)
¼ teaspoon ascorbic acid (trace)
1 tablespoon vital wheat gluten (2.25 mg)
½ teaspoon onion powder (.648 mg)
2 tablespoons extra-virgin olive oil (trace)
2 tablespoons Grandma's Robust or B'rer Rabbit molasses (14 mg)
1 tablespoon brown sugar, packed (10.8 mg)

*You can replace the molasses with a teaspoon of maple extract. Replace brown sugar with Splenda or Brown Sugar Twin. Bulk of carbohydrates after that are in the flour.
†We use Folgers.

3   **tablespoons unsweetened cocoa powder* (3.078 mg)**
1   **tablespoon caraway seeds (1.139 mg)**
2¾ **teaspoons bread machine yeast (5.5 mg)**
¼   **teaspoon fennel seeds, optional (.44 mg)†**

Place all ingredients into the bread machine in the order listed.

Set the machine to White, 2-Pound Loaf, Medium Crust.

When the bread is done, remove it from the pan, place on a rack, and cool before slicing. Store in a ziplock bag to retain freshness.

Nutrient Data per Slice:
Calories: 143.9. Protein: 4.303 g. Carbohydrate: 28 g. Dietary Fiber: 3.023 g. Total Sugars: 5.109 g. Total Fat: 2.362 g. Saturated Fat: .374 g. Monounsaturated Fat: 1.397 g. Polyunsaturated Fat: .366 g. Cholesterol: 0 mg. Trans Fat: 0 g. Total Omega-3 FA: .031 g. Total Omega-6 FA: 0 g. Potassium: 225.5 mg. Sodium: 4.13 mg. Vitamin K: 1.568 mcg. Folic Acid: 27.1 mcg.

❖ SCANDINAVIAN RYE BREAD ❖

ORIGIN: SCANDINAVIA
DIABETIC ADAPTABLE‡

BREAD MACHINE RECIPE

This mild-flavored rye bread is not the deli-type rye you may be accustomed to. Scandinavians love this recipe for their open-face sandwiches. We have used it for our Open-Face Chicken Sandwich (see page 143). The Scandinavians make this bread by hand, but we were able to replicate their bread in a bread machine. Serve hot, warm, or at room temperature. Store in ziplock bag or freeze.

MAKES 1 LOAF   SODIUM PER RECIPE: 143.9 MG
SODIUM PER SLICE (16): 8.993 MG

1   **cup nonfat milk with added vitamins A and D (102.9 mg)**
2   **tablespoons extra-virgin olive oil (trace)**
2   **tablespoons light molasses (14.8 mg)**
1   **tablespoon cider vinegar (.15 mg)**
2½ **cups unbleached bread flour (5.94 mg)**
¼   **teaspoon ascorbic acid (trace)**

*We use Hershey's. Make sure you don't use a mix since they often have salt in them.
†Nutrient Data is figured without the fennel seeds.
‡You will have to replace the molasses with Splenda. This will alter the flavor. Dates have a total of 33.4 g carbohydrates.

1   tablespoon vital wheat gluten (2.25 mg)
½   teaspoon aniseed (.168 mg)
¾   cup medium rye flour (2.295 mg)
½   teaspoon fennel seed (.88 mg)
¼   cup chopped, pitted dates (2.4 mg)
1   teaspoon freshly grated orange zest or orange
       extract (.06 mg)
2   tablespoons potato flour (7.75 mg)
2½   teaspoons bread machine yeast (5 mg)

Place all ingredients into your bread machine pan in the order listed or in the order your manufacturer suggests. Include the dates; they are not added later as is true with most fruits and nuts in bread machine recipes. Set the machine for White Bread, 2-pound-loaf, Light Crust.*

Nutrient Data per Slice:
Calories: 129. Protein: 3.684 g. Carbohydrate: 24.2 g. Dietary Fiber: 1.6 g. Total Sugars: 4.084 g. Total Fat: 2.047 g. Saturated Fat: .292 g. Monounsaturated Fat: 1.311 g. Polyunsaturated Fat: .293 g. Cholesterol: .306 mg. Trans Fat: 0 g. Total Omega-3 FA: .023 g. Total Omega-6 FA: 0 g. Potassium: 152.9 mg. Sodium: 8.993 mg. Vitamin K: 1.429 mcg. Folic Acid: 28.6 mcg.

❈ SWEDISH LIMPA BREAD ❈

ORIGIN: SWEDEN
DIABETIC ADAPTABLE†

BREAD MACHINE KNEAD—OVEN BAKE

There are many varieties of this bread from standard bread dough to batter to varieties that include ale, instant coffee granules, and various spices.

Make this bread by hand, if you prefer. Let rise and shape as a rounded loaf or in a loaf pan. We like this version and have made it often for parties, house guests, and our own use.

MAKES 1 LOAF   SODIUM PER RECIPE: 16.2 MG
SODIUM PER SLICE (16): 1.013 MG

Juice of 1 orange (.86 mg)
Filtered low-sodium water (trace)
2 tablespoons honey (1.68 mg)

*In our tests medium-crust settings caused burning on bottom and sides of the loaf.
†Diabetics can exchange Splenda for the honey to make this diabetic acceptable. Honey has 34.6 g carbohydrates.

2   tablespoons extra-virgin olive oil (trace)⁻
1   tablespoon white wine vinegar (.15 mg)
2   cups unbleached bread flour (5 mg)
1   cup medium or dark rye flour (1.28 mg)
1   teaspoon granulated onion or salt-free onion
       powder (1.296 mg)
1   teaspoon grated orange zest (.06 mg)
½   teaspoons aniseed (.168 mg)
2   teaspoons freshly ground caraway seeds* (.714 mg)
2½   teaspoons bread machine yeast (4.98 mg)

Combine the orange juice with enough low-sodium water to make 1 cup. Heat to 105° to 110°F.

Place all the ingredients into your bread machine pan in the order listed or as the manufacturer suggests. Set for Dough. Check for moisture after 10 minutes of kneading. If the dough is not balling up, add 1 tablespoon of water and wait for a few minutes. If it still does not ball up, add another tablespoon. If the dough is too sticky, then add 1 tablespoon white flour, wait a few minutes, then add another if the dough is still sticky. Lightly spray oil on the lid of the bread machine (you can clean off later) in case your dough rises to the lid. Preheat the oven to 375°F.

When the dough is ready, transfer it to a 10×7-inch lightly oiled loaf pan. Let rise in a warm place or in a proofing oven for about 45 minutes to 1 hour, covered with a lightly floured cloth.

Bake in the preheated oven for 40 to 50 minutes.

Remove from the pan and cool on a rack. Serve hot, warm, or at room temperature. Store in a ziplock bag. You may store it in the refrigerator for up to 1 week.

Nutritional Data per Slice:
Calories: 112.8. Protein: 3.102 g. Carbohydrate: 21 g. Dietary Fiber: 2.508 g. Total Sugars: 3.049 g. Total Fat: 2.146 g. Saturated Fat: .283 g. Monounsaturated Fat: 1.33 g. Polyunsaturated Fat: .343 g. Cholesterol: 0 mg. Trans Fat: 0 g. Total Omega-3 FA: .031 g. Total Omega-6 FA: 0 g. Potassium: 106.9 mg. Sodium: 1.013 mg. Vitamin K: 1.546 mcg. Folic Acid: 24.1 mcg.

*We grind our caraway seeds in a coffee grinder.

◈ WHITE BREAD ◈

ORIGIN: WORLDWIDE
DIABETIC ADAPTABLE*

BREAD MACHINE RECIPE

This white bread is included to support a few recipes in this book. You can make it to produce your own bread crumbs (see pages 167 to 168). Be sure to use this recipe for French toast and for Peruvian Spicy Chicken (see page 115).

**MAKES 1 LOAF (16 SLICES)   SODIUM PER RECIPE: 23.2 MG
SODIUM PER SLICE: 1.448 MG**

1	cup warm low-sodium water, 100°F to 110°F (trace)
1	tablespoon cider vinegar (.15 mg)
3	tablespoons extra-virgin olive oil (trace)
½	teaspoon vanilla extract (.189 mg)
2⅞	cups unbleached bread flour (7.175 mg)
1	tablespoon vital wheat gluten (2.25 mg)
2	tablespoons white granulated sugar or Splenda (trace)
2	level tablespoons potato flour (7.75 mg)
¼	teaspoon ascorbic acid (trace)
½	teaspoon granulated onion (powder) (.648 mg)
2½	teaspoons bread machine yeast (5 mg)

Place all ingredients into your bread machine and set for White Bread, 2-Pound Loaf, Medium Crust.

When done, roll out onto rack and cool. You can freeze these in ziplock plastic bags for up to a month.

Nutrient Data per Slice when Using Sugar:
Calories: 119.5. Protein: 3.035 g. Carbohydrate: 20.3 g. Dietary Fiber: .741 g. Total Sugars: 1.733 g. Total Fat: 2.799 g. Saturated Fat: .382 g. Monounsaturated Fat: 1.906 g. Polyunsaturated Fat: .351 g. Cholesterol: 0 mg. Trans Fat: 0 g. Total Omega-3 FA: .025 g. Total Omega-6 FA: 0 g. Iron: 1.411 mg. Potassium: 60.7 mg. Sodium: 1.448 mg. Vitamin K: 1.594 mcg. Folic Acid: 34.5 mcg.

Nutrient Data per Slice when Using Splenda:
Calories: 113.4. Protein: 3.035 g. Carbohydrate: 18.7 g. Dietary Fiber: .741 g. Total Sugars: .159 g. Total Fat: 2.799 g. Saturated Fat: .382 g. Monounsaturated Fat: 1.906 g. Polyunsaturated Fat: .351 g. Cholesterol: 0 mg. Trans Fat: 0 g. Total Omega-3 FA: .025 g. Total Omega-6 FA: 0 g. Iron: 1.41 mg. Potassium: 60.7 mg. Sodium: 1.448 mg. Vitamin K: 1.594 mcg. Folic Acid: 34.5 mcg.

*Diabetics, most of the carbohydrates are in the flour (273.4 g). The sugar has a recipe total of 25 grams of carbohydrates and can be replaced with Splenda.

Yogurt White and
❖ Whole Wheat Bread ❖

Origin: Mediterranean
Diabetic Adaptable

You'll love this recipe. I first ran into it while traveling the world directing "remotes" for a TV show. It uses vanilla yogurt, vanilla extract, and raisins. (Leave out the raisins if you don't care for them.) The flavor is terrific and so is the texture. Serve hot. Or freeze, then reheat in defrost mode in the microwave for a very short time. Each slice has about 70 calories.

MAKES 12 MINI LOAVES, 3 LARGE LOAVES OR 48 SLICES
SODIUM PER RECIPE: 208.6 MG
SODIUM PER SLICE: 4.346 MG

1¼ **cups warm, no-sodium water, 100°F to 110°F (trace)**
1   **cup vanilla yogurt (low-fat, regular, or nonfat) (161.7 mg)**
1   **tablespoon cider vinegar (.15 mg)**
1½ **tablespoons extra-virgin olive oil (trace)**
1   **teaspoon vanilla extract (.378 mg)**
3   **cups unbleached bread flour (7.5 mg)**
3   **cups white whole wheat flour* (18 mg)**
2   **tablespoons vital wheat gluten (4.5 mg)**
1   **teaspoon onion powder (1.296 mg)**
½   **teaspoon ascorbic acid (trace)**
2   **teaspoons white granulated sugar or Splenda (trace)**
1   **tablespoon bread machine yeast (6 mg)**
½   **cup black seedless raisins or currants, packed (9.075 mg)**

Place all the ingredients except for the raisins or currants into the bread machine pan in the order listed. Set for Dough. At the sound of the Raisin Buzzer, add the raisins and let the machine go through the rest of the cycle. (You may have to help your machine get this one started so that the ball forms properly.)

Roll the dough out onto lightly floured breadboard. Press down gently until 1 inch thick.

If you have an oven with a proof button, turn that on now. If not, you'll need an oven or a space in your house that's at about 80°F.

---

*May be found at Baker's Catalog from King Arthur. Others are available locally in many but not all areas. May exchange with whole wheat pastry flour.

Cut the dough into 3 sections. You can make small mini loaves in mini loaf pans, long loaves in a French bread rack, or standard loaves in loaf pans.

Lightly grease the loaf pans. If making all mini loaves, cut off 12 equal pieces. Or if you are making a combination, cut the dough into sections that will work for your pans.

Shape the dough by rolling. Set into pans, cover with waxed paper, and place into the warm oven or other warm spot. Let rise for 1 hour.

Preheat the oven to 375°F. Bake the loaves for 20 to 30 minutes, or until dark golden brown. Cool on a rack. Serve warm.

Nutrient Data per Slice:
Calories: 70.2. Protein: 2.479 g. Carbohydrate: 13.9 g. Dietary Fiber: 1.245 g. Total Sugars: 1.996 g. Total Fat: .728 g. Saturated Fat: .137 g. Monounsaturated Fat: .361 g. Polyunsaturated Fat: .136 g. Cholesterol: .255 mg. Trans Fat: 0 g. Total Omega-3 FA: .009 g. Total Omega-6 FA: 0 g. Potassium: 68.7 mg. Sodium: 4.346 mg. Vitamin K: .487 mcg. Folic Acid: 12 mcg.

SEAFOOD

$\diamond$ $\diamond$ $\diamond$ $\diamond$ $\diamond$ $\diamond$ $\diamond$ $\diamond$

As a youngster I loved to fish. I had to depend on a friend's father to get us to the lake or river to fish, but it was often enough to keep my fishing vibes calmed.

Later in life when I could get myself to a fishing hole, life was great. Fresh trout from a river or lake was about the best meal I could ever think of. It was up to me to cook them. The first thing a good fisherman learns is how to clean the fish, chill it, and then cook it over a hot camp stove. What could be better?

Soon after I was diagnosed with heart failure, I went out and bought a new bass boat. I explained to my wife, "For every day you fish, you live a day longer." Heck, that was ten years ago at this writing. I can't give all the credit to my low-sodium lifestyle. Some has to go to the fishing, doesn't it?

Not all fish comes from our local lakes or rivers, however. The ocean holds most of the fish the world eats, and it seems that everyone in the world eats fish. Wild fish are so full of nutrients it's no wonder that some cultures survived on fish alone.

I would love to have included many more fish recipes in this book but, alas, we could only include these delicious entrées. And they are good! The Calamari Steaks are definitely a dish not to miss, but then I'd have to say that about each of them.

By the way, it is important to keep your fish cold before preparation. The sooner you put your fish on ice, the less opportunity it will have to take on unpleasant "fishy" flavors and aromas. In that regard, make sure your store-bought fish is cold and not mixed in the same butcher's display case with chicken or other products that might affect the fish, and make sure it's very, very cold but not frozen.

And, yes, you can eat a few shrimp on your low-sodium diet. But make sure you are getting fresh, unsalted shrimp. This may prove a daunting experience in some areas. If a store clerk or butcher displays shrimp and says it's fresh, get brave and ask, "May I see the original bag or container?" They are too often previously frozen and the bag itself will tell you if the shrimp have been salted or not. Supermarket chains seem to carry only presalted, prefrozen shrimp, so watch out for that. Once you've found fresh shrimp, though, you'll love our shrimp tempura. It's a recipe I've had ever since I returned from Japan in the '50s. By the way, play it safe and make the tempura in a cooking appliance designed for deep-fat frying. And use canola for the frying oil.

Wild salmon is usually best from the Pacific and is seasonal, beginning in May of each year. Farmed Atlantic salmon, which has a greater oil content and moistness, and retains most of the color in its rich orange flesh when cooked, is the salmon most Americans see in their markets, especially from fall through spring. Some Pacific salmon is also farmed, but on a much smaller scale. Most Atlantic salmon is farmed salmon. Catching the real thing in the ocean has proved to be too difficult for commercial fishermen to make a living at.

Currently, Atlantic salmon is a major challenge for Alaskans. Atlantic salmon has escaped some of the major-fish farms in British Columbia and the state of Washington and mingled with Pacific wild salmon, which is a scary thought since the Pacific wild salmon is larger, meatier, and much tastier.

The best way to identify an Atlantic salmon is to look for the large black spots on the gill covers and back; they have no spots on their tails. The farm-grown Atlantic salmon is also known to be contaminated with pesticide residuals.

White fish provides us another fish meal that offers a plate just waiting for colorful sides like a mango-tomato-onion salsa or our African Beet and Onion Salad.

We hope you enjoy these recipes. If you would like one of your own recipes for fish adapted to our low-sodium plan, then please visit megaheart.com and e-mail your recipe to heartman@megaheart.com from the site. Place the following filter code into the subject line: From Megaheart Visitor.

❧ CALAMARI STEAKS ❧

ORIGIN: GREECE
DIABETIC ACCEPTABLE

This dish is also served throughout Italy, but they manage to add tomato sauce to it. I first had this tasty dish when filming a stage show for a Greek gentleman who was not only Greek but a man who knew how to eat well, and we enjoyed this meal in a restaurant. This "fried" version is fairly accurate as to what you'd find in an Athens restaurant.

MAKES 2 SERVINGS   SODIUM PER RECIPE: 116.3 MG
SODIUM PER SERVING: 58.2 MG

1 **tablespoon dried tarragon (2.976 mg)**
4 **tablespoons white, unbleached flour* (.625 mg)**
1 **tablespoon rice flour (trace)**
2 **(4-ounce) fresh calamari steaks† (112.7 mg)**
4 **tablespoons extra-virgin olive oil‡ (trace)**

Mix the tarragon with the flour and place on a flat dish or work surface. Dip the calamari steaks in the flour, making sure to coat both sides.

Heat the oil in a medium skillet over medium-high heat.

Using tongs, lower the calamari steaks into the hot oil. Be careful not to splash the hot oil. Cook rapidly on both sides until golden brown.

Serve immediately with Pepper Dipping Sauce (see page 50) that has been warmed, or serve with lemon wedges.

Nutrient Data per Serving:
Calories: 316.4. Protein: 23.5 g. Carbohydrate: 16.9 g. Dietary Fiber: .713 g. Total Sugars: .048 g. Total Fat: 16.7 g. Saturated Fat: 2.503 g. Monounsaturated Fat: 6.979 g. Polyunsaturated Fat: 5.797 g. Cholesterol: 66.3 mg. Trans Fat: 0 g. Total Omega-3 FA: 1.893 g. Total Omega-6 FA: 0 g. Potassium: 443.1 mg. Sodium: 58.2 mg. Vitamin K: 2.224 mcg. Folic Acid: 24.1 mcg.

*Data is based on 3 tablespoons flour since that's the most you'll need to use.
†Probably will be frozen. Average size is 4 ounces but some can be found in 3-ounce cuts and some in 5-ounce cuts. Thaw and dry with paper towels before cooking.
‡Only 3 tablespoons are absorbed, so the nutrient data reflects those 3 tablespoons only.

❋ HALIBUT WITH CHERMOULA SAUCE ❋

ORIGIN: NORTH AFRICA/MOROCCO
DIABETIC ACCEPTABLE

Although this is a fish recipe, it also includes a recipe for a great sauce or paste called Chermoula. Chermoula, which originated in Morocco, is generally a mixture of herbs. It also often includes ground chili peppers, black pepper, cumin, onion, garlic, cilantro, and saffron. There are many different recipes that use many different spices; we included this one.

MAKES 4 SERVINGS   SODIUM PER RECIPE: 491.6 MG
SODIUM PER SERVING: 122.9 MG

½ cup minced fresh parsley (16.8 mg)
½ cup minced fresh cilantro (12.4 mg)
4 garlic cloves, minced (2.04 mg)
2 teaspoons ground cumin (7.056 mg)
2 teaspoons dried red pepper flakes (1.08 mg)
2 teaspoons paprika (1.428 mg)
3 tablespoons olive oil (trace)
3 tablespoons fresh lemon juice (.732 mg)
3 to 4 small halibut or other thick white fish fillets (about 20 ounces total) (453.6 mg)

Mix all but the halibut in a small saucepan until it forms a thick paste. Heat the mixture over low heat until hot. Spread the chermoula on the fish fillets, cover them with plastic wrap, and refrigerate for at least 1 hour.

When ready to cook, preheat the oven to 350°F. Place the fillets in a casserole dish with the chermoula marinade and bake in the preheated oven for about 20 minutes, or until cooked through. These are also delicious barbecued.

Nutrient Data per Serving:
Calories: 211.9. Protein: 19.9 g. Carbohydrate: 4.802 g. Dietary Fiber: 1.291 g. Total Sugars: .744 g. Total Fat: 12.9 g. Saturated Fat: 1.958 g. Monounsaturated Fat: 5.785 g. Polyunsaturated Fat: 4.211 g. Cholesterol: 48 mg. Trans Fat: 0 g. Total Omega-3 FA: .067 g. Total Omega-6 FA: 0 g. Potassium: 527.4 mg. Sodium: 91.4 mg. Vitamin K: 127 mcg. Folic Acid: 0 mcg.

✦ WHITE FISH ✦

ORIGIN: CANADA
PRINCE OF WALES HOTEL, WATERTON, CANADA
DIABETIC ACCEPTABLE

Recently, during a late spring, while the snow was still on the ground, we took a trip on the beautiful Going-to-the-Sun Road in Glacier National Park and ended up at Waterton Lakes. It was such a breathtaking sight that I insisted Don and I spend the night at the gorgeous old Victorian hotel. What a night! A storm whipped off the lakes and the hotel lost its electricity. Our room was next to an automatic door that one had to use manually to access the hallway. So, after each person entered, it would slam shut with a loud bang. Finally, Don had had enough and he took his belt and rigged it to keep the door open. This solved one problem, but the next one was mine. The adjoining room had an open window, a matter that soon affected us. The wind was so strong that it whistled straight through that room into ours through the adjoining door that was not airtight. Oh my, I have never experienced such terrific force, but I was determined to be patient and wait it out. Someone, I thought, had to return to that room. But they never did. Don absolutely loved the sound effects of nature at work, but I became quite miserable.

Finally, I did a little rigging of my own by stuffing the door jamb with my bathrobe belt. It was like trying to caulk a leaking boat. Why I didn't go down and ask the hotel personnel to close those windows, I'll never know. Anyway, it made for an unforgettable experience.

We were able to have a delicious fish dinner that evening before the lights went out and here's our version of that recipe.

SERVES 2   SODIUM PER RECIPE: 176.3 MG
SODIUM PER SERVING: 88.1 MG

½   **cup spoon-size Shredded Wheat (1.715 mg)**
7   **no-salt Kettle or Michael's potato chips* (1.134 mg)**
12 **ounces white fish (orange roughy, halibut, catfish, sea bass, etc.) (173.4 mg)**
½   **lemon, cut into wedges (.295 mg)**

---

*You can make this without the potato chips if you prefer. If so, add just a touch of olive oil to the grill for flavor.

With your rolling pin, flatten out the Shredded Wheat and the potato chips. Place on a flat surface or in a dish to dip the fish.

Clean the fish but don't pat dry.

Spray a nonstick griddle or frying pan with oil and heat over medium-high heat.

Dip the fish in the Shredded Wheat mixture on both sides. Fry on the griddle or pan. Brown on both sides. If the fish starts to brown too rapidly, turn down the heat to medium. Cook for 4 minutes on each side, a bit more for thicker pieces. The fish is done when it flakes.

Serve hot with steamed vegetables, brown rice, and a wedge of lemon.

Nutrient Data per Serving with Potato Chips:
Calories: 307.8. Protein: 34.2 g. Carbohydrate: 14 g. Dietary Fiber: 1.743 g. Total Sugars: .161 g. Total Fat: 12.5 g. Saturated Fat: 2.341 g. Monounsaturated Fat: 4.091 g. Polyunsaturated Fat: 4.516 g. Cholesterol: 102 mg. Trans Fat: 0 g. Total Omega-3 FA: 2.74 g. Total Omega-6 FA: 0 g. Potassium: 681.9 mg. Sodium: 88.1 mg. Vitamin K: 1.736 mcg. Folic Acid: 0 mcg.

Nutrient Data per Serving Without Potato Chips:
Calories: 269.8. Protein: 33.7 g. Carbohydrate: 10.3 g. Dietary Fiber: 1.402 g. Total Sugars: .146 g. Total Fat: 10.1 g. Saturated Fat: 1.565 g. Monounsaturated Fat: 3.393 g. Polyunsaturated Fat: 3.653 g. Cholesterol: 102 mg. Trans Fat: 0 g. Total Omega-3 FA: 2.727 g. Total Omega-6 FA: 0 g. Potassium: 591.6 mg. Sodium: 87.6 mg. Vitamin K: .17 mcg. Folic Acid: 0 mcg.

WHITE FISH WITH
❖ AVOCADO CREAM SAUCE ❖

ORIGIN: CALIFORNIA

**SERVES: 6   SODIUM PER RECIPE: 420 MG
SODIUM PER SERVING 70MG**

THE FISH
1½ **pounds mild white fish fillets, such as halibut or mahimahi**
  1 **teaspoon olive oil**

THE SEASONING
½ **teaspoon ground coriander (.315 mg)**
½ **teaspoon paprika (.357 mg)**
½ **teaspoon freshly ground black pepper (.462 mg)**

THE SAUCE†
½ **cup dry white nonalcoholic wine, such as Fré (8.12 mg)**
2 **garlic cloves, minced (1.02 mg)**
1 **medium Hass avocado*, skin and pit removed (13.8 mg)**

*Or 173 grams of available variety.
†About 6 servings when used as a sauce for fish.

¼ **cup whole milk (24.4 mg)**
¼ **cup half-and-half (24.8 mg)**
2 **teaspoons fresh lemon juice (trace)**
   Dash of cayenne pepper (trace)

Season the fish with the seasoning ingredients.

Bring the wine and garlic to a boil into a small pan and cook, uncovered, for 3 to 4 minutes. Transfer to a blender or use a small handheld blender to puree the mixture with the avocado. Add the remaining ingredients. Process for a few seconds and return the mixture to the saucepan. Reheat and serve warm over fish.

Heat the grill to medium-high heat and cover the cooking surface with the olive oil. Cook the fish for 4 minutes on each side or until cooked through.

For a nice presentation, pour a little sauce on each plate, place the fish on the sauce, and spoon a little more sauce over the top.

Nutrient Data per Tablespoon Sauce:
Calories: 223.6. Protein: 23.1 g. Carbohydrate: 4.314 g. Dietary Fiber: 2.163 g. Total Sugars: .905 g. Total Fat: 12.6 g. Saturated Fat: 2.559 g. Monounsaturated Fat: 5.53 g. Polyunsaturated Fat: 3.044 g. Cholesterol: 72.7 mg. Trans Fat: 0 g. Total Omega-3 FA: 1.912 g. Total Omega-6 FA: .004 g. Potassium: 563.8 mg. Sodium: 70 mg. Vitamin K: 6.768 mcg. Folic Acid: 0 mcg.

PACIFIC NORTHWEST SALMON
❈ WITH BOK CHOY ❈

ORIGIN: NORTHWESTERN U.S.A.
DIABETIC ADAPTABLE*

This recipe is based on a favorite restaurant meal in the Northern California coastal area around Mendocino. It is made with fresh, wild Pacific salmon, and the fresh vegetables make it a real taste treat. You will need a nonstick frying pan and a nonstick† griddle or grill to prepare this dish. Timing with preparation is essential, but easily done.

MAKES 4 SERVINGS   SODIUM PER RECIPE: 375.4 MG
SODIUM PER SERVING: 93.9 MG

*Diabetics, replace sugar with your choice of substitute (Splenda or Stevia). The rice has the bulk of carbohydrates in this recipe with a total of 158.3 grams. The cabbage has 20.6 grams of carbohydrates.
†Why the nonstick? We use nonstick to cut down the need for oil or butter to grill, fry, or sauté. We may use 1 tablespoon of olive oil for flavoring but even that's not needed with a good nonstick cooking surface.

1 cup white basmati rice (2 mg)
4 (5-ounce) Pacific wild Coho salmon fillets* (254.2 mg)

THE SAUCE
1 tablespoon low-sodium water (trace)
2 tablespoons natural rice vinegar (.30 mg)
1 tablespoon sesame oil (trace)
1 tablespoon sugar or Splenda substitute (trace)

THE VEGETABLES
4 ounces mushrooms, sliced (4.2 mg)
½ medium red bell pepper, cored, seeded, and cut lengthwise
    into 12 strips (1.19 mg)
½ pound red cabbage, thinly sliced or shredded (about 4 cups)
    (75.6 mg)
2 small bok choy, cleaned and cut vertically into quarters
    (38 mg)
½ cup low-sodium water (trace)

Prepare the rice according to package directions. This usually takes 15 to 25 minutes depending on the method used. One cup uncooked rice makes about 2 to 3 cups steamed rice.

Prepare the salmon for grilling. Set aside. (The salmon will be especially nice if cooked on a barbecue. Grilling time varies with thickness of fillets, but figure on at least 10 to 15 minutes.)

Whisk all the ingredients for the sauce together in a small bowl. Set aside.

When the rice is just about ready, put the salmon on the grill.

Prepare the vegetables, keeping them separate. Heat the water in a 12- to 14-inch nonstick frying pan over medium heat. Add the mushrooms and red pepper and cook until they begin to soften, 3 to 4 minutes, stirring frequently. Transfer them to a small bowl and keep warm.

Pour the sauce into the pan (most of the water from the mushrooms will have evaporated) and heat over medium heat.

Add the cabbage and sauté until it begins to wilt, about 4 minutes; put the lid on the pan for the final 2 minutes. Transfer to a second bowl and keep warm. When the fish and rice are ready, add a little more water to the sauce. Add the bok choy to the pan, cover with a lid, and steam rapidly for 2 to 3 minutes. The variance in time accounts for keeping the vegetables from overcooking and the cabbage from turning the others red.

Serve individually, putting ½ cup rice on each warm plate and arranging a bed of vegetables next to it. Lay the grilled salmon on top and serve with a wedge of lemon.

*Try to avoid farmed salmon. Farmed salmon is known to have a high level of pesticides.

Nutrient Data per Serving:
Calories: 457.3. Protein: 35.3 g. Carbohydrate: 50.4 g. Dietary Fiber: 3.633 g. Total Sugars: 7.44 g. Total Fat: 12.1 g. Saturated Fat: 2.338 g. Monounsaturated Fat: 4.394 g. Polyunsaturated Fat: 4.385 g. Cholesterol: 62.2 mg. Trans Fat: 0 g. Total Omega-3 FA: 2.114g. Total Omega-6 FA: 0 g. Potassium: 913.7 mg. Sodium: 93.9 mg. Vitamin K: 28.1 mcg. Folic Acid: 112.5 mcg.

❈ SCANDINAVIAN-STYLE COD ❈

ORIGIN: SWEDEN
DIABETIC ACCEPTABLE

Fish is great for our hearts because of the omega-3 fats. Not only is it nutritious, it's very easy to prepare and tasty when prepared correctly. White fish is eaten in practically every country of the world that has its own seaport or fishing village. There are hundreds of names for white fish, with many of them meaning the same fish. For this recipe we like the cod varieties.

MAKES 4 SERVINGS   SODIUM PER RECIPE: 437.5 MG
SODIUM PER SERVING: 109.4 MG

1½	pound cod fillets* (401.2 mg)
¼	cup chopped onion (1.2 mg)
2	tablespoons unsalted butter (3.124 mg)
½	cup low-sodium water (trace)
¼	cup white nonalcoholic wine, such as Fré (.372 mg)
1	teaspoon dried tarragon (.992 mg)
6	whole peppercorns (.132 mg)
	Approximately ¼ cup half-and-half (24.8 mg)
1	tablespoon all-purpose flour (.156 mg)
1	tablespoon unsalted butter (1.562 mg)

Sauté the onion in 1 tablespoon of the butter in a large frying pan over medium-high heat until the onions turn translucent. Add the water, wine, tarragon, and peppercorns. Bring to a boil. Add the cod, reduce the heat to a simmer, and cook for 10 minutes, or until the fish is thoroughly cooked.

Remove the fish, cover, and keep warm.

Strain the cooking liquid into a measuring cup, and add half-and-half to equal 1 cup.

Make a roux with the remaining tablespoon of butter and the flour:

*Data based on lingcod. Pacific cod per 1.5 pounds would be 362.1 mg; Atlantic cod would be 275.4 mg.

Melt the butter in a small saucepan over medium heat, add the flour, and stir until well blended and bubbling. Remove the pan from heat and add the cup of cooking liquid and cream all at once. Stir to make a smooth sauce. Return the mixture to the stove and cook over medium heat until the sauce thickens.

Serve the fish with the sauce poured over it. Peas make a nice accompaniment and taste delicious with the sauce.

Nutrient Data per Serving:
Calories: 253.8. Protein: 31 g. Carbohydrate: 3.519 g. Dietary Fiber: .24 g. Total Sugars: .464 g. Total Fat: 12.2 g. Saturated Fat: 6.902 g. Monounsaturated Fat: 3.343 g. Polyunsaturated Fat: .928 g. Cholesterol: 116.9 mg. Trans Fat: 0 g. Total Omega-3 FA: .105 g. Total Omega-6 FA: .231 g. Potassium: 808.2 mg. Sodium: 109.4 mg. Vitamin K: 1.111 mcg. Folic Acid: 2.887 mcg.

❂ SALMON INDIAN STYLE ❂

ORIGIN: INDIA
DIABETIC ACCEPTABLE

Indian recipes nearly always use coriander and cumin seeds. When you use them on fresh, wild salmon, the two spices add flavor that makes the dish scrumptious. This one is well worth the try, and we recommend it highly. Grill it or fry it. Serve with the Minty Cucumber Sauce with Yogurt (see page 47) or the Tomato-Corn Salad (see page 235).

MAKES 2 SERVINGS   SODIUM PER RECIPE: *165.2* MG
SODIUM PER SERVING: *82.6* MG

2   (6-ounce) wild Pacific salmon fillets (156.4 mg)
    Juice of 1 lemon (.94 mg)
1   teaspoon ground coriander (.63 mg)
2   teaspoons whole cumin seeds (7.056 mg)
⅛ teaspoon ground white pepper (.015 mg)
    Lemon or lime juice for splashing (.118 mg)

Wash the fish fillets.

Mix together the coriander, cumin seeds, and white pepper.

Splash the fillets with lemon juice and then rub in the spice mixture on both sides.

Spray a nonstick grill or pan with oil spray. Grill or fry the salmon over medium-high heat until the first side is lightly browned. Turn and finish cooking on other side; do not overcook.

Nutrient Data per Serving:
Calories: 272.4. Protein: 37.5 g. Carbohydrate: 6.092 g. Dietary Fiber: .849 g. Total Sugars: 1.317 g. Total Fat: 10.7 g. Saturated Fat: 2.184 g. Monounsaturated Fat: 4.046 g. Polyunsaturated Fat: 3.472 g. Cholesterol: 76.5 mg. Trans Fat: 0 g. Total Omega-3 FA: 2.509 g. Total Omega-6 FA: 0 g. Potassium: 833.8 mg. Sodium: 82.6 mg. Vitamin K: .283 mcg. Folic Acid: 0 mcg.

❧ SWEET-AND-SOUR SALMON ❧

ORIGIN: ASIAN
DIABETIC ADAPTABLE*

The idea is to create a dish that is flavorful, colorful, and low in sodium and calories. If you don't have the exact ingredients, don't hesitate to make substitutions with whatever looks good at the market.

Either a wok or a decent large nonstick skillet will work for this dish. Adjust the flavor of the sauce to your liking by adding more apricot preserves or more rice vinegar—the sweet-and-sour parts.

**MAKES 4 SERVINGS   SODIUM PER RECIPE: 366.7 MG
SODIUM PER SERVING: 91.7 MG**

4   (5-ounce) wild (or Coho) salmon fillets (254.2 mg)
1   tablespoon extra virgin olive oil (trace)
2   scallions, thinly sliced (4.8 mg)
1   teaspoon fresh ginger, peeled and minced (.26 mg)
2   garlic cloves, minced (.952 mg)
1   medium carrot, peeled and thinly sliced (42.1 mg)
2   medium zucchini, split lengthwise in half and then cut into 1-inch pieces (39.2 mg)
1   medium red bell pepper, cored and sliced into rings (2.38 mg)
2   tablespoons Don's Soy Sauce Replacement (see Page 37) (3.42 mg)
¼   cup fish stock or Maureen's Easy Chicken Broth (see Page 113) (5.187 mg)
3   tablespoons rice vinegar (.45 mg)
2   tablespoons apricot preserves* (16 mg)
1   teaspoon cornstarch mixed with 1 teaspoon cold water (.175 mg)
1½ cups fresh pineapple, cut into 1-inch cubes (2.235 mg)
4   cups warm steamed long-grain or basmati white rice (7.8 mg)

*Apricot jam can be no-sugar or low-sugar jam if that can fit into your program.

Heat the oil in a wok or skillet over medium-high heat. Add scallions, ginger, and garlic. Cook for 1 minute. Add salmon fillets and lightly brown on both sides, about 3 minutes per side. Remove from the pan and keep warm.

Add the cut carrots, zucchini, and bell pepper to the wok. Stir-fry for 1 minute. Add the soy sauce replacement, fish stock or chicken broth, vinegar, apricot preserves, and cornstarch mixture. When the sauce has thickened, add the pineapple and return the fish to the pan to reheat.

To serve, mound the rice on a serving plate and spoon over the fish, vegetables, and sauce.

Nutrient Values per Serving:
Calories: 328.2. Protein: 32.1 g. Carbohydrate: 24.3 g. Dietary Fiber: 3.181 g. Total Sugars: 17.3 g. Total Fat: 12 g. Saturated Fat: 2.266 g. Monounsaturated Fat: 5.483 g. Polyunsaturated Fat: 3.264 g. Cholesterol: 62.2 mg. Trans Fat: 0 g. Total Omega-3 FA: 2.137 g. Total Omega-6 FA: 0 g. Potassium: 1102 mg. Sodium: 91.7 mg. Vitamin K: 10.3 mcg. Folic Acid: 0 mcg.

◈ TEMPURA SHRIMP ◈

ORIGIN: JAPAN
DIABETIC ADAPTABLE*

While living in Japan for nearly a year I fell in love with tempura. Eat too much of it and you can put on a few pounds, but serve it during special occasions and it's a perfect treat for you and your guests. You can punch up the tempura batter with a little pepper, onion powder, minced garlic, or spicy flavors that you enjoy. You can use this same batter to make tempura vegetables.[†]

MAKES 2 SERVINGS   SODIUM PER RECIPE: 149.4 MG
SODIUM PER SERVING: 74.7 MG

*Most of the carbohydrates are in the white flour (95.4 g), and rice flour (126.6 g). You can cut the yam and broccoli and halve the flour mix to achieve 29.9 grams of carbohydrates per serving.

[†]We recommend for safety reasons that you use an electric deep-fat fryer designed for this kind of recipe. If you don't have one and you still want to try this recipe, then we suggest you use a large pot that is wider than your burner, whether gas or electric. Keep an open box of baking soda within reach (but not next to the pan) and a lid large enough to cover the pan. If you spill or drop oil onto a flame, it will ignite instantly. Baking soda can serve as a fire extinguisher by your dumping it onto the flame source. Immediately place a lid over the pot to starve the fire of oxygen. Visit mega-heart.com/kit_cabinet.html to locate a good electric deep-fat fryer. To make tempura vegetables, prepare the same batter. Clean and dry vegetables. Cut into bite-size pieces. If preparing carrots or yams or eggplant, peel before cutting. Dip into batter and deep-fry just as you would the shrimp.

THE BATTER
1 egg (63 mg)
⅓ cup cold low-sodium water (trace)
½ cup white, unbleached all-purpose flour (1.25 mg)
½ cup white rice flour (trace)

THE TEMPURA
8 large nonbrined, unsalted shrimp (about 3 inches long or
    56 grams weight)* (82.9 mg)
¾ quart expeller-pressed canola oil to deep fry† (trace)

Whisk the egg and water together. Add the flours and stir only until mixed. Do not overmix or it will become lumpy. Set aside.

Clean, shell, and devein the shrimp but leave on the tail. Set aside.

Prepare the oil. To deep-fry with an electric deep-fat fryer, follow manufacturer's instructions for oil quantity needed. Bring the oil up to the recommended temperature.

Dip the shrimp into the batter a few at a time, cook 3 minutes (or per manufacturer's suggestion) until golden brown. Remove and drain on paper towels.

Serve hot, with steamed vegetables such as cubed yams, broccoli florets, diced carrots.

Have some of your homemade Don's Soy Sauce Replacement handy for dipping the tempura shrimp. (See page 37.)

Nutrient Data per Serving:
Calories: 340.5. Protein: 14.8 g. Carbohydrate: 59.7 g. Dietary Fiber: 2.317 g. Total Sugars: 1.929 g. Total Fat: 3.867 g. Saturated Fat: 1.077 g. Monounsaturated Fat: 1.234 g. Polyunsaturated Fat: .83 g. Cholesterol: 148.3 mg. Trans Fat: 0 g. Total Omega-3 FA: .204 g. Total Omega-6 FA: 0 g. Potassium: 202.8 mg. Sodium: 74.7 mg. Vitamin K: .319 mcg. Folic Acid: 48.1 mcg.

*Fresh shrimp from the United States can be found at Trader Joe's and other specialty markets. Make sure it's not salted.
†Nutrient Data for oil is figured only for the oil that binds to the tempura you serve. We use expeller-pressed canola oil for this.

❖ SENEGALESE FISH STEW ❖

ORIGIN: SENEGAL
DIABETIC ACCEPTABLE*

Thebouidienne *(pronounced CHEB-O-DJIN), the national dish of Senegal, has become an African specialty, or classic, if you will. We use olive oil and recommend using it, although peanut oil would be more to the liking in Senegal. (We do understand that many people have strong allergies to peanut oil, so keep this in mind when preparing this dish for others.) In Senegal, this is called a rice and fish stew. We worked to keep the carbohydrates as well as the calories down.*

MAKES 4 SERVING   SODIUM PER RECIPE: 486.6 MG
SODIUM PER SERVING: 121.7 MG

1½   cups chopped onion (7.2 mg)
¾   cup seeded and chopped green pepper (3.352 mg)
⅛   teaspoon cayenne pepper (.067 mg)
1   tablespoon olive oil (trace)
3   ounces or 5 tablespoons no-salt tomato paste† (83.3 mg)
1   cup low-sodium water (trace)
1   pound halibut haddock or other fairly thick fillet of white
     fish (340 mg)
1   large or 2 medium sweet potatoes (71.5 mg) or yams
     (13.9 mg)
½   head Savoy or other mild white cabbage cut into 4 wedges
     (39.2 mg)

Heat the olive oil in a 5-quart Dutch oven and sauté the onion and green pepper in the oil for about 5 minutes, or until translucent. Stir in the cayenne pepper, tomato paste, and water. Bring to a boil, then reduce to a simmer.

Layer the fish on top of the tomato mixture; place the potatoes around the fish and cover them with the cabbage wedges. Cover the pan and cook for 1 hour, or until the potatoes and fish are tender. This stew is often served with boiled rice.

Nutrient Data per Serving:
Calories: 251.1. Protein: 25.5 g. Carbohydrate: 24 g. Dietary Fiber: 4.909 g. Total Sugars: 6.438 g. Total Fat: 6.161 g. Saturated Fat: .88 g. Monounsaturated Fat: 3.343 g. Polyunsaturated Fat: 1.267 g. Cholesterol: 34.7 mg. Trans Fat: 0 g. Total Omega-3 FA: .611 g. Total Omega-6 FA: 0 g. Iron: 2.122 mg. Potassium: 1226 mg. Sodium: 95.2 mg. Vitamin K: 32 mcg. Folic Acid: 0 mcg.

*Most of the carbohydrates are in the sweet potatoes (26.2 grams) and yams (41.2 grams). Yams are much lower in sodium levels.
†Hunt's or Contadina. Hunt's is lower in sodium.

SIDE DISHES

❖ ❖ ❖ ❖ ❖ ❖ ❖ ❖

Side dishes, often referred to as "sides," become a choice for you with each meal. A side dish can be anything from a single ear of corn to more elaborate fixings. In each case, however, we feel you might want to base your side dish on what's available fresh at your local produce or farmers' market.

A side is usually chosen or designed to complement your main course, which may be any meat or seafood dish. Some vegetables complement some meats and seafood more than others do.

The sides in this section are based on side dishes eaten in other countries, with a few from America. Chinese Fried Rice can also be an entrée, but we prefer it as a side to pork, especially sweet-and-sour pork. Our version of the African beet and onion salad makes a terrific side for chicken dishes, whereas curried vegetables work well with beef or chicken.

The Vietnamese Bánh Mì sandwich uses marinated radishes and carrots, but these also work as a great side to a good seafood meal.

In other words, choose side dishes that complement your main course in both color and flavor. If your main course is dark, choose something light in color, like mixed vegetables. If your choice for an entrée is based on a recipe from Thailand, then try to pick a side that also matches a Thai recipe for the side dish.

You'll also do well if you don't bring together two similar dishes that compete with each other and use one as the "side." Remember, too, that monochromatic plates are not as appealing to us as one with color variations. You'll probably find this true for yourself as well.

❧ BEET AND ONION SALAD ❧

ORIGIN: AFRICA
DIABETICS: CHECK NUTRIENT DATA

This side salad will surprise you with its sweet flavor of beets meeting vinegar and onions. It's definitely worth the effort if you like beets. This recipe is very low in fat, and is a terrific salad for lunch or dinner.

MAKES 4 SERVINGS   SODIUM PER RECIPE: 322.5 MG
SODIUM PER SERVING: 53.7 MG

1   **pound beets (about 3 to 4 medium) peeled (318.2 mg)**
1   **small sweet onion, thinly sliced (2.1 mg)**
¼   **cup red wine vinegar (.60 mg)**
½   **teaspoon sugar or Splenda substitute (trace)**

Clean the beets thoroughly and trim them, leaving a ½ inch piece of the top attached.

Place the beets in a pan, cover with water, and bring to a boil. Turn down the heat, cover, and simmer for about 30 minutes, or until tender. Drain in a colander and cool.

When cool enough to handle, slip off the skins and remove the top and any undesirable parts. Slice thinly crosswise and layer alternately with the onion in a small bowl.

Whisk the vinegar and sugar together until the sugar is dissolved and then pour over the vegetables in the bowl. Cover with plastic wrap. Serve at room temperature. Any leftovers may be stored in the refrigerator, but bring to room temperature again before serving.

Nutrient Data per Serving with Sugar:
Calories: 37. Protein: 1.207 g. Carbohydrate: 8.652 g. Dietary Fiber: 2.077 g. Total Sugars: 6.058 g. Total Fat: .125 g. Saturated Fat: .021 g. Monounsaturated Fat: .025 g. Polyunsaturated Fat: .049 g. Cholesterol: 0 mg. Trans Fat: 0 g. Total Omega-3 FA: .004 g. Total Omega-6 FA: 0 g. Potassium: 248.9 mg. Sodium: 53.7 mg. Vitamin K: .183 mcg. Folic Acid: 0 mcg.

Nutrient Data per Serving Using Splenda to Replace Sugar:
Calories: 35.7. Protein: 1.207 g. Carbohydrate: 8.302 g. Dietary Fiber: 2.077 g. Total Sugars: 5.709 g. Total Fat: .125 g. Saturated Fat: .021 g. Monounsaturated Fat: .025 g. Polyunsaturated Fat: .049 g. Cholesterol: 0 mg. Trans Fat: 0 g. Total Omega-3 FA: .004 g. Total Omega-6 FA: 0 g. Potassium: 248.9 mg. Sodium: 53.7 mg. Vitamin K: .183 mcg. Folic Acid: 0 mcg.

❖ CHINESE FRIED RICE ❖

ORIGIN: CHINA
DIABETIC EXCHANGES POSSIBLE

When I returned from the Far East many years ago, I brought back a collection of recipes from Japan with a few additional recipes from other countries I "toured" while wearing the green. This one was always a favorite. Fried rice hawkers in train depots first introduced me to this dish. They would reach through the open windows of train cars and sell small wooden box-type covered trays of rice (a true box lunch) served with chopsticks. The boxes always came with condiments, including lots of soy or teriyaki sauce.

Then I discovered a different flavor. Years later while recording radio commercials for a Chinese restaurant, the Nanking Café, I discovered Chinese Fried Rice using sesame oil and vegetables. Here's my version of that rice dish and it's not far from the original. I think you'll enjoy it.

MAKES 3 SERVINGS   SODIUM PER RECIPE: 184.9 MG
SODIUM PER SERVING (USING 2 EGGS): 61.6 MG
SODIUM PER SERVING (USING 1 EGG): 40.6 MG

1   teaspoon extra-virgin olive oil* (trace)
½   cup chicken, diced into ⅓-inch cubes (38.3 mg)
3   cups steamed white basmati rice (1 cup raw) (2 mg)
3   tablespoons cooked peas, diced (1.45 mg)
2   tablespoons cooked carrots, diced (11.4 mg)
1   tablespoon chopped fresh parsley (2.128 mg)
2   teaspoons Don's Soy Sauce Replacement (see page 37)
       (1.171 mg)
1   teaspoon sesame oil† (trace)
2   large eggs, whisked (126 mg)
2   tablespoons thinly sliced scallions (2.4 mg)
       White pepper (trace)
¼   cup toasted slivered almonds‡, optional (.393 mg)

---

*A good nonstick fry pan or nonstick griddle or wok will allow you to cut the fat and calories by using very little oil (less than a teaspoon). If you don't use a good nonstick pan, use at least 1 tablespoons of extra-virgin olive oil for sautéing the chicken.
†Want to "heat" it up? Use 1 teaspoon sesame seed oil and ½ teaspoon of sesame seed chili oil.
‡I like lightly toasted slivered unsalted almonds but walnuts or peanuts work as well.

Over high heat, heat the olive oil in large nonstick frying pan, griddle, or wok.

Sauté the chicken until nearly done, turning often. Remove from the heat and set aside. If using a griddle, just push it up to the cooler end.

Using the same pan or griddle over high heat, cook the eggs stirring and chopping constantly while cooking. Remove from pan and set aside, or push up with the chicken if using a griddle.

Bring the chicken back to the heat and add the steamed rice. Reduce the heat to medium and cook for 2 minutes, stirring constantly.

Stir in the vegetables. Add the parsley, Don's Soy Sauce Replacement, sesame oil, and the cooked eggs. Cook for 2 to 3 minutes more. Transfer to a large bowl or platter. Sprinkle with sliced scallions and add white pepper to taste. If using the optional almonds, sprinkle over each serving. (Calculate 1 gram of fat per serving for the almonds, and about 60 calories.) Serve the fried rice hot.

Nutrient Data per Serving Using 2 Eggs:
Calories: 351.4. Protein: 13.8 g. Carbohydrate: 56.3 g. Dietary Fiber: 2.707 g. Total Sugars: 1.705 g. Total Fat: 6.979 g. Saturated Fat: 1.524 g. Monounsaturated Fat: 2.926 g. Polyunsaturated Fat: 1.703 g. Cholesterol: 152.4 mg. Trans Fat: .005 g. Total Omega-3 FA: .196 g. Total Omega-6 FA: 0 g. Potassium: 223.2 mg. Sodium: 61.6 mg. Vitamin K: 26.1 mcg. Folic Acid: 150 mcg.

Nutrient Data per Serving Using 1 Egg:
Calories: 326.9. Protein: 11.7 g. Carbohydrate: 56.2 g. Dietary Fiber: 2.707 g. Total Sugars: 1.576 g. Total Fat: 5.323 g. Saturated Fat: 1.007 g. Monounsaturated Fat: 2.291 g. Polyunsaturated Fat: 1.475 g. Cholesterol: 81.9 mg. Trans Fat: .005 g. Total Omega-3 FA: .184 g. Total Omega-6 FA: 0 g. Potassium: 200.9 mg. Sodium: 40.6 mg. Vitamin K: 26 mcg. Folic Acid: 150 mcg.

◈ COLCANNON ◈

ORIGIN: IRELAND
DIABETIC ACCEPTABLE

This side dish was served to Maureen in Ireland. I've not altered it a bit to meet our needs, except for the salt, but I guarantee you it tastes nearly like the original.

MAKE 8 SERVINGS   SODIUM PER RECIPE: 309.7 MG
SODIUM PER SERVING: 38.7 MG

1 **pound Yukon gold or any boiling potato (25.6 mg)**
1 **pound Savoy, napa, or green cabbage (273 mg)**
4 **garlic cloves (2.04 mg)**
1 **cup chopped onion (4.8 mg)**

2   **tablespoons olive oil (trace)**
⅛   **teaspoon ground white pepper (.015 mg)**
2   **tablespoons chopped fresh parsley (4.256 mg)**

Peel the potatoes. Cover with water, bring to a boil, and cook for about 20 minutes, or until a fork slides easily into them.

Mince the garlic and set aside in a small mixing bowl. Sauté the onion in 1 tablespoon of the olive oil until transparent, about 5 minutes.

Chop or slice the cabbage and add to the cooked onion. Pour the remaining tablespoon of olive oil over the cabbage and cook until it begins to wilt, about 10 minutes, stirring occasionally. Sprinkle the white pepper and parsley over the cabbage and onions and mix thoroughly. Lower the heat and prepare the mashed potatoes.

Drain the potatoes, reserving the cooking water. Mix ⅔ cup of the potato water along with the reserved garlic, add the potatoes, and mash.

Combine the mashed potatoes and the cabbage mixture and serve immediately or keep warm over low heat.

Nutrient Data per Serving:
Calories: 86.1. Protein: 2.105 g. Carbohydrate: 12.2 g. Dietary Fiber: 1.783 g. Total Sugars: 1.412 g. Total Fat: 3.586 g. Saturated Fat: .49 g. Monounsaturated Fat: 2.511 g. Polyunsaturated Fat: .428 g. Cholesterol: 0 mg. Trans Fat: 0 g. Total Omega-3 FA: .035 g. Total Omega-6 FA: 0 g. Potassium: 414.7 mg. Sodium: 38.7 mg. Vitamin K: 19.3 mcg. Folic Acid: 0 mcg.

❖ CURRIED VEGETABLES ❖

ORIGIN: INDIA
DIABETIC ADAPTABLE

Vegetable dishes in India usually use curry but with other spices. The mixes or combinations are always a bit different from each other and each, usually, uses salt and some use sugar. When you find such a recipe and it uses sugar, just replace that with Splenda.

Spices are great flavoring for all foods, but the combinations are important so that one doesn't overpower the others. Curry itself is a mixture of spices, so what we have here is a mixture of spices that actually become the curry. In India, this dish is called chorchori.

**MAKES 4 SERVINGS   SODIUM PER RECIPE: 220.3 MG
SODIUM PER SERVING: 55.1 MG**

1   **cup diced Yukon gold potatoes (9 mg)**

1   cup diced or bite-size cauliflower florets (30 mg)
½   cup thinly sliced carrots (42.1 mg)
1   cup green beans, cleaned, stringed, and chopped into 1-inch
      lengths (6.6 mg)
1   cup whole white mushroom caps, cleaned and trimmed
      (2.8 mg)
2   tablespoons expeller-pressed canola oil (trace)
1   teaspoon cumin seeds (3.528 mg)
½   teaspoon mustard seeds (.082 mg)
1   teaspoon turmeric (.836 mg)
1   teaspoon onion powder (1.134 mg)
3   garlic cloves, minced (1.53 mg)
2   dried red Anaheim or Serrano chili, (1.22 mg), or ½
      teaspoon crushed red pepper (.27 mg)
1   cup plain yogurt (113.7 mg)
1   teaspoon white granulated sugar or Splenda (trace)
2   teaspoons cornstarch (.475 mg)

Bring to a boil a large pan with enough water to cook the vegetables. Add the potatoes first and cook for 10 minutes or almost until tender. (Cook the larger, bulkier veggies first so that they aren't overcooked when cooking the others.) Add the cauliflower and carrots, and cook until just done or tender-crisp. Add the green beans and mushrooms last. Drain the vegetables and set aside.

Add the oil to another frying pan, set over medium to medium-high heat. Quickly fry the cumin seeds and mustard seeds in the oil until you hear them popping. Add the remaining spices and garlic, and fry gently until the garlic begins to turn golden. Lower the heat to just below a simmer.

Beat the yogurt, sugar, and cornstarch together.

Add the drained vegetables to the pan with the spices; raise the heat to simmer, while stirring. Slowly add the yogurt-cornstarch mixture, a few tablespoons at a time, and heat gently. Serve hot.

Nutrient Values per Serving:
Calories: 248.2. Protein: 5.067 g. Carbohydrate: 36.6 g. Dietary Fiber: 3.011 g. Total Sugars: 3.459 g. Total Fat: 9.529 g. Saturated Fat: 1.857 g. Monounsaturated Fat: 4.849 g. Polyunsaturated Fat: 2.299 g. Cholesterol: 7.779 mg. Trans Fat: 0 g. Total Omega-3 FA: .691 g. Total Omega-6 FA: 0 g. Potassium: 553 mg. Sodium: 55.1 mg. Vitamin K: 16.2 mcg. Folic Acid: 0 mcg.

◈ FRIED TOMATOES ◈

ORIGIN: JORDAN
DIABETIC ACCEPTABLE

When our friend Scott Leysath[†] first demonstrated his way of grilling vegetables on an outdoor grill over an open flame, he also spoke about frying tomatoes as well as a few other vegetables, and using peppers, spices, or herbs to "punch them up." So, we tried frying many vegetables and came to enjoy tomatoes off the grill or out of the pan more than any others. Then, we learned that Jordanians had been doing this for centuries! So, here is our recipe that apparently began in Jordan and worked its way to us via a sporting chef. Not a bad trip for an excellent side to any meat or vegetarian entrée.

MAKES 4 SERVINGS   SODIUM PER RECIPE: 17.6 MG
SODIUM PER SERVING: 4.405 MG

8 **garlic cloves minced (4.08 mg)**
1 **small jalapeño pepper, minced (.14 mg)**
2 **tablespoons chopped fresh parsley (4.256 mg)**
2 **teaspoons olive oil (trace)**
1 **large firm tomato, thickly sliced (9.1 mg)**
   Black or white pepper (trace)

Mix together the garlic, jalapeño pepper, and chopped parsley. Brush a nonstick griddle or frying pan with ½ teaspoon of the olive oil and place it over medium-high heat. When the griddle is hot, place the tomato slices on the griddle and fry until they begin brown lightly. Increase the heat if necessary, but do not let them burn.

Turn the tomato over and place an equal amount of the garlic mixture on each. Drizzle with the remaining olive oil and when the second side is lightly brown turn them once again for an additional 2 minutes on the garlic-mixture side. Sprinkle with pepper to taste. We serve this as a side dish with Beef and Walnuts (see page 64), and it is delicious.

Nutrient Data per Serving
Calories: 38.8. Protein: .888 g. Carbohydrate: 4.111 g. Dietary Fiber: .839 g. Total Sugars: 1.394 g. Total Fat: 2.409 g. Saturated Fat: .334 g. Monounsaturated Fat: 1.694 g. Polyunsaturated Fat: .315 g. Cholesterol: 0 mg. Trans Fat: 0 g. Total Omega-3 FA: .021 g. Total Omega-6 FA: 0 g. Potassium: 150.3 mg. Sodium: 4.405 mg. Vitamin K: 36.6 mcg. Folic Acid: 0 mcg.

[†]You can find Scott Leysath's wild game cookbook at www.megaheart.com/leysath.html.

❖ JULY FOURTH POTATO SALAD ❖

ORIGIN: U.S.A.
DIABETIC ACCEPTABLE*

When we were young, our picnic tables always had a large bowl of potato salad. The potatoes were white, the eggs were hard-boiled, and the mayonnaise oozed throughout. With the addition of some chopped onions and celery and a little pepper or paprika those salads were the tastiest dishes at the picnic. Today, we have to lose the mayonnaise, but the rest of the salad can still be enjoyed. Here's how we solved the "no-mayo" challenge. This recipe may be doubled or tripled.

MAKES 4 SERVINGS   SODIUM PER RECIPE: 268.8 MG
SODIUM PER SERVING: 67.2 MG

3   medium white, red, or Yukon gold potatoes, unpeeled (38.3 mg)
2   large eggs, hard-boiled, peeled, and chopped (126 mg)
½   cup chopped sweet onion (2.4 mg)
½   cup chopped celery (about 1 rib) (52.2 mg)
1   tablespoon olive oil (trace)
1   garlic clove, minced (.51 mg)
1   tablespoon apple cider vinegar (.15 mg)
⅛   teaspoon ground white pepper (.015 mg)
½   cup sour cream* (60.9 mg)

Boil the potatoes in their jackets for 20 to 25 minutes, testing with a fork to make sure they are done but not soft. Cool or chill. Peel potatoes, cut into 1-inch pieces, and place them into medium bowl.

Mix together the oil, garlic cloves, and vinegar in a container you use for processing, and puree with your handheld processor or in a food processor.

Add the dressing and the pepper to the potatoes in the bowl. Add the onion, celery, egg, and sour cream. Mix together gently.

Nutrient Values per Serving:
Calories: 252. Protein: 7.064 g. Carbohydrate: 29.4 g. Dietary Fiber: 4.351 g. Total Sugars: 3.391 g. Total Fat: 12.1 g. Saturated Fat: 5.033 g. Monounsaturated Fat: 5.2 g. Polyunsaturated Fat: .994 g. Cholesterol: 118.4 mg. Trans Fat: 0 g. Total Omega-3 FA: .149 g. Total Omega-6 FA: 0 g. Potassium: 793.6 mg. Sodium: 67.2 mg. Vitamin K: 8.74 mcg. Folic Acid: 0 mcg.

*Diabetics, the bulk of carbohydrates are in the potatoes (100.4 g).
†Check the FDA label before buying sour cream. Make sure you are not getting a high-sodium product. Sour cream should range from 15 mg per 2 tablespoons to 20 mg.

❖ MARINATED RADISHES AND CARROTS ❖

ORIGIN: VIETNAM
DIABETIC ACCEPTABLE

Use these marinated vegetables with our Vietnamese Bánh Mì sandwich (see page 127). They also work well with other sandwiches, and make a nice vegetable salad.

**MAKES: 1 CUP   SODIUM PER RECIPE: 80.4 MG
SODIUM PER TABLESPOON: 5.024 MG**

¼ **cup chopped red radishes (11.3 mg)**
¾ **cup chopped carrots (66.2 mg)**
1 **cup Marinade for Vegetables (see page 43) (2.838 mg)**

Chop the radishes and carrots together finely. (You can use a processor, but don't turn them to liquid.) Place the mixture into a small bowl and cover with the marinade. Cover tightly and let marinate in the refrigerator for about 6 hours.

Pour off the marinade into another small bowl and use the radish-carrot mixture with sandwiches or salads. Or serve the marinade at the table to sprinkle on salads or sandwiches.

Nutrient Data per Tablespoon:
Calories: 31.7. Protein: .072 g. Carbohydrate: 8.308 g. Dietary Fiber: .199 g. Total Sugars: 7.382 g. Total Fat: .017 g. Saturated Fat: .003 g. Monounsaturated Fat: .001 g. Polyunsaturated Fat: .008 g. Cholesterol: 0 mg. Trans Fat: 0 g. Total Omega-3 FA: .001 g. Total Omega-6 FA: 0 g. Potassium: 32.5 mg. Sodium: 5.024 mg. Vitamin K: .816 mcg. Folic Acid: 0 mcg.

❖ IRISH RED CABBAGE ❖

ORIGIN: IRELAND
DIABETIC ADAPTABLE

While visiting Ireland with my sister, Mary, and my niece, Laurie, we stopped at the Mill Restaurant in Dungarven, where we were pleasantly surprised with a delicious meal of pork chops served with mashed potatoes and red cabbage. I was so taken with the red cabbage that I asked the waitress to please tell the chef how delicious it was and ask if he would share the recipe with me. She came back with the recipe we have here. His, however, was made with red wine. Some may not *wish to cook with wine, so a vinegar version works well also.**

—Maureen

MAKES 6 SERVINGS   SODIUM PER RECIPE: 282.3 MG
SODIUM PER SERVING: 47 MG

1   **medium head red cabbage (about 5 inches in diameter or 2 pounds) (92.3 mg)**
1   **large red onion (4.5 mg)**
1   **tablespoon extra virgin olive oil (trace)**
⅓   **cup red wine vinegar (5.412 mg)**
½   **cup packed brown sugar (42.9 mg)**
1   **cinnamon stick broken into 4 pieces (.149 mg)**
2   **medium tart green apples, peeled and grated (2.76 mg)**
⅛   **teaspoon ground white pepper (.015 mg)**

Core and thinly slice the cabbage. Chop the onion.

Heat the olive oil in a heavy 4-quart pan. Sauté the onion in the heated oil until translucent and turning golden brown.

Add the cabbage and sauté for about 20 minutes. It will release moisture as it cooks down.

Stir in the vinegar, brown sugar, cinnamon stick, grated apples, and white pepper. Simmer for 25 minutes more. Remove the cinnamon stick before serving. Serve hot. Delicious with pork chops as well as other entrées.

Nutrient Data per Serving:
Calories: 167.9. Protein: 2.423 g. Carbohydrate: 37.3 g. Dietary Fiber: 4.456 g. Total Sugars: 29 g. Total Fat: 2.576 g. Saturated Fat: .371 g. Monounsaturated Fat: 1.699 g. Polyunsaturated Fat: .44 g. Cholesterol: 0 mg. Trans Fat: 0 g. Total Omega-3 FA: .116 g. Total Omega-6 FA: 0 g. Potassium: 500.3 mg. Sodium: 47 mg. Vitamin K: 55.9 mcg. Folic Acid: 0 mcg.

◈ RED CABBAGE FOR SAUERBRATEN ◈

ORIGIN: GERMANY
DIABETIC ADAPTABLE

This red cabbage recipe is the one that works best with our German Sauerbraten recipe (see page 119). It's very easy to fix and really would accompany many different meals. If you make it for the sauerbraten, then double the recipe.

*You can also use a nonalcoholic red wine.

½ **head red cabbage (about ¾ pound), sliced as thinly as possible (96.1 mg)**

2 **tart green apples, peeled, cored, and grated (pippin variety works well) (trace)**

1 **cinnamon stick, broken into 4 pieces (.598 mg)**

3 **tablespoons brown sugar (16.1 mg)**

1 **tablespoon fresh lemon juice (.146 mg)**

½ **cup alcohol-free red wine (8.12 mg)**

½ **cup low-sodium water (trace)**

Place all the ingredients into a 3- to 4-quart pan. Bring to a boil. Reduce to a simmer, cover, and cook for 30 minutes. Serve hot as a side dish with sauerbraten.

Nutrient Data per Serving:
Calories: 101.5. Protein: 1.627 g. Carbohydrate: 25.9 g. Dietary Fiber: 3.028 g. Total Sugars: 20 g. Total Fat: .244 g. Saturated Fat: .047 g. Monounsaturated Fat: .023 g. Polyunsaturated Fat: .138 g. Cholesterol: 0 mg. Trans Fat: 0 g. Total Omega-3 FA: .064 g. Total Omega-6 FA: 0 g. Potassium: 342.6 mg. Sodium: 30.3 mg. Vitamin K: 34.6 mcg. Folic Acid: 0 mcg.

❂ SPANISH OR MEXICAN RICE ❂

ORIGIN: LOS ANGELES, CALIFORNIA
DIABETIC ACCEPTABLE*

When Don and I were both youngsters, Los Angeles had a center for Mexican foods and wares; it was known as Olvera Street, and it's still there. I remember it well; it was one of the most popular places to visit when I was a child. One of my favorites was their Mexican Rice, pretty much the same as Spanish rice. Here's the best I can remember from those great childhood days. Give it a try; it's easy to make and I think you'll really enjoy it. And then, if ever in "La Ciudad de Los Angeles," the City of the Angels, make sure to visit Olvera Street. They still serve great Mexican food. And don't forget to try their cactus candy. I'm pretty sure it's sodium free and so delicious.

—Maureen

*The bulk of the carbohydrates is in the rice.

MAKES 4 SERVINGS   SODIUM PER RECIPE: 112.8 MG
SODIUM PER SERVING: 28.2 MG

1   tablespoon extra-virgin olive oil (trace)
1   onion, chopped (at least 1 cup) (4.8 mg)
3   garlic cloves, minced (1.53 mg)
1   tablespoon fresh lemon juice (.153 mg)
1   tablespoon Santa Fe Taco Mix* (.27 mg)
1   tablespoon chopped jalapeño pepper (.07 mg)
1   (14.5-ounce) can no-salt-added tomato puree (105 mg)
¼   cup low-sodium water
1   cup white or brown basmati rice (.976 mg)

Sauté the onion and garlic in the oil in a frying pan over medium-high heat until translucent, about 5 minutes.

Add the lemon juice, taco mix, jalapeño, tomato puree, and water.

Stir and bring to a boil, reduce the heat.

Add the rice.

Cook for 45 minutes, covered. Fluff and serve hot.

Nutrient Data per Serving:
Calories: 400.2. Protein: 33.5 g. Carbohydrate: 79.9 g. Dietary Fiber: 3.721 g. Total Sugars: 3.375 g. Total Fat: 3.603 g. Saturated Fat: .507 g. Monounsaturated Fat: 2.541 g. Polyunsaturated Fat: .357 g. Cholesterol: 0 mg. Calcium: 15 mg. Iron: .154 mg. Potassium: 245.9 mg. Sodium: 28.2 mg. Vitamin K: 2.454 mcg. Folate: 9.465 mcg.

❖ INDIAN DAL ❖

ORIGIN: INDIA
DIABETIC ACCEPTABLE†

When it comes to Indian dal recipes, you'll find many different versions depending on the area of origin. From southern India to northern India, dal recipes are defined by distinct flavors and often by the legumes used in each. (Its legumes range from split peas to lentils.) We use lentils in this recipe. Lentils are low in fat and high in protein and fiber. They also cook quickly.

MAKES 8 SERVINGS (APPROXIMATELY 8 CUPS)   SODIUM PER RECIPE: 76 MG
SODIUM PER SERVING: 9.503 MG

*You can obtain this from www.healthyheartmarket.com, or you may substitute a mixture of chili powder, garlic powder, onion powder, basil, cumin, coriander, and cayenne pepper with the majority of the seasoning coming from the chili powder.
†Lentils have 280 g carbohydrates.

2½ cups lentils (1-pound package) (33.6 mg)
7 cups low-sodium water (trace)
1½ tablespoons extra-virgin olive oil (trace)
3 cups chopped onions (about 3 medium) (14.4 mg)
1 jalapeño pepper, seeded and minced† (.14 mg)
6 garlic cloves, minced (3.06 mg)
1½ teaspoons ground cumin (5.292 mg)
1 teaspoon ground turmeric (.836 mg)
½ teaspoon cardamom (.18 mg)
¼ teaspoon white or freshly ground black pepper (.03 mg)
3 tablespoons fresh lemon juice (.488 mg)
2 cups chopped fresh tomatoes (18 mg)

In a colander or strainer thoroughly rinse and sort through lentils to pick out debris, as you would for any dried beans.

Place the lentils into 4-quart pot. Add 1 cup of the chopped onion and the water. Cover and bring to a boil over high heat. Lower the heat to simmer and cook, partially covered, for 45 to 50 minutes, or until lentils are soft and mixture is thickened.

While the lentils are cooking, heat the olive oil in a frying pan over medium-high heat. Sauté the remaining 2 cups of the onion, jalapeño pepper, and garlic until translucent and softened, about 10 minutes.

Sprinkle the onion mixture with the spices and the pepper. Cook for an additional minute, stirring until well mixed. Add the onion mixture to the lentils. Continue cooking, uncovered, over medium-low heat for 20 minutes. Turn the heat to low. Cover and keep warm until ready to serve.

Just before serving, stir in the fresh lemon juice.

Serve over steamed basmati rice in shallow soup or pasta bowls, and top each serving with ¼ cup chopped tomatoes.

Nutrient Data per Serving:
Calories: 271.1. Protein: 16.2 g. Carbohydrate: 45.2 g. Dietary Fiber: 8.135 g. Total Sugars: 3.999 g. Total Fat: 4.118 g. Saturated Fat: .623 g. Monounsaturated Fat: 2.27 g. Polyunsaturated Fat: 1.064 g. Cholesterol: 0 mg. Trans Fat: 0 g. Total Omega-3 FA: .176 g. Total Omega-6 FA: 0 g. Potassium: 575.7 mg. Sodium: 9.503 mg. Vitamin K: 5.578 mcg. Folic Acid: 0 mcg.

†Remember to wear gloves when handling the jalapeño peppers, and remove all seeds. You don't want to touch the membrane with your fingers.

❖ TABOULI ❖

ORIGIN: LEBANON
DIABETIC ACCEPTABLE

Like many recipes and foods, this one has a controversy attached to it, but one that we think may be a leg-puller. The origin is claimed, by many, to have been the emperor Caesar or Cleopatra. The best we could determine is that it had its origins in the Middle East, primarily Lebanon. For a tabouli to be authentic, it must contain mint.

While I was growing up, my mother had a mint plant just outside the kitchen. Its scent was wonderful and that's why I thought she always kept it growing. Wrong. She loved tabouli and proved it with her own version of this wonderful summer salad.

MAKE 8 TO 10 SERVINGS   SODIUM PER RECIPE: 213 MG
SODIUM PER SERVING (8): 26.6 MG
SODIUM PER SERVING (10): 21.3 MG

1	**cup bulgur (cracked wheat)* (23.8 mg)**
2	**cups boiling low-sodium water (trace)**
2	**cups finely chopped parsley (67.2 mg)**
2	**tablespoons chopped fresh mint leaves (3.42 mg)**
1	**large bunch scallions (to equal 1 cup), chopped† (16 mg)**
4	**garlic cloves, minced (2.04 mg)**
¼	**cup fresh lemon juice (.61 mg)**
2	**tablespoons olive oil (trace)**
1	**medium tomato, chopped finely (6.15 mg)**
	Coarse black pepper (trace)
8	**tablespoon dollops plain yogurt‡ (93.7 mg)**

Put the bulgur in a bowl and cover with the boiling water. Let stand for at least 20 minutes.

Meanwhile, place the chopped herbs in a large bowl. Whisk together the lemon juice and oil.

When the bulgur is softened, drain it in a fine sieve or mesh colander, pressing it with the back of a large spoon against the sides to release as much moisture as possible.

---

*Can be found in most natural food stores or health food sections in grocery stores.
†Or young green onions
‡Slightly more than a tablespoon

Place the drained bulgur in the bowl. Add the chopped herbs, scallions, garlic and chopped tomato and pour the lemon-oil dressing over all. Toss, and season with the pepper. We like to chill it overnight and serve it the next day. The flavors seem to intensify a bit that way and make the tabouli as tasty as you might expect it to be. It is delicious topped with a dollop of plain yogurt.

Nutrient Data per Serving (8):
Calories: 115.2. Protein: 4.01 g. Carbohydrate: 18.2 g. Dietary Fiber: 4.344 g. Total Sugars: .802 g. Total Fat: 3.827 g. Saturated Fat: .547 g. Monounsaturated Fat: 2.588 g. Polyunsaturated Fat: .491 g. Cholesterol: .276 mg. Trans Fat: 0 g. Total Omega-3 FA: .038 g. Total Omega-6 FA: 0 g. Potassium: 287 mg. Sodium: 26.6 mg. Vitamin K: 249.6 mcg. Folic Acid: 0 mcg.

Nutrient Data per Serving (10):
Calories: 92.2. Protein: 3.208 g. Carbohydrate: 14.6 g. Dietary Fiber: 3.475 g. Total Sugars: .641 g. Total Fat: 3.061 g. Saturated Fat: .438 g. Monounsaturated Fat: 2.07 g. Polyunsaturated Fat: .393 g. Cholesterol: .22 mg. Trans Fat: 0 g. Total Omega-3 FA: .03 g. Total Omega-6 FA: 0 g. Potassium: 229.6 mg. Sodium: 21.3 mg. Vitamin K: 199.7 mcg. Folic Acid: 0 mcg.

❖ TOMATO-CORN SALAD ❖

ORIGIN: U.S.A.
DIABETIC ACCEPTABLE

Chilled, light summer salads are great when the heat is up and the fresh fruits and vegetables begin to arrive in our markets or in our gardens. I think you'll like this one. It's easy to prepare and popular when served.

MAKES 4 SERVINGS   SODIUM PER RECIPE: 53.9 MG
SODIUM PER SERVING (3): 13.5 MG

THE SALAD
2   medium ears fresh white corn (27 mg)
16 cherry tomatoes (Yukon if you can get them) (24.5 mg)
¼   medium to large red onion, chopped (1.2 mg)
¼   medium red bell pepper, seeded and chopped (.595 mg)
3   tablespoons slivered fresh basil, optional (.318 mg)

THE SALAD DRESSING
1   tablespoon extra-virgin olive oil (trace)
2   tablespoons white balsamic vinegar (.30 mg)

Parboil the corn for 1 to 2 minutes. Cool and slice off the kernels, placing them into a medium salad bowl. Add the chopped onion, red pepper, tomatoes, and basil to the bowl.

Whisk together the ingredients for the dressing, add to the salad, and toss well.

Nutrient Data per Serving:
Calories: 93.4. Protein: 2.243 g. Carbohydrate: 13.7 g. Dietary Fiber: 2.465 g. Total Sugars: 2.638 g. Total Fat: 4.498 g. Saturated Fat: .652 g. Monounsaturated Fat: 1.972 g. Polyunsaturated Fat: 1.591 g. Cholesterol: 0 mg. Trans Fat: 0 g. Total Omega-3 FA: .034 g. Total Omega-6 FA: 0 g. Potassium: 319.2 mg. Sodium: 13.5 mg. Vitamin K: 9.561 mcg. Folic Acid: 0 mcg.

❖ VEGETABLE TEMPURA ❖

ORIGIN: JAPAN
DIABETIC ACCEPTABLE‡

Great for parties and a real treat, this dish is very low in sodium. Using a good deep fryer will help keep the fat low and give excellent results. This is our best tempura recipe. Choose any of your favorite vegetables, from thin slices or chunks of yams to broccoli, carrots, zucchini, and more.

MAKES 6 SERVINGS   SODIUM PER RECIPE: 65.5 MG*
SODIUM PER SERVING: 10.9 MG

THE BATTER
1 cup white rice flour (trace)
1 cup unbleached, all-purpose flour (2.5 mg)
1 cup ice-chilled low-sodium water (trace)
1 large egg (63 mg)

SUGGESTED VEGETABLES
   Eggplant, peeled and halved, then cut into ½-inch-thick, 3-inch-long pieces
   Zucchini, unpeeled and cut into ½-inch-thick, 3-inch-long slices

*Add in your estimated figures for the vegetables you use.
†Vegetables suggested contain the following listed levels of sodium.
   1 eggplant, peeled (13.7 mg)
   1 large zucchini (9.7 mg)
   1 medium green, red, or yellow pepper (2.38 mg)
   Sweet potatoes or squash (16.9 mg)
   1 cup florets, broccoli (19.2 mg)
   1 medium asparagus spear (.32 mg)
   1 large sweet onion (4.5 mg)
‡Carbohydrates are in the rice and white flour.

Green, red, or yellow bell peppers, seeded and cut into
½-inch-thick, 3-inch-long slices
Sweet potatoes or squash, peeled and cut diagonally into ¼-
inch-thick slices
Broccoli, asparagus tips, or green beans, cut into bite-size
pieces
Vidalia or sweet onion, thinly sliced into rings, rings pulled
apart

Canola oil for frying

Place all ingredients for the batter into a medium mixing bowl. Using a beater or whisk or wooden spoon, mix them together until the largest lumps are broken down. Set one or two ice cubes into the batter, but don't mix anymore. (You want batter to remain cold.)

If using a deep fryer, follow manufacturer's suggestions. If using your stove top and a pot, pour the oil at least 2 to 3 inches deep. Using a candy or fryer thermometer, bring the oil to 325°F.

Dip the vegetables to be fried into the batter and roll around until well coated. Slip into the oil one at a time either with tongs or, if using a deep fryer, place into the tray or basket. (If using the tray, you may put more into hot oil with the tray.)

For the onions only, mix all the rings into the batter, using your hands. Swirl around until you have the "biggest mess in the world" on your hands. Then using tongs for the open type of deep-fat pot, grab a bunch and lower gently into oil. Turn after a few minutes. Let them go to a light golden brown. Remove and set on paper towels placed on a dish, to drain. Let the oil return to 325°F before putting in next batch. These will stay hot in an oven set at about 250° to 300°F, but don't leave them in there for too long.

Serve with or without a homemade, salt-free, dipping sauce. You can make a very low-sodium dipping sauce by combining such ingredients as unsalted horseradish, no-salt-added tomato ketchup, and lemon juice. Or mix together some no-salt-added tomato ketchup with tangy low-sodium honey mustard and a dash of lemon juice.

Nutrient Value per Serving (the batter only plus estimated ½ tablespoon oil per serving):
Calories: 246.3. Protein: 4.767 g. Carbohydrate: 37.1 g. Dietary Fiber: 1.194 g. Total Sugars: .152 g. Total Fat: 8.406 g. Saturated Fat: .889 g. Monounsaturated Fat: 4.575 g. Polyunsaturated Fat: 2.372 g. Cholesterol: 35.2 mg. Trans Fat: 0 g. Total Omega-3 FA: .679 g. Total Omega-6 FA: 0 g. Potassium: 53.5 mg. Sodium: 10.9 mg. Vitamin K: 8.627 mcg. Folic Acid: 32.1 mcg.

YEMISER SELATTA

ORIGIN: AFRICA
DIABETICS: SEE FOOTNOTE*

Serve the lentils as a salad, a side dish, or as a meal in itself. Lentils are loaded with great nutrients and the flavors here will make this one a favorite.

MAKES 8 SERVINGS   SODIUM PER RECIPE: 57.8 MG
SODIUM PER CUP (8): 7.22 MG

1   **pound lentils (38.4 mg)**
3   **tablespoons olive oil (trace)**
6   **tablespoons red wine vinegar (.90 mg)**
10 **to 12 shallots, sliced (18 mg)**
3   **jalapeño peppers or other hot chili peppers, seeded and**
    sliced into thin strips (.42 mg)
    Freshly ground black pepper (trace)

Follow the cooking instructions on the package of lentils. It is usually about 15 minutes when using them for salads. They should be thoroughly cooked but somewhat firm.

Mix the oil and vinegar with a whisk. Pour over the cooked and cooled lentils and add the shallots and peppers. Sprinkle with black pepper to taste. This salad is traditionally served at room temperature, but we thought it was equally delicious served cold.

We experimented by adding other chopped vegetables for added flavor. Here's a list of suggestions. Sodium per serving with the below list added is 15 mg.

2 tomatoes, seeded and chopped (12.3 mg)
½ cup seeded and chopped red bell pepper (1.49 mg)
½ cup chopped celery (49.4 mg)
¼ cup chopped parsley (8.064 mg)

Nutrient Data per Serving Without Addtions:
Calories: 228. Protein: 14 g. Carbohydrate: 31.5 g. Dietary Fiber: 14.8 g. Total Sugars: 3.437 g. Total Fat: 6.063 g. Saturated Fat: .869 g. Monounsaturated Fat: 2.749 g. Polyunsaturated Fat: 2.072 g. Cholesterol: 0 mg. Trans Fat: 0 g. Total Omega-3 FA: .071 g. Total Omega-6 FA: 0 g. Potassium: 519.7 mg. Sodium: 7.22 mg. Vitamin K: 4.095 mcg. Folic Acid: 0 mcg.

Nutrient Data per Serving with Additions:
Calories: 237.5. Protein: 14.5 g. Carbohydrate: 33.6 g. Dietary Fiber: 15.5 g. Total Sugars: 4.768 g. Total Fat: 6.177 g. Saturated Fat: .893 g. Monounsaturated Fat: 2.772 g. Polyunsaturated Fat: 2.135 g. Cholesterol: 0 mg. Trans Fat: 0 g. Total Omega-3 FA: .078 g. Total Omega-6 FA: 0 g. Potassium: 638.6 mg. Sodium: 15 mg. Vitamin K: 38.4 mcg. Folic Acid: 0 mcg.

*Carbohydrates are mostly in the lentils.

BREAKFAST

❖ ❖ ❖ ❖ ❖ ❖ ❖ ❖

Preparing a breakfast meal every day of the week can prove to be something not too inviting for many who lead a racetrack life. Get up late? Who eats? For too many an Egg McMuffin or fried anything from a quick-stop "restaurant" is potentionally heart-damaging if done too often.

Chances are, we've all done it during our lives at least a few times. (I confess, I was the one sitting in the booth next to yours.) We had or have lots of excuses for eating that way. But not any more.

The joke around here when I start "lecturing" about eating right, is that when I attended Marine Corps Basic School at Quantico, Virginia, in the '50s, our breakfast meal often consisted of eggs, steak, pork chops, sausages, hash browns, toast, milk, and coffee. Not just one or the other, but all of it stacked on Melmac plates. A huge sign hung down from the overhead that read: "Take all you want. Eat all you take." I followed orders well.

The sudden change from that diet to one of C-rations in the field was not exactly a change for the better. The high sodium in both types of meals was probably an early-stage introduction to the beginnings of hypertension. Fortunately, neither became a lifetime habit.

In Ireland, breakfast consists of fried food: pork sausages, eggs, bacon rashers, and blood pudding. You can also find heart-healthy oatmeal and Irish brown bread at your table.

In France you'll find a traditional continental breakfast of baguettes, croissants served with jam and butter, and coffee.

When I lived in Japan for a while, local breakfast consisted of steamed rice and sides like grilled fish, pickles, and dried seaweed (the kind used with sushi). They also served miso soup, a stock into which they added or mixed miso paste. This mix is known as dashi. I can tell you from experience that it is very tasty, although I believe it may have been fairly high in sodium.

❖ AEBLESKIVERS ❖

ORIGIN: DENMARK
DIABETIC ACCEPTABLE

The Dutch call these pofferties. They are favorite for our guests and especially our grandchildren who, after enjoying these when visiting our home have all "demanded" that their parents buy an aebleskiver pan. We think you'll really like these just as they have.

MAKES ABOUT 35 AEBLESKIVERS   SODIUM PER RECIPE: 401.3 MG
SODIUM PER SKIVER: 11.5 MG

2	**cups nonfat milk with added vitamins A & D (205.8 mg)**
	Juice of ½ lemon (trace)
1	**teaspoon grated lemon peel (trace)**
3	**large eggs (164.3 mg)**
½	**teaspoon cream of tartar (.78 mg)**
2	**cups unbleached, all-purpose flour (5 mg)**
1½	**teaspoons ground cardamom (.261 mg)**
2	**teaspoons Featherweight baking powder (9 mg)**

Preheat aebleskiver pan on burner at low.

Bring the ingredients to room temperature. (If there is no time to do this, then warm milk to about 90°F.)

Place milk into medium mixing bowl. Add lemon juice and grated lemon rind.

Separate the eggs, placing the whites into a smaller mixing bowl. Put two egg yolks in with the milk. Using clean beater blades, beat the egg whites with the cream of tartar at high speed until stiff. Set aside.

Mix the flour and the cardamom with the milk-lemon mixture. Beat until smooth.

Turn heat up under aebleskiver pan to almost medium.

Add the baking powder to the batter. Mix for about a minute. Gently fold the egg whites into the batter until evenly distributed.

Oil or very lightly butter with unsalted butter each of the skiver cups (trace sodium). (I use Pam olive oil.)

Using a tablespoon or a ¼-cup measuring cup, pour about 1½ tablespoons of batter into each cup. Don't pour over the lip. (This measurement works with the Lodge Pro-Logic Cast-Iron Aebleskiver pan, which you can find at www.megaheart.com/kit_cabinet.html.)

When skivers begin to bubble, use two forks to turn over the skivers. Don't worry if you don't make a perfect turn, you can still save it. Try pushing down with one fork at the beginning of your rolling effort and lifting with the other. You are trying to get the uncooked batter into the bowl of the cup and the cooked portion over it. Let cook for about a minute, then roll the seams in the pan cups to smooth them out.

Serve hot with syrup or jam.

Nutritional Information per Aebleskiver:
Calories: 46. Protein: 1.674 g. Carbohydrate: 6.371 g. Dietary Fiber: .203 g. Total Sugars: .757 g. Total Fat: 1.503 g. Saturated Fat: .276 g. Monounsaturated Fat: .982 g. Polyunsaturated Fat: .187 g. Cholesterol: 12.3 mg. Trans Fat: 0 g. Total Omega-3 FA: .013 g. Total Omega-6 FA: 0 g. Potassium: 71.3 mg. Sodium: 11.5 mg. Vitamin K: .725 mcg. Folic Acid: 11 mcg.

❖ APPLE PANCAKES ❖

ORIGIN: GERMANY
DIABETIC ADAPTABLE

"Apfelpfannkuchen" is one of those words that sound great. But even better are the pancakes the word defines. I have included apples in a lot of recipes but always in this pancake. I think you'll enjoy this breakfast once in a while.

MAKES 4 SERVINGS (4 PANCAKES, 1 PER SERVING)
SODIUM PER RECIPE: 307.7 MG
SODIUM PER SERVING: 76.9 MG

THE PANCAKES
⅔ **cup white, unbleached, all-purpose flour (1.665 mg)**
2 **teaspoons white granulated sugar or Splenda (.084 mg)**
⅛ **teaspoon granulated onion or salt-free onion powder (.1641 mg)**
4 **large eggs, beaten (252 mg)**
½ **cup nonfat milk with added vitamins A & D (51.5 mg)**

THE APPLES
2 **cups unpeeled and thinly sliced apples (2.2 mg)**
2 **tablespoons granulated sugar or Splenda (trace)**
⅓ **teaspoon ground cinnamon (.957 mg)**
   Spritz of olive oil (trace)
   Natural maple syrup or confectioners' sugar for topping

In a small bowl, sift together the flour, 2 teaspoons of sugar, and the onion powder.

In a medium bowl, beat together the eggs and nonfat milk. After they are blended, gradually add the sifted dry ingredients. Beat until smooth. Set the pancake batter aside.

To prepare the apples: Spritz a nonstick pan very lightly with spray olive oil. Sauté the apples in the pan until tender.

In a small bowl, mix the 2 tablespoons of sugar and the cinnamon together. Toss with the apples.

Use a nonstick griddle or pan to make the dish. If you don't have one, you'll have to add either 2 tablespoons of unsalted butter or olive oil during the cooking. We prefer the nonstick to help cut the fats and keep the calories down.

Place a nonstick crepe pan* over medium-high heat. Pour in ¼ cup of the batter to a depth of about ¼ inch or less. When pouring the batter into pan, make a circular motion to create a round pancake shape. Then place one-quarter of the apples evenly on top; cover apples with more batter. When the bottom of the pancake is lightly browned, turn the pancake over and finish cooking on the other side. Repeat with the remaining batter and apples.

If using a nonstick griddle, lightly pour a circle of batter on the griddle; add the apples as above; then pour more batter on top. Fry the pancake until lightly browned on both sides. Repeat the procedure 3 times, until all batter and apples are used, keeping the pancakes warm as you work.

Serve immediately. Provide hot natural maple syrup or confectioners' sugar for a topping.

Serve with sliced fruit such as oranges, bananas, or strawberries.

Nutrient Data per Serving:
Calories: 210. Protein: 9.611 g. Carbohydrate: 31 g. Dietary Fiber: 1.984 g. Total Sugars: 13.3 g. Total Fat: 5.297 g. Saturated Fat: 1.634 g. Monounsaturated Fat: 1.942 g. Polyunsaturated Fat: .799 g. Cholesterol: 212.1 mg. Trans Fat: 0 g. Total Omega-3 FA: .047 g. Total Omega-6 FA: 0 g. Potassium: 197.5 mg. Sodium: 76.9 mg. Vitamin K: 1.484 mcg. Folic Acid: 31.8 mcg.

❖ APPLE STREUSEL MUFFINS ❖

ORIGIN: GERMAN AND JEWISH
DIABETICS: SEE FOOTNOTE**

A bit of history for streusel toppings was provided by friend David Meir-Levi. "Streusel is an old German dish, taken over by Jews in early Middle Ages. Mentioned in diaries of Jews in Germany in the fifteenth to seventeenth centuries. It was brought to Jewish culinary traditions in

---

*If you like crepes and these pancakes, then invest in a great crepe pan. The best we have found is the All-Clad nonstick. You can get one quickly by visiting www.mega heart.com and click on The Kitchen button. Scroll down to the All-Clad crepe pan. As of this writing, no shipping charges.

**The bulk of carbohydrates is in the flour (238.5 g).

eastern Europe either as early as the eleventh century by the German Jews, fleeing the Crusaders in the Rhine valley, or later as the Jews of post-Reformation Germany fled the wrath of German Reformation leaders who renewed their assaults on Jews who rejected the offer to join them in the new Christianity. In any event, it's probably a bona fide German dessert topping that made its way into Jewish culinary traditions in Europe."

Our muffin is very low in fat and sodium and lower than most muffins in calories. This muffin is a bit denser than muffins cooked with oil, but oh so good. (We replaced the oil with homemade applesauce.) I prefer making these in a nonstick muffin tin or one that has been well oiled and flour dusted. They'll pop right out after baking if you do.

**MAKES 12 STANDARD-SIZE MUFFINS   SODIUM PER RECIPE: 313.1 MG
SODIUM PER 12 COUNT: 26.1 MG**

THE TOPPING
1 **tablespoon unsalted butter, softened (2.343 mg)**
⅓ **cup brown sugar, not packed (18.7 mg)**
¾ **teaspoon ground cinnamon (.448 mg)**
½ **cup finely chopped unsalted walnuts (1.17 mg)**

THE BATTER
1⅓ **cups light brown sugar, not packed (73.1 mg)**
⅔ **cup homemade applesauce (see page 51) (.252 mg)**
1 **small to medium unpeeled apple, cored and diced (1.06 mg)**
2 **teaspoons vanilla extract (.756 mg)**
2 **tablespoons orange zest, finely grated (.36 mg)**
1 **large egg (63 mg)**
1 **cup low-sodium buttermilk* (127.1 mg)**
2½ **cups unbleached, all-purpose flour (6.25 mg)**

*Not all reduced-fat buttermilk products are low in sodium. And not all low-sodium buttermilks have reduced fat. Buttermilk with low sodium and reduced fat around the United States include the following brands (sodium data per one-cup serving):
Knudsen (130 mg)
A & P Buttermilk (125 mg)
Borden (130 mg)
Borden Skim-Line (150 mg)
Crowley (130 mg)
Darigold Trim (130 mg)
Weight Watchers (140 mg)

1 **level teaspoon ground cinnamon (.606 mg)**
1 **cup seedless golden raisins, packed (19.8 mg)**
2 **level teaspoons Ener-G low-sodium baking soda (2 mg)**
1 **tablespoon Featherweight or Ener-G baking powder (13.5 mg)**

Preheat the oven to 400°F.

Prepare the topping. Mix together the topping ingredients with a fork. When mostly combined, use your fingertips to bring together completely in large lumps. Set aside.

Spritz a 12-cup muffin pan with spray olive oil if not nonstick, and dust evenly and completely with flour.

In a large mixing bowl, combine the egg, oil, orange zest, sugar, and vanilla with a wooden spoon. When combined, add the buttermilk, stirring as you do.

In a separate bowl, sift together the flour and cinnamon. Stir into the wet batter until smooth. Add the raisins, stirring briefly again with the wooden spoon.

Just when ready to bake, stir in the Featherweight and Ener-G for about 1 minute, or until well mixed.

Now working quickly to preserve the baking powder strength, spoon the batter quickly into the muffin tins up to the top of each cup. Crumble the streusel mixture evenly over each muffin. Immediately place in the preheated oven and bake for 15 minutes. Reduce the oven temperature to 350°F and bake for another 12 minutes. (If making Texas-size muffins, bake at 350°F for another 15 to 18 minutes.) Test with a cake tester or toothpick at the appropriate time as listed above.

Cool the muffins on rack for a few minutes, then remove from the pan and let the muffins cool on a rack or serve hot. Cooled muffins may be stored in ziplock bags. Reheat for a short time in your microwave on a low setting.

Nutrient Data per Muffin:
Calories: 270.2. Protein: 5.267 g. Carbohydrate: 52.8 g. Dietary Fiber: 2.463 g. Total Sugars: 26 g. Total Fat: 5.847 g. Saturated Fat: 1.664 g. Monounsaturated Fat: .997 g. Polyunsaturated Fat: 2.558 g. Cholesterol: 23.5 mg. Trans Fat: 0 g. Total Omega-3 FA: .47 g. Total Omega-6 FA: .038 g. Potassium: 367.5 mg. Sodium: 26.1 mg. Vitamin K: 1.127 mcg. Folic Acid: 40.1 mcg.

✸ BANANA NUT BREAD ✸

SOURCE: U.S.A.
DIABETICS SEE FOOTNOTE*

BREAD MACHINE OR HAND MADE

This recipe was created because of a visitor to Megaheart.com who wanted a bread machine recipe. If your machine has a Batter setting, then this will work well, and be extremely flavorful. If not, bake in the oven; it works just as well.†

MAKES 1 LOAF OR 16 SERVINGS   SODIUM PER RECIPE: 190.2 MG
SODIUM PER SLICE: 11.9 MG

1½ cups white, unbleached, all-purpose flour (3.75 mg)
⅓ cup granulated sugar (trace)
2 tablespoons extra-virgin olive oil (trace)
¼ cup honey (3.39 mg)
1 cup ripe mashed bananas (about 2 bananas) (6.75 mg)
2 teaspoons lemon juice (1.61 mg)
1 teaspoon white wine vinegar (.05 mg)
1 teaspoon banana extract or flavoring (.378 mg)
1 teaspoon ground cinnamon (.598 mg)
¼ teaspoon ground nutmeg (.088 mg)
⅓ cup nonfat milk with added vitamins A & D (34 mg)
2 medium eggs, beaten (126 mg)
½ cup chopped unsalted walnuts (6 mg)
1 tablespoon Featherweight baking powder (13.5 mg)
2 tablespoons walnuts, partially chopped (for top layer)
    (.292 mg)

Mix all the ingredients in a bread machine pan in the order listed. Remember this is not a yeast recipe, so all the ingredients can be at room temperature. The milk can sit on the countertop for about 10 minutes before pouring into the mixture.

If you are using a Breadman, the kneading cycle lasts 29 minutes. If you can catch the 28-minute mark, then add the Featherweight baking powder at that time. If you miss that mark and the machine stops, then

---

*Diabetics may exchange sugar with Splenda to lower carbohydrates.
†We prefer to bake this one in the oven because of the Featherweight's necessity to bake right away.

stir in the Featherweight with a spoon, stirring it somewhat vigorously. If you can pull the blades out now, that will help later when extracting the cooked loaf. If your machine doesn't have a Batter setting, then you can bake this recipe in your oven. (You can't successfully use a standard bread setting on the machine; instead you must use the Batter setting.)

After stirring in the Featherweight, place the unsalted walnut halves over the top, close the lid, and the machine will do the rest.

To bake in the oven, quickly scrape all the batter into a lightly greased 9×7×3-inch loaf pan and bake in a preheated 350°F oven for 30 to 35 minutes.

Nutrient Data per Slice:
Calories: 171.6. Protein: 3.355 g. Carbohydrate: 28.8 g. Dietary Fiber: 1.844 g. Total Sugars: 14.1 g. Total Fat: 5.666 g. Saturated Fat: .812 g. Monounsaturated Fat: 1.532 g. Polyunsaturated Fat: 2.912 g. Cholesterol: 26.5 mg. Trans Fat: 0 g. Total Omega-3 FA: .442 g. Total Omega-6 FA: 0 g. Potassium: 301.4 mg. Sodium: 11.9 mg. Vitamin K: .808 mcg. Folic Acid: 18 mcg.

◈ BASIC CREPES ◈

ORIGIN: FRANCE
DIABETIC ACCEPTABLE

On one of my trips to Paris in the '70s, I ventured down the Champs Élysées, the main boulevard through old Paris. I was with a friend and we decided to stop in one of the many outdoor cafés to have something to eat. Crepes with fruit were on the menu, so I tried them. They were my first crepes and I was in a state of "wow" while eating them. The chef had blended together a selection of berries, wrapped them into the crepes, and sprinkled powdered sugar on top. He'd also set a bit of sugary sauce on the plate.

Since then I have made a variety of crepe combinations, both savory and sweet. This recipe is a reflection of that very first crepe and is really a basic crepe recipe. We suggest you use a crepe pan such as one from All-Clad or the electric Maxim Crepe Maker if you don't like sweating over a hot range and flipping the crepes by hand. Maxim has a neat little device that adds fun to crepe making and leaves out the mess you might otherwise experience. Visit www.megaheart.com/kit_cabinet.html.

3   large eggs (189 mg)
1⅓ cups nonfat or 2% milk with added vitamins A & D (136.9
      mg)
¾   cup unbleached, all-purpose flour (1.875 mg)
¼   teaspoon onion powder (.324 mg)
3   tablespoons melted unsalted butter or extra-virgin olive oil†
      (trace)

Combine the eggs, milk, flour, and onion powder in a medium mixing
bowl or blender bowl and beat together on high speed for about 1 minute
or until smooth. The batter should not be lumpy.

Cover the batter and let rest for about 1 hour. You may also store this
batter in your refrigerator tightly covered for a day. Bring to room temperature before cooking, however.

After the batter has rested, whisk in the 3 tablespoons of melted unsalted butter or olive oil. If you store the batter in the refrigerator overnight,
wait until the batter has reached room temperature before you whisk in
the butter or olive oil.

Heat your 6-, 7-, or 8-inch crepe pan or frying pan over medium heat.
If using an electric crepe pan like the Maxim, follow the manufacturer's directions. If using a nonstick pan, you may proceed without adding oil or
butter to the grill, or you may use it for flavoring. For standard pans, brush
with a little of the melted butter or use a no-stick cooking spray.

Pour in less than a ¼ cup of batter (a 6-inch pan will take 2 tablespoons, a 7- or 8-inch pan will take 3 tablespoons) into your pan. (Follow
manufacturer's instruct if using an electric pan.) Immediately pick up the
crepe pan and tilt and swirl it so that the batter covers the entire bottom
of the pan. Pour excess batter back into the bowl. Remember, crepes are
very thin.

Loosen the edges of the crepe with a plastic or metal turner or spatula.

---

*Crepe pans come in various sizes. We find the 6-inch crepe to be perfect for our eat-
ing plan, but the 7-inch will also work. For 8-inch crepes, reduce the quantity to 20.
You can stretch this recipe with the 6-inch pan, which will yield up to 40 crepes once
you have gained crepe making experience. That would cut the sodium down to about
9 mg and the total fat down to about 1.5 grams with calories per crepe dropping to 27.
†We use olive oil in this and other baked goods recipes since it cuts the fat in half (as
opposed to butter, which takes more when using it) and it cuts down sodium levels
and balances the omega-3 and omega-6 and it produces a healthier meal with zero
trans-fatty acids. Read "Where We Get Our Nutrition Data" (see page xxiii) for more
information.

You can also flip with your fingers, although that may be too hot for some. (I loosen them with the spatula and then turn them with my fingers, using both hands.) Quickly flip the crepe over.

Cook on the other side for less than a minute, or until lightly golden. Slide the crepe out onto a plate. Cover with waxed paper, if building a supply of them. Otherwise fill and roll closed. Serve while hot. Repeat above steps with the remaining batter.

Basic crepes may be filled with jam and sprinkled with a little confectioners' or granulated sugar.

They may also be filled with ingredients like ricotta cheese with some added sugar or Splenda and a touch of cinnamon. Top with whipped cream, confectioners' sugar, or nothing at all.

Fill with freshly cooked or grilled chicken with a light sauce and cooked spinach stuffing or with a pureed cranberry sauce ladled over the top.

Flavor the batter with herbs like an Herbes de Provence mixture and fill with leftover or freshly cooked beef such as a tender roast beef or even a nice ground sirloin.

Dice and fill with strawberries, and roll. Place onto a serving dish and ladle alongside a puree of mixed berries such as frozen blackberries and raspberries. Top with whipped cream, garnish with a half strawberry, and serve.

Best of all? Your own taste buds and your imagination will bring about a tasty success every time.

You may store cooked crepes tightly wrapped for up to 3 days in your refrigerator. They may also be frozen, separated by sheets of waxed paper. Thaw or bring to room temperature when ready to serve after refrigeration or freezing, and reheat in a pan brushed with a little unsalted butter. Heat gently on both sides. Fold into half or quarters and serve accompanied by butter and sugar or preserves.

Nutrient Values per Crepe When Using Olive Oil:
Calories: 34.4. Protein: 1.32 g. Carbohydrate: 2.978 g. Dietary Fiber: .086 g. Total Sugars: .607 g. Total Fat: 1.887 g. Saturated Fat: .354 g. Monounsaturated Fat: 1.196 g. Polyunsaturated Fat: .217 g. Cholesterol: 21.4 mg. Trans Fat: 0 g. Total Omega-3 FA: .015 g. Total Omega-6 FA: 0 g. Potassium: 27.2 mg. Sodium: 10.9 mg. Vitamin K: .838 mcg. Folic Acid: 4.812 mcg.

Nutrient Data per Crepe When Using Unsalted butter:
Calories: 22.2. Protein: 1.135 g. Carbohydrate: 2.553 g. Dietary Fiber: .073 g. Total Sugars: .52 g. Total Fat: .789 g. Saturated Fat: .356 g. Monounsaturated Fat: .255 g. Polyunsaturated Fat: .083 g. Cholesterol: 19.2 mg. Trans Fat: 0 g. Total Omega-3 FA: .006 g. Total Omega-6 FA: .009 g. Potassium: 23.4 mg. Sodium: 10 mg. Vitamin K: .05 mcg. Folic Acid: 4.125 mcg.

❖ BASIC SCONES ❖

ORIGIN: GREAT BRITAIN
DIABETIC ACCEPTABLE*

Scones and biscuits often seem similar in appearance. The difference essentially is that a scone is sweeter with possibly a bit more fat in it. It's really very good and can be served with breakfast or dinner. I make mine in a Nordic scone pan that you can find at www.megaheart.com/kit_cabinet .html. We use this pan for all our scones.

**MAKES 8 SCONES   SODIUM PER RECIPE: 476.7 MG
SODIUM PER SERVING: 59.6 MG**

2¾ cups unbleached, all-purpose or white pastry flour (6.875 mg)
6   tablespoons sugar or Splenda (trace)
5   tablespoons extra-virgin olive oil (trace)
¾   cup Zante currants** (8.64 mg)
2   large eggs (126 mg)
2   teaspoons vanilla extract (.756 mg)
¾   cup nonfat milk with added vitamins A & D
1   tablespoon fresh lemon or lime juice
1   tablespoon Featherweight baking powder† (13.5 mg)
1   tablespoon Ener-G baking soda (trace)

Preheat the oven to 375°F.

When the oven is nearly at temperature, mix all ingredients except the Featherweight and Ener-G with a wooden spoon, stirring until the batter is well combined and ready.

When the oven is at temperature, quickly work the Featherweight and Ener-G into the batter with about 1 minute of kneading.

Scoop the batter evenly into an 8-section scone pan. Put into the oven immediately.

Bake for 23 to 25 minutes.

Rest on rack for about 10 minutes before removing from the pan. Serve hot or cool, or reheat at a later time.

---

*The bulk of carbohydrates is in the flour (262.3 g).
**You can use black seedless raisins instead if you prefer.
†Mix in after the batter is made and just before placing into scone pan. Then bake immediately in a preheated oven.

Nutrient Values per Scone:
Calories: 381.7. Protein: 7.339 g. Carbohydrate: 54.6 g. Dietary Fiber: 2.12 g. Total Sugars: 20 g. Total Fat: 15.2 g. Saturated Fat: 2.302 g. Monounsaturated Fat: 10.5 g. Polyunsaturated Fat: 1.727 g. Cholesterol: 53.3 mg. Trans Fat: 0 g. Total Omega-3 FA: .127 g. Total Omega-6 FA: 0 g. Potassium: 410.3 mg. Sodium: 59.6 mg. Vitamin K: 8.739 mcg. Folic Acid: 66.2 mcg.

❊ MAPLE OAT NUT SCONE ❊

ORIGIN: AMERICA
DIABETIC ADAPTABLE*

Before my heart failure, I used to enjoy the Starbuck's Maple Nut Scones. Alas, not anymore. So, after quite a few tries, I came up with this replacement. It's excellent. I use the Nordic 8-scone pan you can now find at www .megaheart.com/kit_cabinet.html. You may freeze these for up to a month in a sealed container or ziplock freezer bag. Bring to room temperature to thaw.

MAKES 8 SCONES   SODIUM PER RECIPE: 164.2 MG
SODIUM PER SCONE: 20 MG

THE SCONES

1   cup Quick or Old-Fashioned Quaker oats (1.7 mg)
1¼   cups whole wheat pastry flour† (7.5 mg)
1   tablespoon white granulated sugar or Splenda (trace)
2   tablespoons brown sugar, packed (Sugar Twin alternative for diabetics) (10.8 mg)
2   level teaspoons Featherweight baking powder (5.75 mg)
2   level teaspoons Ener-G baking soda (trace)
1   cup lightly chopped, dry roasted, unsalted pecans or unsalted walnuts (1.134 mg)
2   tablespoons natural maple syrup (1.8 mg)

*Carbohydrates are mostly in the oatmeal (38.6 g), whole wheat pastry flour (108.9 g), and the sugars: brown (26.9 g) and white (12.6 g), which can be replaced with brown Sugar Twin and Splenda, respectively.

†Whole wheat pastry flour is available online or in markets from Hodgson Mill, Arrowhead Mills, and Bob's Red Mill, to name a few. You can find the online links at www.megaheart.com/wheretobuy.html.

1   teaspoon maple extract (.378 mg)
2½ tablespoons softened unsalted butter* (3.905 mg)
1   large egg (63 mg)
½   cup low-sodium reduced-fat buttermilk** (65 mg)

MAPLE GLAZE
2   cups confectioners' sugar (2.4 mg)
3   teaspoons maple extract (1.134 mg)
3½ teaspoons water (trace)

Preheat oven to 425°F.

Lightly grease the scone baking dish.

Using your food processor, process the Quaker Old-Fashioned oats to a finer grain but do not overprocess to a powder. If using Quaker Quick oats, you don't need to process them.

Sift together all of the dry ingredients, except for the nuts, in a medium bowl. Stir in the nuts and set aside.

In a smaller bowl, beat together the wet scone ingredients.

When oven has been at 425°F for 5 minutes, quickly mix the dry and wet ingredients together, using a wooden spoon. Stir briskly until it becomes a thick batter.

Scoop even portions into each pocket of your lightly greased scone pan, press down to fill any pockets, and place in the oven immediately.

Bake for 14 minutes.

Remove the scones from the pan and cool on a rack for about 10 minutes.

While they cool, stir together the glaze ingredients in a small bowl. Glaze each scone evenly, covering the top with the maple glaze. Let set an hour before serving.

Nutritional Data per Scone with Unsalted Butter:
Calories: 262.7. Protein: 6.274 g Carbohydrate: 28.3 g. Dietary Fiber: 4.313 g. Total Sugars: 7.814 g. Total Fat: 15.9 g. Saturated Fat: 3.692 g. Monounsaturated Fat: 7.587 g. Polyunsaturated Fat: 3.449 g. Cholesterol: 37.5 mg. Trans Fat: 0 g. Total Omega-3 FA: .188 g. Total Omega-6 FA: .096 g. Potassium: 314.9 mg. Sodium: 20.5 mg. Vitamin K: .912 mcg. Folic Acid: 0 mcg.

Nutritional Data per Scone Without Unsalted Butter:
Calories: 230.8. Protein: 6.236 g. Carbohydrate: 28.3 g. Dietary Fiber: 4.313 g. Total Sugars: 7.811 g. Total Fat: 12.3 g. Saturated Fat: 1.413 g. Monounsaturated Fat: 6.655 g. Polyunsaturated Fat: 3.314 g. Cholesterol: 28 mg. Trans Fat: 0 g. Total Omega-3 FA: .16 g. Total Omega-6 FA: 0 g. Iron: 3.909 mg. Potassium: 313.9 mg. Sodium: 20 mg. Vitamin K: .602 mcg. Folic Acid: 0 mcg.

*Might need a bit more.
**Low-sodium buttermilk brands include Knudsen, A&P, Borden, Borden Skim-Line, Crowley, Darigold Trim, and Weight Watchers.

ORIGIN: BELGIUM
DIABETICS: SEE FOOTNOTE*

It's absolutely true. The original Belgian waffles came from Belgium. But like everything else, we have either changed them for the better or the worse. My first Belgian waffles were served to me by my mother but, alas, the best-decorated and -tasting waffles were served to me in Alaska. This recipe is fashioned after those waffles. The whipped cream and a light dose of fresh fruit to meet your own tastes is pretty much up to you. These waffles work well with natural maple syrup, sour cream, or just plain good homemade strawberry jam.

MAKES 6 TO 8 THREE-INCH WAFFLES   SODIUM PER RECIPE: 406.2 MG
SODIUM PER WAFFLE (6): 67.7 MG
SODIUM PER WAFFLE (8): 50.8 MG

2 **cups unbleached, all-purpose flour (5 mg)**
1 **teaspoon granulated sugar or Splenda (trace)**
2 **teaspoons extra-virgin olive oil (trace)**
2 **cups nonfat milk with added vitamins A & D (205.8 mg)**
3 **eggs, separated (189 mg)**
2 **teaspoons vanilla extract or flavoring (2.34 mg)**
1 **teaspoon orange zest (.06 mg)**
2 **teaspoons yeast† (4 mg)**

Bring the ingredients to room temperature.

Combine the flour, sugar, oil, milk, and egg yolks. Beat the egg whites separately until they stand in soft peaks. Fold into the batter; do not over-mix. Stir in the yeast and cover for 45 minutes to an hour to allow rising.

Heat a waffle iron. Using a 4-ounce ladle, pour ⅛ of the mixture into the hot waffle iron and bake for about 2 minutes. Repeat with the remaining batter. Top with the fruit and whipped cream and serve hot.

Nutrient Data per Waffle (6):
Calories: 248.9. Protein: 10.7 g. Carbohydrate: 37.9 g. Dietary Fiber: 1.44 g. Total Sugars: 5.709 g. Total Fat: 4.523 g. Saturated Fat: 1.145 g. Monounsaturated Fat: 2.17 g. Polyunsaturated Fat: .669 g. Cholesterol: 107.4 mg. Trans Fat: 0 g. Total Omega-3 FA: .04 g. Total Omega-6 FA: 0 g. Potassium: 239.3 mg. Sodium: 67.7 mg. Vitamin K: 1.103 mcg. Folic Acid: 64.2 mcg.

*The bulk of carbohydrates is in the flour (190.8 g).
†May exchange for 1 tablespoon Featherweight Baking Powder. Mix in just before cooking. No rise time necessary.

Nutrient Data per Waffle (8):
Calories: 186.7. Protein: 8.04 g. Carbohydrate: 28.4 g. Dietary Fiber: 1.08 g. Total Sugars: 4.282 g. Total Fat: 3.392 g. Saturated Fat: .859 g. Monounsaturated Fat: 1.628 g. Polyunsaturated Fat: .502 g. Cholesterol: 80.5 mg. Trans Fat: 0 g. Total Omega-3 FA: .03 g. Total Omega-6 FA: 0 g. Potassium: 179.5 mg. Sodium: 50.8 mg. Vitamin K: .827 mcg. Folic Acid: 48.1 mcg.

❖ CINNAMON RAISIN BREAD ❖

SOURCE: U.S.A.
DIABETIC ADAPTABLE

BREAD MACHINE RECIPE

MAKES 1 LOAF OR 16–20 SLICES   SODIUM PER RECIPE: 42.1 MG
SODIUM PER SLICE (16): 2.634 MG

1	cup plus 2 tablespoons low-sodium water, 105° to 115°F (trace)
2	tablespoons granular or soy or soy lecithin (trace)
1	tablespoon olive oil (trace)
1	tablespoon apple cider vinegar (.15 mg)
1	teaspoon vanilla extract (.378 mg)
2⅞	cups unbleached bread flour (7.188 mg)
2	tablespoons potato flour (7.75 mg)
¼	teaspoon ascorbic acid (trace)
2	tablespoons vital wheat gluten (2.25 mg)
4	tablespoons white granulated sugar or Splenda (trace)
¼	teaspoon granular onion powder (1.296 mg)
2½	teaspoons bread machine yeast (5 mg)
1	cup black raisins, not packed, soaked in water for 10 minutes, then drained (16 mg)
1½	teaspoons ground cinnamon (.897 mg)

Place everything but the raisins and cinnamon in bread machine in order listed or in the order your manufacturer suggests. Set for 2-Pound Loaf, Medium Crust, and either White Bread or "Fruit and Nuts" if your machine has this setting.

Add the fruit and cinnamon when buzzer sounds.

When bread is done, cool on rack for about 15 minutes before slicing.

Nutrient Data per Serving:
Calories: 139. Protein: 3.681 g. Carbohydrate: 26.9 g. Dietary Fiber: 1.192 g. Total Sugars: 6.318 g. Total Fat: 2.153 g. Saturated Fat: .318 g. Monounsaturated Fat: .549 g. Polyunsaturated Fat: .829 g. Cholesterol: 0 mg. Trans Fat: 0 g. Total Omega-3 FA: .009 g. Total Omega-6 FA: 0 g. Potassium: 129.5 mg. Sodium: 2.634 mg. Vitamin K: .627 mcg. Folic Acid: 34.6 mcg.

❧ CRANBERRY SCONES ❧

ORIGIN: FRANCE AND GREAT BRITAIN
DIABETIC ADAPTABLE*

I enjoyed the scones (and apple tarts) I found in both Great Britain and France. Although the Brits are well known for their scones, other countries, including France, also have their own unique varieties. Here's a fresh-flavored cranberry scone full of antioxidant-providing cranberries and one that was inspired by scones I found in France. We use a specially designed scone pan for all our scones and we provide links at www.megaheart.com/kit_cabinet.html for that pan and other great cooking utensils. We'll keep those links up-to-date for you in case you want to order online. Otherwise, good scone pans can be found in most kitchen stores where you live.

MAKES 8 SCONES   SODIUM PER RECIPE: 214.3 MG
SODIUM PER SCONE: 26.8 MG

²⁄₃   cup low-sodium buttermilk† (85.8 mg)
1   large egg (63 mg)
1   teaspoon vanilla extract (.378 mg)
3   cups unbleached, all-purpose flour (7.5 mg)
1   teaspoon ground cinnamon (.588 mg)
½   cup unsalted butter, softened (12.5 mg)
½   cup white granulated sugar or Splenda (trace)
1½   cups fresh or frozen cranberries‡ (17.5 mg)
2   level tablespoons Featherweight baking powder (27 mg)
1   level tablespoon Ener-G baking soda (trace)

Preheat oven to 375°F.
    Spray the scone pan with olive oil.

*Most of the carbohydrates are in the cranberries (175.6 g), white sugar (100 g), and the flour (286.2 g). To enjoy the scone itself, you can replace the sugar with Splenda and the cranberries with your favorite nut, such as unsalted walnuts or almonds. Reduce the nut content to ¾ cup. Walnuts contain about 3 grams carbohydrates per ounce, while almonds contain about 5 grams per ounce.
†You may use the same measurement of plain yogurt (113.5 mg) if you prefer or can't find low-sodium buttermilk. Lower sodium buttermilk brands in the U.S. include, Knudsen (130 mg), A&P (125 mg), Borden (130 mg), Crowley (130 mg), Drigold Trim (130 mg), and Weight Watchers (140 mg)
‡Dried cranberries will work if you steep them in boiled water for about 20 minutes. Drain and pat dry with paper towels. Use only 1 cup packed of dried cranberries (before boiling) if you use them. If you use dried cranberries, cut the sugar to ⅓ cup.

In a small bowl, beat the egg with the buttermilk and set aside.

In a larger bowl, blend together the flour and the unsalted butter, using either a pastry blender or two knives held together until the mixture looks granular. Stir in the sugar.

Stir in the buttermilk mixture with a fork until a soft dough forms.

Quickly stir in the cranberries and then the baking soda and Featherweight baking powder. Roll out onto lightly floured board and shape into an 8-inch circle. Cut into wedges like a pie, making 8 pieces. Lift each into the scone pan and pat the sides to fill.

Place immediately into the preheated oven.

Bake for 20 to 25 minutes, or until medium brown. Let cool for 10 minutes in pan.

Remove from the pan and cool completely. A fork helps to get them out if they need a little nudging.

Nutrient Data per Scone:
Calories: 462. Protein: 14.9 g. Carbohydrate: 73.2 g. Dietary Fiber: 10.5 g. Total Sugars: 13.5 g. Total Fat: 13.5 g. Saturated Fat: 7.922 g. Monounsaturated Fat: 3.302 g. Polyunsaturated Fat: .909 g. Cholesterol: 59 mg. Trans Fat: 0 g. Total Omega-3 FA: .193 g. Total Omega-6 FA: .307 g. Iron: 7.367 mg. Potassium: 930.2 mg. Sodium: 26.8 mg. Vitamin K: 1.242 mcg. Folic Acid: 72.2 mcg.

❈ FRITTATA WITH FRESH SALSA ❈

ORIGIN: SPAIN
DIABETIC ACCEPTABLE*

Originally from Spain, this delicious dish incorporates many ingredients that bring strong flavors to it. Our daughter, Maria, who spent some time in Spain immersed in their language for her Spanish language major, brought this recipe home. We often add more diced vegetables, especially green or red bell peppers, onions, and more garlic.

MAKES 4 SERVINGS   SODIUM PER RECIPE: 148.2 MG
SODIUM PER SERVING: 37 MG

2   **medium unpeeled, red potatoes (12.8 mg)**
½   **ripe medium tomato (3.075 mg)**
1   **garlic clove (.51 mg)**
2   **scallions (4.8 mg)**
1   **ounce low-sodium Cheddar cheese (5.88 mg)**

*The bulk of carbohydrates is in the potatoes.

2　large egg whites (109.6 mg)
1　egg yolk (8.16 mg)
1　tablespoon extra-virgin olive oil (trace)
3　tablespoons homemade Fresh Salsa (see page 40)
　　(4.404 mg)

If you don't have red potatoes left over from a previous meal, then cook two or more for this recipe, until almost done but not soft.

Slice the tomato, mince the garlic and thinly slice or chop the scallions. Grate the cheese.

When the potatoes are cool, slice into bite-size pieces and stir-fry in the olive oil in a nonstick pan with the garlic and scallions. When golden brown, set aside. Turn the heat down but let the pan remain warm. Set the tomato slices in with the potatoes and let them rest in the warmth.

Beat the egg whites until fluffy but not stiff. With a fork, gently fold in the egg yolk, making sure to not break down the egg's fluffiness.

Raise the heat under the potato pan to medium-low. Spread the potatoes and vegetables in the pan to the size of your intended frittata. Slide the beaten egg into the pan in one large mass over the mixture of potatoes and vegetables.

Spread the cheese on top and place a lid over the pan. Let it cook for 4 to 5 minutes, making sure it doesn't burn. When cooked on bottom side, gently turn it over and let it cook on other side for 10 to 15 seconds. If the entire frittata has cooked well on the one side, you don't have to do this. Just make sure the egg whites have cooked through.

Serve hot with the Fresh Salsa on top. Top with a dollop of natural sour cream (about a tablespoon).

Serve the frittata with whole wheat or 7-grain toast and your favorite jam.

Nutritional Data per Serving:
Calories: 127.3. Protein: 5.602 g. Carbohydrate: 10.9 g. Dietary Fiber: 1.42 g. Total Sugars: 1.12 g. Total Fat: 6.97 g. Saturated Fat: 2.342 g. Monounsaturated Fat: 3.653 g. Polyunsaturated Fat: .649 g. Cholesterol: 59.4 mg. Trans Fat: 0 g. Total Omega-3 FA: .071 g. Total Omega-6 FA: 0 g. Potassium: 365.4 mg. Sodium: 37 mg. Vitamin K: 5.551 mcg. Folic Acid: 0 mcg.

❖ HOT CROSS BUNS ❖

ORIGIN: ENGLAND
DIABETIC ADAPTABLE*

BREAD MACHINE KNEAD—OVEN BAKE

I asked Maureen, who spent a career teaching grammar school children, if she knew the words to the hot cross "nursery song" that helped make the buns so popular. Sure enough, she sang right out with the Mother Goose rhyme seemingly at the tip of her tongue:

Hot cross buns!
Hot cross buns!
One a penny, two a penny,
Hot cross buns

If you have no daughters
Give them to your sons;
One a penny, two a penny
Hot cross buns

Usually a fruitcake with a cross of buttery or sugary frosting across the top, hot cross buns were sold in the streets of London and other English towns on Good Friday as far back as the early nineteenth century. They helped celebrate the Christian Easter festival.

MAKES 35 BUNS†   SODIUM PER RECIPE: 354.3 MG
SODIUM PER BUN: 11.7 MG

THE DOUGH
1   **cup nonfat milk with added vitamins A & D, warmed (102.9 mg)**
¼   **cup canola oil (trace)**
1   **tablespoon cider or white wine vinegar (.15 mg)**
3   **large eggs (189 mg)**
3¾   **cups plus 2 tablespoons unbleached bread flour (9.688 mg)**
2   **tablespoons potato flour (7.75 mg)**
¼   **teaspoon ascorbic acid (trace)**
2   **tablespoons granular lecithin (trace)**

*You can make this one with Splenda to help lower the carbohydrates. Further changes that can be made include reducing the amount of raisins or omitting them. Most of the carbohydrates are in the flour (372 g), raisins (98.4 g), and powdered sugar (99.6 g).
†Make the buns larger for a yield of 24 buns or smaller for up to 40 buns.

⅓ cup white granulated sugar or Splenda (trace)
1 tablespoon vital wheat gluten (2.25 mg)
¾ teaspoon ground allspice (1.107 mg)
1½ teaspoons ground cinnamon (.897 mg)
1 tablespoon bread machine yeast (6 mg)

THE FRUIT*
⅓ cup chopped unsalted walnuts (.779 mg)
¾ cup golden raisins, packed (14.8 mg)
⅓ cup chopped dried apricots (4.329 mg)
⅓ cup chopped dried apples (.283 mg)

THE CROSS TOPPING
1 cup sifted powdered sugar (1 mg)
1 tablespoon grated lemon zest (.36 mg)
¼ teaspoon vanilla (.094 mg)
2 tablespoons nonfat milk with added vitamins A & D (12.9 mg)

Place all ingredients for the dough in your bread machine pan and set machine for Dough. About 4 to 5 minutes before your machine is finished kneading, add the nuts and fruit. If you miss the timing and the machine stops kneading, reach in, pull the dough out, close the lid, and knead the fruit into the dough. Then return it to the machine and let it rise.

Prepare two baking sheets by lining with parchment paper. For the second rising, set the racks in your oven apart enough for two baking sheets.

Set the oven rack at the bottom third of the oven. Preheat the oven to 100°F. Turn the oven off.

When the dough is finished rising in the machine, roll out onto a lightly floured board and, using a rolling pin, roll gently until you have about ¾-inch-thick piece of dough in either a neat square or rectangle. Mark the dough lengthwise and crosswise (four slice marks by six) to get 35 even pieces. Use a sharp knife to slice.

Shape each piece into a ball by pulling the dough down from all corners to the bottom and pinching shut. Place on baking sheet, about ½ inch apart (5 across and 7 lengthwise on a standard, rectangular baking sheet.) Cover with a piece of oil-sprayed waxed paper and let rise in the same oven in which you will bake the buns.

When the dough has doubled in size, 45 minutes to 75 minutes, re-

*Optional fruit for exchanges or additions are: citron, lemon peel, or orange peel, or an extract or fruit flavor of your choice. I use liquid instead of solid, to reduce the amount of nonfat milk.

move the pan and turn on the oven to 400°F. When the oven reaches temperature, reduce the heat to 350°F. When buns reach a deep golden brown, about 15 minutes, remove from oven. Transfer the buns to a rack for cooling, gently sliding them from the baking sheet to the rack by pulling them to the rack using the parchment paper under them.

While the buns are cooling make your topping. Using a baker's pastry bag and decorating tip, draw a cross on the top of each bun.

Nutrient Data per Bun:
Calories: 150.9. Protein: 3.243 g. Carbohydrate: 27 g. Dietary Fiber: .989 g. Total Sugars: 12.9 g. Total Fat: 3.732 g. Saturated Fat: .466 g. Monounsaturated Fat: 1.404 g. Polyunsaturated Fat: 1.461 g. Cholesterol: 20 mg. Trans Fat: 0 g. Total Omega-3 FA: .282 g. Total Omega-6 FA: 0 g. Potassium: 110.8 mg. Sodium: 11.7 mg. Vitamin K: 2.438 mcg. Folic Acid: 23.3 mcg.

❖ IRISH BREAKFAST SAUSAGE ❖

ORIGIN: IRELAND
DIABETIC ACCEPTABLE

Maureen came home from Ireland on her last trip excited about a few recipes she'd picked up there. We've served these to many friends and family members by now and they are very good for a breakfast. I eat just one but it's worth the effort. We have cut the extra fat, the usual beer or ale Irish recipes have for this, and of course the salt. Don't want to eat pork? This works just as well using lean turkey burger.

MAKES: 18 SAUSAGES   SODIUM PER RECIPE: 267 MG
SODIUM PER SAUSAGE: 14.8 MG

1   slice White Bread, crumbled (see page 203) (1.362 mg)
1   pound lean ground pork (253.1 mg)
½   teaspoon ground black pepper (.462)
½   teaspoon dried marjoram (.231 mg)
¼   teaspoon ground mace (.34 mg)
¼   teaspoon onion powder (.324 mg)
¼   teaspoon dried thyme (.192 mg)
½   teaspoon dried rosemary (.3 mg)
1   teaspoon powdered buttermilk* (11.1 mg)

Dry the bread by toasting lightly. When done, break into crumbs.

Mix together all the ingredients, except the bread crumbs, using your

*You may replace with powdered eggs, or dried milk in the same measurements.

hands. Knead until all the spices and powdered buttermilk are well mixed into the meat.

Add the bread crumbs and knead until they are evenly distributed.

If you can, cover and refrigerate the mixture overnight. The flavor of the sausages will improve.

Fry the sausages in a nonstick pan over medium-high heat, or grill them over a flame.

Nutrient Data per Sausage:
Calories: 74.6. Protein: 4.52 g. Carbohydrate: 1.6 g. Dietary Fiber: .093 g. Total Sugars: .131 g. Total Fat: 5.428 g. Saturated Fat: 1.998 g. Monounsaturated Fat: 2.427 g. Polyunsaturated Fat: .496 g. Cholesterol: 18.2 mg. Trans Fat: 0 g. Total Omega-3 FA: .02 g. Total Omega-6 FA: 0 g. Potassium: 78.1 mg. Sodium: 14.8 mg. Vitamin K: .47 mcg. Folic Acid: 0 mcg.

❈ THE BEST PULL-APART EVER ❈

ORIGIN: U.S.A.
DIABETICS: SEE FOOTNOTE*

BREAD MACHINE KNEAD—OVEN BAKE

This recipe was developed by us for our annual Easter family get-together. I call it a mile-high cinnamon bun (without raisins and nuts). After you bring it out of the oven and set it on your serving platter, you'll see why. We will also serve this to visiting friends who stay overnight. It makes a great breakfast presentation. I don't eat much of it (which shows a great deal of willpower) since the calories are a bit high, but I don't turn it down, either. If you like cinnamon rolls, you'll love this pull-apart, also known as a Monkey Bread.

MAKES 20 SERVINGS† SODIUM PER RECIPE: 422,7
SODIUM PER SERVING: 21.1 MG

THE DOUGH
1½ **cups plus 3 tablespoons low-sodium, reduced-fat buttermilk‡ (208 mg)**
¼   **cup extra-virgin olive oil (trace)**
¼   **cup white granulated sugar or Splenda (trace)**
1   **large egg (63 mg)**
1   **teaspoon vanilla extract (.378 mg)**

---

*Most of the carbohydrates are in the flour (381.5 g).
†This will serve up to 30 people, depending on how much each individual "pulls apart."

1   tablespoon cider vinegar (.15 mg)
4   cups unbleached bread flour (12 mg)
¼   cup potato flour (15.5 mg)
1   teaspoon ground cinnamon (.598 mg)
1   teaspoon onion powder (1.296 mg)
2   level tablespoons vital wheat gluten (4.5 mg)
2   level tablespoons flaxseed meal (trace)
1   tablespoon bread machine yeast (6 mg)

THE SUGAR COATING
1   cup light brown sugar, packed (85.8 mg)
2   teaspoons ground cinnamon (1.196 mg)
8   tablespoons unsalted butter (12.4 mg)

THE TOPPING
1   cup white confectioners' sugar (1.2 mg)
4   tablespoons unsalted butter (6.248 mg)
1–2 tablespoons nonfat milk with added vitamins A & D
      (6.426 mg)

You will need a Bundt pan or tube pan for this recipe. I use a Bundt pan.

Place all the ingredients for the dough into your bread pan in the order listed or in the order suggested by your manufacturer. Set the machine for Dough. I give the inside of the lid a bit of a swipe of oil since this dough rises high and may touch it.

Combine the sugar coating ingredients and set aside.

When the dough is about ready to come out of the bread machine, heat your oven to about 150° to 200°F and turn it off.

Lightly oil or grease your Bundt pan and dust it completely with flour.

When the dough is ready, roll it out of the pan onto a lightly floured breadboard and cut it into 3 or 4 manageable pieces. Either cut or pull the dough apart in pieces that you can roll into 1- to 1½-inch balls. (Some may be larger just to help make the final product a bit more fun for your "tasters.") After forming, roll each ball in the sugar-coating mixture and place into the Bundt pan. Lay the balls evenly around the bottom of the pan, so that they rise evenly. When you are getting to the end of the dough balls, line the outer edge with the last few balls to make a "foot" for the bread to stand on after baking. This dough will rise above the edge of the pan.

Place the bread into the warmed oven, which should be about 150°F now, and cover it with an oil-sprayed piece of waxed paper. Let rise for 30 to 40 minutes, or until the dough is 1 to 2 inches above the rim. Reach in and remove the waxed paper.

Leave the Bundt pan of dough in the oven and turn the oven to 350°F.

Bake for 25 to 30 minutes. Test with a long skewer (metal or wood). If the dough isn't sticky, the bread is done. (The caramel sugar will be bubbling at this point and will stick to the skewer.)

Remove the bread from the oven and let cool for about 5 minutes.

While the bread is cooling, make the topping.

When the bread has cooled, gently turn over the pan and invert the bread onto your serving platter. Spread the topping over the top (as if it is a ridgeline) and then help it drip down the outer sides. Let set before serving. After serving, if any is left, wrap it in plastic and send it home with your guests.

Nutrient Data per Serving (20):
Calories: 275.5. Protein: 4.875 g. Carbohydrate: 41.9 g. Dietary Fiber: 1.195 g. Total Sugars: 19.9 g. Total Fat: 10.8 g. Saturated Fat: 5.094 g. Monounsaturated Fat: 3.917 g. Polyunsaturated Fat: .679 g. Cholesterol: 30.8 mg. Trans Fat: 0 g. Total Omega-3 FA: .082 g. Total Omega-6 FA: .184 g. Potassium: 123.2 mg. Sodium: 21.1 mg. Vitamin K: 2.415 mcg. Folic Acid: 38.5 mcg.

❖ BASQUE OMELET ❖

ORIGIN: SPAIN
DIABETIC ACCEPTABLE

We used to enjoy eating out at a Basque restaurant called Wool Grower's in Bakersfield, California. It was located on the south side road that ran from the main highway up over the Tehachapi Mountains and down into the very hot Mojave Desert. We sat at long tables with other travelers or families out for a good meal. The dinners were spectacular but so were luncheons. That was many years ago and Wool Grower's was fairly new. You can still find them at www.woolgrowers.net. Their history is quite interesting.

Years later, while working in France, I ventured into a Basque restaurant nearly every day with those memories of the Wool Grower's Restaurant and found Basque breakfasts to be just enjoyable. Here's a simple but very delicious omelet closely approximating what I experienced in France. Serve for breakfast or dinner.

MAKES 2 TO 3 SERVINGS   SODIUM PER RECIPE: 254.4 MG
SODIUM PER SERVING (2): 126.4 MG
SODIUM PER SERVING (3): 84.6 MG

3 **large eggs (189 mg)**
1 **medium Yukon gold or new potato, thinly sliced (12.8 mg)**

½ **bell pepper, seeded and diced (1.11 mg)**
½ **small yellow onion, diced or sliced (1.05 mg)**
3 **ounces Don's Authentically Hot Chorizo (see page 95)**
  (48.9 mg)

In a frying pan with very little oil, brown the potato slices. Push aside in the pan and add the onions and bell pepper and sauté until slightly crisp. Whisk the eggs in a small bowl.

Add the chorizo to the pan. Push the veggies and meat aside in the pan, add a bit more oil, and slip the eggs into the open area. Let the eggs cook for a minute over medium-low heat. Bring the veggies and meat to the top of the eggs, cover the pan with a lid, and cook for 2 to 4 minutes over low heat. When nearly cooked, fold it in half, cover, and cook for another few minutes over low heat. Then turn the omelet and cook over for a few seconds to brown the upper side.

Serve garnished with fresh sliced fruit, fresh chopped parsley, or fresh coriander.

Nutrient Data per Serving (2):
Calories: 318.5. Protein: 19.1 g. Carbohydrate: 22.1 g. Dietary Fiber: 2.687 g. Total Sugars: 3.399 g. Total Fat: 16.9 g. Saturated Fat: 5.723 g. Monounsaturated Fat: 6.901 g. Polyunsaturated Fat: 1.944 g. Cholesterol: 347.8 mg. Trans Fat: 0 g. Total Omega-3 FA: .124 g. Total Omega-6 FA: 0 g. Potassium: 785.8 mg. Sodium: 126.4 mg. Vitamin K: 7.997 mcg. Folic Acid: 0 mcg.

Nutrient Data per Serving (3):
Calories: 212.3. Protein: 12.7 g. Carbohydrate: 14.7 g. Dietary Fiber: 1.791 g. Total Sugars: 2.266 g. Total Fat: 11.3 g. Saturated Fat: 3.816 g. Monounsaturated Fat: 4.601 g. Polyunsaturated Fat: 1.296 g. Cholesterol: 231.8 mg. Trans Fat: 0 g. Total Omega-3 FA: .083 g. Total Omega-6 FA: 0 g. Potassium: 523.9 mg. Sodium: 84.6 mg. Vitamin K: 5.331 mcg. Folic Acid: 0 mcg.

PARIS-STYLE PECAN AND
❖ BLUEBERRY FRENCH TOAST ❖

ORIGIN: PARIS, FRANCE
DIABETICS, SEE FOOTNOTE*

Maureen recently returned from a three-week visit to France with much of her time spent in Paris. She called me one evening to let me know about some French toast

---

*Diabetics, this one is a challenge! The carbohydrate exchange might be too high. Replacing the brown sugar (53.5 g) would alter the flavor greatly.

she had had for breakfast. "Wonderful," she purred. Well, I thought, it won't work because "wonderful" nearly always includes a bunch of sodium and salt, lots of calories, fat, and other undesirables. However, she was able to take the recipe she brought home and convert it to this—a most delicious meal to serve any of your guests and to enjoy yourself possibly once a year. (The original recipe has nearly twice the fat, calories, and a lot more sodium.) It takes at least a day to prepare. (First, you'll have to make the French Baguette recipe and, additionally, chill the bread-egg mixture overnight.) The sodium per serving is equal to a bowl of Shredded Wheat with ¾ cup of milk.

This delicious French toast is high in fiber and high in calories as well.

MAKES 8 TO 10 SERVINGS   SODIUM PER RECIPE: 779.4 MG
SODIUM PER SERVING (8): 97.4 MG
SODIUM PER SERVING (10): 77.9 MG

THE FRENCH TOAST
2   14-inch French Baguette loaves (see page 165)
     (16.4 mg)
5   large eggs (315 mg)
3   cups 1% milk with added vitamins A & D
     (322.1 mg)
½   teaspoon ground nutmeg (.176 mg)
1   teaspoon vanilla extract (.378 mg)
½   cup packed brown sugar (42.9 mg)
1   cup unsalted pecans (about 3 ounces) (.85 mg)
4   level tablespoons (½ stick) unsalted butter (6.248 mg)
2   cups fresh blueberries (2.9mg)
¼   cup brown sugar, packed (21.5 mg)

THE SYRUP
1   cup fresh blueberries (1.45 mg)
½   cup pure maple syrup (14.5 mg)
1   tablespoon freshly squeezed lemon juice (.153 mg)

Bake the bread the evening before you make the French toast and keep fresh in ziplock bags.

Lightly grease a 13×9-inch baking dish.

Slice 20 one-inch pieces from the fresh, no-salt baguettes and place into the baking dish in a single layer. In a medium to large mixing bowl, whisk together the eggs, milk, nutmeg, vanilla, and the ½ cup of brown sugar and pour evenly over the bread in the baking dish. Chill this, covered, until all the liquid is absorbed by the bread. Overnight is a good time to let this happen.

Preheat the oven to 350°F.

Spread out the pecans evenly on a baking sheet and toast in the oven or toaster oven for a few minutes, tossing with a teaspoon of the unsalted butter. Remove from the oven and set aside.

Increase the oven temperature to 400°F.

Evenly sprinkle the 2 cups of blueberries and the toasted pecans over the bread-egg mixture. Slice the butter into a pan and heat with the brown sugar, stirring until the butter has melted. Drizzle this mixture over the bread-egg mixture and bake for 35 to 40 minutes.

Either the day before, or while the French toast is baking, make your syrup.

In a medium saucepan, cook the 1 cup of the blueberries and the maple syrup over medium heat until the berries have blended with the syrup, about 3 minutes. Pour the syrup through a sieve to get rid of the solids. Stir in the lemon juice.

Serve the Paris-style French toast with the syrup. Pour syrup over each serving, heated or reheated.

Nutrient Data per Single Serving (8):
Calories: 653.6. Protein: 16.4 g. Carbohydrate: 102 g. Dietary Fiber: 4.529 g. Total Sugars: 43.2 g. Total Fat: 20.9 g. Saturated Fat: 6.336 g. Monounsaturated Fat: 9.398 g. Polyunsaturated Fat: 3.43 g. Cholesterol: 152 mg. Trans Fat: 0 g. Total Omega-3 FA: .24 g. Total Omega-6 FA: .178 g. Potassium: 479.2 mg. Sodium: 97.4 mg. Vitamin K: 12.3 mcg. Folic Acid: 0 mcg.

Nutrient Data per Single Serving (10):
Calories: 521.7. Protein: 13.1 g. Carbohydrate: 81.5 g. Dietary Fiber: 3.623 g. Total Sugars: 34.5 g. Total Fat: 16.7 g. Saturated Fat: 5.069 g. Monounsaturated Fat: 7.518 g. Polyunsaturated Fat: 2.744 g. Cholesterol: 121.6 mg. Trans Fat: 0 g. Total Omega-3 FA: .192 g. Total Omega-6 FA: .143 g. Potassium: 382.7 mg. Sodium: 74.4 mg. Vitamin K: 9.823 mcg. Folic Acid: 0 mcg.

❖ WHOLE WHEAT AND RAISIN SCONES ❖

FRENCH-STYLE SCONE
DIABETICS: SEE FOOTNOTE*

I used to enjoy a great scone from a French restaurant designed and owned by a Vietnamese chef who learned to cook from the French in South Vietnam. The sodium level was very high, but these are low at about 38 mg per

---

*Carbohydrates are mostly in the flour and Ener-G (217.7 g). You may also substitute Splenda for the brown sugar. If you do, add ½ teaspoon maple extract to the mix.

scone, and worth the effort to make. I highly recommend a scone pan.**

MAKES 8 SCONES   SODIUM PER RECIPE: 292 MG
SODIUM PER SERVING: 36.5 MG

2½	cups whole wheat pastry flour† (15 mg)
¼	cup potato flour (15.5 mg)
¼	teaspoon ascorbic acid (trace)
5	tablespoons sugar or Splenda (.63 mg)
1	tablespoon ground cinnamon (2.652 mg)
½	cup unsalted butter, softened‡ (12.5 mg)
3	tablespoons golden brown sugar or Splenda or substitute Twin Brown Sugar (16.1 mg)
2	large eggs (126 mg)
2	teaspoons vanilla extract (.756 mg)
¾	cup nonfat milk with added vitamins A & D (97.5 mg)
1	tablespoon white wine vinegar (.15 mg)
¾	cup black seedless raisins (14.8 mg)
1	tablespoon plus 1 teaspoon Featherweight baking powder (13.5 mg)
1	tablespoon Ener-G baking soda (trace)
	Cinnamon-sugar, optional

Preheat the oven to 375°F.

Mix all the ingredients except the Featherweight with a wooden spoon, stirring until the batter is well mixed. Add the Featherweight baking powder and Ener-G and work into the dough quickly with about a minute of kneading.

Place the dough into the 8-section scone pan in even portions. If not using a scone pan, spread the dough out in a circle ½- to ¾-inch thick on a well-greased silicone baking mat or onto a baking sheet lined with parchment paper. Make crosscuts into wedges so that the dough shows 8 separated sections. Put into the oven immediately.

**I use a Nordic scone pan you can find at www.megaheart.com/kitchen_cabinet.html or use the following link for a direct page to the scone pan: www.amazon .com/exec/obidos/redirect?path=ASIN/B00008UA3H&link=mcode=as2&camp=1789&tag= megahearcomsbook&creative=9325.
†Using special whole wheat/white whole wheat or Bob's Red Mill (online or at your local market) makes a great whole wheat pastry flour.
‡If you're a peanut butter freak like I am, you can exchange from 1 to 4 tablespoons of the unsalted butter with creamy unsalted peanut butter.

Bake for 25 to 30 minutes, or until they begin to turn golden brown and darken on the edges.

Transfer to a rack. Sprinkle with the cinnamon-sugar, while hot. Or cool and serve warm or at room temperature.

Nutrient Values per Scone:
Calories: 382. Protein: 8.565 g. Carbohydrate: 61 g. Dietary Fiber: 5.65 g. Total Sugars: 24.7 g. Total Fat: 13.6 g. Saturated Fat: 7.819 g. Monounsaturated Fat: 3.555 g. Polyunsaturated Fat: .925 g. Cholesterol: 83.7 mg. Trans Fat: 0 g. Total Omega-3 FA: .115 g. Total Omega-6 FA: .306 g. Potassium: 628.2 mg. Sodium: 36.5 mg. Vitamin K: 2.545 mcg. Folic Acid: 0 mcg.

INGREDIENTS USED
IN THIS BOOK

It's a good idea to always have some of these ingredients on hand. Basics, for instance, would include flour, a selection of spices, no-salt-added tomato sauce, tomato paste, and canned tomatoes; pasta and rice. We have listed all the ingredients used not only in this book but also those we keep in our pantry or on our kitchen shelves at all times. When preparing no-salt, low-sodium meals, many of these ingredients are vital. Some may have to be ordered via the Internet or through a catalog such as the Baker's Catalogue from King Arthur. Planning ahead is always a good idea. For unique products, visit www.megaheart.com/wheretobuy.html for links to suppliers.

ORGANIC

For your health, we strongly recommend that, whenever you can, you purchase organic products. Examples include: grass-fed or organic beef, and organic eggs.

Good online sources for organic grains include: www.edenfoods .com, www.bobsredmill.com, and www.healthyheartmarket.com in the United States. In Canada: www.anitasorganicmill.com/. In Great Britain: www.dovesfarm-organic.co.uk/stockists.htm

BAKING INGREDIENTS

If you spot a specialty item in this book or elsewhere that you can't get locally, please check www.megaheart.com/wheretobuy.html. If it's not there, then please e-mail us from the site and let us know what you're searching for. If we can find it, we'll send you a source address.

GRANULATED LECITHIN

Lecithin improves shelf life of yeasted bread and is a good source of choline (250 g per tablespoon), which is a nutrient essential for metabolism. It has a nutty flavor, and may be used in soups, on cereal, in yogurt, and in your homemade granola. Soy lecithin is used by some to replace oil in bread recipes for extended shelf life. The replacement formula of 2 tablespoons for each tablespoon of oil offers little benefit in saving calories or total fats. Vegetable oils average 13.5 grams of total fats per tablespoon. A 2-tablespoon measurement of lecithin, as a replacement for 1 tablespoon of olive oil, contains 18 grams of total fats. The calories are identical. If a recipe calls for 2 or more tablespoons of oil, then replace one with 2 tablespoons of lecithin, and add a nutty flavor, longer shelf life, and choline to your bread. You can obtain lecithin from specialty stores, natural foods departments of some grocery stores, or from online sources. Look for links at www.megaheart.com/wheretobuy.html. Some suppliers you'll find there are Baker's Catalogue, Bob's Red Mill, Hodgson Mills, Arrowhead Mills, and King Arthur, as well as many others.

SPLENDA

A sugar substitute (sucralose), Splenda can be purchased at grocery stores or discount grocery stores. See: Malted Barley Flour.

MALTED BARLEY FLOUR

Used as a sugar or sugar substitute replacement in bread, malted barley flour feeds yeast the way sugar does. Our tests show that it works well in bread, but we recommend 2 teaspoons per 3 cups of flour. Most suppliers recommend 1 teaspoon, but that's based on bread containing salt. Although this serves well as replacement for sugar, we have gotten better results with sucralose (Splenda), especially since malted barley flour doesn't work efficiently with ascorbic acid and gluten. Obtain it from www.bobsredmill.com or from local grocers carrying similar grain products.

Vital Wheat Gluten

This product enhances bread texture. It may be purchased in natural food departments of grocery stores, specialty stores, or online at www.bobsredmill.com or www.kingarthurflour.com/shop/, or visit www.megaheart.com/wheretobuy.html for updates or help to locate vital wheat gluten.

Ascorbic Acid

When used with gluten and sugar or sucralose, ascorbic acid enhances bread rise.

Obtain at www.kingarthurflour.com/shop/ or visit www.mega heart.com/wheretobuy.html for additional sites. As a substitute, you can crush a vitamin C tablet (check that it is pure ascorbic acid) in a mortar using a pestle and use that. You can also use double the amount of Sure-Jell Ever-Fresh and, in a pinch, 1 level tablespoon of finely grated orange or lemon zest for each ¼ teaspoon of ascorbic acid called for. One additional way is to use "not from concentrate" orange juice for the liquid instead of water.

Potato Flour

For potato flour, visit www.megaheart.com/wheretobuy.html.

Potato flour (flour ground from whole, dried potatoes) is invaluable to bakers looking for moist yeast bread with excellent shelf life; the potato starch attracts and holds water. Two to 4 tablespoons of potato flour per loaf—white, wheat, rye, or whole-grain—will banish dry, crumbly bread forever. Potato flour is available in 1-pound bags.

Flaxseed Meal

Exchange 3 tablespoons of flaxseed meal for 1 tablespoon of oil or unsalted butter to help reduce fat and add a very pleasant nutty flavor to your breads. If your recipe calls for 1 tablespoon of oil, then add 1 or 2 tablespoons of flaxseed. We don't recommend replacing all the oil. If your recipe calls for more than 1 tablespoon of oil, butter, or shortening, then exchange 1 tablespoon of oil per flax-seed package instruction and the result will be both healthy and flavorful. Flaxseed meal has been proved to lower cholesterol and we know it adds fiber at 2 grams per tablespoon.

When exchanging flaxseed meal for olive oil, you may find that you need to add 1 to 2 tablespoons of liquid (water, milk, etc.) called for in a bread recipe. We buy our flaxseed meal from Bob's Red Mill (www.bobsredmill.com). Visit www.megaheart.com/wheretobuy.html to locate other suppliers.

Basic Flour for Most Bread Making

We use Stone-Buhr, King Arthur, Gold Medal, Pillsbury, and Arrow-head Mills brands of flour. We purchase bread (high-gluten) flour for bread making. All white flour we use, including all-purpose, is unbleached.

Unbleached bread flour
Organic bread flour (King Arthur)
Whole wheat flour
Whole wheat pastry flour
White whole wheat flour
Unbleached, all-purpose flour
Rice flour
Soy flour
Rye flour (light, medium, and dark)
Corn, white, and whole-grain flour
Corn, yellow, masa, enriched
Malt barley flour
Cake flour (no-salt-added) (Softasilk is an example)

SUPPLIES

Dried or Packaged Fruits
  Raisins
    Golden
    Black seedless
  Cranberries
  Dates
    Medjool
    Deglect Noor
  Candied, Glazed Fruit (used in our Fruitcake and Christmas and Easter breads)
    Citron
    Pineapple
    Cherries
    Lemon
  Crystallized Ginger
Sugar/Sweeteners
  White granulated sugar
  Confectioners' (powdered)
  Brown: light, medium, dark
  Splenda (sucralose)
  Stevia (www.sweetleaf.com)
  Molasses: Grandma's (Grandma's Spanish Pepper Company is owned by a company here in Lenexa, Kansas, by the name of Williams Foods. Their telephone number is 913-888-4343. Please call them and they will be happy to help you.)
  B'rer Rabbit molasses
Tomato Products, Canned
  Tomato sauce, no salt added
  Tomato paste (Contadina or other no-salt-added brand)
  Tomatoes, peeled, diced, whole, no salt added

Honey
  Commercial
  Home produced (hives)
Beans, Canned
  Eden Organic, No-Salt-Added Beans
      Pinto
      Kidney
      Black
      Garbanzo (chickpeas)
      White
      Aduki
Beans, Dried
  Lentils
  Split Peas
  White
Breakfast Cereals, cold and hot (The key here is high fiber and low sodium.)
  Spoon-Size Shredded Wheat
  Barbara's Shredded Wheat (no salt)
  7-Grain (Bob's Red Mill)
  10-Grain (Bob's Red Mill)
  Oatmeal, Quaker old-fashioned (raw) or quick
  Cream of Wheat
Rice
  Basmati
  Arborio
  Sushi rice (also known as "sticky rice")
      Nishiki sushi rice (medium grain), Hinode short or medium grain, or Cal Rose are three you might find in your market.
Cooking Oil
  Extra-virgin olive
  Expeller-pressed canola or regular canola oil
  No-stick oil sprays
Nuts, Unsalted
  Walnuts, English
  Almonds, dry blanched (not in oil)
  Pecans, unsalted
  Peanuts, unsalted
  Cashews, unsalted
Eggs, Organic

Dairy
Nonfat milk, vitamins A & D added
1% milk, vitamins A & D added
Unsalted butter
Sour cream
Light/lite
Regular
Yogurt, plain
Light/lite
Regular
Buttermilk
Low-sodium brands in the United States include:
Knudsen (130 mg)
A & P (125 mg)
Borden (130 mg)
Crowley (130 mg)
Drigold Trim (130 mg)
Weight Watchers (140 mg)

SPICES

Most spices are available at your local grocer. However, some aren't. Special spices we use in this book that are more prevalent in other countries might be found in specialty stores. Such spices include Garam Masala in an Indian store (or health food gourmet store) or Masa Mix in a Mexican store (and some standard grocers), and of course there's my favorite Italian store full of goodies from Italy.

Here is what we consider a good selection of spices for preparing no-salt meals in this and our other *No-Salt, Lowest-Sodium* books.

Allspice
Aniseed
Caraway seed
Cardamom, ground
Celery seed
Chili powder (unsalted)
Cinnamon, ground
Cloves, ground
Coriander, ground
Curry powder, unsalted

Cumin, ground
Cumin seed
Dill seed
Fennel seed
Fenugreek seed (difficult to find)
Garlic powder, unsalted
Ginger, ground
Lemon & pepper seasoning
Mace, ground
Mustard powder
Mustard seed, yellow
Nutmeg, ground
Onion, granulated or powder
Pepper, black
Pepper, crushed red or cayenne
Pepper, white
Poppy seed
Saffron
Turmeric, ground

Herbs You Might Want to Have on Hand

Basil, fresh
Basil, ground
Bay leaf, whole
Chives, raw
Cilantro, fresh (also called Chinese parsley or fresh coriander)
Dill weed, dried
Dill weed, fresh
Garlic, fresh
Ginger, fresh (raw)
Marjoram, dried
Oregano, ground
Parsley, dried
Parsley, raw
Rosemary, dried
Rosemary, fresh
Sage, ground
Spearmint (mint), dried and fresh
Tarragon, dried
Thyme, dried ground and fresh

SPECIALTY MIXES WE MAKE AND KEEP ON HAND

Maureen's Garam Masala (see page 45)
Don's Soy Sauce Replacement (see page 37)
Don's Hoisin Sauce (see page 55)

NONALCOHOLIC WINE

Red
White

COOKING UTENSILS USED IN THIS BOOK

Cooking surfaces recommended are always nonstick. The reasons are simple. Less fat enters your cooked item, and nonstick allows you to lift baked goods out without hassle. But you will have to follow some simple rules to take care of your nonstick cookware.

1. Never wash with harsh detergents.
2. Wash with water and gentle soap, rinse well, and wipe dry.
3. Never subject a nonstick pan to high heat; most will cook safely over medium and lower heat.
4. Never use metal utensils with nonstick cookware; not even if you think you can get away with it.
5. Store nonstick cookware upside down so that other cookware doesn't scratch on it.
6. Take nonstick cookware off the stove top the minute you have finished cooking. Place on a cold burner or on the countertop. Never run cold water over a nonstick pan immediately after removing it from heat.

We may at times ask you to spray a light coat of Pam-type olive oil spray on your nonstick, but that's more for flavoring than cooking, and it doesn't add enough fat to your diet to even try to count it.

BASIC EQUIPMENT LIST

12- to 14-inch skillets, nonstick
4, 8, and 12-quart saucepans
Aebleskiver pan, cast iron

Baking sheet
Barbecue (gas or charcoal)
Basting brush
Blender, handheld, electric
Blender, countertop
Bread knife
Bread machine
Bundt pan, nonstick
Cannoli tubes, preferably 8
Coffee grinder
Colander
Cookie pan
Dutch oven, ceramic, enameled
Egg separator
Electric ovens
Fat separator
Food processor
Gas stove top
Grater
Griddle, nonstick, smooth surface
Hand peeler
Jelly roll pan
Knives, assortment
Loaf pans
Measuring cups
Measuring spoons
Microwave
Mixer, handheld, electric double-bladed stand
Mixing bowls
Mortar and pestle
Muffin pan
Muffin rings
Muffin-top pan
Nonstick crepe pan
Paring knives
Roasting pan
Scone pan
Scrapers
Sieves
Spatulas

Spoons, ladling
Tube pan
Vegetable knife
Whisk
Wooden spoons

DIABETIC *NO-SALT,* *LOWEST-SODIUM* DAILY MEAL PLANNER

❖ ❖ ❖ ❖ ❖ ❖ ❖ ❖

Make up your own Meal Planner using the template below as a start, or one that you may already have. Add or subtract columns you might or might not need.

Use your exchange chart to plan your day with our recipes from any of our books.

Use the nutrient data charts that follow this page to help you calculate each recipe's data.

	SODIUM	*CARBS*	*PROTEIN*	*T-FATS*	
Breakfast					
Snack					
Lunch					
Snack					
Dinner					
Daily Total					

GLOSSARY

You'll find the terms we use in this book in this glossary, along with a lot of other terms you've probably heard through the years or even know now. What fascinated us was that cooking terms we use on a daily basis were not usually originated in our country. Cooking terms number in the hundreds of thousands, so we haven't gone overboard. If we've used a cooking utensil or item in this book that we haven't covered in this glossary, please visit www.megaheart.com and e-mail us from the site. We'll happily answer any questions you have about our recipes.

Aebleskiver: A small waffle or pancake formed in shapes ranging from golf- to tennis-ball size. (See www.megheart.com/kit_cabinet .html for a great aebleskiver pan.) Recipes vary. Some are just plain batter made especially for turning or rolling in the pan. Others may add thinly sliced apples or jam or berries inside the ball. In other words, you can make them your own way. First try the basics, learn how to turn them, and then add what you'd like for fun. The best aebleskivers we've found were at a restaurant in Solvang, California, in the Santa Ynez Valley.

Ahi: Yellowfin tuna used for sushi.

Albóndigas con Arroz: The long way to say: meatballs with nice. Originated in Mexico.

Al dente: The term "al dente" is particularly associated with cooking pasta but has been used by chefs in other food preparations. An Italian term, it means "firm to the bite," or "to the tooth," which pasta should be once it's cooked.

Anaheim Chili: A mildly hot, green to yellow chili pepper, fresh, never dried. It measures from 6 to 8 inches long. Grills well, peels after blanching or grilling, and is used in many dishes. Tasty.

Antipasto: Antipasto literally means "before the pasta," or "appetizer."

Arborio Rice: Follow the instructions when cooking this rice. It is one of the best-known Italian rices, originally grown in Italy's Po Valley. It's a starchy, short-grain rice that was developed especially for risotto, the most famous Italian dish of home and professional chefs. When cooked it develops a creamy consistency.

Artichoke: A member of the thistle family—the unopened flower buds are used (after snipping off the thorns). You can buy delicious artichoke hearts in jars, packed in water, with no salt added, and use these in your own panini sandwich creations with other ingredients like tomato, onion, and no-salt cheese. (Also called globe artichoke or French artichoke).

Baba Ghanoush: A dip. Usually made from grilled eggplant, an oily paste made from ground sesame seeds (known as tahini), olive oil, lemon juice, and pureed cooked garlic.

Baguette: When we say "baguette," Paris comes to mind. Even while in Tahiti, when the morning delivery of baguettes arrived, I thought of Paris. However, the baguette descends from Vienna, not Paris. Not to be outdone, French politicians chose a variety of baguette and officially made it "the baguette of tradition." It is a long, cylindrical loaf with a crispy crust. It does not contain sugar in most cases, although ours has to use a little to help the yeast and gluten leaven the bread. Baste the dough before second rise with a light mixture of egg white mixed with water to help achieve the crispy outer crust.

Baklava (Baklawa): A Middle Eastern, Armenian, or Greek sweet treat made from layers of phyllo dough. It usually contains chopped or ground nuts including almonds, as well as sugar, spice, butter, bread crumbs and so on. It is soaked in sugar syrup or honey after baking; then cut into squares or triangles.

Basil: Ahh, I love the fresh basil from our local farmers' market. A member of the mint family, the fresh green leaves are full of flavor to the senses even before you break it up for cooking. Dried basil is not as aromatic. Basil *is* Italian cooking. It is used with chicken, fish, and tomato dishes; pasta sauce and salads; soups, stuffings, pesto sauce, and salad dressings. If you haven't tried fresh basil, please get some. It will keep on your kitchen countertop for a day or two with its stems clipped, then stuck in a glass of water. Otherwise place it in a ziplock bag and store in the refrigerator vegetable drawer until you use it, preferably the same day you buy it.

Basmati Rice: A dense, thin, long-grain rice, basmati is aromatic and has a nutty flavor. We use it in Indian cooking and for steaming as a side dish. It also works well with our fried rice recipes. It is not suitable for soft or "sticky" rice recipes like sushi, but is the best type of long-grain rice.

Bay Leaf: This well-known leaf from the laurel family is used fresh or dried in soups, stews, and with meats and in many Indian and Italian recipes.

Beans: Bean varieties include kidney, navy, pinto, red beans, garbanzo, (also called chickpeas), black-eyed peas, black soybeans, cannellini (white kidney beans), and more.

Béchamel Sauce: Basic French white sauce made from a white flour and butter roux (see: Roux) and seasoned milk.

Biscotti: An Italian cookie often hard in texture and lightly flavored with anise. You can make this cookie easily without salt or baking powder. Just follow one of our recipes in the *The No-Salt, Lowest-Sodium Baking Book.*

Brine: Be aware of "brined" chicken and pork in your local market. You don't want it. It's happening more and more these days. Brine is salt dissolved and turned into a liquid for soaking meats. Some brine is actually infused into intramuscular or arterial systems—usually in pork.

Bulgur (Cracked wheat): Parboiled and dried wheat kernels processed into grain. Originally used in tabouli and kibbeh (lamb dishes) but used worldwide in everything from salads to bread.

Black Bean Sauce: Fermented black beans with ginger, garlic, rice wine, and other ingredients.

Blanch: To plunge items into boiling water or to bring items to a boil and cook briefly for 2 to 5 minutes. The reason for blanching is to partially cook an item.

Blini: A small, sometimes thick pancake, usually eaten with caviar and chopped vegetables.

Boeuf: French for beef.

Bok Choy: A mild-flavored vegetable from the cabbage family. It is similar in taste to celery. Goes well with fish. It's high in Vitamin K.

Bordelaise: Bordeaux style; also refers to a French sauce made with shallots, red wine brown stock, and bone marrow.

Bouillabaisse: A popular Mediterranean fish soup; most closely identified with Marseille. Traditionally might include dozens of different fish. Cooked in a broth of water, olive oil, onions, garlic, tomatoes, parsley, and saffron. The fish is served separately from the broth, which is poured over garlic-rubbed toast and seasoned with *rouille* a rust-colored spicy mayonnaise made with red pepper, garlic, and olive oil, which is stirred into the broth. Other additions to the stew might include boiled potatoes, orange peel, fennel, and shellfish.

Bouillon: Stock or broth.

Boulangère, à la: "In the style of the baker's wife." Usually it's meat or poultry baked or braised with onions and potatoes.

Bourguignonne, à la: Burgundy style; often with red wine, onions, mushrooms, and bacon.

Braise: To cook meat by browning in fat, then simmering in a covered pot with small amount of liquid.

Brioche: Buttery, egg-enriched yeast bread.

Broccoli: A flowered green cruciferous vegetable that is high in vitamin K but can still be enjoyed if you balance your diet on a daily basis.

Brouillé: Usually scrambled eggs.

Brown Sugar Replacement: Sugar Twin available in stores and online.

Burritos: A tortilla usually filled with shredded or dried meat and mixed with a chili sauce.

Calamari: A squid—not an octopus. Squid are carnivorous and feed on other fish. They can expel ink like the giant octopus when threatened. Squid have an internal bone structure while the octopus has none. Calamari is a popular Greek dish. Often it is served after being breaded and deep-fried. Ours is different for health reasons but exceptionally delicious. We pick up frozen squid at Trader Joe's. See page 209 for our Calamari Steaks.

Cannellini Beans: White oval-shaped beans used frequently in Italian dishes. They are available canned from Eden Organic Beans. Look for the no-salt-added labels. Also referred to as white kidney beans.

Canapé: Originally a slice of crustless bread; now also used to refer to a variety of hors d'oeuvre consisting of toasted or fried bread, spread with forcemeat, cheese, and other flavorings.

Cannoli: This popular Italian dessert consists of a hollow tubular pastry filled with a ricotta or sweet cream filling. (See page 8).

Cardamom: A wonderfully aromatic spice, used often in no-salt cooking. It's a member of the ginger family, and is used in other parts of the world to flavor coffee, yogurt, stews, and bread recipes. There are various types, notably green, white, and brown. It is one of the most aromatic and expensive spices.

Carnaroli: Premium risotto rice from Italy. The outer part of the grain has a soft starch that dissolves during cooking, leaving the inner grain for a firm, snappy bite.

Challah: Pronounced "Hall-ahh" or "hallah." A braided, leavened bread eaten on the Sabbath and other Jewish holidays except for Passover, when Jews are not allowed to eat leavened bread. It is flavorful, fun to make and a delight for your guests.

Chalupas: Made by pressing tortilla dough into an elongated shape with a ridge around the edge. These resemble the *chalupas,* or canoes, from which they take their name. They are sometimes fried and then topped with shredded meat, cheese, and other fillings.

Chili con Carne: Spanish for chili with meat. It's generally a hot spicy stew. We make chili con carne with various cuts of meat or chopped meat including venison, beef, pork, and chicken, and we use Grandma's Chili Powder, which is produced without salt. Choose your chili peppers wisely. If you like it hot, get hot chilies. If not so hot, get mild chilies. In much of the world the dish is referred to as "chili." You can find this dish served throughout Texas and no two taste the same—but they are hot.

Chop Suey: American in origin, chop suey uses odds and ends, leftovers—everything in the same pot. Served over rice and, in our case, with Don's Soy Sauce Substitute (see page 37).

Chorizo: One of our favorite no-salt sausages is Don's Authentically Hot Chorizo (see page 95). Our chorizo is based on the Mexican-style sausage. The Spanish or Basque version is usually drier and flavored with paprika (see page 63).

Chow Mein: Usually stir-fry meat and/or vegetables serve over crispy noodles.

Ciabatta: A flatter-than-usual, teardrop- or slipper-shaped loaf of bread flavored with fresh or dried herbs, no-salt-added olives, or sun-dried tomatoes. Ciabatta has an airy texture inside with a pale crisp crust. Try ours, you'll love it. Great for sandwiches. (See page 173.)

Cilantro: Whether you like fresh cilantro or not, this herb is user-friendly and adds a lot of good flavor to many of our recipes. It's a relative of parsley and is sometimes called coriander or cheese parsley. It is one of the most important spices in Indian cookery and is also found in Latin American cooking. The leaves of the plant can be used fresh and the dried seeds, called coriander, used whole or ground.

Citron: A semi-tropical citrus fruit that is caudled and used in baking.

Citron, orange, or pamplemousse pressé(e): Lemon, orange, or grapefruit juice served with a carafe of tap water and sugar; for sweetening to taste. Grapefruit juice should not be consumed by patients taking heart medications or Coumadin. *Pamplemousse* is French for grapefruit.

Citronelle: Lemongrass, an oriental herb; also lemon balm (mèlisse).

Colander: A perforated bowl used to drain liquids from solid food or liquids used to boil some items like pasta, etc. Usually has handles and a solid base.

Coriander: The dried seeds of the cilantro plant, sold whole or ground.

Conchiglie: A shell-shaped pasta available in a many sizes.

Couscous: Small granular pasta made of semolina, or hard wheat flour; also refers to a hearty North African dish that includes the steamed pasta, broth, vegetables, meats, hot sauce, and sometimes chickpeas and raisins.

Crepe: A large thin pancake—sweet or savory. For Basic Crepes, see page 246.

Crepes Suzette: A hot crepe dessert flamed with orange liqueur.

Cumin: There are two types of cumin seeds: white and black. The white seeds are an important spice in Indian cooking. The black seeds (*kala jeera*) are seldom used. Each may be used whole or ground.

Curry: Curry leaves are small leaves a bit like bay leaves, used in Indian food. They are not the same as curry powder, which is a spice mixture that can include coriander, turmeric, red pepper, onion, and fenugreek.

Dim Sum: The fave in Chinese teahouses, it includes a variety of small dishes such as Chinese rolls or dumplings, usually steamed but also baked or fried.

Dum: Steam cooking. India has her own method for pressure cooking that's been used since they invented it. It's a pot with a close fitting lid, sealed with a ring of dough. The ingredients are then cooked in their own steam under some pressure.

Egg Rolls: Make your own noodle wrapping. Stir-fry bits of pork and shrimp and some chopped vegetables in cholesterol-free oil. Serve in your noodle wrapper.

Empanada: A flavorful Spanish or Mexican pastry-flour turnover. Fill with your choice of fruits and sweets or meat.

Enchiladas: In Mexico, enchiladas usually consist of a corn tortilla "softened" in hot oil (or lard) and often dipped in a red chili sauce. It is then wrapped around a filling of either meat or cheese and garnished with a little more sauce and cheese. In American cooking, enchiladas are often made without the dipping in sauce and are heated after being topped with a large quantity of chili sauce and cheese, and sometimes sour cream.

Entrée: In Europe, the first course. In America, the main course.

Falafel: Small deep-fried patties made using highly spiced ground chickpeas, lots of salt (except with us). Can be served with pita bread.

Farfalle: Bow tie–shaped pasta with crinkled edges.

Fennel: An herb originally from the Mediterranean, with an aniseed flavor. The dried seeds of common fennel are used as a spice in quite a few of our recipes, including bread recipes you'll find in this book. Sprouted Florence fennel is used for winter salads or as a braised vegetable.

Fenugreek: Used as seeds and in fresh or dried leaf form. It is used in many savory Indian dishes. Not easily found in markets.

Five-Spice Powder: You have to have a bottle of this in the house. It's a combination of star anise, cinnamon, cloves, fennel seed, and pepper. A great flavoring tool!

Fettuccine, à la: Flat noodles made from an egg-based pasta dough. Obtainable either fresh or dried.

Flan: A sweet or savory tart. Also, a crustless custard pie. Usually made with milk or cream and eggs.

Florentine, à la: Means "with spinach." Also, a cookie of nougatine and candied fruit brushed with a layer of chocolate.

Flautas: A large corn tortilla rolled around a filling of shredded meat, then deep fat–fried to a crisp golden brown. See Taquitas.

Focaccia: An easy-to-make flat bread shaped as a slab or round. Serve as an antipasto with a dip of olive oil and Italian vinegar.

Fontina (Cheese): A cow's milk cheese, it has a delicate nutty, slightly smoky taste and is much used for "fonduta," an Italian version of the Swiss "fondue."

Fricassée: Classically, ingredients braised in wine sauce or butter with cream added; currently denotes any mixture of ingredients—fish or meat—stewed ot sautéed.

Frijoles: Beans

Fusilli: A spiral-shaped pasta that open during cooking.

Garam Masala: Literally means "hot mixture." Refers to a blend of spices much loved in Northern Indian cookery. Try Maureen's Garam Masala (see page 45).

Gazpacho: a cold soup, usually containing tomatoes, cucumber, onions, and sweet peppers; of Spanish origin.

Granulated Lecithin: Soy lecithin improves the shelf life of yeasted bread and offers up a fresh nutty flavor. You can use 2 tablespoons per 3 cups of flour but we recommend only 3 tablespoons per 5 cups of flour. When using soy lecithin you can often cut back the oil in the bread, which we have taken into account with our recipes.

Gorditas (Sopes): Gorditas are made with tortilla dough (occasionally with the addition of other ingredients such as wheat flour or potato). Shaped a bit smaller than the tortilla, the filling, which like burritos is often beans or shredded meat and cheese, is placed into a pocket. (It is not unlike pita bread that is formed when a small layer of dough puffs up from the top, allowing it to be peeled open.)

Gratin: A dish that is browned under a broiler or in the oven, covered with bread crumbs or cheese that form a surface crust; It also the name of dish in which such food is cooked.

Gruyère Strictly speaking, cheese from the Gruyère area of Switzerland; in France, it can be the generic name for a number of hard, mild, cooked cheeses from the Jura, including Comté, Beaufort, and Emmenthal.

Guacamole: Fresh avocados pureed or mashed and then usually mixed with chopped onions, chili powder or chopped chilies, chopped tomato, lime juice, and not always but sometimes cilantro.

Haddock: Small fresh cod that have been salted and smoked.

Herbes de Provence: A mixture of thyme, rosemary, summer savory, and bay leaf, or a similar variety. It is often dried and blended.

Hoisin Sauce: A thick sweet and pungent condiment of soybeans, peppers, garlic, salt, vinegar, and chilis. See Don's Hoisin Sauce substitute page 55. Delicious.

Hollandaise: An emulsified sauce of butter, egg yolks, and lemon juice.

Hong Choi: Chinese parsley (cilantro), used a lot with Chinese meals.

Hors d'oeuvres: Appetizer; can also refer to a first course.

Jambalaya: Mostly used to define a Cajun or Creole dish of meat, vegetables, and rice. The meat can be chicken or sausage like chorizo, or shellfish, the vegetables are usually tomato based, but include peppers.

Jalapeño Chili: Tapered hot green Mexican chili about 3 to 6 inches long. Handle with care; we advise using gloves. The seeds are very hot.

Julienne: Matchstick strips; usually vegetables or meat.

Julienned Carrots: Wash and peel carrot. Slice off four sides of the carrot to create a rectangle. Cut carrot lengthwise into approximately ⅛-inch slices. Stack the ⅛-inch slices and then cut lengthwise into approximately ⅛-inch strips.

Kebab: Skewered chunks of meat or fish cooked over charcoal, a process over 4,000 years old, which probably originated in the Middle East and imported to India by the Muslims centuries ago.

Kiev: Deep-fried breast of chicken stuffed with herb and garlic butter.

Kim Chee: A heavily seasoned Korean pickled vegetables not often appreciated by Western palates.

Kolache: Derived from a Czech word. See page 196 for our Kolache bread. You can use your own fillings with our recipe. It usually consists of fillings ranging from fruits to cheeses inside a bread roll.

Kung Pao: Tofu or meat, stir-fried with vegetables, unsalted peanuts, and chili peppers.

Lasagne: Flat pasta sheets layered with a variety of ingredients from cheeses to tomato sauce to vegetables, to ground meat. See page 104 for our Italian Lasagne.

Lemongrass: Also known as citronella. It has a strong lemon aroma and is used for cooking, in sauces and soups (see our *No-Salt, Lowest-Sodium Light Meals Book*). It is commonly used in Thailand, Vietnam, and Ceylon.

Macaroni: Short or small hollow-shaped pasta. Great for Macaroni and Cheese. It comes in different sizes, and plain or egg-enriched are available.

Mace: The outer part of the nutmeg. Used in many dishes; a nice addition to pumpkin pie and other puddings.

Mahimahi: Known as dolphinfish or dorado, the mahimahi is not related to the mammal called dolphin. It is not, in other words, "Flipper." However, it is one of the more colorful, if not the most beautiful, fish out there. It has an iridescent bluish-green and gold body, golden yellow fins, and a forked tail. It is easy to prepare and cook. When we grill it, we serve it with mango salsa (see: Mango, below).

Malted Barley Flour: Improves flavor and the appearance of bread. Use about ½ teaspoon per 3 cups of flour. Adds slight sweet flavor with a moist texture. Extends shelf life. If a recipe doesn't call for it, you may still add that ½ teaspoon ratio.

Mango: The mango, for all its trouble to peel, is one of the most popular fruits in the world. It's sweet and juicy, and with its distinctive flavor it allows us to make a great mango salsa. Just chop and combine with chopped onion and chopped tomato, and you've got topping for fish entrées. Select richly colored, firm mangoes, then let them ripen at home for a few days. Frozen mangoes and mangoes in their own juice or water in a jar are also low in sodium and nearly as good as the fresh—and you don't have to jump through hoops to peel them.

Marinade: A seasoned liquid in which food, usually meat, is soaked for several hours. The liquid seasons and tenderizes at the same time.

Masa: This is a fine dough made from corn boiled with lime and ground in a mill designed exclusively to do the job. Masa is used in the making or preparation of tortillas, tamales, and other dishes from Central and South America. Masa is also used as a thickener for sauces and stews, especially with dishes like chili con carne.

Médallion: Usually round or oval slice, usually of fish or meat.

Mein: As in Chow Mein, it means a thin wheat noodle.

Milk with Vitamin A: The USDA has changed the level of sodium in nonfat and other milk that has added vitamin A from 126 mg per cup to 102.9 mg of sodium per cup.

Miso: A fermented soybean paste.

Moo Goo Gai Pan: Great flavors. Fresh mushrooms cooked with sliced chicken.

Moo Shu: Chopped or shredded vegetables stir-fried with egg or meat, eaten in a rice pancake.

Mousse: A light, airy mixture usually containing eggs and cream, either sweet or savory.

Mozzarella: An Italian, unripened, curd cheese made from cow's milk. It is a soft cheese with a rather moist texture and is available salt free in many parts of the United States. Used as a cooking cheese in our pizzas and lasagne.

Murgh: Chicken.

Murgh masala: A specialty dish usually consisting of a whole chicken, marinated in plain yogurt and a selection of spices for 24 hours, then stuffed and roasted.

Naan: An Indian leavened flatbread baked in a tandoor. It is teardrop shaped and 8 to 10 inches long. It must be served fresh and hot. We freeze ours and then microwave "defrost" to perfection. (See: Tandoor.)

Nam Plah: Thai fish Sauce, called "nuacman" in Vietnam.

Niter Kebbeh: (See page 48) for Ethiopian Spice Bread. Niter Kibbeh is usually a seasoned clarified butter used in Ethiopian cooking. It can also be made with olive oil, which you will find with our Ethiopian Spice Bread. Delicious and worth the effort.

Olive oil (Extra-virgin olive oil): Made exclusively from the pulp of the finest-quality olives. Virgin and extra-virgin olive oil have an exciting fruity flavor and a darker green-gold color than light olive oil. It adds an exciting flavor to salad dressings and is used in dishes where strong flavored oil is needed, and especially when we don't use salt. If you don't want the flavor of olive oil to burst out in what you are cooking, then you can use light olive oil, which is still 100 percent olive oil.

Orange Roughy: A white fish, a bit like cod, from the deep. Orange roughy became a "thing" for meals only about thirty years ago when humans figured out how to fish more than a half mile and more down off New Zealand. It is red in body color, large with large eyes and a bony head, and lives in water with a pressure 80 to 100 times that of the surface water. It is rich in oil, with a waxy layer below its skin. It is a white fish on your plate. Although it is native to New Zealand, orange roughy can be found around the world, first being discovered in the North Atlantic around 1889.

Orange Sauce: Make it by cooking orange rind. Puree.

Oregano: Oregano is related to marjoram. It is sold crumbled or ground but not fresh. You can grow it yourself if you want it "fresher" than the commercial kind. Oregano is used in a wide variety of pasta sauces and salad dressings.

Paella: Paella was originally the word for "frying pan" from the Latin word *patella*. Today it can mean the pan or the dish made in it or both.

Panaché: Literally means "mixed," now a liberally used menu term to denote any mixture.

Panini: Generally a toasted sandwich. You can use one of the new panini machines, which are popular at this writing. We bought one to test and make recipes, and accidentally got a great deal. Salton makes the Breadman Panini machine and the same model for other brand names. We bought ours through www.megaheart.com/kit_ cabinet.html for just $39 (at this writing) while the other national brands were offering the very same machine for upward of $139. Toast any sandwich you like, from vegetarian to cheese to meats and veggies. Works with most bread recipes but not the flavored breads.

Paprika: Powdered red pepper. It originally came from Hungary. In some cultures its main use is to give red color to a dish, but in other parts of the world it's used to add a hot spicy flavor.

Parmesan: According to the USDA, a salt-free Parmesan is available in the United States, but we've never found it and neither, apparently, have visitors to www.Megaheart.com. It's one of Italy's best-known cheeses. It is a cow's milk (not goat's milk) cheese made into a large wheel. After fully muturing, it is used for grating and cooking.

Pastina: Also known as soup pasta, it is very small. It is available in many shapes; often used for broths and soups.

Peking Duck: A restaurant favorite: roasted duck breast in a pancake with scallions and hoisin sauce.

Penne: Penne are tubes with angled ends used in Italian dishes and in dishes with chunky sauces. Look for "Penne Pasta" packages.

Peperoncini (Dried red chilies): Hot flakes of dried chilies. Just right for many Italian dishes.

Perch, Ocean: Small rockfish with a flat colorful body. A delicious fish.

Pesto: This is a classic basil sauce from Italy. And you will want that fresh basil mentioned under "Basil." The sauce is also made with pine nuts; a touch of Parmesan is okay when making it for no-salt diets, and we use the virgin or extra-virgin olive oil.

Pine nuts: Tiny cream-colored nuts with a distinctly delicious flavor. Pine nuts are a key component of the popular Italian pesto sauce and they work well when lightly toasted and sprinkled on some salads. Pine nuts are generally expensive in grocery stores but a very large bag costs much less at stores like Costco. Get them unsalted.

Plum Sauce: Try it, You'll like it! You can make it by combining plums, bell peppers, sugar, vinegar, ginger, and Chinese five-spice powder.

Praline: Candy made with boiled sugar and nuts, usually almonds.

Provolone: An Italian curd cheese made from cow's milk. It is used in cannelloni and ravioli. You might find a low-sodium version.

Pugliese: Made with extra-virgin olive oil and soft and chewy with a thin crust, this bread is best eaten warm on the day of baking. On the next day it can be used for a good crostini or Italian Open-Face Chicken Sandwiches made on thin slices of toast (see page 143).

Quesadillas: Usually a corn tortilla, it can also be made with flour. For a no-salt lifestyle, use our Flour Tortillas recipe to make your own (see page 182). Quesadillas are folded over a filling of cheese primarily but you can add other ingredients; usually spices or herbs. Cook on a greased or nonstick surface until the cheese melts.

Quiche Lorraine: A savory custard tart made with bacon, eggs, and cream.

Raisin: A dried grape. Red and white grapes are used.

Ratatouille: A traditional French Provençal dish of stewed vegetables. We make it as a meal or a side dish. See page 149 for our Ratatouille.

Ravioli: A popular filled pasta, almost always square in shape. Often stuffed with spinach and ricotta cheese or herbs. It can also be filled with a meat mixture. Usually cooked when fresh.

Relleno: Spanish word for filling.

Ricotta: Fresh Italian cheese made from the whey of cow's milk. It is unripened, smooth, and mild tasting, and is used in a variety of sweet and tasty dishes including pizzas and in our dessert cannolis.

Risotto: A dish of creamy rice made by stirring starchy Arborio-style rice short-grain rice constantly in stock as it cooks; then mixing in other ingredients for its flavor, such as cheese or mushrooms.

Romanoff: A "Continental" term for fruit, often strawberries, macerated in liqueur and topped with whipped cream.

Romaine Lettuce: Good flavor and crunchy too. Romaine has a good shelf life in the refrigerator. It's the preferred green for Alexander's Caesar Salad (see page 126).

Rouelle: A slice of meat or vegetable cut at an angle.

Roux: A sauce base or binder of cooked flour and butter.

Salade niçoise: A composed salad with many variations, but usually with tomatoes, green beans, anchovies, tuna, potatoes, black olives, capers, and artichokes.

Salsa: Spanish for sauce.

Satay: Beef, pork, or chicken usually but not always on skewers. Often served with peanut sauce.

Sauté: Cooked quickly in fat.

Scant: Slightly less than a full measurement.

Soufflé: A light mixture of pureed ingredients, egg yolks, and whipped egg whites, which puffs up when baked. It can be sweet or savory; hot or cold.

Soy Sauce: Very high in sodium. Made from soybeans, wheat, lots and lots of salt, and fermenting organisms. Invented by the Chinese more than 3,000 years ago. Don's Soy Sauce Replacement (see page 37) was invented just a few years later!

Spaghetti: Spaghetti means "little strings." Usually made from durum wheat. Available fresh or dried. It can be made at home.

Splenda: Sugar substitute. Bake or cook or serve out of the bag or packet. No calories, sugars, or sodium. Also known as sucralose.

Sumac: A ground powder from the cashew family (unsalted, please). It's used as a seasoning in Middle Eastern cuisine.

Sun-dried Tomatoes: Great for many Italian dishes even if added as an extra to sprinkle over the top. Works in pasta dishes, lasagne, and other recipes. Available dry in packets or preserved in olive oil in small jars. These tomatoes are deep red in color and chewy. Before cooking with the dried type, soak them in hot water for a while to soften them.

Sushi: Typically a cold vinegared rice garnished with raw fish, vegetables, eggs, onions, mushrooms, etc. See page 151 for our California Sushi Rolls.

Tacos: Tacos are tortillas wrapped around a filling. They are usually defined by either the type of filling, the type of tortilla (corn or flour), and whether the taco is fried or not. For instance you can find *Tacos al pastor,* which are filled with marinated pork, *Tacos al Carbon,* tacos with char-broiled meats, etc. There are a plethora of such names including those you'll find at various restaurants.

Tabouli (Tabbouleh): A grain salad made with bulgur, tomato, mint, and parsley. See page 234 for our Tabouli recipe.

Tagliatelle: Not always easily found. This is a ribbon-shaped pasta sometime available fresh.

Tahini: An oily paste or nut-type butter made from ground sesame seeds. Usually low in sodium; just watch out for products have added salt.

Tamales: We have a tamale recipe but it's not in this book and neither should it be. We tried to adapt it for this book but there's simply too much sodium, too much fat, and way too many calories. The original tamales were made with uncooked masa, corn husks, and fillings that were too many to list here. But dream about insects, steamed in a tamale and you'll understand why there are scores of regional varieties with almost any ingredient you can come up with.

Tandoor: A tandoor is an Indian clay oven with rounded sides. It stands about 5 feet high, has charcoal in the bottom as the heat source, and its use is not too unlike barbecuing. (It is obviously not a practical oven to install in your home.) Using a tandoor is the traditional Indian way of baking naan bread.

Taquitos (Flautas): Pretty much the same as flautas, these are made with smaller tortillas and deep-fat fried.

Tempura: Vegetables, meat, or seafood quick-fried in a light egg batter of mixed flour and rice flour.

Tofu: A usually soft, moist soybean curd, some are no salt added, some are high in sodium.

Tomates à la provençal: Baked tomato halves sprinkled with garlic, parsley, and bread crumbs.

Tortilla: From the Spanish word "torta," meaning a round cake. Tortilla also means "omelette" in Spain. Today the bread called tortilla is a flat, disk-shaped corn or flour product. It's used in many different recipes from tacos to soup.

Tortellini: This stuffed pasta, is usually stuffed with a variety of fillings like chopped chicken, Italian sausage (make your own salt-free sausage), or cheese and nutmeg.

Tournedos: A center portion of filet mignon, usually grilled or sautéed.

Trace: We use "trace" alongside some ingredients. It means that the ingredient has either a listing of zero (0 mg) with the USDA or so little sodium that it's not worth counting.

Turmeric: Turmeric is a rhizome. The fresh root is used occasionally as a vegetable or in pickles. In Indian cooking, the ground spice is used to give the familiar yellow color to curries. Don't use too much because, used in excess, it will give off a bitter flavor.

Vichyssoise: A cold, creamy leek and potato soup.

Vinaigrette: Used often in salad recipes; it means an oil and vinegar dressing.

Water Chestnuts: A brownish-black skinned, edible tuber of an aquatic plant found mostly in Southeast Asia, available canned in ready-to-use slices.

Wasabi: Similar to horseradish but green and hotter; most American wasabis are dyed horseradish and not true wasabi.

Won Ton: Usually high in sodium and fats, it's a stuffed dough that is often deep-fried in oil.

Yeast: Active dry yeast, bread machine yeast, rapid rise yeast, fresh yeast—all are used to leaven dough. We used Bread Machine Yeast from Fleischmann's, since Fleischmann's adds some ascorbic acid to their yeast, which helps with the rise in no-salt bread. Store dry yeast in a cool, dry place; refrigerate cake yeast.

APPENDIX: NUTRIENT VALUES

BEEF	CALORIES K-CAL	PROTEIN GM	CARB GM	TOT. FAT GM	SAT FAT GM	MONO UNSAT GM	POLY UNSAT GM	CHOLES-TEROL GM	TRANS FATTY ACIDS	OMEGA-3 GM	OMEGA-6 GM	POTASS MG	SODIUM MG	VIT. K MCG
All beef rated at 1-ounce ¼" trim, raw, unless otherwise noted														
Bottom Round, All Grades, 28 g	40.8	6.2	0	1.588	0.541	0.72	0.062	0.003	ND	0.003	0	10-5.2	16.7	ND
Brain, 28 g	40.5	2.079	0.298	2.92	0.828	0.68	0.13	853.3	0.173	0	0	77.7	35.7	0
Brisket, All Grades, ½" trim, 28 g	91	4.656	0	7.882	0.28	0	0	3.595	ND	0.101	0	67.8	17.4	ND
Brisket, All Grades, Flat Half, ¼" trim, 28 g	42	6.081	0	1.758	0.564	0.768	0.065	16.7	ND	0.003	0	98.7	21	ND
Heart, raw, 28 g	31.8	5.024	0.04	1.117	0.392	0.322	0.155	35.2	0.051	0.008	0.003	81.4	27.8	0
Kidney, raw, 28 g	29.2	4.933	0.082	0.876	0.246	0.166	0.155	116.5	0.028	0.006	0.005	74.3	51.6	0
Liver, raw, 28 g	38.3	5.77	1.102	1.029	0.349	0.136	0.132	77.9	0.048	0.007	0.09	88.7	10.6	0.879

(continued)

(continued)

BEEF	CALORIES K-CAL	PROTEIN GM	CARB. GM	TOT. FAT GM	SAT FAT GM	MONO UNSAT GM	POLY UNSAT GM	CHOLES-TEROL GM	TRANS FATTY ACIDS	OMEGA-3 GM	OMEGA-6 GM	POTASS MG	SODIUM MG	VIT. K MCG
Porterhouse Steak, Short Loin, All Grades, 28 g	44.2	6.033	0	2.03	0.726	0.951	0.087	15.9	ND	0.007	0	83.1	16.4	ND
T-Bone Steak, All Grades, lean, 28 g	41.1	5.954	0	1.746	0.602	0.759	0.08	13.6	ND	0.007	0	88.7	16.4	ND
Short Loin, Top Loin, All Grades, 28 g	40.3	6.104	0	1.559	0.593	0.666	0.057	16.7	ND	0.003	0	98.9	16.7	ND
Beef Steak Tartare, ½ cup, 112 g	255.4	20.1	0.551	18.6	7.269	7.986	0.925	19.9	ND	0	0	308.4	134.1	ND
Suet, 28 g	242.1	0.425	0	26.6	14.8	8.936	0.899	19.3	ND	0.244	0	4.536	1.985	1.021
Tongue, 28 g	63.5	4.224	1.043	4.562	1.985	2.053	0.255	24.7	ND	0	0	89.3	19.6	ND
Tripe, 28 g	24.1	3.422	0	1.046	0.366	0.435	0.051	34.6	0.043	0.005	0.003	19	27.5	0
Chuck, Arm Pot Roast, All Grades, lean, 28 g	36.9	6.027	0	1.247	0.451	0.471	0.062	17	ND	0.006	0	105.5	19	ND

Food													
Chuck, Blade Roast, All Grades, lean 28 g	42.2	5.457	0	2.098	0.788	0.933	0.079	18.4	ND	0.006	0	90.4	21.8	ND
Chuck, Clod Roast, separable lean and fat, 28 g	45.9	5.369	0	2.549	0.879	1.052	0.12	17.3	ND	0.024	0	95.5	17.6	ND
Chuck, Tender Steak, separable lean and fat, 28 g	32.3	5.355	0	1.06	0.378	0.568	0.094	15.3	ND	0.009	0	116.8	23.5	ND
Chuck, Top Blade, separable lean and fat, 28 g	42.2	5.406	0	2.121	0.675	0.922	0.095	17	ND	0.013	0	92.7	16.7	ND
Corned Beef, Cured, Brisket, 28 g	56.1	4.162	0.04	4.224	1.341	2.036	0.15	15.3	ND	0.043	0	84.2	345	ND
Eye of Round, All Grades, lean, 28 g	37.4	6.166	0	1.219	0.42	0.505	0.051	15.3	ND	0.003	0	108.6	15	ND
Eye/Small End Ribs (10–12 ribs) Choice, lean 28 g	45.6	5.707	0	2.353	0.916	1.009	0.077	16.7	ND	0.003	0	105.7	17.9	ND
Flank, Choice, lean, 0" trim, 28 g	42.2	6.158	0	1.783	0.741	0.702	0.069	11.9	ND	0.017	0	96.4	16.2	0.34

(continued)

(continued)

BEEF	CALORIES K-CAL	PROTEIN GM	CARB. GM	TOT. FAT GM	SAT FAT GM	MONO UNSAT GM	POLY UNSAT GM	CHOLES-TEROL GM	TRANS FATTY ACIDS	OMEGA-3 GM	OMEGA-6 GM	POTASS MG	SODIUM MG	VIT. K MCG
Ground, 70% lean meat/30% fat, 28 g	93	4.018	0	8.4	3.161	3.685	ND	21.8	0.511	0.041	0.005	61	18.8	0.812
Ground, 75% lean meat/25% fat, 28 g	82	4.413	0	7	2.655	3.069	0.17	21	0.428	0.036	0.005	68.3	18.8	0.672
Ground, 80% lean meat/20% fat, 28 g	71.1	4.808	0	5.6	2.148	2.452	0.146	19.9	0.345	0.032	0.004	75.6	18.8	0.504
Ground, 85% lean meat/15% fat, 28 g	60.2	5.205	0	4.2	1.642	1.835	0.121	19	0.262	0.027	0.003	82.6	18.5	0.364
Ground, 90% lean meat/10% fat, 28 g	49.3	5.6	0	2.8	1.136	1.219	0.096	18.2	0.179	0.023	0.003	89.9	18.5	0.224
Ground, 95% lean meat/5% fat, 28 g	38.4	5.995	0	1.4	0.63	0.602	0.072	17.4	0.095	0.018	0.002	96.9	18.5	0.084
Ground, extra lean, 17% fat, 28 g	66.3	5.301	0	4.837	1.931	2.101	0.201	19.6	ND	0.028	0	80.5	18.7	ND
Ground, raw, 28 g	76.8	4.866	0	6.193	2.499	2.705	0.254	21.6	ND	0	0	70.4	83.6	ND

Food													
Large End Ribs (6–9 ribs), All Grades, lean, 28 g	46.8	5.565	0	2.552	1.04	1.023	0.096	16.7	ND	0.009	0	96.7	18.7	ND
Tri-Tip, Loin, bottom sirloin butt, 28 g	49.9	5.843	0	2.957	1.115	1.473	0.122	19	ND	0.021	0	93.8	15.3	0.397
Tri-Tip, Bottom Sirloin Butt, All Grades, lean, 28 g	43.7	5.999	0	2.2	0.795	1.151	0.095	18.4	ND	0.009	0	96.7	15.6	0.369
Patties, frozen, 100% beef, USDA, 28 g	57.8	4.146	0	4.447	1.795	1.944	0.182	15	ND	0.023	0	76.2	21	ND
Plate, Inside Skirt Steak, All Grades, 28 g	57.8	5.69	0	3.725	1.473	1.789	0.151	17	ND	0.0378	0	98.1	18.1	ND
Ribs, Small End (10–12 ribs), lean, ⅛" trim, 28 g	40	6.331	0	1.429	0.528	0.575	0.062	14.7	ND	0.003	0	98.4	15.9	0.369
Round, Full Cut, Choice Lean, 28 g	39.1	6.246	0	1.386	0.473	0.587	0.06	16.4	ND	0.003	0	106.3	16.2	0.34
Tenderloin, All Grades, 28 g	45.4	5.891	0	2.24	0.836	0.865	0.102	17.6	ND	0.006	0	104	15.3	ND
Tip Round, All Grades, lean, 28 g	35.2	5.985	0	1.077	0.366	0.439	0.051	17	ND	0.003	0	103.2	17.6	ND

(continued)

(continued)

BEEF	CALORIES K-CAL	PROTEIN GM	CARB. GM	TOT. FAT GM	SAT FAT GM	MONO UNSAT GM	POLY UNSAT GM	CHOLES-TEROL GM	TRANS FATTY ACIDS	OMEGA-3 GM	OMEGA-6 GM	POTASS MG	SODIUM MG	VIT. K MCG
Top Round, All Grades, lean, 28 g	36	6.461	0	0.936	0.32	0.366	0.043	16.2	ND	0.003	0	108.6	14.7	ND
Top Sirloin, All Grades, lean, 28 g	36.9	6.022	0	1.247	0.437	0.496	0.06	17.3	ND	0.003	0	102.3	16.4	0.34
Whole Ribs (6–12 ribs), All Grades, lean, 28 g	45.4	5.622	0	2.364	0.95	0.97	0.085	16.7	ND	0.006	0	100.1	18.4	ND
Beefalo (the result of breeding buffalo with steer), Game, Composite, 28 g	40.5	6.605	0	1.361	0.578	0.578	0.043	12.5	ND	0.011	0	123.6	22.1	ND

Weights vary. All meat is raw.

BROILER OR FRYER, CHICKEN

CHICKEN	CALORIES K-CAL	PROTEIN GM	CARB GM	TOT. FAT GM	SAT FAT GM	MONO UNSAT GM	POLY UNSAT GM	CHOLES-TEROL GM	TRANS FATTY ACIDS	OMEGA-3 GM	POTASS MG	SODIUM MG	VIT. K MCG
Liver,* 1 ounce 28 g	33.7	4.7905	0.207	1.369	0.443	0.354	0.232	97.8	0.018	0.005	65.2	20.1	0
Breast, w/skin, 145 g	249.4	30.2	0	13.4	3.857	5.539	2.842	92.8	0.167	0.174	319	91.4	0
Breast, no skin, 145 g	129.8	27.2	0	1.463	0.389	0.354	0.33	68.4	0.029	0.047	300.9	76.7	0.236
Dark Meat, w/skin, 266 g	630.4	44.4	0	48.8	14	20.3	10.5	215.5	ND	0.612	473.5	194.2	6.384
Dark Meat, no skin, 182 g	227.5	36.5	0	7.844	2.002	2.439	1.947	145.6	ND	0.2	404	154.7	4.368
Drumstick, w/skin, 73 g	117.5	14.1	0	6.336	1.745	2.46	1.416	59.1	ND	0.095	150.4	60.6	2.044
Drumstick, no skin, 62 g	73.8	12.8	0	2.12	0.533	0.661	0.508	47.7	0.058	0.056	140.1	54.6	1.798
Giblets, 75 g	93	13.4	1.35	3.352	1.02	0.84	0.817	196.5	ND	0.045	171	57.8	ND
Gizzard,† 28 g	26.6	5.505	0	0.584	0.15	0.145	0.101	68	0.017	0.003	67.2	19.6	0
Leg, w/skin, 167 g	312.3	30.3	0	20.2	5.511	8.083	4.325	138.6	0.175	0.284	330.7	131.9	4.843

(continued)

(continued)

CHICKEN	CALORIES K-CAL	PROTEIN GM	CARB GM	TOT. FAT GM	SAT FAT GM	MONO UNSAT GM	POLY UNSAT GM	CHOLES-TEROL GM	TRANS FATTY ACIDS	OMEGA-3 GM	POTASS MG	SODIUM MG	VIT. K MCG
Leg, no skin, 130 g	156	26.2	0	4.963	1.274	1.534	1.235	104	0.135	0.13	297.7	111.8	3.77
Light Meat, no skin, 147 g	167.6	34.1	0	2.425	0.647	0.573	0.544	85.3	ND	0.073	351.3	100	3.528
Whole Chicken, meat, w/skin, 460 g	989	85.6	0	69.3	19.8	28.7	14.9	345	ND	0.874	869.4	322	6.9
Neck, w/skin, 50 g	148.5	7.035	0	13.1	3.635	5.275	2.84	49.5	ND	0.16	68.5	32	ND
Neck, no skin, 20	30.8	3.51	0	1.756	0.45	0.546	0.0426	16.6	ND	0.042	35	16.2	ND
Thigh, w/skin, 94 g	198.3	16.2	0	14.3	4.123	6.12	3.178	79	0.207	0.194	180.5	71.4	2.726
Thigh, no skin, 69 g	82.1	13.6	0	2.698	0.69	0.835	0.669	57.3	0.073	0.069	159.4	59.3	2.001
Whole Chicken, all parts, 1046 g	2229	191.7	1.36	155.1	44.4	63.6	33.4	941.4	ND	1.883	1977	732.2	ND
Wing, w/skin	108.8	0.982	0	7.825	2.136	3.077	1.597	37.7	0.094	0.098	76.4	35.8	0
Wing, no skin, 29 g	36.5	6.371	0	1.027	0.273	0.247	0.232	16.5	0.02	0.032	56.3	23.5	0

CAPON (Rooster)													
Giblets, 115 g	149.5	21	1.633	5.597	1.886	1.518	1.368	335.8	ND	0.092	259.9	88.5	ND
Meat w/skin, 964 g	2256	180.9	0	164.6	47.7	70.5	34.9	723	ND	1.928	2092	433.8	23.1
Whole, all parts, 2152 g	4993	398.3	1.722	363.7	105.2	154.1	77.5	1872	ND	4.304	4584	1011	ND
ROASTER, CHICKEN													
Dark meat, no skin, 258 g	291.5	48.3	0	9.314	2.399	2.89	2.322	185.8	ND	0.232	585.7	245.1	6.192
Giblets, 113 g	143.5	20.5	1.288	5.695	1.74								
Light meat, no skin, 220 g	239.8	48.8	0	3.586	0.814	1.056	0.88	125.4	ND	0.088	554.4	112.2	5.28
Whole, meat only, no skin 477 g	529.5	97	0	12.9	3.196	3.959	3.196	310	ND	0.334	1135	357.8	11.4
Whole, meat w/skin, 668 g	1443	114.5	0	105.9	30.3	44.4	22.7	487.6	0	1.336	1309	454.2	16
Whole, bone-in, 1509	3214	257.9	1.359	233.3	66.5	96.4	50.2	1298	0	2.867	2958	1041	ND
STEWING CHICKEN													
Dark meat, no skin, 154 g	241.8	30.3	0	12.5	3.203	3.881	3.111	118.6	0	0.323	372.7	155.5	3.696
Giblets, 81 g	135.1	14.5	1.725	7.46	2.13	2.227	1.701	194.4	ND	0.041	183.1	62.4	ND

(continued)

(continued)

CHICKEN	CALORIES K-CAL	PROTEIN GM	CARB. GM	TOT. FAT GM	SAT FAT GM	MONO UNSAT GM	POLY UNSAT GM	CHOLES- TEROL GM	TRANS FATTY ACIDS	OMEGA-3 GM	POTASS MG	SODIUM MG	VIT. K MCG
Light meat, no skin, 130 g	178	30	0	5,473	1,261	1,625	1,352	61,1	ND	0.143	339.3	68.9	3.12
Meat only, no skin, 284 g	420.3	60.4	0	17.9	4.459	5.51	4.459	178.9	ND	0.454	712.8	224.4	5.68
Meat, with skin, 398 g	1027	69.8	0	80.9	22.7	32.8	17.7	282.6	ND	1.075	811.9	282.6	9.552
Whole, all parts, 905 g	2272	158.2	1.72	176.7	49.6	70.8	38.6	787.4	ND	2.263	1846	642.5	ND
Wings, no skin, 25 g	43	6.4	0	1.7	0.5	ND	ND	18	ND	0	ND	19	ND

*Chicken Liver has .138 omega-6.
†Chicken Gizzard has a trace of omega-6.

TURKEY*	CALORIES K-CAL	PROTEIN GM	CARB GM	TOT. FAT GM	SAT FAT GM	MONO UNSAT GM	POLY UNSAT GM	CHOLES-TEROL GM	TRANS FATTY ACIDS	OMEGA-3 GM	POTASS MG	SODIUM MG	VIT. K MCG
Weights vary. All meat is raw.													
Ground, 114 g**	169.9	19.9	0	9.416	2.565	3.534	2.28	90.1	0.312	0.125	265.6	107.2	0.684
Giblets, 244g	314.8	47.2	5.1	10.2	3.074	2.22	2.513	688.1	ND	0.024	771	212.3	ND
Gizzard, 28 g	121.8	18.9	0	4.534	1.299	1.572	0.769	195	0	0.028	318.8	71.3	0
Breast, w/skin 1132 g	1777	247.8	0	79.5	21.6	30.1	18.8	735.8	ND	1.245	3113	667.9	ND
Dark meat, w/skin, 1176 g	1882	222.5	0	103.5	30.3	35.3	26.8	846.7	0	1.882	3069	835	0
Dark meat, no skin, 1017 g	1271	204.1	0	44.5	14.9	10.1	13.3	701.7	0	0.915	2909	783.1	0
Whole, all parts, 5554 g	8720	1131	4.443	431.5	122.2	153.3	107.2	4332	ND	7.776	14940	3721	ND
ROASTER/FRYER													
Breast, w/skin, 433 g	541.2	102.9	0	11.5	3.118	4.33	2.728	303.1	ND	0.26	1195	207.8	0
Breast, no skin, 390 g	432.9	95.9	0	2.535	0.819	0.429	0.663	241.8	0.051	0.078	1143	191.1	ND
Dark meat, w/skin, 532 g	686.3	106.7	0	25.5	7.608	8.246	6.756	462.8	ND	0.479	1234	351.1	ND

(continued)

(continued)

TURKEY*	CALORIES K-CAL	PROTEIN GM	CARB. GM	TOT. FAT GM	SAT FAT GM	MONO UNSAT GM	POLY UNSAT GM	CHOLES-TEROL GM	TRANS FATTY ACIDS	OMEGA-3 GM	POTASS MG	SODIUM MG	VIT. K MCG
Dark meat, no skin, 479 g	531.7	98	0	12.8	4.311	2.922	3.832	388	ND	0.239	1169	330.5	ND
Leg, w/skin, 349 g	411.8	70.3	0	12.5	3.839	3.769	3.385	303.6	ND	0.244	858.5	240.8	ND
Leg, no skin, 329 g	355.3	67	0	71.797	2.632	1.777	2.336	276.4	ND	0.164	835.7	233.6	ND
Light meat, w/skin 561 g	746.1	129.5	0	21.4	5.722	8.527	4.993	426.4	ND	0.281	1419	280.5	ND
Light meat, no skin, 481 g	519.8	116.3	0	2.357	0.77	0.433	0.625	317.5	ND	0.048	1328	250.1	ND
Meat only, 990 g	1089	221	0	15.6	5.247	3.465	4.653	722.7	ND	0.297	2574	603.9	ND
Meat, w/skin, 1093 g	1465	244.5	0	46.5	13.2	16.6	11.6	885.3	ND	0.874	2656	633.9	ND
Whole, all parts, 1509 g	3205	533.8	1.205	102.4	29.4	35.4	25.8	2217	ND	1.687	5829	1470	ND
Wing, w/skin, 128 g	203.5	26.7	0	9.882	2.637	3.955	2.304	125.4	ND	0.166	227.8	71.7	ND
Wing, no skin, 90 g	95.4	20.2	0	1.008	0.324	0.18	0.27	72.9	ND	0.027	180.9	58.5	ND

				7.825	2.136	3.077	1.597	37.7	0.094	0.098	76.4	35.8	0
YOUNG HEN													
Breast, w/skin, 874 g	1460	189	0	72.5	19.7	27.9	17	541.9	ND	1.136	2325	480.7	ND
Dark meat, w/skin, 953 g	1639	177.7	0	97.7	28.5	33.6	25.2	619.5	ND	1.715	2468	6385	ND
Dark meat, no skin, 812 g	1056	163	0	39.6	13.3	9.013	11.9	503.4	ND	0.893	2330	600.9	ND
Leg, w/skin, 656 g	990.6	127.7	0	49.2	15	15	13.4	413.3	ND	0.984	1791	459.2	ND
Light meat, w/skin, 1099 g	1813	236.4	0	89	24.1	34.1	21	681.4	ND	1.539	2934	604.5	ND
Light meat, no skin, 919 g	1066	217.3	0	15.3	4.871	2.665	4.044	533	ND	0.459	2748	551.4	ND
Whole, all parts, 4457 g	7399	8981	4.903	391.3	111	139.5	97.2	3254	ND	6.685	11900	2888	ND
Wing, w/skin, 224 g	470.4	44.6	0	31.1	8.243	12.6	7.213	145.6	ND	0.493	533.1	114.2	ND
YOUNG TOM													
Breast, w/skin, 1789 g	2701	392.9	0	113.4	30.9	42.2	26.8	1199	ND	1.789	5045	1127	ND
Dark meat, w/skin, 1758 g	2672	334.9	0	138.7	40.8	46.8	36.2	1354	ND	2.637	4659	1318	ND
Dark meat, no skin, 1552 g	1884	307	0	63	21.1	14.2	18.8	1149	ND	1.379	4443	1226	ND
Leg, w/skin, 1234 g	1740	241.1	0	78.2	23.9	23.9	21.2	937.8	ND	1.481	3394	950.2	ND

(continued)

(continued)

TURKEY*	CALORIES K-CAL	PROTEIN GM	CARB. GM	TOT. FAT GM	SAT FAT GM	MONO UNSAT GM	POLY UNSAT GM	CHOLES- TEROL GM	TRANS FATTY ACIDS	OMEGA-3 GM	POTASS MG	SODIUM MG	VIT. K MCG
Light meat, no skin, 1771 g	2019	4149	0	27.8	8.55	4.959	7.438	1098	ND	0.708	5561	1187	ND
Light meat, w/skin, 2137 g	3334	462.2	0	150.4	40.8	57.3	35.5	1432	ND	2.351	5919	1346	ND
Meat only, no skin, 3302 g	3863	717.2	0	89.2	29.4	18.8	25.8	2245	ND	1.981	9972	2410	ND
Whole, all parts, 8399 g	12766	1713	6.719	606	172	214	150	6803	ND	10.1	23013	5879	ND
Wing, w/skin, 348 g	654.2	71.2	0	39	10.4	15.7	9.083	250.6	ND	0.626	870	208.8	ND

*USDA does not always supply complete data. Areas where data may be missing are usually carbohydrates, trans-fatty acids. If these subject columns are missing, it means no data (ND) was supplied or that the amount is at unreadable levels. For instance, a whole turkey can be as high as 4443 g carbohydrates. For smaller pieces from those birds, therefore, the USDA readings were so small they don't include them in their ratings. In our recipes we use the word "trace" to demonstrate the possibility of some sodium in ingredients.

**Ground turkey has .684 mcg vitamin K. No data is available for other turkey parts.

PORK, HOG	CALORIES K-CAL	PROTEIN GM	CARB. GM	TOT. FAT GM	SAT. FAT GM	MONO UNSAT GM	POLY UNSAT GM	CHOLES-TEROL GM	TRANS FATTY ACIDS	OMEGA-3 GM	OMEGA-6 GM	POTASS MG	SODIUM MG
All pork rated at 1 ounce, raw, unless otherwise noted													
Back Rib, lean & fat	79.9	4.57	0	6.685	2.475	3.019	0.556	23	ND	0.023	0	66.1	21.3
Belly, Fresh	146.9	2.648	0	15	5.48	7.002	1.602	20.4	ND	0.136	0	52.4	9.072
Center Rib Chop or Roast, lean & fat, 101 g	213.1	20.1	0	14.2	4.909	6.312	1.515	60.6	ND	0.101	0	387.8	42.4
Center Loin/Chop or Roast, lean, 98 g	137.2	21.6	0	4.939	1.705	2.234	0.529	61.7	ND	0.02	0	354.8	64.7
Center Loin/Chop or Roast, lean & fat, 112 g	224	22.5	0	14.2	4.928	6.328	1.523	75	ND	0.101	0	371.8	67.2
Chitterlings	51.5	2.166	0	4.709	2.16	1.522	0.274	43.7	0	0.016	0.013	5.103	6.804
Composite (leg/shoulder/sparerib), lean & fat	61.2	5.372	0	4.238	1.497	1.88	0.439	19	ND	0.026	0	95	15.6
Composite (loin & shoulder blade), lean & fat	56.7	5.537	0	3.657	1.267	1.63	0.388	18.1	ND	L.026	0	99.8	14.5

(continued)

(continued)

PORK, HOG	CALORIES K-CAL	PROTEIN GM	CARB. GM	TOT. FAT GM	SAT FAT GM	MONO UNSAT GM	POLY UNSAT GM	CHOLES-TEROL GM	TRANS FATTY ACIDS	OMEGA-3 GM	OMEGA-6 GM	POTASS MG	SODIUM MG
Composite (loin & shoulder blade), lean only	40.8	6.019	0	1.667	0.576	0.754	0.179	17	ND	0.006	0	108.9	15.3
Ham, Cured, Center Slice, lean*	55.3	7.881	0.085	2.359	0.788	1.083	0.275	19.8	ND	0.026	0	144.6	764
Heart	33.5	4.896	0.377	1.236	0.329	0.289	0.318	37.1	ND	0.023	0	83.3	15.9
Jowl	185.7	1.809	0	19.7	7.161	9.324	2.299	25.5	ND	0.164	0	42	7.088
Loin, Blade, Chop, lean & fat, 110 g	313.5	17.4	0	26.5	9.207	11.8	2.838	79.2	ND	0.198	0	309.1	59.4
Loin, Blade/Roast or Chop, lean only, 82 g	128.7	15.8	0	6.765	2.337	3.059	0.73	52.5	ND	0.025	0	278.8	54.9
Loin, Center rib Chop or Roast, lean w/bone, 86 g	128.1	19	0	5.169	1.78	2.331	0.559	47.3	ND	0.017	0	362.1	38.7
Loin, Center Rib Chop or Roast lean & fat w/bone, 98 g	204	19.8	0	13.3	4.616	5.939	1.421	58.8	ND	0.088	0	376.3	41.2
Loin, Center rib Chop or Roast, lean, boneless, 88 g	133.8	19.2	0	5.702	1.971	2.578	0.616	48.4	ND	0.026	0	370.5	39.6

Loin, Country-Style Rib, lean & fat	68.3	4.817	0	5.304	1.84	2.364	0.567	19.6	ND	0.037	0	85.6	16.4
Loin, Country-Style Rib, lean	44.5	5.463	0	2.339	0.802	1.052	0.241	18.1	ND	0.009	0	96.4	19
Shoulder, Arm, Picnic, lean & fat	71.7	4.732	0	5.724	1.985	2.543	0.612	20.1	ND	0.043	0	82.5	19.3
Shoulder, Arm, Picnic, lean	39.7	5.599	0	1.746	0.604	0.788	0.187	18.4	ND	0.009	0	96.7	23.2
Sirloin Chop or Roast, lean & fat, boneless, 104 g	150.8	21.4	0	6.562	2.267	2.943	0.707	66.6	ND	0.042	0	375.4	52
Sirloin Chop or Roast, lean, boneless, 101 g	129.3	21.3	0	4.262	1.475	1.929	0.454	63.6	ND	0.02	0	373.3	51.5
Sirloin Chop or Roast, lean, w/bone, 94 g	133.5	19.8	0	5.414	1.871	2.444	0.583	59.2	ND	0.019	0	347.8	47.9
Sirloin Chop or Roast, lean & fat, w/bone, 107 g	219.4	20.5	0	14.6	5.05	6.495	1.562	71.7	ND	0.107	0	342.4	57.8
Tenderloin, lean & fat	38.6	5.823	0	1.534	0.53	0.686	0.164	18.7	ND	0.009	0	101.8	13.9
Tenderloin, lean	34	5.951	0	0.967	0.335	0.437	0.105	18.4	ND	0.003	0	103.8	14.2
Top loin Chop, lean & fat, boneless	40.8	6.053	0	1.67	0.569	0.656	0.091	16.2	0.019	0.002	0.008	128.7	50.5

(continued)

(continued)

PORK, HOG	CALORIES K-CAL	PROTEIN GM	CARB. GM	TOT. FAT GM	SAT FAT GM	MONO UNSAT GM	POLY UNSAT GM	CHOLES-TEROL GM	TRANS FATTY ACIDS	OMEGA-3 GM	OMEGA-6 GM	POTASS MG	SODIUM MG
Top Loin Chop, lean, boneless	33.2	6.356	0	0.652	0.201	0.254	0.09	15.6	0	0.003	0.074	134.9	52.2
Top Loin roast, lean & fat, boneless	54.1	5.738	0	3.291	1.14	1.469	0.352	16.7	ND	0.023	0	110.6	12.2
Top Loin roast, lean, boneless	40	6.18	0	1.497	0.516	0.678	0.162	15.6	ND	0.006	0	119.4	12.8
Ground Pork, raw	74.6	4.785	0	6.007	2.231	2.676	0.541	20.4	ND	0.02	0	81.4	15.9

All meat rated at 1 ounce, raw, unless otherwise noted

LAMB/AUSTRALIAN	CALORIES K-CAL	PROTEIN GM	TOT. FAT GM	SAT FAT GM	MONO UNSAT GM	POLY UNSAT GM	CHOLES-TEROL GM	TRANS FATTY ACIDS	OMEGA-3 GM	POTASS MG	SODIUM MG
Foreshank, lean & fat	55.3	5.344	3.595	1.696	1.501	0.169	19	ND	0.045	76.5	27.2
Leg, center slice w/bone, lean & fat	55.3	5.435	3.561	1.648	1.459	0.168	18.4	ND	0.046	90.2	17.3
Leg shank half, lean only	37.7	5.798	1.446	0.569	0.612	0.07	18.1	ND	0.019	93.3	23
Leg, sirloin chops, boneless, lean & fat	59	5.197	4.077	1.956	1.666	0.184	18.7	ND	0.051	87.3	16.7
Leg, sirloin chops, boneless, lean only	37.4	5.792	1.392	0.552	0.577	0.076	18.1	ND	0.02	97	18.1
Leg, sirloin half, boneless, lean & fat	72	4.89	5.67	2.765	2.297	0.233	18.7	ND	0.068	79.1	19.8
Leg, whole (shank & sirloin), lean & fat	61	5.171	4.306	2.066	1.765	0.186	18.7	ND	0.052	83.6	20.7
Leg, whole (shank & sirloin), lean only	38.3	5.8	1.483	0.59	0.621	0.071	18.1	ND	0.02	93.3	23
Loin, separable lean and fat	57.6	5.477	3.793	1.815	1.524	0.153	18.7	ND	0.045	85.6	19.8
Loin, separable lean only	41.4	5.594	1.769	0.758	0.698	0.074	18.1	ND	0.022	92.7	21.3
Shoulder, arm, separable, lean & fat	69.9	4.837	5.355	2.587	2.182	0.22	18.4	ND	0.065	79.7	20.4

(continued)

(continued)

LAMB/AUSTRALIAN	CALORIES K-CAL	PROTEIN GM	TOT. FAT GM	SAT FAT GM	MONO UNSAT GM	POLY UNSAT GM	CHOLES-TEROL GM	TRANS FATTY ACIDS	OMEGA-3 GM	POTASS MG	SODIUM MG
Shoulder, arm, separable, lean only	38.8	5.636	1.647	0.662	0.687	0.077	17.6	ND	0.022	92.1	23.5
Shoulder, blade, separable, lean & fat	74.3	4.672	6.033	2.92	2.432	0.245	19	ND	0.069	73.7	22.1
Shoulder, shoulder, blade, separable, lean only	46.5	5.415	2.577	1.101	1.024	0.101	18.1	ND	0.029	84.5	25.5
LAMB/U.S. DOMESTIC CHOICE											
Composite, lean, 1/4" trim	38	5.752	1.488	0.533	0.598	0.136	18.4	ND	0.02	79.4	18.7
Foreshank, lean, 1/4" trim	34	5.976	0.933	0.335	0.374	0.085	19.6	ND	0.011	67.2	22.4
Foreshank, lean & fat, 1/4" trim	57	5.361	3.793	1.653	1.556	0.301	20.4	ND	0.068	60.7	20.4
Leg, Shank, half, lean, 1/4" trim	35.4	5.817	1.188	0.425	0.479	0.108	18.1	ND	0.017	82.2	17.3
Leg, Shank, half, lean & fat, 1/4" trim	57	5.267	3.824	1.644	1.568	0.306	19	ND	0.068	74	16.2
Leg, Sirloin half, lean & fat, 1/4" trim	77.1	4.802	6.268	2.758	2.574	0.49	20.4	ND	0.113	65.5	15.9
Leg, Sirloin half, lean, 1/4" trim	38	5.826	1.44	0.516	0.578	0.13	18.7	ND	0.02	80.5	18.1

Leg, whole, lean, ¼" trim	36.3	5.829	0.1279	0.456	0.513	0.116	18.1	ND	0.017	81.9	17.6
Leg, whole, lean & fat, ¼" trim	65.2	5.077	4.839	2.106	1.995	0.383	19.6	ND	0.085	70.6	15.9
Loin, lean, ¼" trim	40.5	5.819	1.684	0.604	0.678	0.153	18.7	ND	0.023	78.2	19.3
Loin, lean & fat, ¼" trim	87.9	4.627	7.55	3.334	3.101	0.59	21	ND	0.136	60.7	15.9
Rib, lean, ¼" trim	47.9	5.664	2.617	0.936	1.052	0.238	18.7	ND	0.034	75.1	20.4
Rib, lean, & fat, ¼" trim	105.5	4.116	9.75	4.298	4.006	0.763	21.5	ND	0.176	53.9	15.9
Shoulder, arm, lean, ¼" trim	37.4	5.667	1.474	0.527	0.593	0.136	18.1	ND	0.02	81.4	19.6
Shoulder, arm, lean & fat, ¼" trim	73.7	4.76	5.925	2.594	2.432	0.468	20.1	ND	0.105	67.5	17
Shoulder, blade, lean, ¼" trim	42.8	5.469	2.163	0.774	0.87	0.198	19	ND	0.028	76	19.8
Shoulder, blade, lean & fat, ¼" trim	73.4	4.715	5.914	2.532	2.421	0.476	20.4	ND	0.102	64.9	17.6
Ground, raw	79.9	4.695	6.637	2.889	2.722	0.524	20.7	ND	0.119	62.9	16.7

FISH/SHELLFISH*,† (ALL SERVINGS ARE 3 OUNCES)	CALORIES K-CAL	PROTEIN GM	CARB GM	FAT GM	SAT. FAT GM	MONO UNSAT FAT GM	POLY UNSAT FAT GM	CHOLES- TEROL MG	TRANS FATTY ACIDS GM	OMEGA-3 GM	POTASSIUM MG	SODIUM MG	VITAMIN K MCG
Crab, Blue	74	15.4	0.034	0.918	0.189	0.163	0.329	66.3	ND	0.272	279.6	249.1	ND
Crab, King	71.4	15.5	0	0.51	0.077	0.068	0.111	35.7	ND	0	173.4	710.6	ND
Crab, Dungeness	73.1	14.8	0.629	0.825	0.112	0.142	0.269	50.2	ND	0.269	300.9	250.8	ND
Catfish, Wild Channel	80.8	13.9	0	2.397	0.614	0.717	0.735	49.3	ND	0.455	304.3	36.5	ND
Catfish, Farmed	114.8	13.2	0	5.452	1.503	3.048	1.333	40	ND	0.391	254.2	45.1	0.085
Clam	62.9	10.9	2.184	0.825	0.08	0.068	0.24	28.9	ND	0.168	266.9	47.6	0.17
Cod, Pacific	69.7	15.2	0	0.535	0.069	0.07	0.207	31.5	ND	0.188	342.6	60.4	0.085
Cod, Ling	72.2	15	0	0.901	0.167	0.298	0.255	44.2	ND	0	371.5	50.2	ND
Cod, Atlantic	69.7	15.1	0	0.57	0.111	0.08	0.196	36.5	ND	0.166	351.1	45.9	0.085
Cod, Alaskan, Wild	67.2	15.2	0	0.68	ND	ND	ND	ND	ND	0	368.1	50.2	ND
Flounder, Flatfish, Sole	77.3	16	0	1.012	0.241	0.198	0.28	40.8	ND	0.215	306.9	68.8	0.085
Flounder, Dab, Fluke	76.4	15.8	0	1	0.238	0.196	0.276	40.3	ND	0	303.2	68	ND
Haddock	74	16.1	0	0.612	0.111	0.1	0.205	48.5	ND	0.175	264.4	57.8	0.085

Halibut, Atlantic	93.5	17.7	0	1.947	0.276	0.638	0.621	27.2	ND	0.444	382.5	45.9	0.085
Halibut, Greenland	158.1	12.2	0	11.8	2.056	7.121	1.162	39.1	ND	0.893	227.8	68	0.085
Halibut, Sole, Turbot, boneless	76.4	15.8	0	1	0.238	0.196	0.276	40.3	ND	0	303.2	68	ND
Lobster, Northern	76.5	16	0.425	0.765	0.153	0.221	0.128	80.8	ND	0	233.8	251.6	0.085
Lobster, Spiny	95.2	17.5	2.066	1.284	0.2	0.234	0.502	59.5	ND	0.353	153	150.4	ND
Mackerel, Atlantic	174.2	15.8	0	11.8	2.768	4.638	2.848	59.5	ND	2.27	266.9	76.5	4.25
Mackerel, Pacific, Jack	134.3	17.1	0	6.707	1.91	2.235	1.649	40	ND	1.372	345.1	73.1	0.085
Mackerel, King	89.2	17.2	0	1.7	0.309	0.649	0.391	45.1	ND	0.281	369.8	134.3	ND
Mahimahi, Dolphinfish	137.8	15.5	0	7.955	2.948	2.172	0.955	42	ND	0	320	54.6	ND
Ocean Perch, Atantic	79.9	15.8	0	1.386	0.207	0.531	0.363	35.7	ND	0.315	232.1	63.8	0.085
Ocean Perch, Pacific	77.3	16.5	0	0.782	0.157	0.129	0.313	76.5	ND	0.249	228.7	52.7	0.085
Orange Roughy	58.7	12.5	0	0.595	0.015	0.407	0.011	17	ND	0.002	255	53.6	ND
Oyster, Pacific	68.8	8.033	4.207	1.955	0.433	0.304	0.76	42.5	ND	0.629	142.8	90.1	ND
Oyster, Eastern farmed	50.2	4.437	4.701	0.132	0.377	0.129	0.502	21.2	ND	0.37	105.4	151.3	ND

(continued)

FISH/SHELLFISH*,†	CALORIES K-CAL	PROTEIN GM	CARB. GM	FAT GM	SAT. FAT GM	MONO UNSAT FAT GM	POLY UNSAT FAT GM	CHOLES-TEROL MG	TRANS FATTY ACIDS GM	OMEGA-3 GM	POTASSIUM MG	SODIUM MG	VITAMIN K MCG
Pollock, Atlantic	78.2	16.5	0	0.833	0.115	0.095	0.411	60.4	ND	0.377	302.6	73.1	0.085
Pollock, Walleye	68.8	14.6	0	0.68	0.139	0.106	0.35	60.4	ND	0.329	277.1	84.2	0.085
Rainbow Trout, wild	101.2	17.4	0	2.941	0.614	0.96	1.051	50.2	ND	0.6	408.9	26.4	ND
Rainbow Trout, farmed	117.3	17.7	0	4.59	1.321	1.308	0.1534	50.2	ND	0.838	383.4	29.8	0.085
Rockfish, Pacific	79.9	15.9	0	1.335	0.315	0.281	0.41	29.8	ND	0.338	344.2	51	0.085
Salmon, Atlantic/Coho	124.1	18.4	0	5.041	1.071	1.814	1.693	38.2	ND	1.253	359.6	39.1	0.085
Salmon, Alaska/King (Chinook)	152.2	16.9	0	8.866	2.635	3.739	2.379	42.5	ND	1.991	334.9	40	ND
Salmon, Alaska/Sockeye (Red)	142.8	18.1	0	7.276	1.271	3.506	1.597	52.7	ND	1.108	332.4	40	ND
Salmon, Pink	98.6	16.9	0	2.933	0.474	0.794	1.15	44.2	ND	0.965	274.6	57	0.34
Salmon, Alaska/Chum	102	17.1	0	3.204	0.714	1.31	0.763	62.9	ND	0.629	363.7	42.5	ND
Salmon, farmed (Coho)	136	18.1	0	6.52	1.544	2.831	1.582	43.4	ND	1.089	382.5	40	ND
Scallops	74.8	14.3	2.006	0.646	0.067	0.031	0.222	28.1	ND	0.183	273.7	136.9	0.085

Shrimp	90.1	17.3	0.774	1.471	0.279	0.215	0.569	129.2	ND	0.459	157.2	125.8	0
Swordfish	102.9	16.8	0	3.409	0.932	1.313	0.784	33.2	ND	0.701	244.8	76.5	0.085
Tuna, Yellowfin	91.8	19.9	0	0.808	0.2	0.131	241	38.2	ND	0.207	377.4	31.5	0.085
Tuna, Ahi, Aku, Bonito	90.7	19.6	0	0.798	0.197	0.129	239	37.8	ND	0	373	31.1	ND

* Most seafood contains no fiber, sugars, omega-6, or folic acid (folate).
† ND=No Data. Amounts given are based on USDA SR18, 2005–2006. Nutritional content always varies slightly because of different growing conditons.

DAIRY *††
All milk with vitamin A unless noted. 244–245 g equals 1 cup.

	CALORIES K-CAL	PROTEIN GM	CARB. GM	SUGARS GM	TOT. FAT GM	SAT. FAT GM	MONO UNSAT GM	POLY UNSAT GM	CHOLES-TEROL GM	OMEGA-3 GM	POTASS MG	SODIUM MG	VIT. K MCG
Milk, Whole, 3.25% fat, 244 g	146.4	7.857	11	12.8	7.93	4.551	1.981	0.476	24.4	0.183	348.9	97.6	0.488
Milk, Whole, 3.7% fat, 244 g	156.2	8.003	11.3	ND	8.93	5.558	2.579	0.332	34.2	0.129	368.4	119.6	ND
Milk Lowfat 1%, 1 cup 244 g	102.5	8.223	12.2	12.7	2.367	1.545	0.676	0.085	12.2	0.02	366	107.4	0.244
Milk, Nonfat, 1 cup 245 g	83.3	8.257	12.2	12.5	0.196	0.287	0.115	0.017	4.9	0.002	382.2	102.9	0
Milk, Nonfat, w/o Vit A & D, 1 cup 245 g	85.8	8.355	11.9	ND	0.441	0.287	0.115	0.017	4.9	0.005	406.7	127.4	ND
Milk, Reduced Fat, 2%, 1 cup 244 g	122	8.052	11.4	12.3	4.807	3.067	1.366	0.178	19.5	0.039	366	100	0.488
Milk, Whole, Evap, Canned, Vit A, ½ cup 126 g	168.8	8.581	12.7	ND	9.526	5.785	2.942	0.309	36.5	0.098	381.8	133.6	ND
Milk, Nonfat, Dry, ½ cup 120 g	434.4	43.4	62.4	62.4	0.924	0.599	0.24	0.036	24	0.013	2153	642	0.12
Milk, Nonfat, Dry, 1 tablespoon 19 g	69.5	6.943	9.98	9.98	0.148	0.096	0.038	0.006	3.84	0.002	344.4	102.7	0.019

Milk, Nonfat, Lactose Reduced, 1 cup 245 g	85.5	8.255	11.9	ND	0.441	0.287	0.115	0.017	4.41	0	405.7	126	ND
Milk, 2% fat, Lactose Reduced, 1 cup 244 g	121.2	8.125	11.7	ND	4.685	2.916	1.354	0.173	18.3	0	376.7	121.8	ND
Milk, 1%, Lactose Reduced, 1 cup 246 g	103	8.093	11.8	ND	2.608	1.624	0.753	0.096	9.84	0	384	124.2	ND
Milk, Buttermilk, Low-Fat Cult, 1 cup 245 g	98	8.109	11.7	11.7	2.156	1.343	0.622	0.081	9.8	0.032	370	257.2	0.245
Milk, Buttermilk, Dry, 1 tablespoon 13 g	50.3	4.459	6.37	6.37	0.751	0.468	0.217	0.028	8.97	0.011	207	67.2	0.052
Milk, Buttermilk, Cult, Low-Sodium, 1 cup 240 g	45	9	10	9	4.999	3	ND	ND	25	0	ND	130	ND
Cheese, Swiss, Low Sodium, 1 ounce 28 g	105.3	7.952	0.952	0.367	7.672	4.968	2.032	0.271	25.8	0.098	31.1	3.92	0.672
Cheese, Swiss**, Low Fat, 1 ounce 28 g	50.1	7.952	0.952	0.372	1.428	0.925	0.378	0.05	9.8	0.018	31.1	72.8	0.14
Cheese, Process, Swiss, Low Sodium, 1 ounce 28 g	70.1	5.187	0.441	ND	5.25	3.368	1.48	0.13	17.9	0	45.4	8.61	ND
Cheese, Mozzarella, Low Sodium, 1 ounce 28 g	78.4	7.7	0.866	ND	4.788	3.046	1.358	0.143	15.1	0	26.6	4.48	ND

(continued)

(continued)

DAIRY *,††	CALORIES K-CAL	PROTEIN GM	CARB GM	SUGARS GM	TOT. FAT GM	SAT FAT GM	MONO UNSAT GM	POLY UNSAT GM	CHOLES-TEROL GM	OMEGA-3 GM	POTASS MG	SODIUM MG	VIT. K MCG
Cheese, Process Mozzarella, Low Sodium, 1 slice 21 g	58.8	5.775	0.651	ND	3.591	2.285	1.018	0.107	11.3	0	19.9	5.46	ND
Cheese, Bocconcino Mozzarella 3 balls 100g	70	5	0	0	2	ND	ND	ND	10	ND	ND	20	ND
Cheese, Ricotta, Part Skim, 1 cup 246 g	339.5	28	12.6	0.763	19.5	12.1	5.692	0.64	76.3	0.172	307.5	307.5	1.722
Cheese, Ricotta, Whole Milk, 1 cup 246 g	428	27.7	7.478	0.664	31.9	20.4	8.922	0.947	125.5	0.276	258.3	206.6	2.706
Cheese, Cottage, Low Sodium, 1 cup 246 g	231.8	28.1	6.075	ND	10.1	6.412	2.88	0.315	33.8	0	189	29.2	ND
Cheese, Muenster, Low Sodium, 1 ounce 28 g	103	6.552	0.308	ND	8.4	5.351	2.439	0.185	26.9	0	37.5	5.32	ND
Cheese, Parmesan, Low Sodium, 1 tablespoon 5 g	22.8	2.08	0.185	ND	1.5	0.953	0.436	0.033	3.95	0	5.35	3.15	ND
Cheese, Cheddar or Colby, Low Sodium, 1 ounce 28 g	1114	6.818	0.535	0.137	9.134	5.815	2.573	0.272	28	0.105	31.4	5.88	0.756

Food													
Cream, Half-and-Half, 1 tablespoon 30 g	39	0.888	1.29	0.048	3.45	2.147	0.996	0.128	11.1	0.05	39	12.3	0.39
Cream, Half-and-Half, Reduced Fat, 30g‡	40.5	0.882	1.278	0.048	3.6	2.241	1.04	0.134	11.7	0.053	38.7	121.3	0.18
Cream, Half-and-Half, Fat Free, 1 tablespoon 30 g	17.7	0.78	2.7	1.5	0.42	0.252	0.115	0.016	1.5	0.006	61.8	43.2	0.06
Cream, Sour, Cultured, 1 tablespoon 24 g	51.4	0.758	1.025	0.038	5.03	3.131	1.453	0.187	10.6	0.073	34.6	12.7	0.24
Cream, Sour, Reduced-Fat, 2 tablespoons 31 g	47.1	1.395	2.015	1.984	3.72	2.356	ND	ND	15.5	0	65.1	18.3	ND
Cream, Sour, Fat Free, 2 tablespoons 32 g	29.1	1.504	4.832	2.304	0.416	0.256	ND	ND	2.88	0	70.1	23	ND
Yogurt, Plain, Lowfat, 1 container† 227 g	143.7	11.9	16	ND	3.518	2.27	0.967	0.1	13.8	0	530.7	159.4	ND
Yogurt, Plain, Nonfat, 1 container† 227 g	126.6	13	17.4	ND	0.409	0.263	0.111	0.011	4.086	0	578.6	173.7	ND
Yogurt, plain, Whole Milk, 1 container† 227 g	139.4	7.877	10.6	ND	7.378	4.758	2.027	0.209	28.8	0	350.9	105.3	ND
Egg, White, 1 large 33 g	17.2	3.598	0.241	0.234	0.056	0	0	0	0	0	53.8	54.8	0

(continued)

(continued)

DAIRY *,††	CALORIES K-CAL	PROTEIN GM	CARB. GM	SUGARS GM	TOT. FAT GM	SAT FAT GM	MONO UNSAT GM	POLY UNSAT GM	CHOLES- TEROL GM	OMEGA-3 GM	POTASS MG	SODIUM MG	VIT. K MCG
Egg, Whole, 1 large 50 g	73.5	6.29	0.385	0.385	4.97	1.549	1.905	0.682	211.5	0.037	67	63	0.15
Egg, Yolk, 1 large 17 g	54.7	2.696	0.61	0.095	4.512	1.624	1.995	0.715	209.8	0.039	18.5	8.16	0.119
Egg, Duck, 1 whole 70 g	129.5	8.967	1.015	0.651	9.639	2.577	4.568	0.856	618.8	0.071	155.4	102.2	0.28

*Eggs are not considered a dairy product
**Not Low Sodium
† Approximately 8 ounces
†† ND=No Data
‡ Only the Reduced Fat Sour Cream has fiber: .031 g

FRUIT	CALORIES K CAL	PROTEIN GM	CARB. GM	FIBER GM	SUGARS GM	TOTAL FAT GM	SAT FAT GM	MONO UNS GM	POLY UN GM	OMEGA-3 FA GM	POTASSIUM GM	SODIUM MG	VIT K MG
Apple, 1 med, 154 g	71.8	0.359	19.1	3.312	14.3	0.235	0.039	0.01	0.07	0.012	147.7	1.38	3.036
Avocado, 1 California, w/o seed, 173 g	288.9	3.291	14.9	11.8	0.519	26.7	3.678	17	3.142	0.408	897.1	13.8	36.3
Avocado, 1 Florida, w/o seed, 304 g	364.8	6.779	23.8	17	7.357	30.6	5.958	16.8	5.095	0.292	1067	6.08	ND
Banana, 1 peeled, 118 g	105	1.286	27	3.068	14.4	0.389	0.132	0.038	0.086	0.032	422.4	1.18	0.59
Banana, Plantain, 1 Peeled, 179 g	218.4	2.327	57.1	4.117	26.8	0.662	0.256	0.057	0.124	0.045	893.2	7.16	1.253
Blackberries, 1 cup, 144 g	61.9	2.002	13.8	7.632	7.027	0.706	0.02	0.068	0.403	0.135	233.3	1.44	28.5
Blackberries, Native, 1 ounce, 28 g	15.6	0.142	3.089	ND	ND	0.283	ND	ND	ND	0	ND	0.283	ND
Blueberries, 1 cup, 145 g	82.7	1.073	21	3.48	14.4	0.479	0.041	0.068	0.212	0.084	111.7	1.45	28
Boysenberries, 1 cup, 144 g	74.9	1.037	18.4	7.2	ND	0.562	0.014	0.058	0.317	0	282.2	0	ND
Cantaloupe, 1 cup diced, 552 g	53	1.31	12.7	1.404	12.3	0.296	0.8	0.005	0.126	0.72	416.5	25	3.9

(continued)

FRUIT	CALORIES K CAL	PROTEIN GM	CARB. GM	FIBER GM	SUGARS GM	TOTAL FAT GM	SAT FAT GM	MONO UNS GM	POLY UN GM	OMEGA-3 FA GM	POTASSIUM GM	SODIUM MG	VIT K MG
Casaba, 1 cup, cubed, 170 g	47.6	1.887	11.2	1.53	9.673	0.17	0.043	0.003	0.066	0.037	309.4	15.3	4.25
Cherimoya, 1, 156 g	115.4	2.574	27.6	3.588	ND	0.967	ND	ND	ND	0	419.6	6.24	ND
Cherries, 1 cup, with pits, 170 g	73.7	1.24	18.7	2.457	15	0.234	0.044	0.055	0.061	0.03	259.7	0	2.457
Coconut meat of 1 fresh, 397 g	1405	13.2	60.5	35.7	24.7	133	117.9	5.657	1.453	0	1413	79.4	0.794
Cranberries, 1 cup whole, 95 g	43.7	0.37	11.6	4.37	3.838	0.123	0.01	0.017	0.052	0.021	80.8	1.9	4.845
Crenshaw melon, 1 cup, 170 g	44.2	1.53	10.5	1.36	ND	0.17	0.085	0.017	0.017	0	357	20.4	ND
Figs, 1 medium fresh, 50 g	37	0.375	9.59	1.45	8.13	0.15	0.03	0.033	0.072	0	116	0.5	2.35
Figs, dried, 1, 8.4 g	20.9	0.277	5.365	0.823	4.025	0.078	0.012	0.013	0.029	0	57.1	0.84	1.31
Grapes, Concord, 1 cup, 92 g	58	0.58	15.8	0.644	ND	0.322	0.105	0.013	0.094	0	175.7	1.84	ND
Grapes, Thompson, Red Flame, 1 cup 160 g	113.6	1.056	28.4	0.96	ND	0.928	0.302	0.037	0.27	0	296	3.2	ND
Grapefruit, California, Arizona, ½ fruit, 123 g	45.5	0.615	11.9	ND	ND	0.123	0.017	0.016	0.03	0.006	180.8	1.23	ND

Food													
Grapefruit, California, Florida, Pink, Red, ½ fruit, 123 g	36.9	0.677	9.225	1.353	ND	0.123	0.017	0.016	0.03	0.006	156.2	0	ND
Guava, Common, 1 cup 165 g	112.2	4.207	23.6	8.91	14.7	1.567	0.449	0.144	0.662	0.185	688	3.3	4.29
Guava, Strawberry, 1 cup, 244 g	124.4	2.001	29	13.2	ND	1464	0.42	0.134	0.617	0	693	7.32	ND
Honeydew, ¼ med, 320 g	115.2	1.728	29.1	2.56	26	0.448	0.122	0.01	0.189	0.106	729.6	57.6	9.28
Kiwi (Chinese gooseberry), 1 peeled, 76 g	46.4	0.866	11.1	2.28	6.832	0.395	0.022	0.036	0.218	0.032	237.1	2.28	30.6
Kumquat, 1 whole, 19 g	13.5	0.357	3.021	1.235	1.778	0.163	0.02	0.029	0.032	0.009	35.3	1.9	0
Lemon, peeled, 58 g	16.8	0.638	5.406	1.624	11.45	0.174	0.023	0.006	0.052	0.015	80	1.16	0
Lemon Zest (peel) 1 tablespoon 6 g	2.82	0.09	0.96	0.636	0.25	0.018	0.002	0.001	0.005	0.003	9.6	0.36	0
Lime, 1 fruit, peeled 67 g	20.1	0.469	7.062	1.876	1.132	0.134	0.015	0.013	0.037	0.013	68.3	1.34	0.402
Loquat, 1, peeled, 16 g	7.52	0.069	1.942	0.272	ND	0.032	0.006	0.001	0.015	0.002	42.6	0.16	ND
Mango, 1 cup 165 g	107.2	0.841	28	2.97	24.4	0.446	0.109	0.167	0.084	0.061	257.4	3.3	6.93
Nectarine, 1, 136 g	59.8	1.442	14.3	2.312	10.7	0.435	0.034	0.12	0.154	0.003	273.4	0	2.992

(continued)

(continued)

FRUIT	CALORIES K CAL	PROTEIN GM	CARB. GM	FIBER GM	SUGARS GM	TOTAL FAT GM	SAT FAT GM	MONO UNS GM	POLY UN GM	OMEGA-3 FA GM	POTASSIUM GM	SODIUM MG	VIT K MG
Orange, 1, all varieties, 131 g	61.6	1.231	15.4	3.144	12.2	0.157	0.02	0.03	0.033	0.009	237.1	0	0
Orange, Navel, Calif, 1, 140 g	68.6	1.274	17.6	3.08	11.9	0.21	0.024	0.042	0.043	0.013	232.4	1.4	0
Orange, Valencia, peeled, 1, 121 g	59.3	1.258	14.4	3.025	ND	0.363	0.042	0.067	0.073	0.019	216.6	0	ND
Orange, Florida, peeled, 1, 185 g	85.1	1.295	21.3	4.44	16.9	0.389	0.046	0.072	0.078	0.02	312.6	0	0
Papaya, 1, peeled, cubed, 304 g	118.6	1.854	29.8	5.472	17.9	0.426	0.131	0.116	0.094	0.076	781.3	9.12	7.904
Passion Fruit/Granadilla, 1 peeled, 236 g	228.9	5.192	55.2	24.5	26.4	1.652	0.139	0.203	0.97	0.002	821.3	66.1	1.652
Peach, 1, peeled 98 g	38.2	0.892	9.349	1.47	8.222	0.245	0.019	0.066	0.084	0.002	186.2	0	2548
Pear, 1, 166 g	96.3	0.631	25.7	5.146	16.3	0.199	0.01	0.043	0.048	0	1978.5	1.66	7.47
Pear, Asian, 122 g	51.2	0.61	13	4.392	8.601	0.281	0.015	0.06	0.067	0.001	147.6	0	5.49
Persimmon, Japanese, peeled, 1, 168 g	117.6	0.974	31.2	6.048	21.1	0.319	0.034	0.062	0.072	0.007	279.5	1.68	4.368

Persimmon, Native, 1, 25 g	31.8	0.2	8.375	ND	ND	0.1	ND	ND	ND	0	77.5	0.25	ND
Pineapple, 1 cup, diced, 472 g	74.4	0.83	12.7	1.404	12.3	0.296	0.8	0.05	0.126	0.072	416.5	25	3.9
Plum, 1, 66 g	30.4	0.462	7.537	0.924	6.547	0.185	0.011	0.088	0.029	0	103.6	0	4.224
Pomegranate, 1, peeled, 154 g	104.7	1.463	26.4	0.924	25.5	0.462	0.059	0.071	0.097	0	398.9	4.62	7.084
Prickly Pear, 1, peeled, 103 g	42.2	0.752	9.857	3.708	ND	0.525	0.069	0.077	0.219	0.024	226.6	5.15	ND
Quince, 1, peeled, 92 g	52.4	0.368	14.1	1.748	ND	0.092	0.009	0.033	0.046	0	181.2	3.68	ND
Raspberries, 1 cup, 123 g	64	1.476	14.7	7.995	5.437	0.799	0.023	0.079	0.461	0.155	185.7	1.23	9.594
Strawberries, 1 berry, 12 g	3.84	0.08	0.922	0.24	0.559	0.036	0.002	0.005	0.019	0.008	18.4	0.12	0.264
Strawberries, frozen, package 567 g	198.4	2.438	51.8	11.9	25.9	0.624	0.034	0.085	0.306	0.13	839.2	11.3	12.5
Tamarind, 1 tablespoon pulp	17.9	0.21	4.688	0.383	4.305	0.45	0.2	0.14	0.004	0	47.1	2.1	0.21
Tangerine, Mandarin 1, peeled, 84 g	44.5	0.68	11.2	1.512	8.887	0.26	0.033	0.05	0.055	0.015	139.4	1.68	0
Tangelo, 1, 95 g	44.6	0.893	11.2	2.28	ND	0.114	0.014	0.022	0.024	0	171.9	0	ND
Tomatillo, 1, 34 g	10.9	0.326	1.986	0.646	1.336	0.347	0.047	0.053	0.142	0.005	91.1	0.34	3.332

(continued)

(continued)

FRUIT	CALORIES K CAL	PROTEIN GM	CARB. GM	FIBER GM	SUGARS GM	TOTAL FAT GM	SAT FAT GM	MONO UNS GM	POLY UN GM	OMEGA-3 FA GM	POTASSIUM GM	SODIUM MG	VIT K MG
Tomato, 1, 2 to 3.5" diameter, 123 g	22.1	1.082	4.822	1.476	3.235	0.246	0.057	0.063	0.166	0.004	291.5	6.15	9.717
Tomato, Cherry, 10, 170 g	35.7	1.445	7.888	1.87	ND	0.561	0.077	0.085	0.23	0.009	377.4	15.3	ND
Watermelon, 1/16th wedge, 286 g	85.8	1.745	21.6	1.144	17.7	0.429	0.046	0.106	0.143	0	320.3	2.86	0.286

VEGETABLES*	CALORIES	PROTEIN GM.	CARB. GM.	FIBER GM.	SUGARS GM.	TOT. FAT GM.	SAT FAT GM.	MONO UNSAT MG.	POLY UNSAT FAT MG.	OMEGA-3 MG.	POTAS SIUM MG.	SODIUM MG.	VIT. K MG.
Artichokes, 1	60.2	4.186	13.5	6.912	2.56	0.192	0.045	0.006	0.081	0.022	473.6	120.3	17.9
Asparagus, 5 spears	3.2	0.352	0.621	0.336	0.301	0.019	0.007	0.001	0.014	0.002	32.3	0.32	6.656
Beets, 1 med. raw	35.3	1.32	7.839	2.296	5.543	0.139	0.022	0.027	0.05	0.004	266.5	64	0.164
Bell Pepper, Red, 1	30.9	1.178	7.176	2.38	4.998	0.357	0.07	8	0.186	0.067	251.1	2.38	5.831
Bell Pepper, Green, 1	23.8	1.023	5.522	2.023	2.856	0.202	0.069	0.01	0.074	0.01	208.3	3.57	8.806
Radish, 1, ¾" to 1" diameter	0.72	0.031	0.153	0.072	0.095	0.005	0.001	0.001	0.002	0.001	10.5	1.755	0.058
Bok Choy, 1 ounce, trimmed	4	0.4	0.6	0.3	ND	0.1	0	ND	ND	0	ND	19	ND
Broccoli, 1 stalk	31.9	3.397	5.974	ND	ND	0.399	0.062	0.027	0.19	0.147	370.5	30.8	ND
Brussels Sprouts, 5	40.8	3.211	8.502	3.61	2.09	0.285	0.059	0.022	0.145	0.094	369.5	23.8	168.1
Burdock, 1 root	112.3	2.387	27.1	5.148	4.524	0.234	0.039	0.058	0.092	0.003	480.5	7.8	2.496
Cabbage, Green, 1 cup, shredded head	16.8	1.008	3.906	1.61	2.506	0.084	0.011	0.006	0.042	0.024	172.2	12.6	42
Cabbage, Red, 1 cup, shredded head	21.7	1.001	5.159	1.47	2.737	0.112	0.024	0.013	0.087	0.047	170.1	18.9	26.7

(continued)

(continued)

VEGETABLES*	CALORIES	PROTEIN GM.	CARB. GM.	FIBER GM.	SUGARS GM.	TOT. FAT GM.	SAT FAT GM.	MONO UNSAT MG.	POLY UNSAT FAT MG.	OMEGA-3 MG.	POTAS SIUM	SODIUM MG.	VIT. K MG.
Cabbage, Savoy, 1 cup, shredded	18.9	1.4	4.27	2.17	1.589	0.07	0.009	0.005	0.034	0.018	16.1	19.6	48.2
Cabbage, Napa, Chinese, 1 cup, shredded	9.88	1.14	1.657	0.76	0	0.152	0.2	0.11	0.73	0	191.5	49.4	0
Carrot, 1	25	0.567	5.844	1.708	2.769	0.146	0.023	0.009	0.071	0.001	195.2	42.1	8.052
Cauliflower, ¼ head	35.9	2.846	7.619	3.594	3.45	0.144	0.046	0.02	0.142	0.109	435.6	43.1	23
Celery, 1 med. rib 7" to 8" long	5.6	0.276	1.188	0.64	0.732	0.68	0.017	0.013	0.032	0	104	32	11.7
Cilantro, 1 cup, 46 g	11	0.929	1.996	1.293	ND	0.221	0.005	0.103	0.015	0	234.6	24.8	ND
Collards, 1 cup, chopped, 36 g	10.8	0.882	2.048	1.296	0.166	0.151	0.02	0.011	0.072	0.039	60.8	7.2	183.9
Corn, White, Yellow, 1 ear	77.4	2.898	17.1	2.43	2.898	1.062	0.164	0.312	0.503	0.014	243	13.5	0.27
Cucumber, 1, 201 g	24.1	1.186	4.342	1.407	2.774	0.322	0.026	0.004	0.006	0.004	273.4	4.02	14.5
Daikon Radish, 7"	60.8	2.028	13.9	5.408	8.45	0.338	0.101	0.057	0.152	0.098	767.3	71	1.014

Eggplant, unpeeled, 1¼ lbs 548 g	131.5	5.535	31.2	18.6	12.9	1.041	0.186	0.088	0.416	0.071	1260	11	19.2
Endive, ¼ head	21.8	1.603	4.296	3.976	0.321	0.257	0.062	0.005	0.112	0.017	402.7	28.2	296.3
Fava Beans, in pod, 1 cup	110.9	9.979	22.2	ND	ND	0.92	0.149	0.131	0.431	0.038	418.3	31.5	ND
Fennel, 1 bulb, 234 g	72.5	2.902	17.1	7.254	ND	0.468	ND	ND	ND	0	968.8	121.7	ND
Garlic, 3 cloves	13.4	0.572	2.975	0.189	0.09	0.045	0.008	0.001	0.022	0.002	36.1	1.53	0.126
Ginger, fresh, sliced, ¼ cup 24 g	19.2	0.437	4.265	0.48	0.408	0.18	0.049	0.037	0.037	0.008	99.6	3.12	0.024
Green Beans, also Snap, 10, 4" long	17.1	1.001	3.927	0.99	ND	0.066	0.014	0.003	0.032	0	115	3.3	ND
Horseradish Root, 1 tablespoon fresh	17	0.6	3.9	0.5	ND	0.1	0	0.1	0	0	113	2	ND
Jerusalem Artichoke, 1 cup 150 g	114	3	26.2	2.4	14.4	0.015	0	0.006	0.002	0	643.5	6	0.15
Jicama, 1 small peeled 659 g	250.4	4.745	58.1	32.3	11	0.593	0.138	0.033	0.283	0.092	988.5	26.4	1.977
Kale, 1 cup 67 g	33.4	2.211	6.707	1.34	ND	0.469	0.061	0.035	0.226	0.121	299.5	28.8	547.4
Kohlrabi, peeled, 135 g	36.5	2.295	8.37	4.86	3.51	0.135	0.018	0.009	0.065	0.035	472.5	27	0.135

(continued)

(continued)

VEGETABLES*	CALORIES	PROTEIN GM.	CARB. GM.	FIBER GM.	SUGARS GM.	TOT. FAT GM.	SAT FAT GM.	MONO UNSAT MG.	POLY UNSAT FAT MG.	OMEGA-3 MG.	POTAS SIUM	SODIUM MG.	VIT. K MG.
Leeks, 1, 89 g	54.3	1.335	12.6	1.602	3.471	0.267	0.036	0.004	0.148	0.088	160.2	17.8	41.8
Lettuce, Boston, Bibb, Butter 5" head	21.2	2.201	3.635	1.793	1.532	0.359	0.047	0.013	0.191	0.134	387.9	8.15	166.7
Lettuce, Iceberg, 6" head	75.5	4.851	16	6.468	9.486	0.755	0.097	0.032	0.399	0.28	760	53.9	129.9
Lettuce, Red or Green Leaf, 1 head	49.4	4.11	6.983	2.781	1.483	0.68	ND	ND	ND	0	577.8	77.2	433.5
Lettuce, Romaine, 1 head	106.4	7.7	20.6	13.1	7.449	1.878	0.244	0.075	1.002	0.707	1546	50.1	641.7
Lettuce, Romaine, 1 inner leaf	1.02	0.074	0.197	0.126	0.071	0.018	0.002	0.001	0.01	0.007	14.8	0.48	6.15
Mushrooms, Cremini, Italian 1, 14 g	3.08	0.35	0.577	0.084	0.241	0.014	0.002	0	0.006	0	62.7	0.84	ND
Mushrooms (Enoki), 5	5.1	0.355	1.053	0.39	ND	0.058	0.006	0.001	0.024	0	57.2	0.45	ND
Mushrooms, Shiitake, 4 dried, 15 g	44.4	1.437	11.3	1.725	3.356	0.149	0.037	0.046	0.021	0.002	230.1	1.95	0.105
Mushrooms, Portabello, 100 g	26	2.5	5.07	1.5	1.8	0.2	0.026	0.003	0.078	0.001	484	6	ND

Mushroom, Button, 6, 108 g	231.8	2.259	3.499	1.296	2.009	0.367	0.05	0.006	0.15	0.001	339.1	4.32	0.108
Mustard Greens, 56 g, 1 cup	14.6	1.512	2.744	1.848	0.896	0.112	0.006	0.052	0.021	0.01	198.2	14	278.5
Okra, 1 cup, 100 g	31	2	7.03	3.2	1.2	0.1	0.026	0.017	0.027	0.001	303	8	53
Onion, 1, 2.5" diameter, 110 g	46.2	1.012	11.1	1.54	4.708	0.088	0.029	0.025	0.068	0.002	158.4	3.3	0.44
Onion, Young Green, 1, 4.13" long, 15 g	4.8	0.275	1.101	0.36	ND	0.029	0.005	0.004	0.011	0	41.4	2.4	ND
Parsley, 1 cup, 60 g	21.6	1.782	3.798	1.98	0.51	0.474	0.079	0.177	0.074	0.005	332.4	33.6	984
Parsley, Chinese (Cilantro) 1 cup	3.68	0.341	0.587	0.448	0.139	0.083	0.002	0.044	0.006	0	83.4	7.36	49.6
Parsnip, 1 cup sliced, 133 g	99.8	1.596	23.9	6.517	6.384	0.399	0.067	0.149	0.063	0.004	498.8	13.3	29.9
Potato, Russet, 2.5" to 3.5", 213 g	168.3	4.558	38.5	2.769	1.321	0.17	0.043	0.004	0.072	0.021	888.2	10.7	3.834
Potato, red, 2.5" to 3.5", 213 g	153.4	4.026	33.9	3.621	2.13	0.298	0.055	0.006	0.092	0.03	969.2	12.8	6.177
Pumpkin, 1 cup, 116 g	30.2	1.16	7.54	0.58	1.578	0.116	0.06	0.015	0.006	0.003	294.4	1.16	1.276
Radish, 1	0.72	0.031	0.153	0.072	0.095	0.005	0.001	0.001	.005	0.001	10.5	1.755	0.058
Rhubarb, 1 stalk	10.7	0.459	2.315	0.918	0.561	0.102	0.027	0.02	0.05	0	146.9	2.04	20.9

(continued)

(continued)

VEGETABLES*	CALORIES	PROTEIN GM	CARB GM	FIBER GM	SUGARS GM	TOT. FAT GM	SAT FAT GM	MONO UNSAT MG	POLY UNSAT FAT MG	OMEGA-3 MG	POTAS SIUM	SODIUM MG	VIT. K MG
Rutabaga, 1, 386 g	139	4.632	31.4	9.65	21.6	0.772	0.104	0.097	0.34	0.205	1301	77.2	1.158
Snow Peas, 10 pods, 34 g	14.3	0.952	2.57	0.884	ND	0.068	0.013	0.007	0.03	0	68	1.36	ND
Spinach, 1 cup, 30 g	6.9	0.858	0.1089	0.66	0.126	0.117	0.019	0.003	0.05	0.041	167.4	23.7	144.9
Squash, Acorn, 4" dia., 431 g	172,4	3.448	44.9	6.465	ND	0.431	0.091	0.03	0.181	0.112	1496	12.9	ND
Squash, Butternut, 1 cup cubed, 140 g	6.3	1.4	16.4	2.8	3.08	0.14	0.029	0.01	0.059	0.036	492.8	5.6	1.54
Squash, Crookneck, 1 cup, 130 g	24.7	1.222	5.252	2.47	ND	0.312	0.064	0.023	0.13	0.081	275.6	2.6	ND
Squash, Hubbard, 1 cup, 116 g	46.4	2.32	10.1	ND	ND	0.58	0.119	0.042	0.245	0.152	371.2	8.12	ND
Squash, Spaghetti, 1 cup, 101 g	31.3	0.646	6.979	ND	ND	0.576	0.118	0.042	0.241	0.15	109.1	17.2	ND
Squash, Zucchini, 1, 11 g	2.31	0.298	0.342	0.121	ND	0.044	0.009	0.003	0.019	0.012	50.5	0.33	ND
Sweet Potato, 1, 5" long, 130 g	111.8	2.041	26.2	3.9	5.434	0.065	0.023	0.001	0.018	0.001	438.1	71.5	2.34
Swiss Chard, 1 leaf, 48 g	9.12	0.864	1.795	0.768	0.528	0.096	0.014	0.019	0.034	0.003	181.9	102.2	398.4

Food													
Tomato, 1, 2 to 3.5" diameter, 123 g	22.1	1.082	4.822	1.476	3.235	0.246	0.057	0.063	0.166	0.004	291.5	6.15	9.717
Tomato, Cherry, 10, 170 g	35.7	1.445	7.888	1.87	ND	0.561	0.077	0.085	0.23	0.009	377.4	15.3	ND
Tomato, Italian, Roma, 1, 62 g	13	0.527	0.2877	0.682	ND	0.205	0.028	0.031	0.084	0.003	137.6	5.58	ND
Turnip, 1, 122 g	34.2	1.098	7.845	2.196	4.636	0.122	0.013	0.007	0.065	0.049	233	81.7	0.122
Turnip Greens, 1 cup chopped, 55 g	17.6	0.825	3.922	1.76	0.446	0.165	0.04	0.01	0.065	0.046	162.8	22	138.1
Watercress, 1 cup chopped, 34 g	3.745	0.782	0.439	0.17	0.068	0.034	0.009	0.003	0.012	0.008	112.2	13.9	85
Water Chestnuts, 4, 36 g	34.9	0.504	8.618	1.08	1.728	0.036	0.009	0.001	0.015	0.004	210.2	5.04	0.108
Yam, 1 cup, cubed, peeled, 150 g	177	2.295	41.8	6.15	0.75	0.255	0.056	0.009	0.114	0.018	1224	13.5	3.9

* Vegetables contain no cholesterol, trans-fatty acids, omega-6, or folic acid (folate)
All listed vegetables medium, raw unless otherwise noted
ND=No Data
Amounts given are based on USDA SR18, 2005–6. Nutritional content always varies slightly because of different growing conditons.

BAKING INGREDIENTS	CALORIES K-CAL	PROTEIN GM.	CARB. GM.	FIBER GM.	SUGARS GM.	TOT. FAT GM.	SAT FAT GM.	MONO UNSAT FAT MG.	POLY UNSAT FAT MG.	OMEGA-3 MG.	POTASSIUM MG	SODIUM MG.	VIT. K MG.	FOLIC ACID MG.
All servings are 1 cup, unless otherwise indicated														
Flour/Grain														
All-Purpose, bleached enriched, 125 g	455	12.9	95.4	3.375	0.338	1.225	0.194	0.109	0.516	0.027	133.8	2.5	0.375	193
A-P, White, self-rising, enriched, 125 g	442.5	12.4	92.8	3.375	0.275	1.213	0.192	0.108	0.512	0.027	155	1588	0.375	198
A-P, White, unbleached, enriched, 125 g	455	12.9	95.4	3.375	0.338	1.225	0.194	0.109	0.516	0.027	133.8	2.5	0.375	193
A-P, White, unenriched, 125 g	455	12.9	95.4	3.375	0.338	1.225	0.194	0.109	0.516	0.027	133.8	2.5	0.375	193
Bean, Soy, lowfat, 1 tablespoon, 5.5 g	20.5	2.559	2.089	0.561	1.089	0.368	0.053	0.081	0.208	0.025	141.4	0.99	0.225	0
Arrowroot, 128 g	457	0.384	112.8	4.352	ND	0.128	0.024	0.003	0.058	0.012	14.1	2.56	ND	0
Barley or Meal, 148 g	510.6	15.5	110.3	14.9	1.184	2.368	0.496	0.303	1.141	0.114	457.3	5.92	3.256	0
Barley, Malt Flour, 162 g	584.8	16.7	126.8	11.5	1.296	2.981	0.625	0.411	1.544	0.154	362.9	17.8	3.564	0

Food													
Bran, Oat, raw, 94 g	231.2	16.3	62.2	14.5	1.363	6.608	1.248	2.233	2.6	0.114	532	23.76	3.308	0
Bran, Rice, Ener-G Pure, Raw, 118 g	372.9	15.8	58.5	25.6	ND	24.6	4.922	8.908	8.802	0	1752	5.9	0	0
Bran, Wheat, unprocessed, ¼ cup, 13 g	30	2	66.7	ND	0	3.333	0	0	0	0	ND	0	0	0
Brown Rice, 158 g	573.5	11.4	120.8	7.268	ND	4.392	0.88	1.593	1.574	0.066	456.6	12.6	ND	0
Buckwheat, Whole Groat 120 g	402	15.1	84.7	12	3.12	3.72	0.812	1.139	1.139	0.085	692.4	13.2	8.4	0
Cake flour, enriched, 137 g	495.9	11.2	106.9	2.329	0.425	1.178	0.174	0.1	0.519	0.03	143.9	2.74	0.411	189
Carob, 103 g	228.7	4.759	91.5	41	50.6	0.669	0.093	0.203	0.222	0.004	851.8	36	0	0
Cereal, Wheat Germ, Plain, 113 g	431.7	32.9	56	14.6	ND	12.1	2.068	1.695	7.481	0	1070	4.52	ND	ND
Corn, Masa, enriched, 114 g	416.1	10.6	86.9	10.9	0.73	4.309	0.606	1.137	1.965	0.059	339.7	5.7	0.342	238
Corn Meal, White, Whole Grain, 117 g	422.4	8.108	89.9	11.2	0.749	4.516	0.635	1.91	2.058	0.062	368.5	5.85	0.351	0

(continued)

(continued)

BAKING INGREDIENTS	CALORIES K-CAL	PROTEIN GM.	CARB. GM.	FIBER GM.	SUGARS GM.	TOT. FAT GM.	SAT FAT GM.	MONO UNSAT MG.	POLY UNSAT FAT MG.	OMEGA-3 MG.	POTASSIUM MG	SODIUM MG.	VIT. K MG.	FOLIC ACID MG.
Corn Meal, Masa, Yellow, Enriched 114 g	416.1	10.6	86.9	ND	ND	4.309	0.606	1.137	1.965	0.059	339.7	5.7	ND	238
Corn Meal, Yellow, Whole Grain, 117 g	422.4	8.108	89.9	15.7	0.749	4.516	0.635	1.191	2.058	0.062	368.5	5.85	0.351	0
Germ, Wheat, Crude, 115 g	414	26.6	59.6	15.2	ND	11.2	1.915	1.57	6.911	0.831	1026	13.8	ND	0
Potato Flour, ½ cup, 90 g	315.9	7.2	71.9	ND	ND	0.7	0.2	0	0.3	0	1429	31	ND	ND
Potato Flour, 1 tablespoon, 11 g	39.5	0	8.988	ND	ND	0.088	0.025	0	0.037	0	178.6	3.875	ND	ND
Rice, Brown, Med. Grain, 190 g	687.8	14.2	144.7	6.46	ND	5.092	1.018	1.845	1.822	0.078	509.2	7.6	ND	0
Rice, White, Basmati, Med. Grain, 195 g	702	12.9	154.7	2.73	ND	1.131	0.308	0.353	0.302	0.053	167.7	1.95	ND	433
Rice, White, short grain, 200 g	716	13	150.3	5.6	ND	1.04	0.28	0.322	0.276	0.048	152	2	ND	450
Rice, Wild, raw, 160 g	571.2	23.6	119.8	9.92	4	1.728	0.25	0.254	1.082	0.48	683.2	11.2	3.04	0
Rye & Wheat, 112 g	399.8	12.3	84.4	ND	ND	1.5	ND	ND	ND	0	167	2	ND	ND

Food													
Rye, Dark, 128 g	414.7	18	88	28.9	1.331	3.443	0.396	0.417	1.536	0.216	934.4	1.28	7.552	0
Rye, Light, 102 g	374.3	8.558	81.8	14.9	1.061	1.387	0.148	0.156	0.576	0.082	237.7	2.04	6.018	0
Rye, Medium, 102 g	361.1	9.578	79	14.9	1.061	1.805	0.202	0.212	0.782	0.11	346.8	3.06	6.018	0
Soy, Bean, defatted, 1 tablespoon, 6 g	20.5	2.915	2.379	1.085	1.24	0.076	0.008	0.013	0.033	0.004	147.8	1.24	0.254	0
Soy, Bean, full fat, raw, 1 tablespoon, 5 g	22.7	1.796	1.83	0.499	0.39	1.074	0.155	0.237	0.606	0.072	130.8	0.676	3.64	0
A-P, White, enriched, calcium fortified 125 g	455	12.9	95.4	3.375	0.338	1.225	0.194	0.109	0.516	0.027	133.8	2.5	0.375	193
Triticale, Whole Grain, 130 g	439.4	17.1	95.1	19	ND	2.535	0.413	0.238	1.032	0.069	605.8	2.6	ND	0
Wheat, White, Bread, enriched, 137 g	494.6	16.4	99.4	3.288	0.425	2.274	0.334	0.192	0.996	0.059	137	2.74	0.411	206
Wheat, White, Tortilla Mix, enriched, 29 g	94.2	2.523	16.1	0.899	ND	2.059	0.319	0.835	0.809	0	38	138.6	ND	0

BAKING INGREDIENTS	CALORIES	PROTEIN GM.	CARB. GM.	FIBER GM.	SUGARS GM.	TOT. FAT GM.	SAT FAT GM.	MONO UNSAT MG.	POLY UNSAT FAT MG.	OMEGA-3 MG.	POTAS SIUM	SODIUM MG.	VIT. K MG.
Oils/Shortening*													
Olive, Salad, Cooking, 1 tablespoon, 13.5 g	119.3	0	0	0	0	13.5	1.816	9.977	1.35	0.107	0.135	0	8.127
Butter, Unsalted, 1 tablespoon, 14.2 g	101.8	0.121	0.009	0	0.009	11.5	7.294	2.985	0.432	0.089	3.408	1.562	0.994
Butter, Whipped, unsalted, 1 tablespoon, 9 g	64.5	0.077	0.005	0	ND	7.3	4.544	2.109	0.271	0	2.34	0.99	ND
Oil, Crisco Veg, 1 tablespoon, 14 g	124	0	0	0	ND	14	1.8	4.9	7.3	0	ND	0	ND
Crisco, vegetable shortening, 1 tablespoon, 12 g	106	0	0	0	ND	12	3.1	5.3	3.6	0	0	0	ND
Crisco Non Trans Fat Shortening, 1 tablespoon, 100 g	110	0	0	0	0	12	3	5	4	0	ND	0	ND
Sugars/Molasses/Syrup/Sweeteners													
White, granulated, 1 teaspoon, 4.2 g	16.3	0	4.199	0	4.196	0	0	0	0	0	0.084	0	0
Confectioners' (powdered), 1 teaspoon, 2.5 g	9.725	0	2.49	0	2.448	0.003	0	0.001	0.001	0	0.05	0.025	0

Food													
Brown, packed, 1 teaspoon, 4.6 g	17.3	0	4.477	0	4.426	0	0	0	0	0	15.9	1.794	0
Brown, unpacked, 1 teaspoon, 3 g	11.3	0	2.92	0	2.886	0	0	0	0	0	10.4	1.17	0
Molasses, Sweet, 1 tablespoon, 20 g	58	0	14.9	0	11.1	0.02	0.004	0.006	0.01	0	292.8	7.4	0
Molasses, Grandma's, 1 tablespoon, 20 g	53.2	0	16	0	12.6	0.02	0	0.001	0.01	0	292.8	7	ND
Molasses, Blackstrap, 1 tablespoon, 20 g	47	0	12.2	0	10.4	0	0	0	0	0	498.4	11	ND
Fructose Sweetener, 1 packet, 3 g	11	0	3	0	ND	0	0	0	0	0	0	0.358	ND
Corn Syrup, high-fructose, 1 tablespoon, 19 g	53.4	0	14.4	0	14.4	0	0	0	0	0	0	0.38	0
Syrup, Sweet, Artificial Sweetener, 15g, 1 tablespoon	8.25	0	2.25	0.15	2.25	0	0	0	0	0	4.8	34.5	ND
Syrup, Maple, Natural, 1 tablespoon, 20 g	52.2	0	13.4	0	11.9	0.04	0.007	0.013	0.02	0	40.8	1.8	0
Syrup, Pancake, w/2% maple, 1 tablespoon, 20 g	53	0	13.9	0	12.8	0.02	0.004	0.006	0.01	0	1.2	12.2	0

(continued)

(continued)

BAKING INGREDIENTS	CALORIES	PROTEIN GM.	CARB. GM.	FIBER GM.	SUGARS GM.	TOT. FAT GM.	SAT FAT GM.	MONO UNSAT MG.	POLY UNSAT FAT MG.	OMEGA-3 MG.	POTAS SIUM	SODIUM MG.	VIT. K MG.
Syrup, 2% maple, added potassium, 1 tablespoon 20 g	53	0	13.9	0	13.8	0.02	0	ND	ND	0	4.4	12.2	ND
Equal/Nutrasweet/Aspartame, 1 teaspoon, 3.5 g	12.3	0.076	2.994	0	ND	0.006	0.001	0.002	0.003	0	0.07	0.14	ND
Weight Watchers Sweetener, 1 teaspoon, 3 g	10.9	0	2.82	0	ND	0	0	0	0	0	135	12	ND
Apple Juice, Cider, 1 ounce, 31 g	14.6	0	3.621	0	ND	0.034	0.006	0.002	0.01	0	36.9	0.93	ND
Orange Juice, 1 ounce, 31 g	13.9	0.217	3.224	0	2.604	0.062	0.007	0.011	0.012	0.003	62	0.31	0.031
Other Ingredients Used in this Book													
Vanilla Extract, 1 teaspoon, 4.2 g	12.1	0.003	0.531	0	0.531	0.003	0	0	0	0	6.216	0.378	0
Onion Powder, 1 teaspoon, 2.4 g	8.328	0.243	1.936	0.137	0.852	0.025	0.004	0.004	0.011	0	22.6	1.296	0.098
Baking Powder, Featherweight, 1 teaspoon, 5 g	4.85	0.005	2.345	0.11	0	0.02	0.004	0	0.006	0.001	505	4.5	0

Vital Wheat Gluten, 1 tablespoon, 25 g	30	5.75	1.5	0	0	0.125	0	0	0	0	ND	2.25	ND
Flaxseed Meal (Bob's Red Mill), 1 tablespoon, 6.5 g	30	1.5	2	2	0	2.25	0	ND	ND	0	ND	0	ND
Sesame Seeds, 1 tablespoon, 9 g	51.6	1.596	2.111	1.062	0.027	4.47	0.626	1.688	1.96	0.034	42.1	0.99	0
Lecithin, Granular, 1 tablespoon, 8 g	61	0	0	0	ND	8	1.2	0.878	3.625	0	0	0	ND
Yeast, Baker's Active, 1 teaspoon, 4 g	11.8	1.532	1.528	0.84	0	0.164	0.024	0.102	0	0	80	2	0
Cream of Tartar, 1 teaspoon, 3 g	7.74	0	1.845	0.006	0	0	0	0	0	0	495	1.56	0

* Unsalted butter has .308 of omega-6 fats per tablespoon. Unsalted butter has 30.5 mg cholesterol per tablespoon. Unsalted whipped butter has 19.7 mg cholesterol per tablespoon.

INDEX

Stuffed Dates, 29
Stuffed Flank Steak, 122–23
sugars
    nutrient values, 350–51
    Splenda as substitute, 1
    See also total sugars
supplies, 273–77
    herbs, 276–77
    ingredients, 269–72
    nonalcoholic wine, 277
    speciality mixes, 277
    spices, 275–76
sushi, 154
    California Sushi Rolls, 151–53
Sutherland, LeeAnn, 119
Swedish Limpa Bread, 201–2
Sweet-and-Sour Pork Bites, 123–24
sweeteners
    nutrient values, 351, 352
Swiss Cheese Sauce, 52–53
syrup
    nutrient values, 351–52

Tabouli, 234–35
tarragon sauce
    Maureen's Tarragon Sauce, 46
tempura
    Tempura Shrimp, 218–19
    Vegetable Tempura, 236–37
Texas Barbecue Sauce, 53–54
Thai Sweet and Hot Chili Sandwich, 155–56
tomatoes
    Fried Tomatoes, 227
    Gazpacho, 138
    Greek Chicken with Spicy Tomatoes, 74–75
    nutrient values, 338
    Tomato-Corn Salad, 235–36
total fats, *xxvi–xxvii*
total sugars, *xxvi*
    Splenda as sugar substitute, 1
trace, *xxix*
trans-fatty acids, *xxvii*
Tupano, Rene, 38
turkey
    Don's Mock Sausage, 106
    Maureen's Uniquely American Meat Loaf, 111–12
    nutrient values, 313–16
    Panini Pesto Sandwich, 158
turmeric, *xviii–xix*
Tuscan Bread, 192–93
Tzatziki Sauce, 54–55

vanilla
    French Vanilla Pudding, 19
    Vanilla-Flavored Cupcakes with Orange Zest Topping, 30–32
Vegetable Tempura, 236–37
Vietnamese Bánh Mì, 127–28
vital wheat gluten, 271
vitamin K, *xxviii*

waffles
    Belgian Waffles, 252–53
walnuts
    Banana Nut Bread, 245–46
    Beef and Walnuts, 64–65
    Chocolate Cookies, 5–6
    Date-Walnut Cookies, 16–17
    Maple Oat Nut Scone, 250–51
    Persimmon Pudding, 26–27
    Stuffed Dates, 29
    Walnut Cookies with Dates, 17–18
water
    filtered water, *xxix*
    low-sodium water, *xxix*
weight measurements, *xxix*
Wetstein, Jurgen, 164
whipped cream fillings, 11–12
White Bread, 203
White Fish, 211–12
White Fish with Avocado Cream Sauce, 212–13
Whole Wheat and Raisin Scones, 265–67
wine
    Avocado Cream Sauce, 24
    Boeuf Bourguignon, 66–68
Wingers, Marlene and Jack, 122
Wool Grower's restaurant, 262
Worcestershire sauce replacement, 81–82
wraps
    Orange-Glazed Chicken Wraps, 145–46

Yemiser Selatta, 238
yogurt
    Chinggis Raan, 98–99
    Greek Meat Loaf, 100–101
    Hungarian Chicken Paprika, 101–2
    Minty Cucumber Sauce with Yogurt, 47
    nutrient values, 331
    Tzatziki Sauce, 54–55
    Yogurt White and Whole Wheat Bread, 204–5
Yugoslavian Grilled Sausages, 62–63